A *Sisters Today* Jubilee

A SISTERS TODAY JUBILEE

BLOW the TRUMPET at the NEW MOON

Edited by DANIEL DURKEN, o.s.b.

THE LITURGICAL PRESS

Collegeville   Minnesota 56321

Library of Congress Catalog Card Number: 79-27505

ISBN 0-8146-1016-1

CONTENTS

Part Four: Questions and Answers

Part Five: The Vows

Part Six: Wholeness and Holiness

Part Seven: Adaptation and Renewal

Part Eight: Ministries and Apostolates

Part Nine: Bulletin Board

Part Ten: Sisters Today and Tomorrow

POEMS

INTRODUCTION

This collection of editorials, essays, interviews, and poetry has been selected from the pages of *Sponsa Regis/Sisters Today* to commemorate the fifty years of publication of the magazine.

The title of the text is provided by that ancient composer of the festive prayer that invited God's people to "Sing joyfully to God our strength; . . . sound the timbrel, the pleasant harp and the lyre. *Blow the trumpet at the new moon*, at the full moon, on our solemn feast" (Ps 81:2-4).

Trumpet, timbrel, harp, and lyre are not the sort of accompaniment that a conductor would choose for a quiet concert of nostalgic numbers played to lull an audience into pleasant reverie of "the good ol' days." A trumpet or a bugle is an obvious attention-getter, then, now, and in the future. St. Paul, for instance, tells us that "at the sound of God's trumpet those who have died in Christ will rise first" (1 Thes 4:16). The trumpet that announces this book plays a wide range of melodies. It sings of deaths and risings. Here are tunes that will at times sound oh-so-familiar to older ears and somewhat strange to younger ones, and then vice versa.

The original score for this medley was simply going to bring together the best of the past, a kind of "Top Forty" from a half-century of writing and reading. But as the trumpet was a-tuning, a new and different melodic line was heard. This was the song of the throng that outnumbered the crowd of elders and the elect who stand before the throne of God in an apocalyptic heaven (Rev 4 and 7). This was the music that thousands of Sisters during the last fifty years have sung and hummed, worked to, danced to, wept over, and rejoiced at. Sometimes harmonious, sometimes cacophonous, this was the score that had a definite story to tell.

The articles in this volume tell the story of the life and times of American women religious perhaps better and more clearly than that life and times could ever be told by a single author. It has been and remains a good life, full of determination, dedication, and devotion. It has been and remains "a time for every affair under the heavens. A time to be born, and a time to die; a time to plant, and a time to uproot the plant; a time to rend, and a time to sew; a time to be silent, and a time to speak . . ." (Ecc 3:1, 2, 7).

The articles selected speak for themselves. They have been arranged in parts that seem to highlight the major aspects of religious life — for example, lasting fundamentals like prayer, the vows, renewal, and ministries. The articles speak loudly and clearly of the impact that external adaptation and interior renewal have made on religious life particularly during the last quarter century.

But most of all, this collection proclaims the ongoing vitality of Sisters today. Few if any Sister readers will need to apologize for the past as they read and wonder, "How did we ever survive?" For Sisters yesterday, like Sisters today, did much more than survive. They lived as fully as their hearts would let them. This volume is a tribute to the stout hearts that have lived and continue to live lives that are uncommonly generous, occasionally rigorous, and unmistakably vigorous.

So let the trumpet salute the new moon. But let it not forget that the moon has its wax and its wane. The full moon of renewal will undoubtedly be dimmed, and the trumpet's echo will fade away. And then it will be time to declare a new feast of the Spirit and to proclaim a new song "to God our strength." The next fifty years of Sisters Today will hopefully remain a faithful record of the ebb and flow of religious life. May the festive trumpet with timbrel, harp, and lyre sound again and again to challenge the reader to the ongoing conversion that will last as long as music. The reader will then say, "It seems to me I've heard that song before. / It's from an old familiar score. / I know it well that melody."

My appreciation is given to the editors, authors, and readers of Sponsa Regis/Sisters Today who have planned and played the melodies of this score. Their voices make a concert that brings together old favorites and new tunes to stir the heart to "sing joyfully to God our strength." Special gratitude is reserved for Sister Audrey Synnott, R.S.M., present poetry editor of Sisters Today, who selected the poems that grace the pages of this volume and have their own song to sing; for Sister Mary Charles McGough, O.S.B., who created the cover design of this volume and added one more artistic contribution to those already made since her initial cover on the December, 1967, issue; and for Sister Dolores Schuh, C.H.M., who assisted in the preparation and completion of this book.

Space considerations have made it necessary to excerpt some of the articles.

Daniel Durken, O.S.B.
Editor

Collegeville, Minnesota
September 8, 1979

Blow the Trumpet
at the New Moon

PART ONE

EDITORIAL DEVELOPMENTS :

An Array of Anniversaries

"If the trumpet's sound is uncertain, who will get ready for battle?" St. Paul asked the Corinthians (1 Cor 14:8). But there is nothing uncertain about the clarion call to readers — "Spouses of the King" — sounded by the first editor of *Sponsa Regis/Sisters Today*. As the editorial comments in this section reveal, the policy and purpose of this "first review for our American sisterhoods" seem to be clear and concise. Father Joseph Kreuter, O.S.B., the founding editor of the journal, states in his introductory essay, "It is for the better attainment of this your high calling that the editors of *Sponsa Regis* have started this new review." The magazine's objective is further clarified a page later with the words: "*Sponsa Regis* does not aim at science or at learning. It contains nothing new. On the contrary, the editor's ambition is to be wholly traditional and ancient. It shall endeavor, with God's help, to kindle sparks of divine love in souls, who, in the midst of dark times, are truly seeking him."

Ten years later, in 1939, Fr. Kreuter's religious superior, Abbot Alcuin Deutsch, O.S.B., acknowledged that his initially reluctant consent to this publication project had caused him no regrets. A contributor, Father Francis Remler, C.M., reviews the first decade of the journal's mission as "a counsellor, an instructor, a guide to souls consecrated to God in religious life." He selects two examples of how the magazine has been of particular help to religious, namely, its treatment of the subject of Victim Souls, and its warnings of certain evils that all religious should guard against.

The silver jubilee of *Sponsa Regis* is commemorated in 1953 with a note of thanks from editor Father Paschal Botz, O.S.B., to "the most unique, the most loyal and devoted family of readers of any publication printed" and with his wish to engage those same readers in a "jubilee of prayer." The founding editor, Fr. Kreuter, returned to comment on the initial scope of the journal — "the closest imitation of Christ"— and how that scope was extended to promote in readers their "intense sharing in the Church's sacred liturgy."

In 1965, a new note was introduced to the trumpet's tune. This was the year when editor Father Ronald Roloff, O.S.B., announced a contest for choosing a new title for the magazine. He wrote, ". . . a Latin title, however good it may have been in the past, is no longer appropriate at a time when the whole Church is striving to identify itself as a vital force in the contemporary world . . . . A magazine which claims to be pertinent for all religious women should not ignore the *aggiornamento* lest it be thought that the spiritual lives of Sisters are still being lived in an archaic past."

In the September, 1965, issue the winning title was chosen from the hundreds of suggestions submitted. Henceforth *Sponsa Regis* would be called *Sisters Today*. In addition to the new name, the magazine's subtitle was changed from the very general, "A spiritual review for Sisters" to a more embracing and challenging statement of purpose: "To explore the role of the religious woman in the Church in our time." Not purporting to represent a new purpose or approach, this statement rededicated the journal to bring "revealing insights" into such areas as prayer, work, virtue, personal relations, and psychological maturity and thus enable the Sister reader to "understand her role in the Church with greater clarity and fulfill it with greater fruitfulness."

During the golden jubilee year (1979) of *Sisters Today*, four past editors met with the journal's present editor, Sister Mary Anthony Wagner, O.S.B., "to look to the future by taking into account the experience of the past." Before "old editors just fade away" it was good of them to exercise a little nostalgia and sing a chorus of "Those Were the Days." They also make it clear that male chauvinism was not the main reason why fourteen years elapsed between the first and final search for a Sister editor of *Sisters Today*.

Sponsa Regis, September, 1929

To Our Readers

Joseph Kreuter, O.S.B.

Spouses of the King! What a wonderful dignity it is to which God has called you! To be spouses of a King, when that King is none other than the King eternal, the only begotten of the Father, united with him in a divine unity whose bond is the all-consuming fire of love, the divine Paraclete! Called in a special way to partake of this divine love, and to live the sublime and holiest innocence of him who is the immaculate Lamb of God!

The holy vows of religion wed your soul to Christ, who thereby becomes your spiritual bridegroom. Your vowed life is the life of the spouse of Christ the King. It is the life of a heavenly queen, endowed with all the spiritual graces and devotion of soul that will ever reflect in you the image and the life of your royal bridegroom.

The life of a queen! It can be of two kinds. A queen by her espousal to the king partakes by that very fact of the royal dignity and splendor of her spouse. Yet she may not rise interiorly to a higher level by that fact. In her own person, she may undergo no change, no transformation in harmony with the new position she now holds. She will then indeed move in the royal atmosphere, she will bear the name of queen, but she will not be a queen in heart. She will differ from other persons only externally, not in her inner soul. She will be a queen in name but not in fact.

Quite otherwise, the royal spouse who is queen in fact as well as in name and external position. She will not rise to full queenhood in one day. But she will grow ever more to real queenhood of heart from the moment she assumes the title and rank of queen. Day by day, her heart and mind, her soul, will mould themselves according to the soul of the king. To the external royalty which she has put on there will be added increasingly a royalty of heart and soul that will truly make of her another king.

3

Queenhood means for her a new inner life — not merely a new condition of life, but truly a new inner life. Life is constant growth; and her queenhood will be an inner transformation, a constant growth in all the grand qualities of soul, in all the virtues that will enable her bridegroom to recognize his own royal dignity in her.

Called to be a spouse of Christ means called to a special life of inner growth in Christ. Such is the desire of Christ by which he deigned to make you his chosen ones. As spouses of Christ your life is destined in a special manner to reflect the perfect life of the Church, who is pictured by St. Paul as the spouse of Christ. Christ gave himself for the Church "that he might present it to himself a glorious church, not having spot or wrinkle, or any such thing; but that it should be holy, and without blemish" (Eph 5:27). Even so, when you vowed yourself over entirely to Christ your King in the holy act of your espousal, Christ also gave himself to you. It was in the power and the sanctity of the Church that this took place. And it took place that you might be in holiness like the Church: "Not having spot or wrinkle, or any such thing: but that you should be holy, and without blemish."

Thereby you were vowed to a life of special holiness, the holiness of the Church of God, the holiness of Christ. It was not the final consummation of an action, but rather the beginning of what is to continue in ever-increasing love — your life in Christ. Every day you must grow in Christ, become transformed step by step into truer queens of your royal Bridegroom, so that your every thought, your every action, your daily prayer, and your daily occupation become one act of devotion to your heavenly King, one great and never-ending expression of your queenly souls. Your daily devotion to him must become in his eyes an ever more evident expression of his own soul, his own life.

It is for the better attainment of this your high calling that the editors of *Sponsa Regis* have started this new review. May it prove in truth what it shall endeavor to be, a modest beacon, shining in the strength of him who called himself the Way, the Truth, and the Life. May you in word and action help to make its efforts fruitful and help it attain its aim: namely, that the life of Christ may increase without end in the hearts of those whom he in his love has chosen, and chosen to the end that they reflect in their daily lives the fuller splendor of his own life before God and man!

In the pursuit of this aim, *Sponsa Regis* will carry articles on all questions of religious life, ascetical and mystical, historical, liturgical, educational, on Catholic Action, on the best religious and spiritual books appearing today, on current events and activities in religious life, etc.

The co-operation herewith solicited from all readers by the editors should be more than passive or merely receptive. It should also be active on the part of the readers. How so? By their contributions to the pages of *Sponsa Regis*, by the sending of articles, letters, data and facts, questions for information, etc. Thus will the new venture partake of the corporate life that should be realized wherever souls strive together for the better attainment of the higher life in Christ, the one supreme Highpriest and King and Bridegroom and Head, in whom all are one unto the life of eternal glory that shall be without end.

Reading *Sponsa Regis*

Many letters have reached us from all parts of the United States and Canada in the course of the past four months. Bishops, priests, superiors of motherhouses, provincial and local superiors have written most enthusiastically relative to our project of publishing the first review for our American Sisterhoods. Many devout prayers were offered by the Sisters for the success of this new venture. Within a comparatively short time more than a thousand subscriptions had been paid or promised.

As we had anticipated, the need of just such a publication as we had in mind was being felt in all convents, by practically every religious. Many assured us that they were looking forward with eager anticipation to the coming of the first issue. They expected much of *Sponsa Regis*. It would have been impossible for them to state precisely just what these expectations were. For it was to be the first review of its kind in the English-speaking countries. All they could do was to laud "the idea" and the appropriate title, while the general prospectus which was sent to all convents raised their hopes to a high level. Now the first issue is before them. Will they be disappointed? We hope not.

Sponsa Regis does not aim at science or at learning. It contains nothing new. On the contrary, the editors' ambition is to be wholly traditional and ancient. It shall endeavor, with God's help, to kindle sparks of divine love in souls, who, in the midst of our dark times, are truly seeking him. It intends to nourish the languishing souls with that spiritual food which is no other than the divine Word, the essential Truth, the living Bread from heaven, the King of souls.

The existence of *Sponsa Regis* is sufficiently justified by the great advantage accruing to souls eager for perfection, from the possession of exact, simple and clear principles, which will enable them to glean with discernment and reproduce in their conduct that which they should imitate in the example and teaching of their divine Bridegroom. For want of such discernment false and inexact notions gain free circulation, and often the very books that are intended for edification serve to foster delusion.

Furthermore, we may be assured that a soul's advancement in perfection does not depend upon the number of ideas which are put before her mind, but upon her really digesting some of them. Our Lord said one day to

Sister Benigna Consolata: "At the last judgment I shall not ask souls if they have read much, but what fruit they have drawn from their reading." In point of fact, nothing is of any worth in the spiritual life but that which ends in practice. Doctrine is proved by acts; high thoughts and sentiments that do not produce solid virtue are of no value.

The characteristic of our faith is that it ever tends to apply to ourselves all the truths that it teaches us, that all its theories are meant to be reduced to practice. If we wish to live by faith only, we must be honest with ourselves and draw all the logical consequences from our belief. In other words, it is the courageous doers of God's word that will be called saints.

You will then do well to look more for principles than for sentiments in the pages of *Sponsa Regis*, truths calculated to encourage action rather than to satisfy the mind. It shall be our ambition to lead our readers to practical knowledge of the "only true God, and Jesus Christ whom he has sent" (Jn 17:3), rather than to feed even the most legitimate curiosity.

Trusting our devout readers will peruse the pages of *Sponsa Regis* in this spirit and will prayerfully ponder upon them with a view to practical application, we place the review under the patronage of Christ, the King and Center of all hearts, and of Mary, his august mother, protectress of all religious.

Sponsa Regis, September, 1939

Ten Years of *Sponsa Regis*

Abbot Alcuin Deutsch, O.S.B.

When I granted permission ten years ago to Father Joseph Kreuter to undertake the publication of a monthly magazine for Sisterhoods, I did so with considerable hesitation. I knew that it is not a small matter to issue a monthly magazine, even though the volume be small. I feared that the enthusiasm which prompted the request might spend itself before many months had passed. Then, too, there was a possibility of illness or death, and I doubted whether I could find another man in my community with the ability and enthusiasm to carry on the work. However, I finally gave a reluctant consent.

I take pleasure in saying that I have had no cause to regret the consent. Father Joseph has stuck to his magazine for ten years with the utmost fidelity. He has had other work to do — teaching and preaching and conducting of retreats. But he has not complained, nor has he ever permitted his interest in *Sponsa Regis* to flag.

Nor have his readers, the Sisters throughout the country, as a whole been unfaithful to him. Many have been the words of appreciation and gratitude that have come to him in these many years. While the number of subscribers has not run into the tens of thousands, in many a community dozens have listened to the public reading of the one copy subscribed to by the community. Thus the number of those that have profited spiritually by *Sponsa Regis* has gone far beyond ten thousand. There can be no doubt but that the magazine has been a powerful factor in the spiritual development of the religious communities in the United States and elsewhere.

What is particularly striking in the character of *Sponsa Regis* and its spiritual message is the consistency with which it has emphasized prayer and sacrifice, the two means by which we cooperate most efficaciously with the divine action for the perfecting of our lives according to the pattern of our Lord Jesus Christ. May *Sponsa Regis* continue to inculcate, without wearying of the repetition, use of these most powerful antidotes to the activism which characterizes our times and threatens the spiritual life even of our religious women. And may it do so bravely and effectively for a long, long time. God bless it and prosper it!

A Song of Beauty

I have seen You watching
    out from the abyss of eternal space
    with the white eyes of stars.
I have known You
    in the scattering of warm fragrance
    from the plum thicket in June.
I have walked with You
    down dark aisles of forest
    strong with the scent of wood flowers.
        You are in the canyon
        when the white moon
        sheds its mist down the rock walls.
I have watched You in the sumac
    lifting red loveliness
    to the music of the breezes' gypsy band.
I have found You
    in the face of a buttercup
    dipping its yellow brilliance
    into a mountain stream.
        You are in the snowflakes
        dropping a chaste carpet
        over a sullied world.
I would take You from these things
    and hide You in my heart,
    but You slip away and leave me empty.
A still voice speaks:
    "These are but shadows, Child,
    of that which is to come.
    These are glances
    of the Beauty whom you want.
    These are only mirrors reflecting
    the countenance of Him
    who is Beauty."

Sister Margaret Mary, O.S.B.
Sponsa Regis, December, 1955

Sponsa Regis, October, 1939

Sponsa Regis and Its Mission

Francis J. Remler, C.M.

The founding of *Sponsa Regis* ten years ago is to our mind not a matter of chance but rather of providential design. Under the direction of the all-embracing Providence which "reaches from end to end mightily and orders all things sweetly," all things happen according to plan and design, so that there is no such a thing as chance or accident. This applies also to such a seemingly ordinary event as the founding of a magazine especially devoted to the spiritual interests of religious communities.

The mission of *Sponsa Regis* is to be a counsellor, an instructor, a guide to souls consecrated to God in religious life. By means of selected articles it is meant to elucidate and explain more fully the principles of the supernatural life and to convey other information that is of interest to those who are banded together in religious communities for the promotion of the glory of God and their own personal sanctification.

That this magazine has been true to its mission during the past ten years may be judged from the numerous expressions of appreciation and commendation that have reached the editors from religious persons both in the United States and elsewhere. They all indicate that the contents of *Sponsa Regis* have proved to be a valuable help to numerous souls.

A few remarks about the propriety of publishing a magazine intended for members of religious communities will not be out of place here. Is it not the accepted thing that organizations of all kinds have their special journals and periodicals as an aid to the furtherance of their particular work? The professions, trades, labor unions, etc., all have their official publications. Why then should not our large body of Sisterhoods have a publication the purpose of which is to aid souls consecrated to God in their endeavor to make the most of the graces and advantages attached to the life of the evangelical counsels?

Should anyone object and say that there is no need for such a magazine since religious women have many excellent spiritual books at their disposal, our reply is this: All this is very true; but it does not destroy the usefulness of *Sponsa Regis* as a medium of furtherance of sanctity. A book usually explains one subject only, and that often in a drawn out way, so that only those who have sufficient time to give to close reading can profit by it. And it is a well known fact that due to the pressure of work that many religious persons are called upon to do, the leisure that is needed for extensive reading is simply impossible to secure. And yet the soul must be fed regularly with spiritual food if it is not to succumb to starvation. A certain amount of spiritual reading is practically indispensable.

Sponsa Regis proves to be a great help in this difficulty. It treats in briefer form various subjects that the editor judges to be necessary or useful to religious women. These articles are therefore more easily understood and mastered especially by those who do not have sufficient time to devote to books, or by those who may not have had the advantages of higher education.

This has been the aim of *Sponsa Regis*, and we feel confident that it is just because of the judicious presentation of selected articles on the different phases of the spiritual life that it has been a great help to many religious eager for fuller information, but which was inaccessible to them for the one reason that they did not know where to look for it.

Let us give just an example or two. We have no hesitation to affirm that the enlightening articles which appeared in the pages of this magazine on the subject of Victim Souls must have been a veritable God-send to many a religious that was sorely tried in one way or another by suffering, either physical or spiritual, or perhaps by both. It is unhappily only too true that there are not a few religious persons that have never learned the real meaning and purpose of suffering, nor the secret of bearing it with perfect surrender to the adorable will of God, even though they seem to be well instructed in other spheres of the supernatural life.

Such persons often bear their sufferings very ungraciously, with many murmurings against God and their surrounding and with an unexpressed persuasion that God is dealing very unjustly with them. The sad result is that far from bearing them with perfect resignation and patience and intimate union with their crucified Spouse, and thus converting them into a source of wonderfully rich merit, they rather render themselves deserving of punishment by their impatience. If they rightly understood, they would suffer cheerfully, offering up their pains as atonement for their own sins, for the sins of others, for the welfare of the Church, the conversion of sinners, the spread of the faith, the sanctification of the clergy, and similar intentions; thus participating very intimately with Christ on the cross in the great work of the redemption and opening heaven to thousands of souls that might otherwise be lost forever.

Now it cannot be denied that the articles on Victim Souls have done a valuable service to suffering members of religious communities by showing them how to convert their seemingly inactive life into a very meritorious one, and how, despite their seeming uselessness, they can do more for the promotion of God's interests than many of those who give themselves up feverishly to works that attract attention and often tend to further the material rather than the spiritual good of their Order and of the Church.

There is another department in which this magazine has tried to fulfill its mission. It has not shrunk from taking upon itself at times the rather unpleasant task of acting as a monitor or mentor to the members of our Sisterhoods. Fully realizing the great danger in which all religious persons and all communities are of leaving their first fervor and growing lukewarm with the risk of final apostasy, the editors have opened its pages to writers who were not afraid to point out certain evils that all religious must seek to guard against as much as they guard against the contagion of virulent epidemic diseases.

No doubt, some of the strictures passed and warnings given were far from being flattering; they rather hurt and even provoked feelings and utterances of resentment. But that is only what is to be expected. The only apology *Sponsa Regis* can make under these circumstances is the one St. Paul used in one of his epistles: "Have I then become your enemy because I tell you the truth?"

We must face situations as they are. If certain evils have crept into religious houses — and who will deny that they do creep in, especially in these days of close contact with the world — then the only hope of salvation for these houses consists in removing them. If not removed they will eventually ruin the community and render it useless in the Church. The fate of the barren fig tree will overtake it. "May no fruit grow on thee henceforth forever!"

There is another reason why such warnings should be given more insistently today perhaps than was necessary in former times. Our present day communities are not only in very close contact with the world which is always anti-Christian, but their members are for the most part recruited from the ranks of young people who are brought up in the midst of refined luxuries and creature comforts of which past generations had not the slightest idea, and hence know next to nothing of the spirit of mortification and self-denial. How abhorrent to many candidates must be the standards of that penitential and mortified life insisted on by Christ, and how strongly they must be tempted gradually to surround themselves with all kinds of contrivances that minister to sensual gratification in one way or another. But this is inimical to a truly religious life. It is nothing less than an attempt to do the impossible, namely, to acquire the perfection of the love of God while "walking in the broad way that leads to destruction."

This being the case, *Sponsa Regis* is fulfilling a real mission and doing a very valuable service to all well meaning religious souls when it points out to them frankly and courageously the various evils that easily insinuate themselves, often without their being perceived, even into the most regular and fervent communities. The best friend we can have is one who is not afraid to tell us our faults; he may hurt us, but he is in truth our greatest benefactor, provided we have the good sense to profit by his warnings. The same applies to *Sponsa Régis* in its relations to religious families.

In a great variety of ways, then, is *Sponsa Regis* working for the greater glory of God by offering to its religious readers a large variety of instructive and edifying articles and treatises. It is our fond hope that this highly useful work, begun so auspiciously and carried on so successfully for the last ten years, will continue to prosper and be blessed with success for many years to come. This surely is the heartfelt wish of everyone that is interested in the promotion of God's glory and the welfare of the Church through the prayers, labors, and sufferings of that vast army of religious women who for the love of their crucified Savior have abandoned the things of earth to devote themselves exclusively to the things of heaven.

Poem

My poems wear blue denim skirts and jeans.
They follow psalms around from dawn to dark.
They take personally news of invasions,
assassinations, plots to overthrow
one regime after another.
Hidden deep within their cowls,
they weep silently, their fragile eyes
balancing the world without regret.
Wed to silence, they offer hospitality
if you are listening for their names.

Sister Thomas Jeanne Doriot, S.P.
Sisters Today, June–July, 1979

Sponsa Regis, September, 1953

Our Twenty-Fifth Anniversary

Paschal Botz, O.S.B.

The timeless Creator and Dispenser of time has graciously given us this beginning of *Sponsa Regis'* silver jubilee. While it is not a long time, as anniversaries go, yet it does offer us an occasion to pause and reflect, to offer thanks and examine our conscience.

It was on the feast of the Nativity of Our Lady, September 8, 1929, that the "Spouse of the King" first appeared. Dedicated to Christ the King and his glorious Mother, our magazine made its appearance humbly, cautiously, and yet with a clear consciousness of its high mission. While there has been a change of editorship, the founding editor, Father Joseph Kreuter, O.S.B., is still with us contributing articles. His presence has been a guarantee of continuity of spirit and purpose. Even the first issue of our little magazine placed the emphasis on meditative reading and practical spirituality, which (we hope) still characterizes its pages. We thank him and all our faithful, generous contributors of these past years.

Most of all, *Sponsa Regis* is proud of its great and devoted body of readers, Sisters, priests, bishops, laymen, spread over the continents and islands of the whole world. We have repeatedly maintained, with justifiable pride, that we have the most unique, the most loyal and devoted family of readers of any publication printed. For this loyalty and devotion, steadily increasing and becoming stronger, we are also deeply grateful. Twenty-five years is a long enough time to try the patience of any group, but we beg God in humble prayer, that he may continue to give us a justified existence by offering our readers a greater "advantage for perfection," to use the phrase of the first editor in the first issue. We want to be concerned entirely about our readers and not about ourselves. For that reason, too, we deem any high pressure advertising out of place, even during a jubilee year.

There will be further and more important reminders of the anniversary year, mainly in the form of articles. The editor's immediate wish is to engage all readers in a jubilee of prayer, for all graces received, for the interior growth and perfection in Christ of all our readers, for the sanctity of the Church, the universal *Spouse of Christ*, and of religious in particular, for a new corporate spirit of charity of all souls wedded to Christ the King. In that prayer we want to see the pattern for all others who are in any way celebrating their silver jubilee.

Poem

humble one(gifted with

illimitable joy)
bird sings love's every truth

beyond all since and why

asking no favor but

(while down come blundering
proud hugenesses of hate

sometimes called worlds)to sing

e. e. cummings
Sponsa Regis, February, 1961

Sponsa Regis, October, 1953

Twenty-Five Years of *Sponsa Regis*

Joseph Kreuter, O.S.B.

Sponsa Regis is the first spiritual review published in the interests of English-speaking Sisterhoods, wherever they live and labor and, in particular, of those in the United States and Canada. Before its first appearance a quarter of a century ago, many a Sister leading the contemplative life in her cloister or being active in the missions, in schools, hospitals, orphanages, houses for the aged and neglected, had longed for the day when a monthly copy of a review she might call her own would reach her as a welcome aid on the path to religious perfection.

It was evident that a vast amount of good would accrue to many thousands of souls from the devout reading of such a spiritual monthly review. Religious vocations would be aroused, strengthened and maintained, and even the children taught by the religious, or the sick and infirm under their care, would greatly be benefited, at least indirectly, by the intensified spiritual and religious living that was bound to follow in the wake of the publication.

Bishops, priests, and religious superiors, likewise, had long felt that a review for our many Sisterhoods would be most welcome and fill a gap in the lists of our Catholic periodicals. When in the early part of 1928[1] the Bishops, the major superiors of religious communities, and the editors of Catholic papers and periodicals of the United States and Canada received a letter announcing that in September the first monthly review for Sisters under the title *Sponsa Regis* would make its appearance, letters began to come in from all sides giving the newly contemplated venture an enthusiastic welcome and pledging it full support.

---

[1]It was actually in 1929 that the initial work on *Sponsa Regis* began.— Ed.

15

The first issue of *Sponsa Regis* came from the press of the Wanderer Publishing Company in St. Paul, Minnesota, in September 1928[2], with sixteen pages of solid reading matter, under the approval of Rt. Rev. Alcuin Deutsch, O.S.B., superior of the editor, and of members of the hierarchy. In the following year the number of pages was raised to twenty-four. Considering the life of religious observance and the hard work generally incumbent on Sisters, this amount of solid and practical spiritual reading was adhered to till last year, when the twenty-eight page issue became necessary.

SCOPE

The Holy Year 1925 and, in particular, its crowning event, the institution of the feast of Christ the King, had given the first impetus toward the founding of the review, and even the selection of the title *Sponsa Regis*, Spouse of Christ the King, goes back to that year and feast. But two more years elapsed before the plan reached its fruition. Meanwhile the scope was worked out in regard to the coming review. As its title indicated, it must be the foremost endeavor of editor and contributors to spur their readers on to the closest imitation of Christ, their King and Spouse, following the example of Mary, model of religious. This sublime and overall program would call for intense spiritual living with Christ, that is, the cultivation of interior recollection consequent upon the realization of the special indwelling of the Triune God within the soul by sanctifying grace.

This interior living is, indeed, the shortest path leading to sanctity. Only truly recollected souls, moreover, are capable of efficaciously building up Christ's Kingdom on earth. Such exalted spiritual living must be the ambition of all religious in their endeavor to sanctify themselves and aid in the work of the apostolate of souls. At the same time, interior living is the great antidote to the baneful secularism, activism, mediocrity, and other anti-spiritual tendencies in fallen human nature. Imitation of and configuration to Christ, the Savior of souls and supreme Victim for a sinful mankind, call for intense sacrificial living with him on behalf of the countless souls who do not know him or refuse to follow him.

Such victim living with Christ does not consist in imposing all sorts of sufferings upon oneself, but it rather comprises the vast number of sacrifices, self-denials, and intense efforts that are required on the part of generous souls who wish to establish themselves in interior recollection. Religious, in virtue of their vows and dedicated life in communities and the apostolate, are called to be among the closest followers of their divine King and Spouse, hence are expected to live the victim life with Christ. These fundamental truths and facts have for years been stressed in the pages of *Sponsa Regis*. As a result, many thousands of *Sponsa Regis* readers have embraced the victim life and are experiencing its wonderful effects in bringing about a more intimate union with Christ, their Spouse and King.

[2]The first issue was dated September 8, 1929.— Ed.

SCOPE EXTENDED

Intensification of the readers' spirituality by due emphasis on *ascetical or victim living* characterizes the initial phase of *Sponsa Regis'* endeavor. This must ever be so, for fallen human nature is powerfully drawn to mediocrity, self-seeking, and immortification. The spiritual life, that is, Christ's life in the soul, calls for a thorough purification from all that is opposed to the divine will. Once the soul is well on the way of this cleansing process, the Holy Spirit is ready to begin his work of enlightening the soul and leading it on to gradually increasing intimacy with Christ, King and Spouse.

On this way to higher degrees of perfection the religious is given a new incentive and impetus when it is made to realize the sanctifying effects of thorough *liturgical* living. Having been purified in some degree, it is enabled to see the necessity of intimate living with the Church, Christ's Mystical Body, and of becoming an ever more sanctified member of the eternal King and Spouse. Intense sharing in the Church's sacred liturgy will henceforth be one of its preoccupations.

For this reason *Sponsa Regis*, although not professedly liturgical, endeavored to arouse in its patrons that interest in divine worship which becomes religious as privileged members of the Church. Ascetical or victim living joined to liturgical piety combine with mystical contemplation unto the highest goal of genuinely interior souls. A lively interest in this particular sphere of spirituality has of late years been stimulated in many religious, and even in not a few members of the laity, through the publication and study of mystical works. It may truthfully be asserted that today the number of contemplative souls is on the increase.

PRESENT STATUS

Considering the extensive spiritual program our Sisters' review has followed during the past twenty-five years, it is not to be wondered that its subscription list has neared the saturation point. Of eight thousand subscriptions to date the majority come from motherhouses and dependent convents, where the monthly copies are first read in public and then in private by individual Sisters, and finally bound so as to be available for reading to old and new members of the communities. Parents, brothers, sisters, and friends have for years been in the habit of subscribing to the periodical for the benefit of their beloved ones in religion. More prelates, priests, and lay persons are among the readers of the review than one would suspect. Victim Souls are far in excess of ten thousand.

ACKNOWLEDGEMENTS

Sponsa Regis can boast of a host of clerical, religious, and lay promoters and friends. The following deserve special mention: Rt. Rev. Abbots Alcuin

Deutsch, O.S.B. (deceased), and Baldwin Dworschak, O.S.B., Rev. Rembert Bularzik, O.S.B., literary editor for many years; Brother Elmer Cichy, O.S.B., and his co-workers in the subscription department, the many contributors to the pages of the review and especially also Rev. Paschal Botz, O.S.B., present editor since 1946, and his group of co-workers.

SOULS IN PERIL

The mission of our Sisters' review is becoming more and more urgent as time goes on. Although there is a notable increase of religious vocations during the past decade, the opportunities for work in schools, hospitals, home and foreign missions have vastly multiplied at the same time. The sublime spiritual program, as outlined in these pages and followed by *Sponsa Regis* during the past twenty-five years, is a guarantee that, with the special divine blessing, our Sisterhoods will continue their manifold activities on the same high level as heretofore, unto the greater honor and glory of God and the salvation and sanctification of ever greater numbers of souls.

Wooden Tabernacle

Most of my life,
except for a few retreats
into the deep forest of God,
I've stayed in the city,
remained at the edge of the woods,
writing poems
about the edge of things,
singing sad songs
about my loneliness,
about the color of surfaces,
about these gods of mine,
flowers at the edge of my woods,
at the edge of the tabernacle,
flowers so easy to uproot,
so soon to fade,
so unlike the trees
in the heart of the forest.

Andrew Costello, C.SS.R.
Sisters Today, January, 1979

Sponsa Regis, March, 1965

Looking for a New Name

Ronald Roloff, O.S.B.

We are now in our 36th year of publication under the title *Sponsa Regis*. Reactions to this title have been predominantly favorable, and previous suggestions that it be changed have not produced very much enthusiasm.

However, it seems to us that a Latin title, however good it may have been in the past, is no longer appropriate at a time when the whole Church is striving to identify itself as a vital force in the contemporary world. Whatever may be one's personal attitude, this is the age of the vernacular; and if we cling too tenaciously to the idiom of a former day we implicitly proclaim our willingness to be excluded from the developments that are taking place all around us. Admitting that not all of these developments may be good or fruitful, it seems to us that a magazine which claims to be pertinent for all religious women should not ignore the *aggiornamento*, lest it be thought that the spiritual lives of Sisters are still being lived in an archaic past.

We therefore propose to adopt an English title beginning with the first number of Volume 37, which will appear in September, 1965. To assist us in selecting a name that will be in harmony with the contents and purpose of the magazine, we invite you to submit titles of your choice. Brevity is desirable by all means, and the title must be in English. We will accept suggestions that are postmarked up to and including June 1, 1965, and will award a prize of $25 for the title which is finally adopted. (We would really like to offer a larger prize, but are afraid that we might be so buried with suggestions that we could never reach a decision!) You do not need to be a subscriber. If two or more suggest the prize-winning name, the earliest postmark will have to decide the winner.

19

Here are some considerations: we are an exclusively spiritual review; we are concerned exclusively with Sisters; most of our readers are engaged in active apostolic work of some kind; they are becoming more conscious of themselves as parts of the whole Church; the many contemporary developments in the Church are causing both Sisters and others to re-evaluate the role of the Sister in the modern world; this re-evaluation has profound implications for the spiritual life of the individual Sister. If you can reduce some or all of these ideas to one or two or three words, you will deserve a reward!

For My Daughter Emily

What is all this juice and all this joy?
— GERALD MANLEY HOPKINS

It was only
one white tulip

she wanted
to see blowing

in the soft wind:
spring's first candle

speckled for her
and balanced

by God's finger.

David Pearson Etter
Sponsa Regis, November, 1964

Sisters Today, September, 1965

New Name and Subtitle

Ronald Roloff, O.S.B.

Our contest for a new name for the magazine proved to be a stimulating experience. We received hundreds upon hundreds of suggestions, from all parts of the country, from Canada, Bermuda, and Puerto Rico, and from such distant lands as England, Italy, Australia, and Rhodesia. So many of your suggestions were accompanied by praise for the magazine that it almost became embarrassing sometimes. On the other hand, a number of letters remarked that the task of thinking of a name caused the thinker to make a new evaluation of religious life, or at least compelled her to attempt to phrase the concept in precise terms. We had not anticipated this result of the contest, but apparently we were not the only ones to profit from this enterprise.

Some of the suggestions were accompanied by drawings of a possible cover design — even by some full-sized scratch-board work. A surprising number explained their choice by references to Scripture or theology (sometimes this ran into several pages), and these explanations not only gave evidence of their concern that we select a good title, but also illustrated the excellent thought and principles upon which the spiritual life of the writers is based. Perhaps more than anything else these explanations made us feel that Sisters today are walking with eyes open and feet firmly planted on the ground, in spite of the winds of controversy and uncertainty which seem to be assailing them from so many sides.

We are sorry that we finally had to decide not to select a title that had biblical or theological implications. Many of those suggested were applicable to ordinary Christians; many more were applicable to men religious as well as women. Many, too, expressed a wonderful concept which nevertheless is only one aspect of religious life. Since our magazine is for

21

Sisters, but Sisters of every kind, we wanted a title that would exclude nothing of the complex reality that is the life of Sisters today.

In the last two paragraphs the phrase, Sisters today, has already appeared twice. The writing really was not planned that way; but now that it has occurred it may serve to indicate the ease with which one falls into that phraseology whenever there is discussion of a topic like this. Perhaps it was inevitable that our judges should acknowledge this fact. After going over the mass of suggestions and culling those which seemed especially commendable, we consulted a board of five Sisters (from five different Orders or Congregations) and several monks of Saint John's Abbey who have been occupied in work with Sisters. The result of our consultation was a surprising unanimity about the title, *Sisters Today*.

Our new title identifies the magazine at once, and does so without restricting the concept of the religious life of women. If Sisters attain the ideal of their religious life, then the very word "Sisters" will conjure up all those ideas of commitment and involvement, of witness and response, of apostolic work and contemplative prayer, of love and generosity, of idealism and unselfishness, which were expressed in a hundred different ways in the titles you suggested. On the other hand, if Sisters do not pursue these ideals, then an expression of such noble aspirations in the title of this magazine will only be an embarrassment. What is perhaps equally important, the image of the Sister may undergo changes of many kinds in the years that lie ahead, and *Sisters Today* will be a title that will have validity at any time.

The winner of the contest was Sister Catherine, S.H. (Sisters of Notre Dame de Namur), who teaches at Sacred Heart School, Salinas, California. Because there were a number of others who suggested this title, we have decided to offer additional prizes as well. Sister Giovanna Mapelli, O.S.B., of Saint Lucy's Priory, Glendora, California, suggested the name only three days after Sister Catherine did, and we are giving her a two-year gift subscription.

We are turning from the very general subtitle, "A spiritual review for Sisters," to a more embracing and challenging statement of purpose: "To explore the role of the religious woman in the Church in our time." Actually, this does not represent a new purpose or approach. During the past several years we have been doing just this, and we expect to keep our pages open for articles on any of the multifarious aspects of religious life.

As your suggestions implied, the life of religious women is a witness and an apostolate, an involvement and a perfection, which includes prayer, work, virtue, personal relations, psychological maturity, and many other things. We hope to present articles that will bring revealing insights into as many of these areas as possible, and we hope that this "exploration" will enable each of you to understand her role in the Church with greater clarity and fulfill it with greater fruitfulness.

Sisters Today, January, 1979

Old Editors Just Fade Away . . .

Interview with Past and Present Editors—
Paschal Botz, O.S.B.
Kilian McDonnell, O.S.B.
Roger Kasprick, O.S.B.
Daniel Durken, O.S.B.
Sister Mary Anthony Wagner, O.S.B.

Sister Mary Anthony: At one time each of you bore the title and task of editor of *Sponsa Regis/Sisters Today*. During this year when we celebrate the fiftieth anniversary of this publication, it is good to look to the future by taking into account the experience of the past. I would like, first of all, to ask each of you which years you served as editor of the periodical and how much of your workload was devoted to this task.

AN OVERVIEW OF EDITORS

Father Daniel: Let me give a quick overview of this half-century of editors. Fr. Joseph Kreuter started *Sisters Today* which was first called *Sponsa Regis* back in September, 1929. He continued as editor until October,1946 — a good span of years. Fr. Joseph relinquished the editorship to carry on a mission of mercy to a number of abbeys and Catholic homes in Germany shortly after World War II. He gave many retreats (including my own ordination retreat in 1956) and served as a hospital chaplain until his death in 1963. Someday someone must do justice to this venerable pioneer in American spirituality with a good biography — and a lively one it would be! When Fr. Joseph began his new work in 1946, Fr. Paschal Botz was named editor and continued until 1958. Fr. Kilian McDonnell then took over until 1963. Fr. Ronald Roloff, who is no longer a member of our community, was editor from 1963 to 1967. He was assisted by Fr. Roger Kasprick. But each can speak for himself.

    Fr. Kilian: During my years as editor (1958-63), the job was considered about one-fourth of a full work load, but I don't think it actually took that much time.

Fr. Roger: I was appointed managing editor in the summer of 1963. This was in addition to a three-fourths teaching load. I continued in this capacity for several years, also doubling as review editor. When the business office in The Liturgical Press assumed some of the work, I remained the book review editor. For several years I also did some occasional primary editing and proofreading. A while later I became simply the review editor when I had introduced other media such as records and tapes and when many more people and publishers were submitting books for review. While Fr. Daniel was on assignment in Decorah, Iowa, and New York City, I held down the home front as managing editor until I resigned in 1975.

Fr. Daniel: I assumed editorship in the fall of 1967 at which time I was also novice master of the community and was teaching a college theology course. As to the work load, it was a kind of "fitting into the cracks" condition. My editorial work expanded according to the amount of time I could give to it.

THE TENOR OF THE TIME

Sister Mary Anthony: What was the tenor of the time in which you were editor, and how did that affect the contributions which you either accepted or sought for publication?

Fr. Kilian: My pre-1963 days were pre-Vatican II, of course, so things were pretty quiet. All religious were wearing the habit. Souls were being saved. I do not think there were any major problems until the times became more troubled when Cardinal Suenens' *The Nun in the World* appeared. I did introduce a poetry editor, Father Raymond Roseliep.

Shortly after I became editor I established a National Advisory Board of Sisters for the magazine. I think this was a good idea, but it was not a very successful one. I tried to get in contact with the Sister Formation Movement. I went to Sister Mary Emil's office in Washington to talk to the directors, and I did get a bit of response and permission to use their names. But when I really tried to involve them in the magazine, the results were very disappointing. I wanted them to tell me what kind of a journal they wanted, what articles they wanted, and what kind of writers they wanted. I asked for their input regarding the direction of the magazine; I wanted their critique of what we were doing.

Sister Mary Anthony: Did you ever assemble the group?

Father Kilian: No. We had no funds to bring these people together. I kept in contact with them through correspondence.

Fr. Roger: I would like to add that Fr. Kilian tried to raise interest in the magazine and in the quality of its appearance. It was he who was able to get the new type faces and the design of the magazine. He asked me to work on covers, and it was then that we began working with texts in a new way. It was quite a deliberate change. Mr. Frank Kazmarcik was artistic consultant for a time.

THE VICTIM SOUL APOSTOLATE

Fr. Daniel: I think it would be important here for Fr. Paschal to speak about the change that he brought about when he became editor. Fr Joseph, beginning the magazine in 1929, brought it to a certain point. Fr. Paschal really turned a corner when he took over in 1946. Under Fr. Joseph, *Sponsa Regis* had become a vehicle for promoting the Victim Soul Apostolate — a way for people to offer their sufferings in a salvific way.

Fr. Paschal: At the time I assumed editorship in 1946, Fr. Joseph was the recipient of many personal letters which he received from "Victim Souls" and which he in turn shared with the readership of the magazine. He was teaching ascetical theology at the seminary then, and I also recall that he gave a retreat to the monastic community on the "Spirituality of Victimhood."

After I became editor, the number of letters was significantly reduced in the magazine. It seemed questionable to make the reality of the matter a public affair. At that time the names of 10,000 Victim Souls had been sent to the European center for Victim Souls in Austria. The idea of Victimhood meant very much, especially to persons who had prolonged illnesses or suffering. In a way, I regretted the loss of emphasis upon Victimhood. What was a vital reality to many of these Christians was the fact that they were sharing in the vicarious love of Christ's own victimhood of total love to the Father. This would still be valid today.

I also began to put more emphasis upon the theological aspects of spirituality, and to indicate more the sacramental influences upon spirituality. For example, this was the time of the restoration of the ancient rite of Consecration of Virgins for religious women. I was also on the staff of *Orate Fratres/Worship* magazine. Though the main thrust of this journal was the promotion of liturgical thought and practice, *Sponsa Regis* did not have that as its goal — although it was in no way contra-liturgical.

THE IMPACT OF VATICAN II

Fr. Daniel: When we are talking about the tenor of the time, I think the real change, of course, came with Vatican II. We just mentioned Cardinal Suenens' book, *The Nun in the World*, and the great impact that it had on women religious. Suddenly convents became alive in the sense that now they could go out into the world; the whole notion of cloister changed. You know about that, Sister.

Sister Mary Anthony: During 1958 to 1963, the beginning years of the Benedictine Institute of Sacred Theology at St. Benedict's Convent, that was one of the books Fr. Paschal used to focus interest and discussion among the Sisters who were involved in graduate theological study. I suppose that was just symptomatic of what was happening universally.

Fr. Daniel: I believe Fr. Ronald Roloff sensed that. I give him much credit for making the magazine a kind of vehicle for the new consciousness arising out of Vatican II. Sisters were looking for some way they could express new interests, some way they could be updated, and for a magazine that would help them do this.

Circulation figures seem to support this change. It is interesting to note that the lowest circulation figure from 1961 to the present was in 1963, shortly after the beginning of the Council. It had reached a low of about 9,000 subscribers. Right after that, as the Council continued, we see the circulation rising — 10,000, 11,000, 13,000, 15,000. When I took over in 1967, the circulation was 14,000, and it just sort of took off from there until it reached a peak of some 23,000 a few years ago and then levelled off and settled down.

Now, what is the correlation? Either we were writing things that Sisters wanted and needed to read, or we were providing a way for them to express what was happening. The journal was also used as an educational medium for communities that needed to know the principles and practices of updating religious life.

I remember the first "Bulletin Board" I wrote. I had made up my mind when I accepted the editorship that I was not going to let the magazine become a kind of soap box for a harried debate over hemlines and horariums. Some of those issues were not settled yet, but I did not feel that the magazine was the place to resolve matters of that sort.

EARLY EFFORTS TO INVOLVE SISTERS

Fr. Roger: I can fill in a few of those years since Fr. Ronald is not here. When I first became associated with the magazine, Fr. Ronald asked me to try to cultivate Sister reviewers of books. He had concluded that Sisters were placing confidence and credence only in priest book-reviewers. I found, in fact, that there was a resistance by many readers to Sister reviewers who lacked theological preparation.

In the mid-60's we made some tentative efforts to involve Sisters more in the magazine. In fact, when I first joined Fr. Ronald in the fall of 1963, I asked him about the Advisory Board since I was aware of the work Fr. Kilian had done in this respect. Because of its inactivity, he was unable to involve it in the publication. In my first two years I sought for book reviewers among that group of advisors. However, I did not get much response from them. Many of them, I presume, were very busy people.

A couple of years later when we were very low in subscriptions, a Sisters' section became a frequent feature of *The National Catholic Reporter*. *America* magazine was also publishing articles of interest to Sisters. My suggestion to Fr. Ronald at that time was that we either get a Sister editor for *Sister Today* or that we consider stopping publication, since the subscriptions were down to 9,000 and the magazine was not showing an increase of readership. Sisters had these opportunities to go out to other apostolates, and we were encouraging them, as a policy of the magazine, to expand their horizons. However, the management of The Liturgical Press told us at that time that they definitely wanted to continue to publish *Sisters Today*.

THE FIRST SEARCH FOR A SISTER EDITOR

It was then that Fr. Ronald and I contacted a number of Sisters to ask them if they would be interested or knew someone who would be interested in being editor of the magazine. This was about 1965. The responses were uniformly negative, but for different reasons. When I try to draw up a summary of that endeavor, the answers fall into two categories. In the first category were those in which the Mother Superior or the Sister involved indicated that we as priests, as men, would have greater freedom to do the work that was necessary for Sisters than they, as Sisters, as women, could do "under the local bishop." They felt we could do the things necessary and be of greater help to them. The other category was comprised of those Sisters or superiors who said they would only get into trouble if they were to take the job of editor. Ultimately we did not get any applicants, and within a year or two business was looking up again with an increase of subscriptions.

At that time I suggested the name change from *Sponsa Regis* (the Church was getting into the vernacular) to something more contemporary. Fr. Ronald and I sat down one evening and planned a contest for the name change. We tried to figure out what some of the suggestions would be. We supposed it would be something like "Today's Sister," or "Sisters Today," or "Sisters of Today." We expected those to be the most commonly suggested names, and as a matter of fact they were. So even though we did not get a Sister editor, we did get a new name.

Fr. Daniel: I think Fr. Roger's comments are interesting and important in that all the years that the monks of St. John's Abbey have edited and published *Sisters Today* it was a kind of male citadel, but it was not really chauvinistic. Sister readers just were not ready for a Sister editor.

AGGIORNAMENTO

Fr. Paschal: At the time I took over the editorship in 1946, it was a completely different world than what had preceded it. I had been continuously in contact with Sisters through retreats and summer sessions in which I taught courses in theology. I had been involved in ministering to the spiritual growth of Sisters throughout many parts of the United States. Now to begin to explore the situation of "Sisters in the world" was a complete reversal to the previous stance I had taken. When we published the first articles on aggiornamento, I was amazed at first at some of the naivete with which some of the message was being received. I remember hearing from a Sister in England who thanked me for publishing an article on renewal within the Church, for as a result she no longer needed to obtain permission of her superior to wind her watch every day!

The renewal, together with the vehicle of new categories of existential thought, had much that was good for religious life, but not all. The "new liberty" was misunderstood in many instances, though I think it had been accepted in good faith. It appears that the aggiornamento had made it easier for religious to free themselves of their permanent vow commitments. There were also inadequate understandings of obedience.

A genuine renewal ought to be not a rupture from the past but a gradual growth: all we are now is what we were plus the new development. We ought to come of age without losing the identity of who we were and are in Jesus Christ.

During this time many of the contributors to *Sponsa Regis* dealt with articles on the psalms, on prayer, on the scriptural theology of the religious vows, and on the identity of our religious life with the Gospel.

THE BEST OF TIMES

Fr. Daniel: When I began editing in 1967, the Second Vatican Council was over, and it was the best of times. I pushed and pulled a bit with advertising and reminding people that their subscriptions were running out and needed renewal. But these were just good times. Religious life came into a rebirth. Sisters began to come alive in new and exciting ways, and they were doing more things than they had ever done before, with all the growing pains that this involved. They were looking for direction and inspiration. The apostolates were expanding.

I remember doing a composite article ten years ago in which I asked Sisters to write about what in the world they were doing. The results were amazing. One Sister was studying and teaching in a Japanese university; another was working in the inner city; one was teaching in a Baptist seminary; another was doing volunteer work at a state institution; still another was nursing in a nonsectarian hospital. It was sort of mind-blowing to learn how seriously Sisters were taking the directives of Vatican II and beginning to carry the Church into the modern world.

I really wonder what would have happened in the Church ten years ago if bishops, priests and lay people had taken Vatican II as seriously as Sisters did.

SISTERS AS AUTHORS

Sister Mary Anthony: When did Sisters begin to write articles for the magazine? You mentioned, Fr. Roger, that they had hesitated doing book reviews.

Fr. Roger: We began to have the first articles by Sisters in any sort of quantity in the mid-60's. I think we were lucky at that time if we had one article by a Sister each month. But it was our policy to encourage qualified Sister authors to contribute. One of the difficulties was that we were getting a number of warmed-over term papers from summer sessions. But the quality gradually improved, especially as formation directors encouraged younger Sisters to submit articles.

Fr. Kilian: One of the things I tried to do in those early years was to get away from a magazine which was published almost exclusively on articles that were volunteered or free-lanced. I thought it was a bad policy and would inhibit having a magazine with definite direction. So I attempted to go out, especially to Sisters, and ask them to write on specific topics. That was one of the functions of the Advisory Board — to give me topics and authors so that the editorial policy would be formed instead of simply being allowed to drift. I do not think that movement was very successful, but I did get some response.

Fr. Daniel: If that was your policy, I have changed directions. When I came in as editor, I had a certain amount of backlog material that had been passed on to me. Articles just seemed to keep coming in without my having to go out and look or ask for them. One faithful reader told me to always print the best articles that I had on file as soon as possible. Good quality would result in even better quality. I have tried to follow that principle. At times I would ask a few people for specific articles or arrange to interview people on certain topics. I realize I should have done more of this, and I see this as a new direction the magazine ought to take — soliciting articles on specific themes or issues.

CONTACTS WITH SISTERS

Sister Mary Anthony: I would like to pursue another area. In what way were you in contact with women religious in the Church at the time, and did that influence your editorial policies? Fr. Kilian, you have already indicated that you made a deliberate effort to keep in touch through your Advisory Board. What about the rest of you?

Fr. Roger: I was invited to teach at the College of St. Benedict, and so I had Sisters in class and associated with them for coffee or lunch. I also had a sort of residual respect and love for Sisters. This was undoubtedly because I had never gone to a Catholic grade or high school, so I had never gotten those prejudices against Sisters that some priests seemed to have had in earlier days.

Sister Mary Anthony: I was also thinking of Fr. Paschal when I asked that question because I know how involved he was in giving retreats to Sisters and initiating the Benedictine Institute of Theology here at St. Benedict's. He had constant contact with Sisters and also had some association with the Sister Formation leadership group.

Fr. Roger: There is one other thing that certainly influenced me, and that was my going to summer school at the Catholic University of America during the years that Sisters were experiencing many of the changes in the Church and in their convents. Meeting Sisters summer after summer in those days and discussing more freely their concerns was an important new contact for me.

Fr. Daniel: I must give credit to some Sister friends of mine and to the Sisters I got to know through retreats or teaching. They were a great help and support. I always regretted that my other duties did not allow me time to attend some of the early Sisters' conferences such as the National Association of Women Religious.

EDITORIAL OBJECTIVES

Sister Mary Anthony: Did any of you have a different editorial objective than that described in the magazine now that says the purpose of *Sisters Today* is "to explore the role of the religious woman in the Church in our time?"

Fr. Kilian: The policy during my time as editor was different. It was much more restricted and it reflected the period. I had gone to the Sister Formation group and asked them what they wanted the magazine to be, what Sisters needed. Their answer was, "Give us a magazine that we can take into chapel for our meditation."

Sister Mary Anthony: That is interesting. Evidently the Sisters then were not taking the Scriptures with them as the source of their meditation.

Fr. Kilian: No, they weren't taking the Bible with them, but they wanted something to feed themselves spiritually. Either they thought that exploring the role of religious women in the Church in our time was not something the magazine would do well or that there were other instruments which were doing that.

Sister Mary Anthony: Was it even an open question of exploration at that time?

Fr.Kilian: Yes, I think Sister Formation was very much into that, reacting already against the stereotype of the nun. It was an actual question. But it was these women who were so concerned about the role of religious women who asked that *Sisters Today* be the kind of magazine they could take into chapel with them. They wanted spiritual food, spiritual reading.

THE PRIORITY OF PRAYER

Fr. Daniel: I have always been conscious of trying to maintain some kind of a balance between a sort of "how to do it" manual (how to find a place in the inner city, or how do Sisters get out of teaching into something else), and a vehicle for spirituality. We are writing for women who are essentially women who have a spirituality. So articles on prayer have always been a priority of mine. If I receive an article on prayer that is coherent, clear and somewhat unique in its content and form, I buy it and print it. I think that is one thing Sisters are interested in day by day, month by month. The day that ceases, I wonder what will happen to them and to the magazine.

Sister Mary Anthony: It is their role to be special women of prayer in the Church?

Father Daniel: Yes. Do you doubt that?

Sister Mary Anthony: I was just wondering if it is their role more than that of any other Christian in the Church today.

Fr. Daniel: Maybe the charismatic renewal has changed that now, but I do consider that if Sisters are not women of prayer they are not religious women. *Sisters Today* should continue to serve this aspect of their lives.

Fr. Kilian: In times past the concept of religious women as women of prayer was tied to a model; but even in their new freedom, they still have a special call. They do not necessarily have a higher state, but they are a different sign of the Kingdom. The role that prayer has in their lives helps to constitute the difference in that sign as over against married life.

Sister Mary Anthony: I think in fact they have shown that, even if they became liberated. In many ways they have become more serious about prayer.

RECOMMENDATIONS

What recommendations or suggestions do you have for the present or the future of *Sisters Today*?

Fr. Paschal: It is important that *Sisters Today* continue to project a strong theological thrust, orthodox and reflective of the faith. I would hope that it would always maintain the "catholic sense" of things. We have to do what we can to restore confidence in the Church.

Fr. Daniel: We have to find a Sister editor of the magazine. After fifty years, Sisters certainly deserve a Sister editor.

Sister Mary Anthony: Do you think the image of the magazine should be changed?

Fr. Kilian: I think it should be changed by going out and getting more Sisters involved in writing to give the magazine more direction. Prospective authors should be given suggestions for topics. This takes more time, of course, and cannot be done between two or three other jobs. I also think that if we get not only Sisters but also top quality male writers whom Sisters recognize as willing to give of their talents, Sisters will not object to male writers as long as they do not dominate or sound paternalistic.

THE FUTURE

Sister Mary Anthony: Does *Sisters Today* fulfill a purpose? Does it deserve to be in existence?

Fr. Daniel: I think that is a question the new editor ought to ask herself. I think it would certainly create a gap for some readers if the magazine were discontinued, especially for Sisters who have grown up with it and depend on it because it gives them a certain amount of support, information and inspiration.

But perhaps some hard questions have to be asked. Do Sisters need another magazine, and if so, what should it be? I would hope that *Sisters*

Today is not going to continue just because it has been in existence for fifty years. In fact, this may be a good time to discontinue it if it has ceased to explore the role of the woman religious in the Church in our time. I think a new editor should ask questions like "What is our objective? What are we trying to do? Where are we going?"

Annuals

('Plants that flower the first season
the seed is sown, and then die.')

All I planted came up,
balsam and nasturtium and
cosmos and the Marvel of Peru

first the cotyledons
then thickly the differentiated
true leaves of the seedlings,

and I transplanted them,
carefully shaking out each one's
hair-fine rootlets from the earth,

and they have thriven,
well-watered in the new-turned earth;
and grow apace now -

but not one shows signs of a flower,
not one.
            If August passes
flowerless,
and the frosts come,

will I have learned to rejoice enough
in the sober wonder of
green healthy leaves?

Denise Levertov
Sisters Today, July, 1966

PART TWO

EARLY ASPECTS AND ATTITUDES :

The Days of Victimhood and Detachment

It can hardly be overestimated how seriously religious in general and Sisters in particular have taken these words of Jesus: "Whoever wishes to be my follower must deny his very self, take up his cross each day, and follow in my steps. Whoever would save his life will lose it, and whoever loses his life for my sake will save it. What profit does he show who gains the whole world and destroys himself in the process?" (Lk 9:23-25)

The articles selected for this section give sure and simple witness to the way these words of the Lord were accepted and put into practice by an earlier generation of his disciples. More than a mere shadow of Jesus' cross seemed to have fallen across the lives of those who professed to turn their backs on "father and mother, . . . brothers and sisters, indeed their very selves" (Lk 14:26). Religious had been called to "take up," not just to tolerate that cross.

One way to guarantee that the cross of Christ was being carried and not dragged was through the acceptance of suffering. Before the days of the charismatic renewal with its emphasis on the healing power of Jesus and his willingness to bring relief not grief, the vocation of suffering was seen as a special invitation to imitate the Suffering Servant, Jesus Christ, who was "pierced for our offenses, crushed for our sins" (Is 53:5). He who was victim before he was victor was calling for generous followers to be identified with him as victim, A Victim Soul.

A unique task of *Sponsa Regis* during the first two decades of publication was to consistently encourage its readers to take up the apostolate of suffering as Victim Souls and thereby "form an inner circle of real friends of the Man of Sorrows." To prove the truth of a saying of St. Francis de Sales that "An ounce of suffering is worth more than a pound of action," religious

33

were invited to offer themselves as victims, "nailed to a cross of physical or spiritual suffering." With the consent of their confessor, religious were to make an act of oblation of their sufferings and submit their names to the editor of *Sponsa Regis* for transmission to the headquarters of the Association of Victim Souls in a European convent of the Institute of the Daughters of the Sacred Heart. In 1937, the editor could report that this Association "counts a membership of more than 200,000 souls, belonging to all classes of society in different nations." Sisters comprised a significant segment of that membership. Two articles have been chosen among the dozens published to further describe a movement that gave meaning, direction, and dedication to countless women religious.

The article "On Detachment" from 1930 highlights the attachment given to this particular aspect of religious life a generation or two ago.

"Proper Custody of the Eyes" is based on the conviction that "There is no true striving after perfection and holiness without the proper custody of the eyes. The pursuit of perfection and holiness requires that 1) we close our eyes, 2) we use them at the proper time."

"The Gracious Nun" is a short and delightful call for balance in the pursuit for piety lest it be true of more convents what a forty-year professed Sister said of hers: "After being forty years with 'saints,' I understand why Christ preferred the company of sinners."

"Failures of Religious Vocations" is one of a lengthy series of articles signed by "A Missionary" in which the dangers to religious life are attacked with vigor and little compromise. The graphophone (today's record player), the telephone, and the radio are seen as the devil's "handy means for promoting worldliness among religious persons, and through that the decay and decline of religious communities." It is an easy matter to imagine what "A Missionary" would write about the blight that television has brought to religious communities and individuals where a 21-inch screen becomes a kind of tabernacle or altar for a new liturgy of the hours . . . and hours . . . and hours. Or perhaps convents, unlike monasteries, are still able to schedule community affairs on Monday evening during the pro-football season. So how about a Saturday meeting during the Lawrence Welk show?

Sponsa Regis, April, 1936

Victim Souls: The Vocation of Suffering

A Carmelite Sister

Only the other day, a six year old boy who was bearing suffering patiently was touched by the cries of other children about him in the hospital ward. "Oh," he said wistfully, "if it would only just hurt me and not them!"

In many pure and generous hearts the desire for vicarious suffering may almost be termed an instinct. And he who bore our infirmities bends down to these little creatures whose thoughts are echoes of his own. He teaches them many things unknown to the worldly wise. They soon understand that they can make use of every trial, every sorrow that comes to them, that all can be offered to the Man of Sorrows, and that he will unite these drops — or, it may be, these streams — to the fathomless sea of his own sufferings, whence he will draw healing waters to cleanse souls from the leprosy of sin.

A certain nun who loves to think of our Lord's public life, to picture him as teacher and physician, believes that a delightful story — fiction, but enshrining truth — could be written about a little invalid girl whom Jesus did not heal. The scene might be laid in a cottage near Nazareth. The mother of the child stands at the doorway, watching a receding figure. She says, half aloud: "If the carpenter's son is indeed a wonder-worker, why has he not healed my child?" A sweet voice calls her, and she kneels beside the little sufferer's bed. The child's face is drawn with pain, but the eyes are radiant with happiness.

"Mother, do not ask him to cure me! I would not wish it. Come closer. I will tell you a secret. We have made an agreement, the Master and I. He is lord of a beautiful kingdom, where all is peace and love. He wishes to win all our hearts and to have us dwell with him in that kingdom. But his soldiers do not make use of swords. He has told me that prayer and

35

suffering are two most powerful weapons. And I am to help him win subjects for his kingdom. Just as the beautiful white lambs are slain in the temple, so I am placed on an altar of sacrifice. I give him every moment of my pain. He tells me that I am far more privileged than many of those he has healed. It may be that he touches them once; then he says, 'Go in peace!' Some of them never meet him again. But he does not dismiss me. Even when I do not see him, I often have a sense of his presence. Lately I feel that almost constantly. And I am so happy! I would not change places with any of those whom he has healed!"

This little confidante of Jesus is a type of the victim souls. They form an inner circle of real friends of the Man of Sorrows. They are not of the number of those who hear his commands from afar; they do not merely come in contact with him; they regard all things from his point of view; they think his thoughts. There is hardly need of words in their intimacy. They see "no one but only Jesus." They love their pain — not for its own sake, for they are human and pain is always pain — but because it has won for them a place close to the tenderest of hearts, and chiefly because suffering is the purchase-price of souls.

Our Lord selects his friends from all lands and classes of society. In a truly Catholic home in cultured France, a child tastes the bliss of winning to repentance the criminal Pranzini whom she styles her "firstborn." Henceforth, no earthly joy can detain her from the Carmelite cell in which she must love and suffer; aiding Jesus in his work for souls. Her plea for a legion of little victims rings across the ocean and finds an echo in the hearts of a knightly boy, Gerard Raymond, the Quebec seminarian, who thus offers his life to the King: "With thee, I shall go up to calvary; I shall stretch myself upon the cross, I shall let the nails be driven in, the blood flow."

In September, 1930, less than two years before his death, Gerard, who was following the exercises of a students' retreat, wrote in his diary: "O Jesus, I hardly dare to formulate this desire. Receive it, if it please thee, as a pledge of my love . . . To thee I sacrifice my life, with my hopes of the priesthood and of martyrdom, for this object in exchange — that of all the pupils who are following this retreat with me, not one may be lost eternally, that all may love thee and may work for the extension of thy reign upon earth." Two days later: "Thou hast not accepted my offering for today, but for another time. But, O Jesus, if in reality some companion is not yet with thee, I pray thee, accept my offering. Or, grant that I may suffer all my life, and receive my suffering, united to thine, for this same object!"

It is not only in refined homes and in centers of learning that the victim-vocation finds responsive hearts. In the recently founded Carmel of Borneo there died, some months ago, a child of one of the least civilized of Borneo's pagan tribes. She had been rescued and instructed by missionary Sisters. When still very young she entered Carmel, where she was named Alice of the Blessed Sacrament. She yearned for the conversion of her countrymen and felt inspired to offer herself as a victim of love. God accepted the sacrifice. She, who had hitherto enjoyed robust health, was attacked by an illness that defied medical skill. She made her profession upon her death-bed; and at the age of twenty, having spent only sixteen months in Carmel, she was called to the eternal nuptials. As soon as this little grain of wheat had fallen into the ground, a harvest began to appear. Heavenly favors, conversions, vocations to Carmel, attest the holiness of the heroic child who died for her people.

Why has not our Lord a greater number of willing victims? Partly because the value of suffering is not understood. Those who enter the service of the King wish to accomplish much for his glory, to build temples in his honor, to follow the sound of the trumpet which calls to action and to victory. Helplessness, obscurity, enforced leisure which seems to avail nothing, apparent failure — none of these is attractive to hearts that are burning with zeal. Perhaps only those who have endured pain can understand the meaning of the saying of St. Francis of Sales: "An ounce of suffering is worth more than a pound of action."

But there is another — and less worthy — reason for a soul's reluctance to place itself upon the altar of sacrifice. There is a natural apprehension of the trials which may follow. One day, when St. Teresa of Avila was on her way to found the Carmel of Burgos, she and her little party of nuns had one of the annoying experiences which seemed to be their lot on such expeditions. The road was so flooded that it became dangerous to continue their journey by carriage. Reminding the nuns that they need not fear since they were doing God's work, the saint led the way through the torrent. She lost her footing and was in danger of being carried away by the current. Within her soul she heard the voice of our Lord: "It is ever thus that I treat my friends." And Teresa replied: "Ah, Lord, that is the reason thou hast so few."

We smile at the flash of wit, the playful intimacy of the bride who would not surrender her share in the trials of the Bridegroom for all that the world could offer. But we regretfully admit the truth of her words. Even among those called to the special service of the King, there are not enough Teresas. There are many who say that they love Jesus, who do love him in a sense, but very few who reply "We can" to the wistful question: "Can you drink the chalice that I shall drink?" There are few who can plead as did Gerard Raymond, who wrote beneath a picture of the agony in the garden: "Jesus, grant that I may drink this chalice with thee! I wish to be a victim for sinners! I wish to be a martyr."

Today the King whom we know to be worthy of all love is being reviled, insulted, hated. His enemies are planning to drive him from the earth; if they could, they would dethrone him from his heaven. Shall we who dwell in his house, who are daily fed with his eucharistic banquet of delight, we who know him so intimately, shall we not fight his battle — with the best of weapons? We must turn our eyes to Calvary if we would know what that weapon is. He won his greatest victory when he seemed to fail; he was strong against death when he seemed weakest. Have we courage to tell him that, if he desires it, we will let ourselves be nailed to a cross of physical or spiritual suffering, so that, in our persons, he may continue his life of reparation? On the cross, his hands and feet could not move; they could only suffer. Yet he was using them as instruments in his work of saving souls. We are members of his mystical body. Shall we not cooperate with our head?

But when we offer ourselves as victims, we must beware of choosing the manner of our execution. The lambs destined for the temple-sacrifices must go meekly, whither they are led. Let us place ourselves in the tender hands of the divine high priest. It may be that unusual trials are not in store for us. Let us be too little to ask for them, for we could not bear them without God's grace.

Ours may be the cross of uncongenial tasks, of physical and mental weariness, of daily annoyances which are pin-pricks that set the nerves on edge. Or ours may be the harder trial of spiritual darkness and coldness which are all the more painful because we have known the joys of divine intimacy. Any of these sufferings may cause a long martyrdom requiring all the more heroism because it appears inglorious. Let us not seek to know what particular trial may be in store for us. The King to whom we offer ourselves loves us with an infinite love.

He calls for volunteers. He deigns to wish for our help. He has said to one of his little confidantes: "Souls are not saved by doing nothing." By prayer, by sacrifice, by self-immolation, we can lift his banners high. Shall we not demean ourselves as spouses of the King?

Sponsa Regis, October, 1936

A Call for Victim Souls

Xavier Hasler, O.S.B.

Once on the feast of Corpus Christi a soul asked our divine Savior: "Lord, what is your wish on this great feast?" The Savior replied: "A legion of victim souls. It is to walk in procession before me, and from it flames of love and sacrifice are to ascend as votive-offerings to my heart. O, how I thirst for victim souls!"

Do not be frightened at the word "victim soul." It indeed sounds harsh, but it means something quite different from what it appears. It conceals an apostolate of unlimited fruitfulness and a promise of unsuspected holiness. Is this not the sum total of what a devout soul may desire?

There is a great dearth of priests and missionaries in many parts of the world. Multitudes of souls are in danger of being lost forever. Yet our divine Savior will not suffer that his beloved children should perish. His immense mercy prompts him to seek auxiliaries who are to aid his priests in the work of saving souls. Apostolic souls, victim souls are to be found who must help to keep the world from utter ruin.

Is it possible that God calls religious and lay people to take part in the work of redemption? Yes, and blessed are they whom he calls to save souls; they will share in his glory. But souls are saved more through prayer, sacrifices, and sufferings than by instruction and preaching. St. Theresa, the Little Flower, was so convinced of this that she would say: "By suffering more souls are saved than by the most eloquent sermons." The priests sow the seed of the word of God, the victim souls water it by their prayers and sacrifices. The sufferings of Christ redeemed the world, the sufferings of men in union with his passion must complete the work of redemption.

God alone knows how many victim souls throughout the world are already exercising their sublime apostolate in all secrecy by a life of sacrifice. There are such charming examples of heroic love that they are capable of arousing the enthusiasm of multitudes of souls. St. Margaret Mary, the Little Flower, Benigna Consolata, Gemma Galgani, Teresa of Konnersreuth, and many others by their words and examples inflame thousands of generous men and women, even children, to follow in their footsteps. Only at the last judgment will it be manifest what these simple souls as apostles of the divine heart have accomplished for the salvation of mankind.

But why does the Savior desire so vehemently to arouse the victim spirit in great multitudes of souls? Because there are so many of his children on earth who do not know him, who do not even wish to know him, who do not love him, who even give themselves over to a life of sin. Moreover there are so many lukewarm souls, souls that have no zeal, that do not endeavor to become holy, that waste their precious time on the world and its vanities, in short, souls that are neither bad nor good, but just mediocre. All these he longs to save, many of them even to lead to greater holiness; but the pace is too slow for him. He needs generous victim souls, souls that forget themselves in order to serve only the interests and the love of the Sacred Heart without counting the cost. In union with him and his sufferings these souls will rescue the world from the brink of perdition.

Now there are so many lovers of the Sacred Heart in the whole world, especially in religious communities. From them Jesus loves to choose his hidden victim souls. Many of them only seem to wait for an invitation from the Sacred Heart to consecrate themselves entirely to him with all their being and possession. And when the Savior calls and the soul hears the blissful and urgent invitation, what must be its response? It is to accept the call without the least fear and hesitation, and to give to the Savior unreservedly all it has, its faculties and powers, its body with its senses, all it does and suffers, all its prayers and merits, even all that it receives from others in life and in death. All without exception must be given to the Savior that he may dispose of it according to his designs for the salvation and sanctification of souls.

Many souls give to the heart of Jesus an occasional good work or sacrifice; some others are perhaps even quite generous. The victim soul gives him all, offers him every single sacrifice without exception; yes, its entire life is one continuous heroic act of perfect, unselfish love. More than that! If it sees that it has no more to bestow, it requests the Savior to dispose of its body and spirit according to his good pleasure.

The victim soul then does not make a gift of some fruits merely but of the entire tree together with all its fruits. It is like a burning candle that quietly and entirely consumes itself for the divine heart. It is like a grain of incense that dissolves itself on the altar of sacrificial love and ascends as sweet smelling odor in the sight of God. It is like a mine of gold or a field of diamonds whence the Sacred Heart can draw ever new and more ransom money for the salvation of sin-bound souls.

As soon as religious have become victim souls, the Savior himself takes their training into hand. He adorns them with all graces, encourages them anew to the practice of self-denial, strengthens their interior life, increases their love for God and neighbor, fills them with the presence of God. He makes of them true apostles, genuine saints of his heart.

Now there are some who say: "I am not worthy to become a victim soul." I answer: "It is not necessary to be worthy. The Savior is satisfied with your earnest good will and your persevering efforts to suffer in union with him whatever your life imposes upon you."

Others try to excuse themselves saying: "I have no taste for such a life of love." But the Savior has promised that he will teach his victim souls the science of love and open to them the treasures of his heart. Some again believe themselves unfit for the victim life because they cannot pray well. This precisely is what the Savior will teach them, if they embrace the victim state.

Finally there are those that are full of fear and apprehension. But how can a soul that seriously strives for perfection fear so easy a means to become an apostle of the divine heart! One day such a soul saw how a constant stream of light and grace flowed from the Blessed Sacrament onto the victim souls and how these therefrom received strength and love for their sacrifices.

All victim souls are favorites of the divine heart, so full of goodness, love, beauty that there seems to be no greater blessedness than to become such a favorite. The Savior in his goodness and gratitude goes so far as to give them power over his heart. "They shall possess power over my heart." Whatever they confidently ask for themselves or others they will receive from his heart. Like for like. The divine heart will not be surpassed in generosity by any of his best friends. To the soul that gives all the Savior also gives all.

Let no one take offense at the word "victim soul." Let no one imagine that all victim souls must drink the chalice of sufferings to the dregs. Of many the Savior requests merely the ordinary, but he will give them the graces to do all well. Only few he permits to taste sacrifice and suffering in full measure. But these are the most blessed and privileged. They are most admirably transformed and sent forth as saints to heal the world.

Perhaps some generous soul will ask: "What am I to do in order to place many spiritual treasures at the disposal of the Savior? I am indeed willing, but I do not know how to proceed." As previously stated, the Sacred Heart at first demands very little. It is satisfied if the soul performs its ordinary duties well and will inspire it to do them still better as time goes on.

Religious should observe their vows in all respects and lovingly yield submission and punctual obedience to their rule and their superiors; for every act, if done for the love of God, brings a great reward. They should bear patiently whatever pains or trials fall to their lot, mortify their senses, wherever it can be done, and love to worship the Sacred Heart in the tabernacle. The Savior does not demand great things of them, but desires to see his victim souls faithful in small matters. By this fidelity heaven is again opened to many sinners.

The small matters of which our Savior speaks are precisely: great fidelity to duty, our daily crosses and the various smaller sufferings, our devotion to the Precious Blood and sacred wounds, the offering up of our divine Savior's sufferings and merits as a means of expiation and petition, and above all, the holy Sacrifice of the Mass.

How should one offer herself as a victim soul? Through the hands of the Blessed Virgin Mary and in union with the passion and death of our divine Savior. Mary, our good mother, will add thereto from her own works and merits and thus render the sacrifice still more acceptable to God. But some already have given over all to the poor souls in purgatory by the Heroic Act. Even these souls should donate themselves and their all to the Sacred Heart. God knows how to apply our gifts in the best possible manner. He may apply all to the poor souls, if he sees fit. At any rate the poor souls will certainly not be the losers.

Finally many souls have consecrated themselves to the Blessed Virgin according to the method of the "True Devotion to Mary" as taught by the Blessed Grignon de Montfort. These souls and their sacrifices are likewise desired by the Sacred Heart. Moreover, they already are generous souls who have given themselves entirely to Mary. Let them now go through Mary to Jesus, for this precisely is the purpose of every surrender to Mary.

And now one more word to victim souls. Bring to your Savior as many other victim souls as you can find. He is not content with but a small number; he desires to have a whole army of them.

By means of these little victims many souls are saved, others are sanctified, and finally the world is won for the heart of Jesus. Therefore, find victim souls! This can only be done through prayer and suffering. The Little Flower of the Child Jesus prays so fervently: "Humbly I beg of thee. O Savior, look down upon the many little souls and draw them to thy Sacred Heart. I conjure thee, O my God, select for thyself from among men a whole army of little, humble victims, who are worthy of thy love!"

Let therefore the oblation be made by whomsoever the divine heart calls. As of old, so now again our Lord seeks apostles, but apostles of a different kind, apostles of love, prayer, and sacrifice. As of old, he now again addresses himself to souls, but to almost countless ones, saying: "If thou wilt be perfect, leave all thou possessest and follow me!" Save what may yet be saved, for the time is short!

Sponsa Regis, September, 1930

On Detachment

An Ursuline Sister

Every one of you that does not renounce all that he possesses cannot be my disciple" (Lk 14:33). How our hearts shrunk at the thought of this requirement when first the Lord whispered his sweet invitation to give ourselves to him! And yet, urged by his love, the eyes lifted to the holy mountain, we some day cast aside all earthly possessions, friendships, family ties, our own free will, and full of happiness we said: "Now my Beloved is mine; he is all I have, and I am wholly his."

Did we realize the full meaning of this? If we look over the years passed since, we shall probably say: "I was sincere, but how little did I know what it meant! How little did I know my own poor human heart, which, at every occasion, especially in the little daily occurrences, tries to get back a crumb or two of the big offering it made!" Our vows, our rules, we try to keep them faithfully; but if we examine the detachment of our hearts, we make unexpected discoveries. Is my Beloved my all when I listen to the many earthly desires regarding my work, my surroundings, food, clothing, my superiors and companions, which turn up at every discomfort and difficulty?

If we are detached we accept discomfort, we even impose it freely, yet prudently, on ourselves. It is easy to appear detached in our own eyes and in those of others as long as we want nothing; only when a thing is taken from us can we see the real disposition of our soul, and generally it is then only that we can become truly detached. Renouncement in fact is necessary to reach the detachment of the heart, as humiliations are necessary to attain humility.

Detachment is above all a matter of the spirit that vivifies; exterior abnegations without the right spirit do perhaps no more than nourish our pride. God is the great factor in the work of detachment; we can only prove our good will by making ourselves God's partners in the task of destroying all undesirable attachments either to the world around us, or to ourselves, or even to the consolations of God.

When we think of detachment, we have primarily the first field in view: the world around us. It is here that we find the most numerous occasions for active cooperation with the promptings of grace. The fervent soul eagerly listens to what the Lord says within her and willingly cuts the threads that bind her to a cherished object, to a beloved person. "God alone" is the sword with which she fights unceasingly; for no sooner have we severed old ties, than we form, often unconsciously, new ones.

Two dangers beset us in this work: imprudence and pride. A wise director can do much to ward them off. Often, too, God himself takes the lead. He, the scrutinizer of hearts, knows best our bad tendencies, and if he finds good will on our part, he will use unsparingly the pruning shears and free us from all wild growth, yet not without pouring into the bleeding wound the healing balm of his strong love. The soul has nothing to do but to submit to the painful dispositions of his all-wise providence — a providence that may even regulate such trivial matters as food and clothing. Is this not the case in sickness?

What renunciation in this respect did he not impose on the religious in Europe during and after the war? Nothing was left them but the bare necessities of life together with a still darker outlook for the future. No director would require so much from a soul committed to his care, but the Lord did; and there was no danger of pride about it.

Another case. We might resolve to counteract an overgreat sympathy by setting narrow limits to our intercourse with a friend. God, instead, lets indifference, misunderstandings, coldness take hold of the friend's heart. Not only do we feel keenly the disruption of tender ties; we are humiliated, often painfully humiliated, at the same time. Detachment and humiliation go with him hand in hand.

This brings us to the second field of detachment: detachment from self. We must learn to renounce our self-love and, therefore, all that makes us love and esteem ourselves, such as natural gifts, talents, accomplishments. How slow are we in discovering the opportunities for this self-effacement by suppressing our views for those of others as far as they are right, by letting others reap the success that our efforts made possible.

Knowing our weakness and inability to give up our inner self, the Master comes again to our aid. How much detachment is there not included in a prolonged illness, in a change of place? Or he permits our best efforts to meet with failure, our ideas to be ridiculed, our intentions suspected, our character misunderstood, our actions misrepresented to superiors; those on whose sympathy and advice we relied show suspicion and ill-feeling. If such a condition lasts, the soul becomes uncertain of her own self, her character seems changed to her, she loses all hold, her inner life is clouded in doubts whose solution seems hopeless, is hopeless indeed, because God wants this state for her purification.

It is not seldom that the nerves break down under the strain of such trials, adding new difficulties to the old ones. Her nervous weakness is considered lack of good will. Why should she not be able to do what she did before? There is nothing left for her but to sink down at the feet of the Lord with a heartfelt *"Kyrie eleison."* And her Lord and God, seeing his work accomplished, the soul detached from self, will not despise her cries, but lift her up with tender mercy. Yes, "the word of God is more piercing than any two-edged sword, reaching unto the division of the soul and the spirit, of the joints also and the marrow" (Heb 4:12).

This is especially true in the third field of detachment where the soul is entirely passive under the knife of the divine Surgeon: detachment from God's consolations. As long as God leaves to the soul the feeling of his love for her, she finds the strength to bear any privations and trials. Is not his love sweeter than any pleasure of the earth? What joy greater than to be loved by the Almighty? Even from this joy she must be detached. Therefore the Lord abandons her, her prayers seem not to reach him, she is weighed down by the crushing consciousness of her faults, there seems to be no longer any God for her. And yet, now only does she cling to him purely, unselfishly; now she seeks God alone.

Painful as the practice of detachment may be, our Lord requires it with the kindest, most merciful purposes in view. For only as far as the heart is free from self-love can God fill it with his divine love, our only true happiness. To gain this love, we should eagerly do our part in renunciation; we should implore the Lord to spare us not, and thank him for every bond he severs. Then we can say with the saints: *"Deus meus et omnia."*

Sponsa Regis, July, 1947

Proper Custody of the Eyes

A.D.

"The light of thy body is thy eye. If thy eye be single, thy whole body will be lightsome; but if thy eye be evil, thy whole body will be darksome" (Mt 6:22-23). History records that the heathen philosopher Crates one day carried all his money and possessions to the sea and cast them into the waves. He wished thereby to detach himself from everything earthly in order to be able wholeheartedly to devote himself to the contemplation of truth.

The heathen philosopher Democritus went still further. He thrust out his eyes in order not to be distracted in his contemplation and quest for truth.

How these men loved truth! One might understand why a man may make use of his money to seek the truth, but to cast away all his possessions for its sake is inconceivable. One may also see the reason why a person might seclude himself behind closed doors and curtained windows in order not to be disturbed in his thoughts; but to thrust out one's eyes, to render oneself blind in order to devote one's time to contemplation is hard to understand.

These philosophers strove to detect truth which God placed in creation through various laws. We strive after the eternal, uncreated truth, the Creator of nature. Ought we to allow ourselves to be outdone by the heathens in the pursuit after truth?

In order to possess God eternally, to enjoy the eternal truth, we have given up all our possessions at the time of our holy profession. We have renounced our claim to everything earthly in order to travel more freely and unhindered the way to our heavenly home. We have entered the cloister, retiring into the solitude of the enclosure away from worldly temptations and distractions in order to concentrate our attention more freely on God. Must we religious go to the extent of depriving ourselves of our eyes in order to close the door to every distraction? That would be preposterous. However, even though we are able to possess our priceless treasure, the eyes, we must guard them at all times. There is no true striving after perfection and holiness without the proper custody of the eyes. The pursuit of perfection and holiness requires that 1) *we close our eyes*, 2) *we use them at the proper time*.

I

At the present time, great emphasis is placed on the care of the eyes, not only by health dilettantes but also by eye specialists. It is said that all internal organs are reflected in the eye and that all organic changes are indicated therein. The fact is that eye diagnosticians have discovered severe maladies which escaped the notice of many physicians. It is quite certain, however, that one's inner life, the life of the soul, is reflected in the human eye. We sometimes say: "One can look straight into his eyes," "He can't look straight into your eyes," or "His eyes betray him."

Just as the whole life of the soul is reflected in the eye, so also does the soul receive the most impressions through the eye. Indeed, through the eye more impressions are received than through all other organs together. It is true, we hear much. But the ear has not a great range of perception. Under favorable circumstances one can hear a normally speaking person at most sixty meters away. The field of vision, however, is very much greater, and therefore are the impressions received through the eyes more numerous.

From these purely natural facts it follows that we religious have a sacred duty to guard our eyes well. If our soul receives the most impressions through our eyes, then we, who earnestly strive for perfection, ought also to be solicitous that only good impressions are made on the soul. We must guard our eyes.

This custody of the eyes and the caution to be exercised in our looks is of primary importance outside of the cloister in our association with the world. "The world is seated in wickedness" (1 Jn 5:19), which is true for all times. The world is wicked, is corrupt in its modes and fashions, vicious in its pictures and literature, corrupt in its displays and advertisements. Woe to the religious who, as it were, swallows alive through the eyes everything that is worldly, indecent and scandalous. Then shall be verified what St. Augustine says: "A thought is preceded by a glance, then follows the delight, and delight begets consent."

Did not all the misery of mankind have its origin in an unguarded look? Holy Scripture very clearly describes the fall of our first parents: "And the woman saw that the tree was good to eat, and fair to the eyes, and delightful to behold; and she took of the fruit thereof and did eat, and gave to her husband who did eat." Had Eve not looked at the forbidden fruit, she would not have fallen.

How many have sinned through their eyes which they failed to guard! How many have been aroused to sensuality by sinful looks and led to commit the greatest sins against holy purity because of a too great freedom of the eyes. David was a man according to God's own heart, a friend of God. An unguarded look indulged in resulted in his becoming an adulterer and a murderer. Had he resisted and guarded his eyes, he would have spared himself much misfortune.

It is true that not all looks have these dire consequences and lead to sensuality and sin. But how many distractions at prayer, how many inordinate desires, urges, and impulses may be traced to unguarded eyes! Holy Scripture says: "Look not round about thee in the ways of the city" (Sir 9:7). A religious who does not heed this admonition will hardly make any progress in the spiritual life. For everything received by the senses, especially the eyes, comes to life again in our moments of solitude and appears before our mind at prayer, meditation, during holy Mass, and even while receiving Holy Communion.

If one's own salvation already requires the custody of the senses, then the good example which we owe to seculars all the more demands a proper restraint in the use of the eyes. Nothing is more unbecoming for a religious than to gaze about fixedly while passing through the streets. Such a one can only arouse the admiration and ridicule of passersby besides being offensive in her conduct. On the contrary, a Sister greatly edifies others who modestly goes about her way, looking neither left nor right, and is blind as it were to everything about her. Her conduct is a living sermon to all who see her.

Every Sister, when going out in public, should aim to follow the example of St. Francis of Assisi. This saint one day said to one of his confreres, "Come, let us go and preach." They started out, going down one side of the mountain, then through Assisi and back again. Throughout the entire journey they proceeded with eyes cast down, saying not a word. Coming back to the cloister, St. Francis was asked by his companion: "Father, didn't we want to go and preach?" St. Francis gave the well known answer: "Brother, we have just given our sermon. Through the restraint of our eyes, which others have observed in us, we have preached to them."

The custody of the eyes is also necessary within the cloistral walls. A religious who throughout the year, and perhaps throughout her whole life, does not come in contact with the world may nevertheless be unrestrained and distracted if she does not guard her eyes. For that which is unnecessary and to no purpose, and which arouses her curiosity and attention also robs her of interior recollection throughout the day and renders her spiritual exercises very difficult of accomplishment. Moreover, even though religious life and discipline may flourish in a cloister, there will be many failings and imperfections. We ought, however, to disregard such imperfections in our surroundings and not uncharitably criticize our fellow religious on account of their shortcomings. If then we do not guard our eyes but allow them to scrutinize everything that goes on in the cloister, every existing imperfection comes to our notice and we easily lapse into uncharitable criticism of those in whom we observe these imperfections. A religious who has not the power to restrain her eyes from wandering about will hardly in the end refrain her tongue from uncharitable speech.

Through such criticism great harm is inflicted on the soul. The constant daily observation of what is imperfect and its condemnation in our interior engenders eventually a dissatisfaction in our heart. This dissatisfaction leads to fault finding and carping, not only against the failing Sisters but also against the superiors, and the entire household with its daily order and routine.

The more we complain, the more our dissatisfaction grows until a point is reached when the soul's attitude hardly differs from that which is characteristic of a Bolshevist out in the world. And all this may be traced back to the lack of vigilance of the eyes. *"Averte oculos meos ne videant vanitatem.* — Turn away my eyes, that they may not behold vanity." These words of the Psalmist should be our daily prayer. The guarding of our looks, the restraint of the eyes is of the greatest importance for our spiritual progress on the road to perfection. Yet, sometimes, it may also be our duty to keep our eyes open.

II

To have our eyes cast down in the cloister is always desirable. But this can go too far when we no longer see the things we ought to see — for instance, when a Sister fails to see the dust and filth that gathers in the rooms or corridors. Such lack of observation must be corrected by the superior without delay. It is true, our rooms should not resemble the boudoir of the modern woman of the world; nevertheless, scrupulous cleanliness and tidiness should reign supreme. Spider webs in the corners, layers of dust which would invite one to draw figures on tables and window sills should be unknown in the cloister. This cleanliness, however, is only possible when one keeps her eyes open.

Legend has it that St. Bernard, after having lived in his cell for a whole year, did not know how the ceiling looked. This may possibly be true. It may be that spiders were unknown in his cloister. However, if a Sister nowadays would fail to examine the ceiling for a whole year, the spiders would soon dance upon her head. Cleanliness and tidiness require that we keep our eyes open to remove all dust and dirt.

Charity amongst the Sisters also demands an open eye. The principle that no Sister should meddle in the affairs of another is ever true. Nevertheless, Sisters should help one another in their work and lighten the burden for one another. However, it requires an open eye to lend a helping hand to another Sister who is crowded with work and labors in the interests of the community. A Sister who seeks her own convenience is blind to sisterly charity as well as to the means of salvation.

A watchful eye is also needed in the care of children. It would be regrettable if a Sister were to face the children in the classroom without watching them. If the eye cannot rule and control the class, then all other educational means are of no avail. In the training of children, the eye plays a very important role. Therefore the watchword should be, have an eye on the children, large and small. See to it that nothing disorderly creeps in, that no child sidesteps the rules or becomes corrupted. Where many children are together, it easily happens that one may go wrong or at least become morally tainted. If the teacher fails in vigilance, such a child may entirely go to ruin and drag others along into the abyss.

These principles also hold over against domestics and all those who by reason of employment or education form part of the religious community. Despite their condition, they still remain human and will manifest their weaknesses as soon as an opportunity is afforded them. It does not necessarily argue distrust, false suspicion or rash judgment closely to observe them. It is a matter of duty to see to it that they take part in the religious exercises. It may easily happen that domestics fail to make their Easter duty. This would indicate a lack of watchfulness on the part of the superior. It is her duty to take care that the work entrusted to them be duly performed, that their conduct be checked throughout the day and that the hours of retiring be punctiliously observed. Failure in this matter may result in grave scandals and vicious talk throughout the neighborhood.

Care is also needed in nursing the sick. Perhaps a patient has died without the sacraments because a Sister failed to see any danger ahead. It is true that sudden deaths do occur. Complications may set in which a Sister may not foresee. As a general rule, a Sister will sense the danger of death in due time if she keeps on the alert.

Finally, every position of trust requires an open eye. Whether one has work assigned in church, in school or in any other place in the management of the household, every office of responsibility exacts the faithful fulfillment of duties on the part of every Sister. The vow of poverty requires that we avoid extravagance and waste, and its observance depends upon a vigilant eye.

Of all the responsible positions in a community, that of Superior is the most important, and it is she who must exercise a careful watch over her flock. A superior should be according to the mind of God the guardian of religious observance. She must endeavor to keep those under her charge from evil, strengthen them in virtue and lead them heavenward on the road to perfection. Such is the primary and most important duty of a superior. We know very well from our own personal experience that we commit many faults despite the best of intentions. This is a consequence of fallen human nature. If a superior has no eye for such failings she is unable to reprimand or correct them. The result then will be that these failures become more frequent and tend to undermine religious discipline. Therefore, a superior who does not keep her eyes open may easily bring about the ruin of community life.

In striving after perfection the eye as well as every other sense organ must be used properly. Our association with the world and the life in the cloister sometimes demand proper control of our eyes. On the other hand, our vocation, position of trust in the community, sisterly charity and general order in the cloister call for watchfulness and alert use of the eyes. If then we open and close our eyes at the proper time, place, and occasion, as the will of God may demand, we shall be deemed worthy one day to behold and enjoy the vision of the all holy God for all eternity.

The Cat As Cat

The cat on my bosom
sleeping and purring
- fur-petalled chrysanthemum,
squirrel-killer -

is a metaphor only if I
force him to be one,
looking too long in his pale, fond,
dilating, contracting, eyes

that reject mirrors, refuse
to observe what bides
stockstill.

     Likewise

flex and reflex of claws
gently pricking through sweater to skin
sustain their own tune,
not mine. I-Thou, cat, I-Thou.

Denise Levertov
Sisters Today, June, 1966

Sponsa Regis, July, 1939

The Gracious Nun

W.E. Mulroney, S.J.

An old nun who had lived for forty years in the convent with other nuns that should have been saints remarked one day: "After being forty years with 'saints,' I understand why Christ preferred the company of sinners."

There is, no doubt, a certain note of sarcasm in the old nun's remark; but there is also, unhappily, a certain amount of truth. For it is strange but true, that the so-called very pious nun is often hard to get along with, is selfish and ungracious. That, no doubt, makes others recoil from piety. For they reason, wrongly of course: if, being pious, one becomes so unattractive and odd, then it is better not to be pious.

When we strive to find out why the overly pious nun is so unfriendly and often non-human, we discover that it is because her prayer is not enlightening. Prayer is never meant to be a sedative, confirming one blindly in one's oddities and eccentricities. It should be a searchlight, penetrating into the soul's greatest depths to discover all that is not Christlike.

Very often nuns who are extremely scrupulous about the exact performance of their duties and the living up to their rule in every detail are lacking in the natural virtues of politeness and courtesy. They would consider it a sin to break silence or to fail in some minor detail of their rule. Yet their consciences never bother them when they are unkind to their Sisters.

A Christian, and more so a nun, should be as much ashamed of roughness as of falsehood. Where God's grace has full swing, perfect graciousness always follows. Remember, it is not the severe morals of Christianity that attract, but the winsomeness of the approach of Christians. A Christian's "Good Morning" should be different from that of a person of the world. It should be an evangel of the Lord. Convents should not only be homes of prayer and piety, but also places where the perfection of courtesy and refinement is found. Remember, grace can only build on the natural; in other words, grace requires natural graciousness as an atmosphere for growth and development.

It is true that sometimes in God's saints we discover certain external faults as regards behavior and conduct. But remember that they are saints in spite of these things, not because of them. Roughness is not a virtue, even though it may be found in the saintly. And those whom the Church has canonized, in spite of certain faults, possessed unusual and extraordinary virtues which indeed offset but which did not efface this lack of perfect refinement.

Christianity should always refine and make gracious, and where it does not, the grace of God is not given full swing. It is very true that our convents are filled with nuns who are not only pious, but perfectly gracious. And this is as it should be. For a nun should be Christ-like, and Christ was perfect not only in grace but also in nature.

Regrets All Old Unkindnesses and Harms

Loam Norton
considers Belsen
and Dachau.

The Lord was their shepherd.
   Yet did they want.
Joyfully would they have lain in jungles or pastures,
Walked beside waters. Their gaunt
Souls were not restored, their souls were banished.
In the shadow valley
They feared the evil, whether with or without God.
They were comforted by no Rod,
No Staff, but flayed by, O, besieged by shot a-plenty.

The prepared table was the rot or curd of the day.
Anointings were of lice. Blood was the spillage of cups.

Goodness and mercy should follow them all the days of their death.
They should dwell in the house of the Lord forever.

Where they dwell, they save a place for me.

I am not remote,
Not unconcerned.

Gwendolyn Brooks
Sisters Today, January, 1966

Sponsa Regis, June, 1931

Failures of Religious Vocations

A Missionary

The Graphophone

"They are of the world; therefore of the world they speak" (1 Jn 4:5).

It may seem childish to go into particulars in this matter. But since it is our aim to point out as many causes of religious failures as we can, we must speak of the little things as well as of the great ones. Besides, there is really nothing little when there is question of serious losses. It is said that there are no trifles in the service of God. If this is so, then it must also be said that there are no trifles in the development of infidelity in his service.

Let us begin with the graphophone. By means of this truly wonderful invention of modern times a contact with the world has been made possible for religious, even for cloistered ones, which did not exist so much as half a century ago. Those who have bidden farewell to the world in order to shut themselves in behind the walls of their convent or cloister to remain there as lifelong prisoners of the love of God are no longer able to visit places of worldly amusement such as the opera, theater, dance hall, and the like.

But somehow or other the world manages to follow them into their retirement. It has succeeded in spreading its poisonous atmosphere even within the sacred enclosure of monastery and cloister and convent. By means of modern inventions its speeches and songs, its music of jazz and opera, and other means of amusement can now be enjoyed in the recreation rooms of religious communities just the same as in the dance hall or theater. Surely this must be considered a form of participation in the pleasures of the world which we feel sure every founder of a religious community would roundly condemn.

Is not the enjoyment of these diversions out of harmony with the spirit of unworldliness and self-denial which religious, to be true to their voca-

54

tion, must strive to practice continually? Moreover, may it not be that for many there is particular danger in again listening to jokes and songs and music which before their entrance into religion may have been for them the occasion of grievous sin, now recalling to their minds actions and events which had better be forgotten, lest they become again the source of sin or at least of violent temptations.

Let it be understood that we do not condemn the graphophone or any other invention as a thing of evil; we only wish to point out that it, too, may prove to be a hindrance to religious perfection, and along with other means of worldliness, a promoter of religious failures.

The Telephone.

"Set a watch, O Lord, before my mouth, and a door round about my lips" (Ps 140:3).

Another point of contact with the world which was unknown before 1875 is the telephone. What a source of distraction and interference with religious retirement this marvelous invention has become in many convents and cloisters, even in such as profess strict seclusion from the world!

While is is true that the telephone makes it possible to save much time that would be consumed in going on errands and making necessary calls, it is also true that it leads to much loss of time and to dissipation by individuals who make it a practice to call their relatives and friends or arrange to be called by them. And when a conversation has once been started, it often seems impossible to end it. Besides, how useless, trifling, and childish such conversations often are: were some serious and important business to be transacted, no one could find fault with even a very long talk; but to talk merely for the sake of talking and for the pleasure there is found in speaking with some friend or acquaintance is certainly not in accordance with the principles of the spiritual life.

If visits from relatives and friends and interviews with them in the parlor are subject to very precise rules, then surely the use of the telephone for conversations with them must also be placed under the strict supervisions of superiors. If this is neglected, then the door is opened wide to many abuses and to a decline of the religious spirit. And if the idea of true religious life is to bid farewell to father and mother and brother and sister and the home and the attractions of the world so as to be free to live to God alone, then certainly it must also keep at a distance such means of close contact with them as is established by the telephone.

When some of our modern inventions were first introduced into religious houses, some of the old members were convinced that the devil had something to do with their working. They could not be prevailed upon to make use of them or even to go near them. Possibly they were not as mistaken as we think they were. If the devil is not in these contrivances, he at least finds them handy means for promoting worldliness among religious persons, and through that the decay and decline of religious communities.

The Radio

"Mind the things that are above, not the things that are upon the earth" (Col 3:2).

If the telephone can easily be abused so as to become a means of loss of the religious spirit, what shall we say of that most marvelous of all inventions of these modern times—the radio?

We must give credit where credit is due. This wonderful instrument can be made the vehicle of a very large amount of varied information that formerly was inaccessible to a great number of people. Instructive lectures on all kinds of topics can be listened to at almost any time: reports on the weather, on the markets, on the movements of vessels at sea, the returns of games, of races and elections, and of similar things can be learned by those who are interested; while those who love music can hear the best there is to be had. In themselves these things are good, and no one can find fault with them.

But these things must be looked upon as dangerous when they become obstacles to perfection and serve to minister to the gratification of the desire to enjoy the pleasures of worldly amusements and diversions. As a matter of fact, they have become for many religious a source of distraction and dissipation of mind and therefore a hindrance to progress in holiness and virtue.

First of all, the use of the radio establishes a most intimate contact with the world in every imaginable department. To tune in at any hour of the day or night and to listen to speeches, songs, musical productions, jokes, reports of markets, of games, sports, as well as to sermons by non-Catholic preachers of every denomination, surely can result in nothing else except in the filling of the mind with all sorts of distractions which make it utterly impossible for religious to foster that habitual recollection and union with God that is so essential for the attainment of religious perfection. Their minds are so taken up with purely worldly matters that they cannot apply themselves to the things of God.

In the second place, there is the frequent waste of valuable time, of time which should be devoted to the serious duties of the religious life. If those who listen in can do so only by neglecting their prescribed prayers, visits to the Blessed Sacrament, rosaries, spiritual readings, and other exercises, must it not be said that they are not only losing much precious time but also sustaining irreparable spiritual losses?

Thirdly, there is the violation of the rule of silence which is inseparable often from this form of amusement. It can be safely asserted that the radio is playing havoc with the rule of silence. This is especially true of that stricter form of silence which the rules of all communities enjoin from the time of night prayers till after breakfast the next morning. Usually the most interesting programs are broadcast during the hours of the evening till late into the night, so that those who listen are spending this time of strict silence and recollection in the state of diversified distraction. Besides this there is often found actual violation of silence for the reason that several persons are gathered about the instrument to enjoy the program and discuss its merits. And worse still, it not rarely happens that loud speakers are used which can be heard over a large part of the house, so that others too are disturbed in their endeavor to be recollected and kept from getting much needed sleep.

Fourthly, those who remain up late at night to listen will often be absent from the spiritual exercises of the next morning. They will make up for the sleep they lost. In this way meditation will often be neglected, possibly too, the holy sacrifice of the Mass and Holy Communion. And a day begun without the proper attention to prayer is not likely to be one of fidelity and fervor in the service of God.

One more reflection. The use of a common radio by a community is bad enough; but what is to be said when religious make use of individually owned outfits? Is not the possession of such a means of amusement plainly contrary to the accepted idea of religious poverty? We greatly wonder what the saintly founders of the various communities would do if they were to come back from the other world and undertake a visitation of their respective orders and congregations, and see the many means which their disciples have at their command for enjoying in an almost unlimited degree the pleasures and amusements of the children of the world. Would they not be horrified at the prevailing unrestrained use of modern conveniences, luxuries, and amusements, and order them to be abolished and removed immediately—at least many of them—and would they not insist that the members of their communities return to the practice of self-denial, mortification, and abstention from all necessary contacts with the world?

St. Gregory's Abbey

Nazianzus celebration of morning faces
turned down in sweat over cycle and plow,
others bare chested in cut-offs grooming
an Arabian horse.

Lauds at 4 before dawn when old deaf
Dom Joseph is just going to bed.
In the loft an abbatial crosier
of fork and shovel, tools of
Terce and consecration.

In soil and turf the sedge of Michigan,
lake and stonehenge barn shielding an
aura of light through blistered and open hands.

In summer boys through the woods
find the privately stable pond
with fishes and subliminal landscapes
of mud.
At night Augustine wakens
the monastic sleep by colloquial prayers
with Grieg in the cottage at the end of the lane.

At the close of the intermitted day
all gather in choir, a separate
duty of militant praise.

Brothers, pray for the vision of our lives:
Roy Brinkley, architect;
for Albert missing in Vietnam;
for Sheila in jail;
for John and Dick and their problems.
Also for the Goldstein's first child.

And three rivers cross at the end of the descendant hill.
Below Coon's Hollow Road winds back
to the holy din of the city, village,
town and borough where, on all the stony houses,
widow's walks are transfused with sun.

Sister Alla Renee Bozarth
Sisters Today, November, 1969

PART THREE

LASTING FUNDAMENTALS:
Truly Seeking God

In order for it to have survived the rains and winds of renewal, religious life has copied the wise builder's blueprint and set its house solidly on rock (Mt 7:24-25). The articles of this section examine some of the strata of that firm foundation.

The very bedrock of religious life is God. Our God is the "God of Gratuitous Love" (the title of a splendid article), whose most distinctive trait is to love his people first and to love them freely, for nothing. Because our Father's love has sent his Son Jesus to save us, Thomas Merton in one of his not infrequent contributions reminds us in "Christ, the Way" that "what matters above all is not this or that observance, this or that set of ethical practices, but our renewal, our 'new creation' in Christ." The enduring solidity of our situation is assured through the Spirit. A conference entitled "In the School of the Holy Spirit" teaches us that "The beginning, progress, and consummation of the spiritual perfection depend on our fidelity to the inspirations of the Holy Spirit."

Since the Lord God has been content to deal with his people in human, worldly ways through other people, rituals, symbols, and rules, religious folk have found no satisfactory substitute for this method. The God who interacts with patriarch, matriarch, judge, king, queen, prophet, and sinner always in the context of community continues to use the religious community as the arena of his activity. Evidently community was such a *sine qua non* for early editors and writers that the concept of community as such is not directly dealt with during the first half of the magazine's existence! One will look in vain throughout the first twenty-five years of *Sponsa Regis* for an article with "community" in its title. But why write or talk about community when everyone *had* community? In 1955, when

Volume 26 was half finished, the article "Community Life" appeared and considered the blessings of that "one large family in which the superior holds the place of the mother and the members are sisters to one another." More recent aspects of community are considered in several articles of Part Seven.

The primary place of the Holy Rule is presented in "The Holy Rule, Your Way of Life": "The Rule shows us how to do God's will every minute of the day and night." What the Rule did not regulate, local customs did. Such customs as bowing to another in passing, kneeling before the superior when requesting permissions, refectory ceremonies, and prayers while dressing are evaluated in "Sacramental Value in Religious Customs." The positive values of the clothes that seemed to make the Sister are emphasized in "The Religious Habit." In "Spiritual Direction," Thomas Merton presents the spiritual father of religious as "a kind of 'sacrament' of Christ Himself. It is Christ who lives, speaks and acts in the spiritual father: for we have but one master and one father, Christ the Lord."

The prayer life of religious is surely the one aspect that has received the most consistent attention during the half century of this publication's history. For the readers who ask, "Teach us to pray," articles abound. The essay on "Teaching True Piety" was chosen because it gives the four simple rules for prayer that the founding editor later practiced and repeated in his popular retreat conferences. "Helps for Meditations" overflows with methods while "The Particular Examen" offers an order to be followed during this daily spiritual exercise.

One of the most significant contributions of *Sponsa Regis* was to explain and promote the liturgical life in convents throughout the English-speaking world. Thanks to the creative work of Father Virgil Michel, O.S.B., the founder of The Liturgical Press at St. John's Abbey and the first editor of the liturgical review, *Orate Fratres* (later *Worship*), the Church's liturgy was coming to be identified less with clerical rubrics and more with this well-known description of Pope Pius X from his 1903 *motu proprio*: "Active participation in the most holy mysteries and in the public and solemn prayer of the Church is the primary and indispensable source of the true Christian spirit."

To carry that description beyond words into reality for Sisters, a concerted effort was made to instruct readers in the pearls of great price that the Church offered those who wished to worship in spirit and in truth. The founding editor of *Sponsa Regis* in an early issue wrote "The Liturgical Movement in Convents." Articles such as "Holy Mass in the Life of Religious," and a meditation on the Eucharist ("I Live, Now Not I") helped to highlight the Mass. "More Fruitful Confession" sought to show "how to receive the sacrament of Penance with the greatest profit and make of it a powerful instrument in our spiritual progress." "Liberty of Conscience" deals with the canonical safeguards for insuring Sisters full freedom in choosing their confessor — no small problem in the days when confession was a weekly exercise and when Sisters lacked the mobility of our times.

The greatest difficulty in the liturgical renewal of convents was the weaning of religious from their diet of private prayer and persuading them to the public recitation of the Divine Office. The answer to a common concern of "How Long is the Roman Office?" was "Not as long as you think it is; in fact no longer than the present prayer time." Obviously there were more questions being asked, so some thirteen years later Father Clifford Howell, S.J., an international leader of the liturgical movement, wrote "The Religious Life and the Liturgy" to again encourage communities to pray the Church's own Office. This he felt would "do enormous good to our Sisters, enrich their spiritual lives, help them to pray and think with the Church, and is likely to attract more and better postulants than are now presenting themselves as recruits."

If the Church's liturgy is the prime source of the true Christian spirit, it is not the only font. "Religious and the Rosary" attempts to demonstrate "how imitation of Christ is made more easy by the spirituality of the Rosary." "A House of Prayer" details the genesis of a new development in prayer in the late 1960's. "Prayer and the Psychology of Women" deals with woman's emerging self-awareness as related to prayer.

The final essay, "Fostering Vocations," concerns a topic that has never lost its importance or interest during the past fifty years. And if there is to be a centennial addition to this book, the topic will hopefully remain a lasting fundamental. A sentence in this same article —"For the one or other community a lack of adaptation to their environment may be the cause for keeping off candidates"— seems to be the first tentative note of adaptation to be sounded in the magazine's pages. Like the lost chord, it is a note that will remain hidden and unnoticed for a decade or more until it becomes the "middle C" of religious renewal.

Sponsa Regis, September, 1963

God of Gratuitous Love

Robert Guelluy

If the Lord has arranged all things that we might spend our lives in his house and in his service, it is without doubt in order that we may learn through one another and with one another to know him better and to love him more. This is really the only "conversion" that is demanded of us in the religious life: to know who the Lord is and to be occupied with him. Oh, of course, we have many faults to correct, many problems to solve; but what is asked of us is something far more profound. We are not just to look deeper into ourselves, to exert more effort on our own persons. No, what is asked is more startling than this; it is no longer to look at ourselves at all.

This is the conversion we need to make: to learn to live for the praise of God, not just to "do good" but to glorify God in thinking no longer of self but of him.

To be a Christian is to be liberated. The Christian is not someone concerned about making something of himself. The Christian is not a person occupied with himself, even with his virtuous desires; the Christian is someone disengaged from self, taken up with God and the neighbor. It is that which is supernatural about Christian life.

Really, in its most profound meaning, the evangelical call is a call to abandonment; but this does not mean simply "giving up" or "letting go." An even greater stripping and a more total detachment are demanded. We are no longer to think of self at all, no longer to be busy with self, no longer to esteem the good we do or to dramatize the evil we commit. To be free from self is truly the greatest detachment, the most thorough kind of stripping. And it is this to which we are summoned, nothing else: to holy littleness, childlike obedience, confident surrender.

In other words, we are asked to be so open that God may accomplish *his* work in us, a work exceeding all our dreams, and this in spite of all our sham. We must learn to surrender to him both our desires and our disappointments, all our egotistic thoughts, whether they be noble ideas to which we remain very humanly attached or disappointments which depress us because our pride is hurt by them. The conversion we need demands that we become more occupied with God than with ourselves, more taken up with what he is doing for us than with what we wish to do for him. It is the spirit of faith which will effect this in us.

Usually we are led to one of two extremes in our thinking. When all goes well we are happy, hugging a righteousness and well-being based on pride; or else, when nothing goes right — and there is always something wrong with ourselves or with others! — we are upset, embittered, hostile to others as well as to ourselves. Every life knows this alternation between satisfied pride and hurt pride; although the forms may vary, the same wretchedness prompts them all. This is because we lack the basic humility of one who lives by virtue of a gift, who lives in the disposition of having received all.

It is necessary to break through this infernal circle of flattering self-satisfaction and fretful discontent. Only a firm belief in love can free us. Once we understand how we are loved, once we realize the Father's utterly gratuitous and unmerited affection for his children, we will be liberated from this deep-rooted attachment to ourselves. As it is, a humility that is truly oblivious of self escapes us in the very measure that we try to cultivate it, for we exert ourselves, once again by pride, in an effort to become humble.

We should strive to dwell on what God is doing for us rather than on what we are doing for him. Perhaps we should make an examination of conscience different from our usual type: an examination on the *present*. This examen would awaken and sustain in us sincere gratitude. Before meditating on our sins, we should meditate on what is in order, on all the concrete evidence of divine predilection. This will help us to believe in the absolutely gratuitous affection of the Father and to live in the joy of being loved. We so lack this spirit; yet it alone will change us. We resort to pseudo-conversions: "I'm determined to overcome myself. Till now I haven't done too well, but I'll not be caught napping again." So with a little pride and self-assertion one establishes a bit of equilibrium. Actually, we only adjust the proportions of self and sin, and the balance remains the same.

The great problem is to be content with God. If only we were content with God! We are deterred before we start by a nagging sentiment of self love. We murmur, "I don't want to be like a new convert; I'm not a first communicant. I don't want others to say, 'At last he has understood!' This idea is so simple and childlike that it is unworthy of me." Yes, it is difficult to be practically, concretely content with God in such a way that nothing else matters at all, in such a way that one consents simply to walk every day in the joy of being loved.

This is not to be a more refined type of self concern; it is to be enamored of God. The Lord calls us to live in a communion with him, in a loving exchange, recognizing who he is. But we, on our part, raise the great objection that we know who we are. We murmur within, "I know myself well and I see quite clearly what's going to happen." This is not the problem; what matters is to know the Lord. We do not know him enough. It is only in his light that we can really know ourselves. It is only a belief in divine love that will enable us to pass from the visible motives we have for feeding our pride to the invisible motives for being profoundly happy: happy to be loved.

This is the desert march, the radical stripping, the great renouncement: to be free from all in the joy of being with the Lord. This is the Christian life: to leave aside the non-essentials in order to endure the privations of the desert while being led to the promised land, yet throughout the journey reveling in the company of God. So it was with the Hebrew people in the desert when God was closer to them than ever before.

The Christian life is somewhat like the reflection heard so often during the wartime evacuations: "Perhaps we shall recover nothing, maybe everything will be destroyed. It doesn't matter if only we stay together, if only the family is not split up." So in Christian living: trials and demands count little if only we are with the Lord. God tried to make his people in the desert understand this, but they forgot his hidden presence and sighed for the fleshpots of Egypt. They ceased to think of him and instead bemoaned the long way they had yet to travel and the difficulties they were bound to encounter.

There are some pertinent verses for us to consider in the Book of Deuteronomy. At the outset, Moses tells how the law, which is the people's response to God's free election of them, should be understood. Fidelity to this law is simply a way of expressing confidence in unmerited love. We must accept the law, knowing the goodness of the Father, understanding that what he asks of us he asks for our good. We are to see in it the form which his predilection takes and the manifestation of his grace, and to obey him through trust in his love.

These first chapters of Deuteronomy insist on the greatness of God, describing and revealing him so that the Israelites may be moved to observe his law as it deserves: to think more of the Lord than of themselves. The emphasis is on the unique character of the God of revelation: he is the one who loves for nothing, the one who loves first, the one who has freely chosen us. What poverty of spirit this demands on our part! Knowing that everything comes solely from grace, from his sheer magnanimity, we are destitute of *any* claim deriving from ourselves.

"If Yahweh has attached himself to you and chosen you, it is not because you are the most numerous of all peoples; for you are the least numerous among all peoples" (Dt 7:7). These words have value not only for the Hebrew people but for each one of us. If God has chosen us, it is explained only by his love. Were he a shrewd businessman or an enterprising executive, had he in addition a sense of efficiency and a methodical spirit calculating what he would draw from humanity by way of profit, it is obvious that neither you nor I would have been chosen to follow him. If God has chosen us, it is not because we were particularly interesting or because he could expect something from us; it is not through a spirit of bargaining, but simply because his heart is good. This is what you must consent to; this is what you must welcome: *the joy of being loved for nothing*.

We poison our lives by the vain desire to be loved for something, or by the despair of always having empty hands. We must accept supernaturally, in the joy of being loved, our insufficiency and the limitations of our existence. This joyous acceptance will at the same time liberate us from all comfortable self complacency, all that pride which makes us disdain others.

If God has attached himself to you and chosen you, it is certainly not because there was some prior worth in you. It is surely not because he found there something to his advantage, some profit you could bring to him. One finds in quite reliable books that God has created the world for his glory. Let us reflect a little on what this really means. If I approach the matter seriously I must admit that I will give God very little glory and that without doubt he has more peace without me than with me; I cause him more trouble than satisfaction. Nor am I alone in this situation. If God has created the world so as to be magnified by it, he has poorly calculated the results; the venture is quite disappointing.

In truth, the glory of God is *to love for nothing*. That is the glory for which he has created all things. And heaven will consist in our wondrous astonishment at being so loved. It is thus that I shall glorify God for all eternity. What I want to bring him is my joy in receiving everything; this is the need he has of me. What he expects of me is this marveling welcome in regard to his totally gratuitous affection. What do you expect to bring him if not what he has already put into your hands?

Heaven will be comprised of people happy to be there for nothing. The others — those who proudly esteemed themselves to have succeeded in life — will be disputing in hell. One will find them arguing with their predecessors and collaborators: "You have reaped what I have sown, you have benefited from the fruits of my labor." Those who think they have earned something will spend eternity quarreling. Heaven is going to be a community of persons thrilled to be there *gratis*. This will be our initial amazement on arriving, one of which we will never weary and from which we will never recover. We will be forever in awe at this divine marvel. We will ask ourselves: "How did I ever get here? I can't understand it at all. It is certainly not because I was the strongest of all persons!"

Behold the Christian life: to strive earnestly to merit heaven, yet to receive it finally as being beyond all merit; to struggle courageously to win eternal happiness, but knowing we can never gain it except by gift; to do our best while rejoicing that all is given us. Even our effort itself is a grace, a divine favor which has more of God in it than of ourselves.

Consider well: if God has attached himself to you and chosen you, it is not because you are the greatest of all persons; it is not that you are worth the trouble. Be humble; be grateful that you are not worth his trouble and then bow before this ultimate explanation of your existence in this world and in your community: love. Unreasonable as it may seem, God loves you dearly. To look at you one would not think so, but faith assures us it is so. God is held captive by the love and fidelity promised to your fathers. He is prisoner of his own goodness; what he has begun he cannot discontinue.

How striking is that prayer of Jesus on the cross: "Father, forgive them, for they know not what they do" (Lk 23:34). In the gospels, it is obvious that our Lord does not make a great tragedy of the adulterous woman, of Mary Magdalene, of Zacchaeus the publican — these cases do not appear very grave to him. What does appear fatal is the refusal of God out of a sense of self-sufficiency, the hardness of heart of the Pharisees. Yet even in regard to them, on what note does our Lord end? "Father, forgive them . . ." We are much like these Pharisees, but we can take heart. How could the Father refuse to hear the plea of his beloved Son on the cross, this prayer of Jesus in agony? It is evident that we know not what we do.

The text of Deuteronomy continues: "But it may be the thought will come into your mind, 'These nations outnumber me; shall I have the strength to dispossess them?' " (Dt 7:17). So also you reason in your hearts: "The difficulties are stronger than I; how can I possibly surmount them?" You are thinking of yourself, of what you are going to do, even while I speak to you of the Lord! You give yourself halfheartedly to contemplation, remaining preoccupied with self, rather than discerning the heart of the Father, the invisible presence encompassing us, the divine life surging within us at this moment. Instead of being busy with him, we remain terribly taken up with ourselves; we say, "But the difficulties are so great, the nations to be conquered are so much stronger than I. How shall I ever arrive at the promised land?"

And the answer comes: "Away with these fears!" Fundamentally, you and I are afraid, and this fear is the basis of our problems. You have given up because you have despaired of becoming a saint, of reaching the promised land. But Scripture says, "Away with these fears! Remember what the Lord did to Pharaoh and to the rest of the Egyptians, the great plagues you witnessed, the portents and the marvels, the constraining force the Lord your God used, the display he made of his power to rescue you" (Dt 7:18-19). Think of the difficulties already overcome, of all the things you formerly feared but through which you have safely emerged. "Do not be frightened, throw off your paralysis, because in your midst is Yahweh, your God."

Together we have to rediscover, above all else, this living presence. God is in our midst, the strong and mighty God. This God who loves you and who has chosen you for nothing is the God who will do his work in you, being all-powerful. But not all at once will this happen. "Little by little, now here, now there, Yahweh your God will destroy these nations. Perhaps to you the conquest will seem too long — you would prefer to exterminate the enemies at a single blow. If you were to empty the country of all its inhabitants — this promised land which you are not yet capable of enjoying — it would be to your detriment, for the wild beasts would be multiplied" (Dt 7:22). These words are said *to us*. Our enemies, for the moment, are useful to us; our failures are salutary. They deepen faith in us; without difficulties, we would live in a purely superficial manner, we would feel no need of the Lord, we would not think of him. Difficulties are beneficial, and if God permits them it is again because he loves you indeed, because he wills your good.

"And now the Lord God means to settle you in a rich land, a land that has water coursing down in streams, and deep wells that break out from plain and hill; a land of wheat and barley, of vine and fig tree and pomegranate and olive, a land where oil and honey flow. Here without fear of want you will win your livelihood; all shall be yours in abundance; the very stones of that land will yield iron, and there is copper to mine from its hillsides; here you may eat your fill and bless the name of the Lord your God for the wonderful land he has given you. Nevertheless, it will be a land of trials where life will be difficult. You will be in danger, then, of forgetting the Lord your God, of neglecting the laws and decrees and observances you have learned this day. You will eat your fill, you will build yourself fair houses to dwell in, you will have herds and flocks; gold and silver and all good things shall be yours. But beware lest your heart swell with pride, and you forget the Lord your God! He it is who rescued you from bondage . . . . Never are you to flatter yourself that valor of your own, strength of your own, has won you wealth; rather, remember the Lord God and the strength that he gives you" (Dt 8:7-14, 17-18).

If you were perfect; if recollection were easy for you; if you could pray without any difficulty, as it were, spontaneously; if you were the embodiment of patience and a paragon of kindness; if the whole world were drawn to praise your mildness, your self possession and your fidelity to duty; in short, if you were a living model of virtue, then certainly would you need to be on guard! You would be in a fearful situation, for you could be content with yourself. And you could say in your heart: "It is the strength of my hand that has accomplished this supremacy; my power has worked these marvels." Rather, "Remember the Lord your God; it is he who has given you this power, faithful to the covenant sworn to your fathers."

What constant peril we are in! If we manage to withstand the trials of departure, we are soon tempted to despair, remembering the fleshpots of Egypt. And if we are in the promised land, we find ourselves faced with the exigency of living as if in the desert, since we are not to be attached to all the riches God has given us.

The procedure is, indeed, what we pointed out in the beginning: to renounce discouragement and discontent as well as the independence which makes us take ourselves seriously. We must stop being guided by the visible so that we may commit ourselves in faith to the invisible, live in the joy of being loved, and walk happily under the eyes of the Father, aware that his most distinctive trait is to love for nothing, to love first. He loves in a way that nothing can precede or anticipate. It is he who has taken the first step toward us and he never stops doing so. This divine initiative is fundamental in our Christian faith.

One can find generosity, endurance and devotedness outside Christianity. What belongs properly to Christian life is building our lives on faith — faith in a choice which has selected and called us simply because the heart of the Father is good and because he is faithful to the promises made to our fathers in the faith and to his love in Christ Jesus our Lord.

Today, we must reaffirm our faith in this love; we must forget ourselves in order to be occupied with what faith tells us of our God. He has first loved us; that is tremendous! He has no need that an object be lovable before he loves it; that is startling. To love what is worthy — even I can do that. What is unique in God is that he loves *first*, without the object being worth the trouble. That is gratuity, divine spontaneity.

Let us try to understand the Lord, to know the heart of the Father. Oh, that we might know the Father! This is the great liberation, the great revelation; no other is necessary. All our effort must be channeled to concentrating on him, to living more for his praise. In the throes of our disappointments and disillusionments, our sufferings and failures, let us renew in ourselves this faith in the invisible and this unshakable confidence in God's unwavering love.

Sponsa Regis, January, 1962

Christ, the Way

Thomas Merton

Perfection is not a moral embellishment which we acquire outside of Christ, in order to qualify for union with him. Perfection is the work of Christ himself living in us by faith. Perfection is the full life of charity perfected by the gifts of the Holy Ghost. In order that we may attain to Christian perfection, Jesus has left us his teachings, the sacraments of the Church, the religious state with its vows, and all the counsels by which he shows us the way to live more perfectly in him and for him. Under the direction of the Church herself, we seek to correspond generously with the inspirations of the Holy Spirit. Inwardly guided by the Spirit of Christ, outwardly protected and formed by the visible Church with her hierarchy, her laws, teaching, sacraments and liturgy, we grow together into "one Christ."

We must not regard the Church purely as an institution or an organization. She is certainly visible and clearly recognizable in her teachings, her government and her worship. These are the external lineaments through which we may see the interior radiance of her soul. This soul is not merely human, it is divine. It is the Holy Spirit himself. The Church, like Christ, lives and acts in a manner at once human and divine. Certainly there is imperfection in the human members of Christ, but their imperfection is inseparably united to his perfection, sustained by his power, and purified by his holiness, as long as they remain in living union with him by faith and love. Through these members of his the almighty Redeemer infallibly sanctifies, guides and instructs us, and he uses us also to express his love for them. Hence the true nature of the Church is that of a body in which all the members "bear one another's burdens" and act as instruments of divine providence in regard to one another. Those are most sanctified who enter most fully into the life-giving communion of saints who dwell in Christ.

Their joy is to taste the pure streams of that river of life whose waters gladden the whole city of God.

Our perfection is therefore not just an individual affair, it is also a question of growth in Christ, of deepening our contact with him in and through the Church, and consequently of deepening our participation in the life of the Church, the mystical Christ. This means, of course, a closer union with our brethren in Christ, a closer and more fruitful integration with them in the living, growing spiritual organism of the Mystical Body.

This does not mean that spiritual perfection is a matter of social conformism. The mere fact of becoming a well-working cog in an efficient religious machine will never make anyone into a saint if he does not seek God interiorly in the sanctuary of his own soul. The common life, regulated by traditional observances and blessed by the authority of the Church, is obviously a most precious means of sanctification. It is, for the religious, one of the essentials of his state. But it is still only a framework. As such, it has its purpose. It must be used. But the scaffolding must not be mistaken for the actual building. The real building of the Church is a union of hearts in love, sacrifice and self-transcendence. The strength of this building depends on the extent to which the Holy Spirit gains possession of each person's heart, but on the extent to which our exterior conduct is organized and disciplined by an expedient system. Human social life inevitably requires a certain order, and those who love their brothers in Christ will generously sacrifice themselves to preserve this order. But the order is not an end in itself, and mere orderliness is not yet sanctity.

Too often, religious men and women waste all their efforts on the scaffolding, making it more and more solid, permanent and secure, and paying no attention to the building itself. They do so out of a kind of unconscious fear of the real responsibilities of the religious life, which are solitary and interior. These are difficult to express, even obliquely. They are almost impossible to communicate to anyone else. Hence one can never be "sure" whether he is right or wrong. One has very little evidence of progress or perfection in this interior sphere — while in the exterior, progress can be more easily measured and results can be seen. They can also be *shown* to others for their approval and admiration.

The most important, the most real and lasting work of the religious is accomplished in the depths of his own soul. It cannot be seen by anyone, even by himself. It is known only to God. This work is not so much a matter of fidelity to visible and general standards, as of *faith*: the interior, anguished, almost desperately solitary act by which we affirm our total subjection to God by grasping his word and his revelation of his will in the inmost depths of our being, as well as in obedience to the authority constituted by him.

The *Credo* which we triumphantly chant in the liturgy, in union with the whole Church, is real and valid only insofar as it expresses the inner self-commitment of each one to God's will, as manifested exteriorly through the Church and her hierarchy, and interiorly through the inspirations of divine grace.

Our faith is then a total surrender to Christ, which places all our hopes in him and in his Church, and expects all strength and sanctity from his merciful love.

SANCTITY IN CHRIST

From what has so far been said, it should be clear that Christian holiness is not a mere matter of ethical perfection. It includes every virtue, but is evidently more than all virtues together. Sanctity is not constituted only by good works or even by moral heroism, but first of all by ontological union with God "in Christ." Indeed, to understand the New Testament teaching on holiness of life we have to understand the meaning of this expression of St. Paul. The moral teaching of the epistles always follows upon and elucidates a doctrinal exposition of the meaning of our "life in Christ." St. John also made it quite clear that all spiritual fruit in our life comes from union with Christ, integration in his Mystical Body as a branch is united with the vine and integrated in it (Jn 15:1-11).

This of course does not by any means reduce virtues and good works to insignifiance: but these always remain secondary to our new being. According to the scholastic maxim, *actio sequitur esse*, action is in accordance with the being that acts. As the Lord himself said, you cannot gather figs from thistles. Hence we must first be transformed interiorly into new men, and then act according to the Spirit given to us by God, the Spirit of our new life, the Spirit of Christ. Our ontological holiness is our vital union with the Holy Spirit. Our striving to obey the Holy Spirit constitutes our moral goodness.

Hence, what matters above all is not this or that observance, this or that set of ethical practices, but our renewal, our "new creation" in Christ (see Gal 6:15). It is when we are united to Christ by "faith that works through charity" (Gal 5:6) that we possess in ourselves the Holy Spirit who is the source of all virtuous action and of all love. The Christian life of virtue is not only a life in which we strive to unite ourselves to God by the practice of virtue. Rather it is also a life in which, drawn to union with God in Christ by the Holy Spirit, we strive to express our love and our new being by acts of virtue. Being united to Christ, we seek with all possible fervor to let him manifest *his* virtue and *his* sanctity in our lives. Our efforts should be directed to removing the obstacles of selfishness, disobedience and all attachment to what is contrary to his love.

When the Church sings in the *Gloria, Tu solus sanctus* — Thou, O Christ, alone are holy! — we can interpret this to mean, surely, that all else that is holy is holy in and through him. It is through Christ that the sanctity of God is communicated and revealed to the world. If then we are to be holy, Christ must be holy in us. If we are to be "saints," he must be our sanctity.

For, as St. Paul says: "To those who are called, Christ Jesus is the power of God and the wisdom of God . . . . Christ Jesus has become for us God-given wisdom and justice and sanctification and redemption; so that, just as it is written, 'let him who takes pride take pride in the Lord' " (1 Cor 1:24,30). But this all demands our own consent and our energetic cooperation with divine grace.

Jesus Christ, God and Man, is the revelation of the hidden sanctity of the Father, the immortal and invisible King of ages whom no eye has seen, whom no intelligence can contemplate, except in the light which he himself communicates to whomever he wills. Hence, Christian "perfection" is not a mere ethical adventure or an achievement in which man can take glory. It is a gift of God drawing the soul into the hidden abyss of the divine mystery, through the Son, by the action of the Holy Spirit. To be a Christian, then, is to be committed to a deeply mystical life, for Christianity is the greatest of all mystical religions. This does not mean, of course, that every Christian is or should be a "mystic" in the technical, modern sense of the word. But it does mean that every Christian lives, or should live, within the dimensions of a completely mystical revelation and communication of the divine being. Salvation, which is the goal of each individual Christian and of the Christian community as a whole, is participation in the life of God, who draws us "out of darkness into his marvelous light" (1 Pt 2:9). The Christian is one whose life and hope are centered in the mystery of Christ. In and through Christ, we become "partakers of the divine nature — *consortes divinae naturae*" (2 Pt 1:4).

It is through Christ that the power of divine love and the energy of divine light find their way into our lives and transform them from one degree of "brightness" to another, by the action of the Holy Spirit. Here is the root and basis of the inner sanctity of the Christian. This light, this energy in our lives is commonly called grace.

The more grace and love shine forth in the fraternal unity of those who have been brought together, by the Holy Spirit, in one Body, the more Christ is manifested in the world, the more the Father is glorified and the closer we come to the final completion of God's work by the "recapitulation of all things in Christ" (Eph 1:10).

GRACE AND THE SACRAMENTS

Our divine sonship is the likeness of the Word of God in us produced by his living presence in our souls, through the Holy Spirit. This is our "justice" in God's sight. It is the root of true love and of every other virtue. Finally it is the seed of eternal life: it is a divine inheritance which cannot be taken from us against our own will. It is an inexhaustible treasure, a fountain of living water "springing up into life everlasting." The First Epistle of St. Peter opens with a jubilant hymn in praise of this life of grace, freely given to us by the divine mercy, in Christ: the grace which leads to our salvation, if only we are faithful to the love of God that has been given to us when we were dead in our sins, raising us from death by the same power which raised Christ from the dead:

> Blessed be the God and Father of our Lord Jesus Christ, who according to his great mercy has begotten us again through the resurrection of Jesus Christ from the dead unto a living hope, unto an incorruptible inheritance — undefiled, unfading, reserved for you in heaven. By the power of God you are guarded through faith for salvation, which is to be revealed in the last time. Over this you rejoice; though now for a little while, if need be, you are made sorrowful by various trials, that the temper of your faith — more precious by far than gold which is tried in the fire — may be found unto praise and glory and honor at the revelation of Jesus Christ. Him, though you have not seen, you love. In him, though you do not see him, yet believing, you exult with a joy unspeakable and triumphant; receiving as the final issue of your faith the salvation of your souls (1 Pt 1:3-9).

To say that the Christian religion is mystical is to say that it is also *sacramental*. The sacraments are "mysteries" in which God works and our spirit works together with him under the impulse of his divine love. We should not forget that the sacraments are mystical *signs* of a free spiritual work of divine love in our souls. The visible, external action by which a sacrament is conferred is not something which "causes" God to give grace, though it causes us to receive grace. It is a sign that God is freely granting us his grace. The sign is necessary for us, but not for him. It awakens our hearts and our minds to respond to his actions. His grace could equally well be given *without* any external sign, but in that event most of us would be far less able to profit by the gift, to receive it efficaciously and correspond to it with the love of our hearts. We therefore need these holy signs as causes of grace in ourselves, but we do not, by them, exert a casual pressure on God. Quite the contrary!

If God has willed to communicate to us his ineffable light and share with us his life, he must himself determine the way in which this communication and sharing are to take place. He begins by addressing to man his *word*. When man hears and receives the word of God, obeys his summons and responds to his call, then he is brought to the font of baptism, or to the cleansing rivers of penance. He is nourished with the Blessed Eucharist in which the body of the Lord is given to us to be our true spiritual food, the pledge of our eternal salvation and of our nuptials with the Logos. Jesus wants us to "come to him" not only by faith, but also in sacramental union: for union with Christ in all the sacraments and particularly in the Blessed Eucharist not only signifies and symbolizes our complete mystical integration in him, but also produces that which it signifies. "He who eats my flesh and drinks my blood abides in me and I in him. As the living Father has sent me and I live by the Father, so he that eats me, he also shall live because of me" (Jn 6:57-58).

When we speak of this mystical way to God through the sacraments, we must be careful not to give the impression that sacramental mysticism is a kind of magic. This would be the case if the sacraments produced grace infallibly, without any reference to the dispositions and correspondence of the one who received them. It is true that the power of the sacraments, working *ex opere operato*, produces a salutary effect even when the worshipper is not able to elicit subjective sentiments of fervent devotion. In other words, the sacramental system is objective in its operation; but grace is not communicated to one who is not properly disposed. The sacraments produce no fruit where there is no love.

THE LAW OF LOVE

The sanctity of Christian life is based not on love of an abstract law but on love of the living God, a divine Person, Jesus Christ, the incarnate Word of God, who has redeemed us and delivered us from the darkness of sin. Hence our moral life is not legalistic, not a mere matter of fidelity to duty. It is above all a matter of personal gratitude, of love, and of praise. It is a "eucharistic" morality, a code of love based on thanksgiving and appreciation of our new life in Christ. This appreciation implies a deep understanding of the divine mercy which has brought us to share in the death and resurrection of Christ. It implies a spiritual awareness of the fact that our Christian life is in fact the life of the risen Christ active and fruitful within us at every moment. Our morality is then centered on love and on praise, on the desire to see the risen Lord and Savior fully glorified in our lives.

We must realize that our acts of virtue and our good works are not done simply in order to satisfy the cold obligation of an impersonal law. They are a personal response of love to the desire of a human heart filled with divine love for us. The Sacred Heart of the risen Savior communicates to our own inmost being every least impulse of grace and charity by which he shares with us his divine life. Our response is then an answer to the warm and sensitive promptings of the Lord's personal love for us. This realization not only diverts our attention from ourselves to him, but it also arouses a deeper and more vital hope, and awakens in our heart a more fruitful and dynamic faith. It fills our Christian life with the inexpressible warmth of gratitude and with a transcendent awareness of what it means to be sons of God because the only begotten Son of the Father has loved us even to the point of dying for us on the Cross.

Not only are we grateful for our deliverance from sin by Christ, but Paul also makes clear that our "eucharistic" morality of grateful love is nourished by a sense of deliverance from a seemingly inescapable conflict. While we were under the law, says the Apostle (Rom 7:13-25), we realized only our incapacity to be holy and to satisfy its stern demands. But now, by the grace of the loving Savior, we have been able to keep the law and go much farther than the law prescribed, in the perfection of love, because Christ himself has come, has put to death sin in our hearts, and has brought forth charity within us.

It is only because we have Christ dwelling in us that we can now satisfy the demands of the law. But the way of our doing so is to fix our eyes not on the law, but on Christ. We must occupy our hearts not with the thought of arduous and cold obligations which we do not fully understand, but with the presence and love of the Holy Spirit who enkindles in us the love of good and shows us how to "do all things in the name of Jesus Christ." The Christian way of perfection is then in every sense a way of love, of gratitude, of trust in God. Nowhere do we depend on our own strength or our own light: our eyes are fixed on Christ from whom come all light and strength. Our hearts are attentive to his Holy Spirit. The Lord himself then gives us power and guides us in a way that we do not understand.

Our only concern is to be constantly and generously faithful to his will. Our whole morality is to trust him even when we seem to be walking in the darkness of death, knowing that he is life and truth, and that where Jesus leads us there can be no error. The whole Christian way is summed up by St. Paul:

> There is therefore now no condemnation for those who are in Christ Jesus, who do not walk according to the flesh. For the law of the Spirit of the life in Christ Jesus has delivered me from the law of sin and death. For what was impossible to the Law in that it was weak, because of the flesh, God has made good (Rom 8:1-3).

FLESH AND SPIRIT

The only thing the Apostle asks of us is to "walk" (that is, to live) not according to the "flesh" but according to the "spirit." This means several things. The flesh is the generic term not for bodily life (since the body along with the soul is sanctified by the Holy Spirit) but for *mundane* life. The "flesh" includes not only sensuality and licentiousness, but even worldly conformism, and actions based on human respect or social preoccupation.

We obey the "flesh" when we follow the norms of prejudice, complacency, bigotry, group-pride, superstition, ambition or greed. Hence even an apparent holiness, based not on sincerity of heart but on hypocritical display, is of the "flesh." Whatever may be the "inclination of the flesh," even when it seems to point to heroic and dazzling actions admired by men, it is always death in the sight of God. It is not directed to him but to men around us. It does not seek his glory, but our own satisfaction. The spirit, on the other hand, leads us in the ways of life and peace.

The laws of the spirit are laws of humility and love. The spirit speaks to us from a deep inner sanctuary of the soul which is inaccessible to the flesh. For the "flesh" is our external self, our false self. The "spirit" is our real self, our inmost being united to God in Christ. In this hidden sanctuary of our being the voice of our conscience is at the same time our own inner voice and the voice of the Holy Spirit. For when one becomes "spirit" in Christ, he is no longer himself alone. It is not only he who lives, but Christ lives in him, and the Holy Spirit guides and rules his life. Christian virtue is rooted in this inner unity, in which our own self is one with Christ in the Spirit, our thoughts are able to be those of Christ, and our desires to be his desires.

Our whole Christian life is, then, a life of union with the Holy Spirit and fidelity to the divine will in the depths of our being. Therefore it is a life of truth, of utter spiritual sincerity, and by that token it implies heroic humility. For truth, like charity, must begin at home. We must not only see ourselves as we are, in all our nothingness and insignifiance; we must accept completely the reality of our life as it is, because it is the very reality which Christ wills to take to himself, which he transforms and sanctifies in his own image and likeness.

If we are able to accept the presence of evil within us, we will be calm and objective enough to deal with it patiently, trusting in the grace of Christ. This is what is meant by following the Holy Spirit, resisting the flesh, persevering in our good desires, denying the claims of our false exterior self, and thus giving the depths of our heart to the transforming action of Christ.

> You are not carnal but spiritual if indeed the Spirit of God dwells in you . . . If Christ is in you, the body is indeed dead by reason of sin but the spirit is life by reason of justification. But if the Spirit of him who raised Jesus Christ from the dead dwells in you, then he who raised Christ Jesus from the dead will also bring to life your mortal bodies because of his Spirit who dwells in you (Rom 8:9-11).

Hence, when we are united to Christ by baptism and love, there may be many evil tendencies still at work in our body and psyche — seeds and roots of "death" remaining from our past lives. But the Holy Spirit gives us grace to control these, and our will to love and serve God in spite of these tendencies ratifies his lifegiving action. Thus what he "sees" in us is not so much the evil that was ours but the good that is his.

Sponsa Regis, June, 1931

In the School of the Holy Spirit

Joseph Kreuter, O.S.B.

Pentecost must ever continue in us. The action of the Holy Spirit is unceasing. It is his constant and unchanging desire that we should at all times and to the best of our ability praise, revere, and serve God, becoming ever more closely united to him.

"Like covets like," says the philosopher, and consequently the soul thirsts after the noblest and most perfect of its kind, the Divine Spirit. He being infinite and uncreated, the created and finite spirit may satiate and fill itself with him and in him. All created beings, finite and limited as they are, cannot satisfy the soul; it soon grows wearied of them and goes in search of the proper food or pasture of a spirit. Thus the divinity is the infinite, profound center where the soul can find rest. "As the stag longeth for the running streams, so longeth my heart for thee, my God. My soul thirsteth for God, the strong, the living. When may I come and stand before the face of God?" (Ps 41:2-3)

This thirst for God under the influence of grace is the root of our soul's internal quest for God. This ardent longing for God will abide within us till our last breath, unless under the weight of passion and sin it is lost sight of. It is identical with the quest for happiness.

And what is the real reason for this searching of the soul for God? It is because God is in search of us. It is because God has loved us and made us for himself that nothing created can satisfy the hunger of our soul. Through the action of grace this searching for God becomes, as it were, the beginning, progress, and end of our spiritual life. In virtue of the will's being always impelled to elevate itself to God and of being, moreover, aided by grace, we begin the quest of God. As the Holy Spirit adds greater vigor to this impulse, our efforts to find him who alone can satisfy our thirsting soul become more numerous.

Here we must guard ourselves against one great mistake, viz., that of following our own caprice instead of taking the Holy Spirit as the supreme master of our spiritual life. Left to our own natural light we grope in the dark, apt to lose the direction and eventually find ourselves seeking not God, the Creator, but self, the creature. How important, then, it will be to take as our supreme teacher and guide him who has been appointed by God as our light and director, the Holy Spirit!

And he is never far from us. He is ready at every moment to aid us. It is only to those who seek him earnestly that he reveals himself. "To him who thirsteth I shall give." To taste him is to thirst more for him and less for the things of earth.

But man is free. In his fallen state he feels a strong attraction from without and a powerful impulse from within to turn him away from God. Therefore there is a need for us to purify our soul and mind, for it is with them that we look out on life. If we submit them to the purifying and sanctifying action of the Holy Spirit, we shall find and possess him, find and possess eternal life.

The Holy Spirit desires to be our constant teacher and guide. We must, therefore, enter his school. He gives us the light of discretion for all we should do, avoid, suffer. "He proceeds with the soul, not violently, but sweetly, graciously, leading it on little by little; and, as it were, extorting from her the abandonment of deliberate inordinate affections; thus, by denuding the soul of the clouds of passion, whereby the natural reason is obscured, it is able to see much more clearly the light and help imparted by him, to distinguish good from evil, to see its way in the spiritual life, and to correct its faults" (Father Baker, O.S.B., *Life of Gertrude More*, 35).

"The spiritual life consists in observing and following the divine light and inspiration, in humbling and subjecting the soul to God and to all creatures according to his will, in loving God above all things, in pursuing prayer, and performing it according to divine guidance — all qualities proceeding from the divine operation, a state into which none but the Holy Spirit can bring the soul" (*Op. cit.*, 143).

It is obedience to the inspirations of the Holy Spirit that matters in the spiritual life. One who yields not this obedience, knows not what he ought to do, or omit; or he acts with some natural, human motive, such as fear, shame, habit, or desire to please another, or with some other reason having no reference to God. Thus his works become tainted by self-seeking, not being done principally out of regard to God himself. And will they not lose their value before God? On the contrary the soul that is obedient to divine inspirations not only does, shuns, or suffers all that is necessary, but also acts with perfect liberty and only for the love of God, rejecting all motives that end in self. Thus it is God himself who works all in the soul, and the works become, as it were, divine works, and entitled to a divine reward.

As a result of this fidelity to God's calls, peace and happiness will fill the soul. "O Lord, thou wilt give us peace; for thou hast wrought all our works for us" (Is 26:12); and again: "God has wrought all things for himself" (Prv 16:4). God, then, not only moves the soul to do the works, but also to do them for him, and to exclude every other end and purpose. Thus purity of intention is produced, and God becomes to the soul "all in all," the beginning, the middle and end of all that it does, refrains from, or suffers. Besides, such supernatural works that are undertaken under the influence of the Holy Spirit commonly attain their end, whereas works taken up out of our own initiative and caprice usually end in nothing.

This correspondence with divine inspiration must especially be exercised in regard to prayer and mortification. It is by no means the number and length of prayer that counts, but prayer said in obedience to the divine call as expressed either by the rule and constitutions of the institute to which one may belong or else by the secret inspiration from God. In like manner it is not the number of acts of mortification done under the guidance of one's natural light that will produce the habit of mortification, which consists in the spiritual death to self-love and created things; it is rather the correspondence of the soul with God's inspirations by which the soul is lifted out of self into God, or in other words, lost in him.

The beginning, progress, and consummation of the spiritual perfection depend on our fidelity to the inspirations of the Holy Spirit. The works of souls that are ruled by divine inspirations are performed in true humility and obedience based upon the knowledge of God and herself. They are moreover protected against the attacks of Satan and other enemies of the soul. Such persons can say with the psalmist, "The Lord is my light and my salvation: whom shall I fear?" (Ps 26:1)

The lack of this humility and obedience explains why so many souls who have spent thirty, forty, or more years in religion and have done and suffered much exteriorly are still as unresigned, proud, and self-willed interiorly as they were at the time of their entrance into the cloister. Yes, it may even be that they are worse, for in the beginning of their religious life they at least followed the divine inspirations more or less faithfully; but gradually they grew careless, disregarded them altogether, and daily increased more and more in self-love.

The Holy Spirit, then, must be accepted and obeyed as our spiritual teacher and guide. He will preside over our entire spiritual life if we but correspond to his inspirations. This will insure rapid progress, impart confidence to the soul both in life and in the hour of death, for it enjoys God as her own. Neither need such a soul care as to the nature of the work which is allotted to her, provided it be a work that God wants her to do, and that she undertake and perform it purely because it is God's will that she do it, renouncing all personal advantage and end. Nor will she concern herself about the external success of her work, for that also is referred to God's holy will.

The religious who says the Office with attention will notice that the psalmist is very insistent that we seek the face of God. The reason for this insistence is because the quest of God is the very soul and meaning of life itself. It is indeed truest wisdom to seek God. "Seek and you shall find." God will surely be found by the one who faithfully attends to his inspirations. A strong desire of this gift must be cultivated within us. This desire will urge us on to apply for this gift in fervent prayer. "But if any of you want wisdom, let him ask God, who giveth to all men abundantly, and upbraideth not" (Ja 1:5). "For every best gift and every perfect gift is from above, coming down from the Father of lights with whom there is no change, nor shadow of alteration" (Ja 1:7).

Our Lady of the Angels

fire, on the first of December

Who remembers?
Who remembers the Children?
The children who shall ever be the children the
Children whose cries are crushed in crushed embers.
Who remembers
The Children who shall cry and die on the firsts
                                    of all Decembers?

Who is not going to forget the breath
And body of the fire that brought death
After hurt to the Hundred,
To the children
To the children who shall ever be Children the
Children whose cries are crushed in crushed embers.

Who remembers
The Children who shall cry and die on the firsts
                                    of all Decembers?

Gwendolyn Brooks
Sisters Today, December, 1965

Sponsa Regis, February, 1955

Community Life

A. Biskupek, S.V.D.

Religious life is community life. Religious form one large family in which the superior holds the place of the mother and the members are sisters to one another. All members are under the same obligation to observe the rule and the common order, and thus to strive after perfection. All are employed in the work of the Congregation according to their abilities; all enjoy the same rights as to the spiritual privileges and suffrages of the Congregation in life and after death. It is clear that the Congregation will fulfill its mission, and the members will find their happiness in it, only if they observe the proper attitude toward it, and that is an attitude of esteem, love, and loyalty. To acquire and keep such an attitude it is well to be mindful of the blessings and requirements of community life.

BLESSINGS

Undoubtedly the greatest blessing of community life in convents throughout the world is the nearness of God, the religious atmosphere that pervades the convent. The very building is sacred, in the wider sense of the word, a *bonum ecclesiasticum*, dedicated to a holy purpose. Everything that smacks of the world or would open the door to the spirit of the world must be kept out.

The heart and center of the house is the chapel with the presence of the God-man in the tabernacle; if in a small house the Blessed Sacrament is not preserved in the house, it is not far away. There is the daily Sacrifice of the Mass and Holy Communion. Through the presence of the Blessed Eucharist the religious house becomes a place more sacred than the temple of old, more venerable than the ground surrounding the burning bush, more

81

awe-inspiring than Mount Sinai on which God gave the Ten Commandments amid thunder and lightning.

Religious life is a life dedicated to the pursuit of perfection. Perfection
is charity; charity is the great commandment, the fulfillment of the whole
law. Charity contains within itself all other virtues; but virtues can be
acquired only by their practice. Community life offers all necessary opportunities for their acquisition. Charity wishes well, is eager to help, eager to
share with others whatsoever good we possess, to lighten the burdens of
others, to make joyful and happy.

There is an abundance of spiritual poverty also in the religious community, in constant need of charity. Let us look upon all those who suffer
from faults and failings as spiritually poor, as not possessing the treasures
of the desired virtues, as sick, lacking in spiritual health and vigor. So our
charity, kindness, sympathy, patience go out to the vainglorious, the irritable, the inconsiderate, the selfish and narrow. Their condition is more
pitiful than that of those who are poor in material goods. The practice of
such charity is not easy. To lighten the burden Jesus identifies himself with
the poor, accepting as done to himself whatever is done for them.

Charity will open our eyes to let us see the good that is in others, the
good example which they give to members of the community. The majority
of canonized saints have been members of religious communities. This is
an evident proof that community life offers the best opportunities for the
attainment of sanctity. These saints must have distinguished themselves by
heroic practice of virtue during their lives; they did not become saints after
death.

But the Church is holy, and there must be saints living also in our days.
Indeed, God has his chosen souls in every religious community. Even
though their virtue does not find its deserved appreciation in lifetime — in
fact, it would not be good for them — it nevertheless works like a leaven,
like a light showing the way to that perfection after which all are bound to
strive. The full splendor and power of inspiration of such good example
usually appears only after the saint has departed from this life. In the
sanctity of a fellow religious lies a particularly encouraging incentive, since
she has attained to holiness in the same community, amid the same living
conditions, and thus proved that holiness is within reach of all members.

The blessings of community life pointed out so far have reference more
or less to the individual religious. But the religious state has also a mission
for the world at large, a special task to fulfill in the Church. The individual
religious as a rule cannot do very much in that regard. The blessing of
community life is that it makes possible the attainment of aims which the
individual religious alone could never accomplish. Unity makes strong. To
lift a ton is impossible for one person; the combined strength of a hundred
can easily do it.

The task entrusted to the Church is immense. The weight of sin must be
lifted from earth; the gospel must be preached to all nations; the blessings of

redemption must be brought within reach of all. To accomplish these ends the concentration of the energy of many is necessary. Such transformation of individual into mass energy was the idea of founders of religious orders. They saw the vastness of the work to be done and realized their inability to do much about it alone, and therefore they sought and associated with themselves companions by whose help they would be able to carry out their ideas.

REQUIREMENTS FOR COMMUNITY LIFE

We do not have in mind here the regulations of Canon Law for the admission of candidates, but some more general and fundamental requirements which are necessary to make the community a real religious family, a living organism and not merely an assemblage of persons. As such may be mentioned common sense, solidarity, patriotism.

Webster defines common sense as good, sound, ordinary sense; specifically, good judgment and prudence in managing affairs, especially as free from emotional bias and intellectual subtlety, "horse sense." The very term suggests that it is productive of a manner of speaking and acting that is approved by the vast majority of people of the same state or social and religious persuasion.

The absence of common sense is disturbing: it manifests itself ordinarily in provoking mannerisms, oddities, eccentricities, and in a stubborn refusal to correct such things. The remedy for such a condition is humility and charity. Humility will prompt the religious thus afflicted to accept the verdict of superiors and others as to the existence of the defect, and then to submit to correction and guidance. Charity will prepare the religious to realize the annoyance and provocation she causes to her fellow religious and to spare the latter such afflictions.

The sense of solidarity, which we may call the very soul of the community spirit, the esprit de corps, is the common spirit pervading the members of a body or association. It implies sympathy, enthusiasm, devotion and zealous regard for the honor of the body as a whole. Solidarity in the religious community stands for esteem and love of the founder and his or her work, for the manner of life given by him or her to the community, devotion to the cause for which the community was founded.

Such solidarity will make allowances for the human imperfections of the members and in every way possible endeavor to raise the spiritual level of the community. Destructive criticism is diametrically opposed to this spirit, wheras constructive criticism, brought to the attention of authorities, is a sign of its presence. Once the community has been approved by the Holy See and accepted for cooperation in the mission of the Church, this community spirit and solidarity is in the end nothing but an expression of the *sentire cum Ecclesia*.

Patriotism is usually defined as love of, devotion to one's country, obedience rendered, work done with love to further its interests. Our Lord himself showed such patriotism; he loved his country and his people with a particular love and therefore felt so deeply its blindness and final rejection. Such patriotism has its place also with regard to the religious community. Though we must esteem and love all religious institutes as parts of the Church and because of their work for God and souls, our own community must have a special place in our affection.

It cannot be denied that here and there such patriotism is wanting in members of a religious community, and a great deal of bitterness takes its place. There is little love, not to say positive dislike, for the Congregation, an attitude of indifference toward its condition, a desire to quit if it could be done without too much trouble. Whence such a lamentable condition? The cause is a deficiency of the religious spirit, the absence of solid virtue, too much egotism, narrow-mindedness that sees only one's own comfort, ambitions, and advantage.

Let us open our eyes to the good that is in our own community and to the place it holds in God's designs. And if our community is small and insignificant, let us remember that God loves variety. In his garden there are found not only the mighty oak and red cedar but also the humble violet and pansy, and it is hard to say which one of these proclaims the glory of God more impressively. The individual Sister will do most for God and souls in the place which God has assigned to her through her vocation. Hence, let all take the words of St. Paul as addressed to them: "Therefore I, a prisoner in the Lord, beseech you that you walk worthy of your calling . . . with all humility and meekness, with patience bearing with one another in love, careful to preserve the unity of the Spirit in the bond of peace" (Eph 4:1).

Sponsa Regis, January, 1955

The Holy Rule, Your Way of Life

Anselm Lacomara, C.P.

THE WAY

Actual grace may be likened to a continual stream descending from the limitless reservoir of God's bounty. There is never a minute in the whole day which does not contain its supply of this divine commodity. For this reason Pere de Caussade, S.J., calls actual graces sacraments of the present moment. Each moment carries within itself grace-bearing potentialities. If we use these moments throughout the day, we cannot fail to grow holier with every twenty-four hours that pass.

We religious are most fortunate in this matter, because we have a definite way of life, safe, sure and guaranteed to produce results of a supernatural order. The Holy Rule is that way of life and, in following the rule, both as to the spirit and the letter, we shall obtain our full quota of actual graces.

Thus the religious life, a road to perfection, is well defined as to its route, is safeguarded from danger, and certain as to its successful outcome through the grace of God obtained by fidelity to the Holy Rule.

THE SAFE GUIDE

The Holy Rule is a safe guide to follow because it comes from God's inspiration given, in a limited sense, to some particular individual for a specific purpose. In this sense we might call every holy founder inspired by God. Please do not misunderstand me. You know that inspiration in the true and theological sense refers only to Holy Writ. Inspiration, in the strict sense, is that divine process whereby God guides and directs the sacred authors to write all and only those things which he wants written and in the way he wants them written.

However, God may be said to inspire founders of religious institutes in this sense: every age has characteristics hostile to the interests of God and souls. Thus, in the beginning of the Renaissance the accent was placed on material riches, pagan concepts of luxury and sensuality, and unbridled adherence to the god of mammon. In the eighteenth century the accent was on the superiority of the human intellect over the intellect instructed by faith.

A chosen soul recognizes this opposition to Almighty God and, precisely because he or she is a chosen soul, close to God and most solicitous for the divine good, begins to pray for the alleviation of this evil. In prayer the idea is gradually conceived that prayer must be bolstered up by good works, not the good works of only one man or one woman, but by the activity of a solid, unified group of men or women who will go forth and do battle with this evil through a way of life. In the warfare for God's glory which will inevitably ensue, the persons chosen by God to follow this new way will gain sanctity.

In order to combat the particular abuse the founder usually does two things. First, through his spirit of prayer and his genuine holiness, he devises by God's grace a plan of life totally opposed to the spirit of the age in which he lives. Where the age is filled with sensuality, penance will predominate. Where the age is filled with the spirit of materialism, poverty will come to the fore. Where the age is filled with pride of intellect, humility will prevail.

The second phase in the genesis of practically every rule denotes the particular work a given institute will do. It may be preaching, teaching, nursing, care of the poor, etc. It may be purely active in its scope; it may be purely contemplative. Usually it is a combination of both, called apostolic. In any event, it will be a characteristic activity opposed to the prevailing abuse or spirit of the times.

So we are justified in saying that every rule is, in a certain sense, inspired. The age has its abuse; a holy man or woman sees and prays over the abuse; in prayer God sheds his light, and the result is some definite form of action. The rule is finally approved by God's supreme authority on earth, the Church, and each man or woman who takes membership in the society thus approved has the infallible guarantee that this way of life, if faithfully followed, can produce only holiness, good works and, eventually, eternal life.

THE SURE GUIDE

The Holy Rule is likewise sure. It is guaranteed to produce results of a supernatural order. One proof of this lies in the results which have followed upon its observance by others. Go through the lives of the saints and observe for yourself how many of them were founders of religious orders or congregations. St. Augustine, St. Benedict, St. Scholastica, St. Bernard, St. Dominic, St. Francis of Assisi, St. Vincent de Paul, St. Paul of the Cross, St. John Bosco, to mention only a few (and, forgive me, nearly all men), founded religious orders. What is the rule of their institutes but a continuation of their way of life? Living the rule is an imitation of them in the way they imitated Christ. Every holy founder can say with St. Paul, "Be imitators of me as I am of Christ" (1 Cor 9:1).

Furthermore, the rule, because it throws ramparts around the vows, safeguards the fundamental means to perfection. The religious, having renounced worldly obstacles through voluntary poverty, is told by the rule exactly what the vow of poverty means and how it is to be kept. It gives the religious what she needs and reduces her use of goods and money to definite limits. In like manner for the other vows. Chastity is guarded through wise directions regulating conduct at home and abroad. Obedience is safeguarded by defining to whom the religious owes obedience and the manner in which she is to obey. The rule simplifies everything connected with the vows and shows us how best to observe them. If we follow the rule, we can be absolutely certain that we are keeping the vows, and in keeping the vows we shall attain perfection.

But the greatest assurance the rule gives us is even more fundamental in its scope, and this is where actual grace superabounds. The rule shows us how to do God's will every minute of the day and night. It would not be incorrect to state that the rule is God's decree for us here and now. What time does God want us to rise in the morning? When the bell rings. What time does God want us to hear Mass? At whatever time the rule says. When are we to study, do our spiritual reading, eat, sleep, take recreation, work, pray, all according to the will of God? Follow the table of hours constituted by the rule. What kind of work shall we do to please God? Read the rule. How shall we accomplish our task for God's glory. The rule will tell us. What clothing shall we wear to serve God? Consult the Holy Rule. Where shall we live in the household of God? Where the rule sends us. And in every one of these circumstances we can say with all honesty, "God wills it."

In his infinite mercy God has called us to this manner of life. The very fact that we have taken our vows and still have them proves that conclusively. Divine Providence has so arranged matters for us that we are able to live from day to day as God wishes. We are never in the unfortunate position of not knowing what God wants of us. If we desire to know what we are to do at any given time, we have simply to consult a little book, a book approved by God's authority.

VIOLATIONS COURT DISASTER

In the light of these truths, it is easy to see that deliberate violations of the rule lead to disaster on many counts. They lead to disaster in the institute itself. The congregation to which we belong has been established in the Church for a definite purpose. Because of it, many souls will be saved and great material as well as spiritual good will be accomplished. However, once the good which should flow from the specific end of the society ceases to diffuse itself, the society has only one destiny: suppression.

Nothing can produce this sorry state of affairs more quickly than deliberate and constant violations of the rule. Where such violations exist, the institute becomes internally lax. Once the internal organization becomes loose, once the members of the congregation lose sight of the rule's exactions at home, the external works of the order will soon suffer. The plan of God calls for a detailed regime of life and discipline. If this plan is flouted and flagrantly ignored, the spirit and life of the order cease to be.

Pick up even a superficial history of the Church and see how true this has been through the years. There can be no doubt that religious orders fail and are suppressed, not because of external circumstances, but because they rot from within.

PERSONAL DISASTER

Nor can the religious who deliberately and constantly violates the rule escape disaster in her own life. Through her deliberate violations of rule she throws aside the means to perfection God wants her to have. How can that religious be said to seek God when she deliberately rejects the only safe and sure method of finding him? What is she doing? When God says, "Be poor," she succumbs to the concupiscence of the eyes and allows herself privileges contrary to the rule of poverty. She reestablishes personal ownership and dominion; she retracts a gift once given. When God says, "Be chaste," she endangers herself because "the rule is old-fashioned and European, unrealistic for Americans." When God says, "Be obedient," she complains, groans, gripes and completely ignores what her rule says about cheerful obedience. And so one could continue with spiritual exercises, prayer, penance, silence and all the other points upon which most rules lay particular stress. This religious is a sham; she rejects, day in and day out, the many graces God offers her through her rule.

DISASTER TO THE CHURCH

Moreover, violations of the rule bring harm to the Church. Neither religious institutes nor individual religious act apart from the Church. The good as well as the evil they do affects the general holiness of the Church, Christ's Mystical Body. The good of any religious order stems from the purpose for which the Church allowed the order to exist in the first place. When the rule is disregarded and the works of the order are not accomplished, the Church suffers in having a faulty limb.

Those of us who are called to a life of special friendship with God in religion have the obligation of contributing greatly to the holiness of Christ's Mystical Body. We can contribute that holiness only by living according to the plan laid down for us by the teaching and legislating authority of that same Mystical Body. When we, by violating the rule, refuse this obligation, we contribute only imperfection and sin.

A PERSONAL MATTER

Each of us must consider the observance of the rule as a personal matter. Each of us knows that point or, perhaps, those points of rule where most of the tripping is done. It may be with regard to the vows, spiritual exercises, silence, etc. It may be anything and everything. It is vital, therefore, to our successful religious living that we investigate humbly and prayerfully into these points and, as it were, take ourselves firmly in hand and put a stop to this flying in the face of God. We took our vows and embraced a way of life for one purpose, to become saints. The rule alone can guide us to this end. Unless we follow the guide, we shall be lost.

We should, therefore, esteem, cherish and love the rule. It is a treasury from which God's bounty flows. It is the means through which we can achieve the highest goal of our desire: God. If we look upon our rule in this way and not as a set of restrictions, then we shall be able to serve God day by day and daily grow in his love. And if we do , we shall merit to hear from the lips of Christ himself our reward exceedingly great, "Well done, good and faithful servants; because thou hast been faithful in the few things imposed on thee and promised by thee, enter thou into the joy of thy Lord."

Sponsa Regis, April, 1951

Sacramental Value of Religious Customs

Sister Mary Urban, O.S.B.

To the beginner of the religious life one of the most perplexing problems with which she is confronted is the maze of custom and ritual which seems to fill her daily life. The simple, everyday actions of living suddenly become complicated and take on an unwarranted importance because of many strange ceremonies and practices.

In some convents the candidate is introduced to the customs of local usage by means of a little handbook which contains the do's and don't's, the bows and inclinations, the various traditional practices which are peculiar to the house. In others the example of the elders is a living guide to manners and morals.

As time goes on, the newcomer becomes accustomed to these practices and they become easy through repeated use. In fact, they frequently become so completely a routine part of life that they lose much of their significance, at least to the individual. When this is the case, the customs of religious life tend to lose their efficacy, their power to clothe even the most commonplace acts with the splendor of sacramental grace and the urge to sanctify. A little reflection on their derivation and meaning in connection with the sacramental life of the Church should serve to aid us in using them as they were intended to be used, not as mere social observances, but as sources of grace for ourselves and of glory to God.

The customs of a religious house frequently derive from usages common to the particular country where the order had its origin. The founders of each order incorporated details calculated to suit their followers who came from a certain locale and followed a specific culture. These details in subsequent years became part of the tradition of the order and were often carried from the original house to new foundations. For example, in many communities there is the practice of using certain phrases of the French or German vernacular.

More frequently, however, it is possible to trace the various customs to the ceremonies of the Church, and if this is done it becomes immediately apparent that the customs carry with them a sacramental quality derived from their source. It follows that because of this quality, such customs are a means of obtaining great grace and merit. Viewed in this light, they gain new importance and meaning for the religious.

Perhaps some examples will help to illustrate this point. In most religious houses it is the custom for religious to make a slight inclination when passing each other. The action itself bears a definite resemblance to the movement of the celebrant at the altar when he gives the kiss of peace, the symbol of fraternal charity and communion. A thoughtful *"Pax vobis"* would charge the smallest action with an infusion of charity that would renew during the day the bond sealed at the altar in the morning sacrifice.

In requesting permissions in many houses it is the custom for the subject to kneel before the superior. Besides being an indication of humility, kneeling to ask for what is needed recalls the supplication that is made in the *Pater noster* of the Mass, when we beg God our Father for our daily bread. We are reminded too that the superior takes the place of God in our house. The declaration of faults and the acceptance of commissions of obedience in a kneeling posture likewise emphasize the humility and submission of the prodigal son or willing servant, as the priest reminds us by his profound bow at the *Confiteor* or at the *Munda cor*.

The ceremonies of the refectory are all designed to make the partaking of food one of the most solemn actions of the day. Here again we can note a similarity to the ceremonies of the Mass where the giving of Eucharistic Bread is surrounded by prayers and actions intended to make us realize the solemnity of what we are about to do.

The prayers prescribed for recitation while dressing coincide almost literally with the prayers which the priest says while vesting for Mass. They serve as a reminder to the religious of the priestly character of the Christian and, more particularly, of the religious life. At the same time, the offering of the day in the sacrifice of the Mass is prepared for by the divestment of self and the "putting on of Jesus Christ," the Priest and Victim.

One final example — the use of holy water and the sign of the Cross. Besides the fact that both are enriched with many indulgences, we can find their sacramental meaning made still more significant in connection with the Mass. The use of water in the *Asperges* denotes the cleansing of the soul from sin. The sign of the Cross, used repeatedly in the Mass and all the functions of the Church, symbolizes the blessing of the Trinity. Used thoughtfully through the day, the sign of the Cross and the holy water may serve as reminders of our baptism, when we were first cleansed from sin and signed with the sign of the Trinity, and of our consecration in religious profession, when we solemnized our vows "in the name of the Father and of the Son and of the Holy Ghost." Thus in addition to remitting temporal punishment for sin, these symbols also become sources of actual grace and positive inspirations to holiness.

Many more examples could be mentioned, but these are sufficient to illustrate the relationship between the various religious customs and the sacramental system of the Church.

a waspoem

watching the trees
              blush
as
summer picks up her
           bucketfulofblooms
i
wander through
          yesterday
while the
cattails
         wave their sighs of
             gonenow
and
the
         crinkledwas leaves of
yellowed maybes
crunch
under
        october's foot
. . .& the mockingbird laughs
           never
flying south

Sister Frances Barrett, O.S.B.
Sisters Today, October, 1967

Sponsa Regis, April, 1955

The Religious Habit

A. Biskupek, S.V.D.

In ancient as well as in modern times, among pagan nations as well as among Christians, it has been customary that persons dedicated in a special manner to the service of God wear a distinctive dress. In the Old Testament, God himself prescribed in detail the dress to be worn by Levites and priests performing acts of divine worship; in the New Testament the Church insisted from quite early times upon a special dress for priests and sacred ministers when conducting divine services. A distinctive garb was made obligatory for clerics even in ordinary life.

A distinctive dress for persons dedicated to the service of God in the religious state is likewise of early origin. At the present time Holy Church insists upon it for all religious. Even though in some countries conditions make it advisable that the full religious garb be not worn in public, especially by religious men, it is always to be worn in the house. If Holy Church insists upon the observance of this law, there must be good reasons for it. Indeed, the wearing of the religious garb is a striking profession of faith and offers considerable help towards the attainment of the object of the religious life, i.e., self-sanctification and the sanctification of souls.

PROFESSION OF FAITH

By its very appearance the religious habit is an impressive profession of faith. It marks the wearer as one who believes in God as our Creator and Lord, to whom service is due, as one who believes that the primary end and purpose of life is to know God, to love and serve him and thus to save our souls. True, God does not demand the same perfection of service from all, but no better use can be made of life than to spend it in his exclusive service, and it is such exclusive service of God to which the religious has given her life.

This profession of faith made by the religious is the profession of the Catholic faith. The very sight of the religious in her habit tells the observer that here is a member of the Catholic Church who believes this Church to be the only true Church founded by Jesus Christ for the salvation of the world, and considers the work of the Church so noble and holy as to consecrate to it her whole life. If notwithstanding the rigorous demands as to perfection of life and personal sacrifice, the religious state can attract thousands of men and women, it must be admitted that the very appearance of the religious habit in public is a telling demonstration that the Spirit of Christ lives on in the Church.

Religious do not give up their human nature, either in the choice of their vocation or in the work that is demanded of them. They too remain sensitive to the things that appeal to people in general: independence of action, a worldly career with its agreeable associations, its comforts and pleasures. If they have renounced these things definitely and for life, what can be their motive? Perfection of life and service of God.

Perfection is the closest possible imitation of our divine Savior in his life and work with the full realization that as we now share in his labors, we shall also share in his glory. Before the splendor of this glory pales into nothingness all that the world could offer or promise. The great Apostle has expressed this thought strikingly, "I reckon that the sufferings of the present time are not worthy to be compared with the glory to come that will be revealed in us" (Rom 8:18).

Hence the religious garb proclaims before the world that there are ideals, spiritual and heavenly ideals, that are capable of captivating the whole love of a human heart, ideals richer and more soul-satisfying than all the riches of the world, ideals of spiritual greatness, of immortal glory and happiness in a world which, though unseen, is nevertheless real and certain to follow after this life.

INCENTIVE TO PERFECTION OF LIFE

If such is the idea of the religious habit and the effect which its appearance produces in the world, it surely must influence also the Sister who wears it. We cannot carry a flaming torch to illumine the way for others without seeing it ourselves. If the habit speaks to men about God and his service, should it not be a constant reminder to the religious of the ideals of the religious life? If her very habit proclaims the Sister to be dedicated to the work of the Church, should she not love that Church, its worship, its discipline, its activity, and so foster within herself the *sentire cum Ecclesia*?

If, finally, the very shape and color of the habit speaks of contempt of the world and dedication to a life of perfection, should the Sister be satisfied with the mere avoidance of sin and mediocrity of virtue that is so common among the faithful living amid the distractions and temptations of the world? Must not the thought of eternity and heaven give a very definite impress to the life of the religious, to her manner of judging and acting?

PROTECTION

A practical awareness of the above thoughts will prove to be a strong protection for the religious. Nature remains weak in the Sister, notwithstanding the sacred state which she has chosen, but she has kept a profound respect for this state, and this respect makes her shrink from doing things which might desecrate it and eventually become the cause of ruin for others. There is, after all, in the human heart, unless thoroughly wicked, a certain abhorrence of deceit and hypocrisy. Will she wear the religious garb and live like a worldling in the sight of those who venerate and love the religious state? No, the religious will not do so, certainly not without torturing qualms of conscience.

Her habit will tell the Sister which places she cannot visit without disgracing it, which associations she cannot foster without becoming a traitor to her sacred profession, which things she cannot do or speak about without becoming guilty of shameful cowardice and inconsistency. With a little humility and self-knowledge we will admit our weakness and our need of protection and be thankful to Holy Church for the religious habit.

EDIFICATION OF THE FAITHFUL

Deep down in the human heart, especially of the believing Christian, burns the longing desire for something better and nobler than this world has to offer. It is not always felt with the same intensity, but from time to time it reveals its presence with irresistible force and clearness. He experiences the difficulties of the Christian life in consequence of the corruption of nature through original sin and looks for encouragement and help to assist him in his struggles. He receives such help by the work and example of religious. Hence that spontaneous pleasure which Catholics generally experience at meeting a good religious, that reverence and attachment shown on such occasions.

The religious habit speaks to them of a life consecrated to God and his service, of the glory and happiness of such a life; they are breathing in, so to say, a spiritual, heavenly atmosphere, and feel strengthened anew to do their work and carry their cross in the state to which God has called them. It surely would be a blessing for themselves and for the world, if Sisters became more vividly aware of the fact that their very appearance in public is an object lesson for the faithful and also for those not of our faith; right then and there they have not only the opportunity, but also the obligation to preach the gospel of peace, sometimes by words, but always by their example, and the official garb for their preaching is the religious habit.

Such a view of the religious habit will surely be helpful in the attainment of the object of the religious life. To wear it must be considered an honor and privilege, a sign of divine predilection and predestination for eternal life. And when at last the Sister has reached the end of her life and is laid out in the garb of her Order or Congregation, may this be not just the conventional way of doing it, but the symbol of her devotion and loyalty to her Order or Congregation of gratitude for the blessings that came to her through her habit, or her lifelong efforts to wear it with honor and distinction. And so the religious habit becomes the nuptial garb in which she, the *Sponsa Christi*, appears before her heavenly Bridegroom to celebrate the eternal nuptials of the Lamb.

Prayer Upon Waking

These winter mornings
a thickened light
glides in
between the blinds,
congealing shadows
on the objects in my room:

A half-burnt candle,
a basket spewing waste,
a celibate veil
hanging like a pod,
a bastion of unopened books.
Here is the lurking gorgon
we must be delivered from —
this petrifying nuance
of unremitting gray:

Were it brighter
I would rise and sing;
were it darker
I could pray.

Sister Sonia Gernes
Sisters Today, February, 1972

Sponsa Regis, June, 1959

Spiritual Direction

Thomas Merton

When we speak of spiritual direction we normally mean a continuous process of guidance in which a Christian is led by a trusted and friendly spiritual advisor through the obstacles that lie in the way of perfect union with God in Christ. As we shall see, in the full traditional sense of the word, what we call today a director is much more than the name implies. He is more than an advisor or a counsellor. He is a spiritual father who brings the Christian to closer union with Christ not only by his words and advice, but by his prayers, his example, and his whole life.

In the earliest days of Christian asceticism the spiritual father was not simply an advisor who was consulted from time to time when there were problems to be solved. The neophyte lived in the same cell with the spiritual father and not only received verbal instruction, but imitated the father in everything that he did. Thus his own ascetic life became a reproduction of the life of one who was in all truth his spiritual father. In the monastic tradition the spiritual father (originally the abbot or a venerable senior) is to the monk a kind of sacrament of Christ himself. It is Christ who lives, speaks and acts in the spiritual father: for we have but one master and one father, Christ the Lord.

Before we consider the meaning of spiritual direction today let us dispose of a few preliminaries.

Is spiritual direction necessary? Strictly speaking, spiritual direction is not absolutely necessary in the Christian life. That is to say that the ordinary contacts of the faithful with their pastor and confessors are sufficient to take care of their minimum needs in this regard, even without any more intensive and intimate guidance.

In the religious life, a certain minimum of spiritual direction is implied by the very nature of the life itself. Novices must be formed in the spirit of the order, and this means more than merely learning how to keep the rules and following the customary practices of piety. Professed religious have to continue in the way of perfection, and in doing so they may meet with many and serious obstacles which they can hardly negotiate as they should without the intimate guidance of someone who knows and understands them, in an atmosphere of informality and trust which may perhaps not be easy to achieve with the superior.

It is not necessary to add that through the course of the ages, spiritual direction has become a special function, separate from that of the superior and even from that of the confessor. In early monasticism, the abbot was at the same time not only the canonical superior of all the monks but at the same time their spiritual director and confessor. Today the superior is forbidden to hear the confession of his subjects except in certain rare cases. He can, however, be their spiritual director. Very often spiritual direction is separated from confession, and direction is given by a specially qualified priest, perhaps on rare occasions. Today most people are lucky if they can find someone who can give them direction when they are burdened by accumulated problems. The ideal would be for everyone to have a father to whom he or she could go for regular direction.

However, spiritual directors are not easy to find, even in the religious life. Even where there are several priests at hand, this does not mean that they are all suitable as directors. The scarcity of really good spiritual directors for religious may perhaps account for the magnitude of the problems in certain communities. Sometimes religious do not receive a really adequate formation, and they are nevertheless professed with unfortunate consequences. After profession, the effects of a good novitiate may vanish into thin air, through lack of a director to continue the work that was well begun. No doubt many losses of vocation could have been prevented by a really solid and firm spiritual direction in the first years after the novitiate.

When one has been aided by spiritual direction to lay down a solid foundation, she may be able to go on building by herself the structure of her religious life in mature years. Those who are firmly grounded and who can share their knowledge and their strength with others receive in this process lights which are of inestimable value for their own religious lives. Nevertheless, a timely conference with a good director may resolve many apparently hopeless problems and open one's eyes to unsuspected dangers, thereby preventing a disaster.

At all times, spiritual direction is of the greatest value to a religious. Even though it may not be strictly necessary, it is always useful. In many cases, the absence of direction may mean the difference between sanctity and mediocrity in the religious life. Naturally, one who has sought direction and not found it will not be held responsible for its lack, and God himself will make up to the soul what is wanting to it in his own way.

We have said above that good directors are rare. This, in fact, is a rather important matter. If we really desire spiritual directors for our communities and for others let us seek them. We can at least pray for this intention! In the last ten years there has been an amazing growth in the publishing of spiritual books and in the study of the spiritual life. This growth has come at a time when it was needed and desired by the faithful. If it is realized that there is not only a need for spiritual direction but also a very real hunger for it on the part of religious, directors will soon begin to be more numerous, for God will send them. He will raise up priests who will desire to give themselves to this kind of work, in spite of the difficulties and sacrifices involved. But there is always a danger that the priest qualified for this kind of work will be overwhelmed by the demand for his services. His first duty, if he wants to be an effective director, is to see to his own interior life and take time for prayer and meditation, since he will never be able to give to others what he does not possess himself.

Setting aside this urgent problem, let us suppose that one has found a director. How can he make the best use of this gift of God? In the first place, those who have regular spiritual direction ought to realize that this is a grace of God, and even though they may not be thoroughly satisfied, they should humbly appreciate the fact that they have direction at all. This will enable them to take better advantage of what they have, and they may perhaps see that supernaturally they are much better off than they realized. Gratitude will make them more attentive to the direction they receive, and will attune their faith to possibilities which they had overlooked. Even if their director is not another St. Benedict or St. John of the Cross, they may come to realize that he is nevertheless speaking to them in the name of Christ and as his mouthpiece.

What are we normally entitled to expect from spiritual direction? It is certainly very helpful, but we must not imagine that it works wonders. Some people, and especially some religious who ought to know better, seem to think that they ought to be able to find a spiritual director who with one word can make all their problems vanish. They are not looking for a director but for a miracle worker.

In point of fact, we very often look for someone else to solve problems that we ought to be able to solve, not so much by our own wisdom as by our generosity in facing the facts and obligations that represent for us the will of God. Nevertheless, human nature is weak, and the kindly support and wise advice of one whom we trust often enables us to *accept* more perfectly what we already know and see in an obscure way. A director may not tell us anything we do not already know, but it is a great thing if he helps us to overcome our hesitations and strengthens our generosity in the Lord's service. However, in many cases, a director will reveal to us things which we have hitherto been unable to see, though they were staring us in the face. This, too, is certainly a great grace.

One thing a good director will not do is make our ill-defined, uncon-scious velleities for perfection come true with a wave of the hand. He will not enable us to attain the things we wish for, because the spiritual life is not a matter of wishing for perfection. Too often, people think that all they need to turn a wish into the will of God is to have it confirmed by a director. Unfortunately, this kind of alchemy does not work, and one who seeks to practice it is in for disappointment.

It often happens that so-called pious souls take their spiritual life with a wrong kind of seriousness. We should certainly be serious in our search for God — nothing is more serious than that. But we ought not to be constantly observing our own efforts at progress and paying exaggerated attention to our spiritual life. Some who lament the fact that they cannot find a director actually have all the opportunities for direction they really need, but they are not pleased with the available director because he does not flatter their self-esteem or cater to their illusions about themselves. In other words, they want a director who will confirm their hope of finding pleasure in them-selves and in their virtues, rather than one who will strip them of their self-love and show them how to get free from preoccupation with them-selves and their own petty concerns, to give themselves to God and to the Church.

This does not mean that all that passes for spiritual direction is really adequate. On the contrary, very often the direction given after confession is nothing more than a short, impersonal homily delivered to each penitent individually. It may be doctrinally correct, and perfectly good as a sermon. But direction is, by its very nature, something *personal*. It is quite obvious that a Sister who knows she is receiving exactly the same vague, general exhortation as the twenty who went before her to confession hardly feels that she is receiving spiritual direction. Of course she is not.

Even then, she should try to make the best of it. If she is humble enough to accept at least this, she will find that the Lord has his message for her in it all. And the message will be personal.

On the other hand, a priest who might be glad to give direction pertinent to the individual case is sometimes unable to do so because the penitent has not made a sufficiently clear manifestation of conscience.

A manifestation of conscience, which is absolutely necessary for spiritual direction, is something apart from sacramental confession of sins. In actual fact, sometimes our real problems are not very closely connected with the sinful acts which we submit to the power of the keys. Or if they are connected, the mere confession of the sins does nothing to make the connection apparent.

Actually, sin usually presents itself to the confessor as something rather impersonal — it is the same in everyone. In consequence, the best he can do is to respond with advice that is more or less general and universal. It may be good advice in itself, and perfectly in accordance with moral theology, and yet not get anywhere near the real root of the problem in the soul of the penitent.

Sponsa Regis, February, 1943

Teaching True Piety

A Group of Religious

Novices do not enter the novitiate to be trained for teaching, nursing or performing the Martha services in the community. Neither does God send them to us primarily for any one of these purposes. Every newly vested novice that crosses the threshold of a novitiate is a saint in the making, and the whole purpose of the novitiate is to assist her in achieving this sublime end. A saint is one who constantly endeavors to live intimately with God. To show her novices the way to this union is the first and chief duty of the Novice Mistress.

What is this way to God? It is true piety or godliness. It is the only way which will never fail. "Train thyself in godliness — for it is profitable in all respects," St. Paul exhorts Timothy (1 Tim 4:8). St. Augustine says: "Every being lives in the measure in which it attains to unity." The novice must perform many acts, she must strive to acquire many habits, to cultivate many virtues. Only in the measure in which she fuses all these into one will she simplify and unify her spiritual life in God. Piety is the secret of this unity. It gives to every human act its final purpose, its direction toward God, its real value. It alone is the passport to eternal glory in heaven.

Piety must become a virtue, a habit which enables the soul to see, to love, and to seek God in all things. St. Paul, in his inimitable way, admonishes the Ephesians to acquire this virtue: "Practice the truth in love, and so grow up in all things in him who is the head, Christ" (4:15). This habit of seeing, loving, and seeking God in all things is not as frequently found among religious as some of us imagine. If it consisted in a multitude of devotions, or even in the frequent reception of the sacraments, it would be quite common.

The fact is, a novice may attend every spiritual exercise required by the daily order and yet fail to acquire the true spirit of prayer, of piety. Indeed, it is possible to recite many formulas of prayers and not pray at all. Neither are prayers, practices, and penances that are suggested by natural dispositions, caprices and tastes, signs of true piety. For piety is born of God alone and of his will; it sees, loves, and follows the will of God in all things and thus constantly promotes his honor and glory.

PIETY VERSUS PIETISM

Piety that is self-seeking is not genuine. It is pseudo-piety or pietism. Much of the piety of today is of this anemic sort. Pietism stresses the *multa* or quantity of prayer. Piety looks to the *multum* or quality. Pietism seeks self first and then God. Piety, on the other hand, seeks God above all and self only because of God and in God. The prayer of the truly pious soul is essentially unselfish. For her, God's honor and glory come first, then her own spiritual advantage; and then again, she desires her own spiritual progress in order to be able the better to advance the glory of God. As God-seeker she surrenders herself totally and without the least reserve to him who is her highest good. She loves to be with God, to suffer for God , to work with God. She is entirely dedicated to him, for real piety to her is utter devotedness to God. Our rule must be: "Seek first the kingdom of God and his justice, and all these things shall be given you besides."

Piety, then, is the sum total of all our spiritual living: it is the great virtue from which all other virtues flow and whither all virtues tend. St. John calls piety "walking in truth." "I have no greater joy than to hear that my children are walking in the truth" (2 Jn 4). No religious possesses the virtue of piety until she has acquired a readiness in seeing, loving, and seeking God in all things to the exclusion of all conscious self-seeking. These sobering reflections should give us the standard by which to judge piety in ourselves and in our novices.

THE ALL-IMPORTANCE OF PRAYER

Piety is thorough devotedness to God. Prayer is the "breathing" of the pious soul. As in the natural life our physical well-being requires continuous breathing, so our spiritual well-being in the supernatural life demands prayer. The law of prayer may be called the most fundamental law of the spiritual life. Eternal Truth expressed it in these words: "Without me you can do nothing" (Jn 5:15), or "We must always pray and not lose heart" (Lk 18:1). St. Paul teaches: "Not that we are sufficient to think anything of ourselves, as for ourselves . . . (2 Cor 3:15), and again "for it is God who worketh in you, both to will and to accomplish" (Phil 2:13).

The necessity of prayer is based on our need of actual grace in all that we think, desire, say, do, and suffer. It is a truth of faith that without such grace we are utterly incapable of obtaining salvation and still less of attaining perfection. He alone who has begun in us the good work of perfection can bring it to a happy close. Only he who has called us unto his eternal glory can perfect and confirm and establish us in our striving for holiness and perfection. We truly have to rely upon the divine favor.

Our dependence upon God is absolute. Absolute also must be our confidence in his assistance. Confidence not based on prayer is presumption, for God has not pledged himself to give it except through prayer. God assuredly knows all our wants and needs before we express them in prayer, yet he wills that prayer be the spring that sets in motion his loving mercy, so that we may acknowledge him as the author of the gifts he bestows on us. God commands us to do what we can and to ask his assistance for what we cannot do. He even must help us to ask for it in the right manner.

LEARNING TO PRAY WELL

If you wish to receive from God what is needed for the attainment of perfection, you must observe the following rules:

1. Desire ardently what you need.
2. Ask for it again and again until you receive it.
3. Try to practice what is demanded on your part in the matter.

God then seeing your ardent desire, hearing your continued prayer, and noting your persistent efforts at practice will grant the favor in his time and measure. However, there is one more point to be observed: It must all be desired, prayed for, and practiced for the greater honor and glory of God, not for any selfish purpose.

Now apply this to the gift or spirit of prayer. (1) We must desire it ardently, that is, hunger for it, hope for it from God. The hungry he will fill with good things, but the self-satisfied he will send empty away. Religious believe that they need prayer to persevere, but how many of them have a keen relish for the gift of prayer? In fact, some are afraid to be considered pious. As a child no one of us ever asked for what we did not want, nor have we done so ever since. The first requisite to obtain the gift of prayer is to ardently desire it. This desire need not be expressed in word; it can be hidden in the soul. God sees it.

(2) We must persevere in asking for the grace of prayer. "We must always pray and not cease." This petition need not be expressed in formal terms either. The request can be made in the fraction of a second; it can flash from earth to heaven with lightning speed. "Lord, teach me to pray." Ask for this grace hundreds of times. This is the greatest gift we can obtain from God. Ask for it constantly. "Ask and it shall be given you," our Lord says. Then be patient and wait on the Lord, trusting that he knows best when and in what measure he should give it to you. Thus self-will is excluded and the will of God made to rule our life.

(3) We must try to practice it. Here is the crux of the matter. Here is the parting of the road for the fervent and the lukewarm religious. There is little profit in learning how to meditate, how to make an examen of conscience,

how to say our Office, how to study, how to teach and catechize, how to practice the various virtues unless we, at the same time, endeavor to acquire true piety, or at least cultivate a strong desire for it. As it is the essence of all spirituality, the fervent religious will make efforts to obtain it, ask for it, and try to practice it.

(4) It is self-love, self-seeking that keeps us from attaining the life of prayer. We have no other end in view but our own interests. Self-love only thinks of prayer as a request, a petition made to God to obtain from him some benefit. It rarely rejoices with God because God is God, because God is so great and so beautiful, so holy, so all-perfect. It seldom gives thanks for his great glory which really constitutes our true happiness. Self-love seeks to put God in our service. It considers God a friend to be utilized rather than served. Such devotion is very imperfect because it is selfish.

The religious as a select member of the Mystical Body of Christ must make this more perfect kind of prayer — the prayer of praise, thanksgiving, and expiation — her own. God must be first. God must be ALL in ALL. "We praise thee, we bless thee, we adore thee, we glorify thee. We give thee thanks for thy great glory." This is directly unselfish prayer, and yet it is the right way of seeking self. "First find God, and in God you will find self" has been the life maxim of every saint.

Religious do not frequently and persistently enough ask for the great gifts they need most for their spiritual progress. To beg for such fundamental needs of our soul, e.g., the gift of prayer, of faith, love and humility, seldom occurs to them. They do not ask for the spirit of prayer because they do not actually realize the truth of the words of eternal Truth: "Without me you can do nothing."

Only those religious who live this text, "Without me you can do nothing," will learn how to pray well. They will give God what is his due: adoration, gratitude, expiation for their sins and faults, and petition above all for his glory, then for their neighbor's salvation including their own. And as they cannot do this by themselves, they will persist in asking for the gift of prayer. "Lord, teach me to pray well, to pray always" will become one of their favorite ejaculations for life. It embodies the wisdom of all the saints.

"I affirm," says Father de Ravignan, "that all deceptions, all spiritual deficiencies, all miseries, all falls, all faults, and even the most serious wanderings out of the right path, all proceed from this single source — a want of constancy in prayer. Live the life of prayer; learn to bring everything, to change everything into prayer: pains and trials and temptations of all kinds."

Sponsa Regis, July, 1952

Helps for Meditation

Winfrid Herbst, S.D.S.

PRAYER BEFORE MEDITATION

My God, I firmly believe that thou art here present, and I humbly adore thee in union with the angels and saints. I am sorry for having sinned, because thou art infinitely good and sin displeases thee.

I love thee above all things and with my whole heart. I offer thee all that I am and all that I have — my soul with all its faculties, my body with all its senses.

Enlighten my understanding and inflame my will that I may know and do what is pleasing to thee. I beseech thee to direct all the powers of my soul, all my thoughts and affections to thy service and thy glory as well as to my own sanctification and salvation. Amen.

OUTLINE FOR FORMAL MEDITATION

I. *Memory*: Who? What? Where? Whereby? Why? How? When?
II. *Understanding*:
       1. What general consideration?
       2. What truth for my everyday life?
       3. What motives? How fitting? useful? pleasant? easy? necessary?
       4. How observed theretofore?
       5. What to do in future?
III. *Will: Resolutions and Affections*:
       1. Resolution. A special one for today. When? At what occasion? Which hindrances are to be removed? What means are to be applied?

2. Affections and ejaculations. Adoration.
Praise. Thanks. Humility. Sorrow. Love.
Petition, etc. — Colloquy.

TWELVE METHODS OF MEDITATION

1. Meditation properly so-called or the textbook method. You take a certain holy consideration — heaven, for instance — and apply to it the powers of the soul: memory, understanding, and will, according to the above outline. Try to arrive at affections towards God and definite resolutions.

2. This method is sometimes called "contemplation" in the broad sense of the word. Take some mystery of the life of Christ or of the Blessed Virgin, and ask yourself: "Who are the persons? What are they saying? What are they doing?" Persons, words, actions. Seek to arrive at union with God in love.

3. This is called the application of the senses. Direct the imagination and senses of the body to some truth or mystery. Take the temptation of the Savior in the desert, for example. With the sight, hearing, taste, smell, and touch, imagine all you can about those temptations.

4. Here we have the examination of conscience method. Take the commandments, the seven capital sins, the vows, the rules, and while trying to see what sins you have committed, arouse devout desires to be better, compunction, resolutions of amendment, perfect love, and contrition.

5. A very simple and often most fruitful method. Take any vocal prayer, like the Our Father, Hail Mary, or the Apostles' Creed. Say one word or a group of words and meditate upon the same, going to the next only when the mind and heart seem to have utilized to the full the spiritual nourishment contained in each. Seek again to arrive at affections, love of God, resolutions.

6. A still simpler method, but one that is still meditation. Take some vocal prayer, the "Soul of Christ," for instance, and say it very slowly and thoughtfully, pausing between each word or phrase for the length of time it takes to draw a breath. Strive for affections towards God.

7. This we might call the spiritual reading method. It is spiritual reading united with consideration. Read a few lines or a paragraph with close attention. Pause over it, ponder it well, let it sink into the heart and make its impression there. When you have extracted all the spiritual honey, so to speak, go on with your attentive reading. Be like a bee that pauses longer at one flower than at another. Let each reflection draw you to God. Make use of frequent ejaculations and aspirations.

8. This is the prayer of resignation. Do what the Son of God did in the Garden of Olives when he repeated the selfsame words: "My Father, if it be possible, let this chalice pass from me; yet not my will but thine be done!" "Thy will be done." Some souls have more abundant occasions for this form

of prayer than others. It is a most profitable method. "Thy will be done" is one of the best acts of love.

9. Make a pilgrimage to the holy places associated with the earthly life of Jesus Christ. Offer thanks for all he endured for us. Visit all the places where the Blessed Virgin Mary ever was. Or if you have been in Rome or at famous shrines, revisit those places in spirit.

10. This method consists of the adoration of the divine perfections. You praise God. You call upon the whole of his creation to praise and bless him with you, as in the beautiful hymn *Benedicite*, first of the prayers in the priest's formal thanksgiving after Mass. "Let all the works of the Lord praise, bless, and glorify him!"

11. Meditation strictly so called may be impossible for some souls, but surely everyone can breathe forth a sigh of love like "My God, I love thee!" or make other acts and aspirations of faith, hope, thanksgiving, adoration, oblation, contrition, petition, conformity to the will of God. Rest with all simplicity in the arms of your heavenly Father. Be happy to be in his presence, to feel his presence within you as in his temple.

12. But if you cannot meditate in any of these ways, nor in any other, if your mind wanders and wanders still and you cannot fix its attention, then you can at least make acts of humility and patience. "Dear Jesus, I cannot even pray!" Acknowledge that you are wholly ignorant and weak and that you can do nothing apart from the grace of God. Be patient and offer the Savior your distractions and dryness and unworthiness in all humility. If you do what you can, God will give you what you desire. He loves you not only in spite of your miseries, but because of them. One of the dispositions of prayer is a lively desire fervently to devote oneself to prayer, a firm resolution to pray daily in spite of dryness, barrenness, work, suffering or temptation.

A METHOD OF MAKING THE COLLOQUIES

Make three. Let each last five minutes. Go to Mary and tell her all about your meditation and offer her your resolution, or at least your affections and gratitude, to present to Jesus. Finish with a Hail Mary. Then with Mary taking you by the hand, go to Jesus and tell him about it, in the same or in some other way, and let Mary present to him your resolution, affections, gratitude. Finish with the *Anima Christi*. Thereupon with Jesus and Mary go to the heavenly Father and tell him and make your offering. Finish with an Our Father. These colloquies may well be the most important part of your meditation and even the most genuine mental prayer. Never omit them.

PRAYER AFTER MEDITATION

O my God, I give thee heartfelt thanks for all the graces thou hast conferred on me during this meditation. Pardon me, I beseech thee, all the negligence and all the distractions of which I have been guilty. Give me strength to carry out my good resolves. Help me to practice virtue, to avoid sin, to do good — for thy glory. Sweet Virgin Mary, help me. Dear St. Joseph, help me. My good Guardian Angel, help me. Amen.

THE REFLECTION ON THE MEDITATION

This may even be considered a part of the meditation. If you make an hour's meditation, ten minutes may be given to this reflection. Ask and candidly answer the following questions:

1. Did I carefully prepare the "points"?
2. Did I call them to mind before falling asleep — or at least the subject of my meditation — at awakening and while preparing to go to chapel?
3. Did I place myself in God's presence just before the preparatory prayer?
4. How well did I make the preparatory prayer?
5. Did I make the "preludes" well?
6. How did I employ the powers of my soul: memory (questions), understanding (my circumstances), will (affections, resolutions)?
7. Did I make numerous ejaculations?
8. Did I make definite resolutions?
9. Did I try to avoid distractions and weariness?
10. Did I make the colloquies with all fervor?
11. Did I assume an edifying posture?
12. Did I use the whole time for meditation?

Sponsa Regis, March, 1930

The Particular Examen

A Master of Novices

A single day lost in your business of salvation is a great loss. It cannot be retrieved. A clever business man balances his books to note the loss and gain for every day. Religious must do the same to see whether they make headway or go backwards; otherwise they may go blindfolded to perdition. The particular examen, as the name indicates, considers only one defect each day.

Like everything else, it must be learned and practiced in the novitiate. Once the habit is acquired, it will follow the religious through life and become the most important and fruitful exercise for the interior life. In order to form this habit, the novice would do well to observe the following rules:

In the morning put yourself on your guard for the day. Offer God the day, bewail your faults of the preceding day, renew the resolution anent your predominant fault and ask God's grace to keep the resolution. Only a short time, perhaps a minute, is required for this.

At noon and evening examine how you have kept the resolution, following this order: 1) Give thanks for graces received. 2) Ask the Holy Ghost for light. 3) Examine into your faults. 4) Make your act of contrition for them. 5) Renew your resolution. 6) Ask for the grace to keep it and impose a light penance in case of a fall.

Devote one fourth of an hour or at least ten minutes to the particular examen. The greater part of this time must be spent in making the acts of contrition, resolution, and petition for grace, as these are the more essential points on which depend all strength and fruit of the examen; for it is certain that one avoids a fault more carefully, the more he abhors it. Let your resolution extend only from one examen to the other.

Never take more than one fault for your particular examen. In fact, you should divide the investigation of one fault into different parts, taking one single point for some time. For example, if you wish to combat pride and acquire humility, divide this very extensive field thus: 1) Not to speak a word in your own praise. 2) Not to covet the esteem of others, nor to attract the attention of anyone to yourself. 3) Not to exhibit any joy when someone praises you. 4) Not to excuse your defects, neither exteriorly or interiorly. 5) To reject immediately all thoughts of vain glory. 6) To consider yourself inferior to others interiorly and to prefer others exteriorly in your behavior. 7) To seize and accept any opportunity for humiliations as coming from the hand of God. 8) To make exterior and interior acts of humility, joining thereto fervent petitions for a deep humility.

In this manner you will concentrate on eradicating the vice in all its ramifications and instilling the opposite virtue. Do not change the subject of your particular examen until you have corrected the fault thoroughly, even if it should require a long time. Remember: eradicating one fault a year soon makes a saint. Remember also: violence is necessary to conquer heaven.

In regard to particular examen as in all other important matters of the spiritual life take counsel from a wise spiritual director who knows your needs. He will point out the subject of examen, how long you should continue on the same subject, the penance you may perform in case of a lapse.

Sisters who are actively engaged in various works will do well to observe these same rules, at least as far as the time allotted by their rule for particular examen will permit.

Each day spent under the inspiration of a good particular examen will intensify your love for God and allow you to taste how sweet the Lord is for those who conquer self in order to belong entirely to him, our "God and our All."

Sponsa Regis, September, 1933

The Liturgical Movement in Convents

Joseph Kreuter, O.S.B.

"That Christ may be all in all" (Col 3:11).

There are at present few religious in our convents who have not heard or read of the Liturgical Movement occasioned by the first *Motu Proprio* of the saintly Pope Pius X. Many Sisters, yes, even entire convents already have caught the liturgical spirit which is none other than the spirit of the early Christians, the true spirit of Christ himself and of his Church. Pius X declared that "active participation in the most holy mysteries and in the public and solemn prayer of the Church is the primary and indispensable source of the true Christian spirit." The Pontiff had adopted as the motto of his pontificate the words of St. Paul to "re-establish all things in Christ" (Eph 1:10) so that "Christ may be all in all" (Col 3:11). He looked upon the Church's liturgy as the most potent means to realize this lofty purpose. His *Motu Proprio* became the inspiration for the Liturgical Movement which since has spread in many countries in Europe and taken a firm foothold in the New World.

A convent is by its very nature a place where the movement must find special favor. As Christ is the very center of the liturgy, the spouse of Christ must feel drawn to the liturgy and all that stands in any relation to it. It must be her ambition to enter into its spirit as thoroughly as possible in order to find in it the means of her holiness and to draw from these "living fountains of the Savior" all the strength and encouragement she will need in her efforts toward greater perfection.

If a religious prefers her private devotions — no matter how legitimate in themselves — to the Church's official liturgy, she has not yet fully entered into the mind of Christ and the spirit of his Church and loses thousands of precious opportunities of coming closer to him.

In a convent, where each and every religious aims at a fuller understanding of the liturgy and a closer participation in it, the bond of union of all with Christ and with each other is more readily preserved and appreciably strengthened; and in consequence of this, sanctity has a better opportunity to develop and reach loftier heights. For it is precisely the function of the liturgy to foster the Christ-life in souls. And inasmuch as genuine Catholic Action or the spirit of the apostolate can only flourish where the Christ-life is cherished, the liturgical spirit is the powerful promoter of all efforts that tend to further God's greater glory and the salvation of immortal souls.

Superiors can do themselves and their subjects no better service than to encourage in their convents the study of the sacred liturgy and the development of the liturgical spirit. If responsibility for the souls of their charges weighs heavily upon superiors, they need but let the liturgy dominate the daily lives of the religious to experience its sanctifying power, inspired as it is by the Holy Spirit himself, the supreme director of souls.

Religious who hitherto struggled along as best as they might on the arduous path of perfection, but often became a prey to discouragement, may well examine into their methods of prayer and work. Perhaps they will find that they have let go the guiding hand of Mother Church and preferred to walk the byways of private devotions instead of keeping close to their divine Bridegroom. His choicest graces of holiness are dispensed to souls who endeavor to live with his Church.

How many religious are given to undue self-introspection, torturing their minds by more or less constant examination into past or present failings, shortcomings, imperfections — instead of opening their souls widely to the sanctifying influence of the Church's liturgy? Comparatively few religious master the art of living with God because they fail to live intimately with his Church. Back to the liturgy, to living with Christ in his Church — this must become their slogan if they desire to make rapid progress in perfection! Fuller understanding and appreciation of holy Mass and the Divine Office, consciousness of the divine life in the soul, realization of their membership in the Mystical Body of Christ and their consequent duty and privilege of active participation in the most holy mysteries of the Church, together with the members of the community and the body of all the faithful, will open up before their souls new splendid vistas and avenues of spiritual blessings that had hitherto been practically unknown to them.

How many religious teachers have had reason to complain of lack of results in their efforts to make solid Christians of their pupils! In school days the children were faithful enough in the practice of their religion and gave promise of becoming good practical Catholic men and women. But in later years not a few of them disappointed their parents, teachers and priests, began to neglect Sunday Mass, reception of the Sacraments, perhaps even married against the laws of the Church.

Was it perhaps because they had not been thoroughly grounded in their religion, because they had not been taught by word and example to appreciate holy Mass, the center of the liturgy, to live with Mother Chuch in her liturgical year? "Let our teaching communities get the proper appreciation of holy Mass, and the children of our schools will soon share in their enthusiasm," we read in an editorial of *Orate Fratres* (Vol I, p. 318). Better, more fervent and intelligent Catholics will go forth from our schools once our teachers will have caught the liturgical spirit and become apostles of the liturgy.

It is not sufficient to attract aspirants to the cloister and train them in the ordinary ways of the religious life and the work the community is doing. They must also be led to understand and appreciate the liturgy and learn to participate intelligently in the most holy mysteries and in the public and solemn prayer of the Church. This will strengthen them in their vocation and place at their fullest disposal the rich treasures of grace and holiness which Christ has handed over to his Church. Moreover, they will then, under the guidance of the Holy Spirit, develop the true spirit of the apostolate or Catholic Action, and become efficient instruments in the hand of God for the salvation of souls.

Many convents find it impossible to obtain the necessary number of recruits for the work they have undertaken. Will the Holy Ghost, the giver of vocations, not inspire many generous souls in the world to take up the religious life in convents where his liturgy is fervently fostered and exploited unto God's honor and the spread of his Kingdom on earth?

The liturgical spirit will go far in making the members of a religious community realize more vividly their spiritual unity as a family, where each one is a living member of Christ's Mystical Body and is called to make united efforts unto the greater glory of God and their mutual sanctification.

Let our readers, therefore, old and young, strive with all the energy and means at their disposal to become deeply interested in the liturgy of the Church. They will then soon realize that more intimate contact with it results in an increasing knowledge and understanding of the things of God, especially of the mission of Christ's redemption as transmitted to his Church and operating in her divine life. They will become desirous of entering more fully into the liturgical life; they will feel urged to take up the cause of the apostolate and to initiate others into the ranks of promoters of the liturgical revival work.

We ask again: Must it not be the ambition of the "Spouse of the King" to strengthen his Kingdom upon earth and thus to become a cooperator in the mission of Christ which he delivered to his Church and which she exercises primarily through her liturgy?

Sponsa Regis, August, October, 1939

Holy Mass in the Life of Religious

V.S.

The Sacrifice of the Cross is the central act of all history, the midmost moment of all time, the pinnacle of all religious ceremonies, the masterpiece of omnipotent love.

On the cross was wrought the redemption of mankind — the purchase for him of pardon, grace, and salvation.

In the Sacrifice of the Cross, Jesus gave to God infinite praise, adoration, satisfaction, and thanksgiving.

This supreme act of worship, however, did not cease with the death of Christ. God willed to perpetuate this holy sacrifice until the end of time, and so he instituted the Mass. In the Mass, Calvary is daily renewed. Daily, under Eucharistic veils, Jesus offers himself anew to his Father and applies to men's souls the fruits of the redemption.

In the Mass, Jesus, the great highpriest and victim, continues to immolate himself for the same ends as in that first bloody sacrifice, consummated upon the cross.

The Mass, then, is a treasure of infinite value, for it comprises the infinite merits of the passion of Jesus, his blood, his wounds, his cruel death. Never has omnipotent love made anything so priceless, so beautiful and excellent as holy Mass.

"A single Mass," theologians tell us, "gives more glory to God and procures more grace for men than all the prayers of the saints, the sufferings of the martyrs, or the burning love of the seraphim."

In the Mass, Christ not only offers to God himself and his mystical members, but he allows these members to share in his priesthood and his victimhood. He permits them to unite with him in offering to God the divine victim; moreover, to offer themselves, together with him, in his sublime sacrifice.

114

Sharing in his priesthood implies also the sharing in his victimhood. The role of both co-priest and co-victim is realized in our union with Christ in the Mass.

Religious who by their profession have consecrated themselves to a life of oblation share in a special way in this sacerdotal office. By their vows, and for some by an added act of victim oblation, they have dedicated themselves as victim-spouses of the Victim-Bridegroom. By union with Christ in the Mass, they cooperate with him in the work of redemption, "filling up those things which are wanting in the sufferings of Christ."

Union with Christ in the Mass means for the religious the making of her body, as St. Paul exhorts, "a living sacrifice, holy, pleasing unto God." To be a "living sacrifice" means really to live the Mass. To live the Mass is to carry out in her life the spirit of the divine Victim — the spirit of sacrifice. It is to identify herself with Christ by love and union with him in his unending sacrifice, offering to the eternal Father every hour his blessed Son, the divine Victim on the altar of the cross and of the Mass.

Daily, as a victim-host of "Jesus Hostia," she can offer herself as a little host of praise in union with her Victim-Lover. Daily she may seek transformation into him through mystical consecration. Hourly she may strive for union with him in silent prayer and communion.

The Mass has its principal parts: offertory, consecration and communion.

The life of a religious, it is obvious, has its parallel in holy Mass. Religious profession may be considered her offertory; the substitution of Christ for self and transformation into an *alter Christus* will constitute her consecration; loving union with him will be her communion and the prelude of eternal union with him in heaven.

In another sense, each day may be for the religious a day of mystical immolation. Each morning she may set up in her own heart an altar of sacrifice. Her crucifix will surmount this mystical altar, and faith will light up the sanctuary, as tapers before the Most Holy. Her missal, the rule book, will state in explicit terms God's will for the rubrics of her sacrifice. Clothed in the liturgical robes of her holy habit, she will offer herself with Christ, a victim of immolation. Placing herself as a little host on the paten with Jesus in his sacrifice, she will take from his hand the chalice he gives for her daily oblation.

Into that chalice she will place every breath, every word, every prayer, labor and suffering. These she will mingle with the wine of her love and the vows of her victim-oblation. "Praising," she "will call upon the name of the Lord" that her offertory may be acceptable to God, sanctified by the Holy Spirit, and transformed into the likeness of Jesus crucified.

Not only at her morning devotions, but often throughout the busy day, the heart of the fervent religious will be lifted Godward in the renewal of her mystical offertory, and this in union with the Masses being said throughout the world. All her trials, crosses, mortifications offered in union with the supreme Victim will become purifying, expiatory and transforming, preparing her for the second principal part of her Mass — the consecration.

The consecration in the Mass is the essence of the holy Sacrifice.

When Christ through the mouth of his priest pronounces over the snow-white host and the wine the words of consecration, there is no longer bread and wine upon the altar, but Jesus, the King of glory. The altar becomes a mystical Calvary where Christ, in self-sacrificing love, presents anew to his heavenly Father his cruel death upon the cross.

The consecration, in the Mystical Mass of the religious, likewise is of vital importance. It means transubstantiation — a changing of self into Christ her divine model. Is not this after all the object of her consecrated life? Is it not her one great aim and ambition to be divested of self, to put on Christ, to be so identified with him that she may no longer live, but that Christ may live in her?

Such being the case, she must make every effort to secure this transformation. If she will be like him, a victim, holy and pleasing unto God, she must by prayer, effort, and sacrifice strive to resemble her Victim-Bridegroom.

Jesus was silent under opprobrium, patient, humble, unselfish. He loved the cross. He loved man, even his enemies. He was poor and obedient even unto death. He sought not to please himself but to do the will of his Father. He abandoned himself in loving trust in that dark agony on the cross.

The religious who would be "another Christ" must manifest these same dispositions. She must imitate the virtues of her divine model. She must carry the cross. She must love the cross. She must die daily in mystical crucifixion, even as her Victim-Bridegroom. She must be one with him in mind and heart and will. She must disappear and be lost in him that he may be her all. She will give herself so completely to him that substituting himself in place of her poor ego, he will think and speak and act in her and for her. She will strive to be so Christ-like that men may see reflected in her the divine image. The Christ-in-her must be "lifted up" all day long in the elevation of her life's Mass that human hearts may, in turn, be lifted up to him, who from the altar of his cross "would draw all men to himself."

Thus will the Spouse of Christ reach the fulness of her life's consecration, and truly be able to say, "I live, now not I, but Christ liveth in me."

We have now come to the third principal part of the Mass, the eucharistic banquet. Herein Jesus, the infinite God, in infinite love bestows an infinite gift — himself. Having received our gifts at the offertory, and sanctified them in the consecration, Jesus now returns them to us at the communion, no longer as the little white host, but his own self, body and blood, soul and divinity. The grace and merits of Calvary, the fruits of the holy Sacrifice, flow into the souls of the communicants who become saturated with divinity — one with the dear Victim of the Mass.

And what shall we say of the spouse of Jesus? Who can tell what communion means to her! She becomes a living ciborium. In her loving heart rests Jesus, her Spouse and Savior, the object of all her love. Jesus has raised her to intimate participation in his divinity. He communicates to her something of his own life and being as a token of his goodness and his union with his bride.

Fortunately for her, this union does not cease with the disappearance of the sacred species. Christ, yes the Blessed Trinity itself, dwells continually in her soul. Union with God is prolonged and projected into every action of her spiritual day.

Her Mystical Mass has not only sacramental communion but also a spiritual communion — union of heart and mind and will with Jesus, the divine guest in her heart and union with him in every holy Mass celebrated throughout the world. In him she "lives and moves and has her being." Even during the busy hours of her daily schedule, the spirit of Jesus encompasses her. She lives and works and loves in him and never lets go his hand. She is so close to the heart of Jesus that he deigns to fulfill her wishes by the substitution of himself for her in the center of her soul.

Yes, the mystic Christ lives and reigns on the altar of her heart — her Host of love in sweet communion. Compenetrating her whole being with his power, wisdom and love, he prepares her, day by day, for the everlasting union with himself, her Bridegroom, in the eternal nuptials of heaven.

By frequent visits to the tabernacle; by silence, aspirations, and glances of love; by the renewal of her holy vows and of her victim oblation in union with the Mass — she keeps close to her Beloved who is always present on the altar of her heart.

She belongs entirely to God. She is his in glad surrender. Even the cross cannot sever her union with her beloved Spouse. When the hour of bitter sorrow strikes for her and she must pass through the darkness of Gethsemane, she does not forsake Jesus in cowardly fear. She clasps his hand the tighter and presses closer to his thorn-crowned brow. His victim-heart and hers shall suffer and bleed together in a holocaust of love. Her crucifixion joined with his shall be a source of strength and greater love. "With Christ" she can declare with St. Paul, "I am nailed to the cross."

She seeks communion with her Creator above all in the immortal creatures of his love. For union with Christ means union also with his mystical members; hence she will seek union with Christ in her neighbor. Because of her oneness with him in his representatives, she will act with faith, obedience, reverence and humility toward her superiors. Likewise, she will treat with charity, meekness, and self-sacrificing love her Sisters in religion, her charges, and all with whom she may come in contact.

By "living the Mass" the spouse of Christ follows the lead of the supreme Victim and unifies her spiritual activity into seeking but one essential goal — the object of her religious life — her one and only desire, namely, divine love.

Love requires the gift of self — offertory.

Love transforms and makes lovers alike — consecration.

Love tends to union with the Beloved — communion.

"Living the Mass" means self-annihilation and sacrifice; but sacrifice is the language of love. To follow Jesus, we must take the road to Calvary; but Calvary is not only the mount of sacrifice, but the mountain of love. In the Sacrifice of the cross, love reached its climax. The Mass is the renewal of that masterpiece of love.

Advent

I was seven when I first knew waiting.

I thought those swings at Denison Park
would take me all the way.

Sister Mary Lucina, R.S.M.
Sisters Today, December, 1973

Sponsa Regis, September, 1935

"I Live, Now Not I"

Philip F. Burns, C.P.

On the night before he suffered, Christ, with the full dignity of his eternal priesthood, offered himself to the Father in sacrifice. He solemnly dedicated himself to his passion, and perpetuated for all time that timeless offering of himself by leaving us the Sacrifice of the Mass. By means of the Mass he made it possible for every human being to offer with him the one perfect Sacrifice to the Father.

St. Augustine tells us that every sacrifice is in reality but an outward sign of man's inward gift of self. By sacrifice we dedicate ourselves to God in love and adoration. Unless we truly give ourselves, our sacrifice remains an empty gesture.

Christ, as we have seen, by giving us a share in his priesthood has made it possible for us to offer with him. But that did not satisfy his love. He would also make it possible for us to *be* that which we offer. In other words, he would make it possible for us to become one with the sacred Victim offered. For this end he instituted the sacrament of the Eucharist.

The Eucharist is above all a sacrifice, mankind's gift to God. But it is also a sacrament, a precious gift of God to man. Every sacrament is an outward symbol to which Christ has attached some marvelous grace — a grace which is best described by the very symbol which imparts it. The Eucharist is given us under the symbol, under the appearance of bread and wine because bread and wine have always symbolized the most invigorating and substantial of nourishments. The bread and wine are then a sign to us that the reality which they symbolize is the greatest of all nourishments, the body and blood of the all holy Christ.

But the bread and wine are not the only symbols in the Eucharist. They are not the ultimate symbol. There is yet another symbol beyond the bread

119

and wine. Christ is, as we so ardently believe, really and truly present, body and soul, humanity and divinity, beneath the sacramental species. But tremendous as it may sound, the all holy Christ has deigned to constitute himself a symbol, a symbol of the grace he imparts in the Eucharist. He in his physical body is at the same time a symbol of his Mystical Body — a symbol and yet the greatest of all realities.

Christ instituted the sacrament of the Eucharist to build up his Mystical Body. All food is of its very nature body-building. And it is not otherwise with the Bread that came down from heaven. It also is body-building, Mystical-Body-building.

Christ does not come to us in communion merely as a guest, as a transient visitor. He comes as the mighty builder. He comes to transform us into himself. It is only when we have received the Eucharist, at least in desire, that we belong completely and entirely to the Mystical Body of Christ. Baptism, it is true, incorporates us into the Mystical Body, but only on condition that the Eucharist is to follow. So true is this that even infants, as St. Thomas tells us, communicate spiritually at the time of baptism. Just as the Church supplies for them the act of faith, so too she supplies for them the desire for the Eucharist. Baptism is the initiation, but the Eucharist is the fulfillment, the completion of our incorporation into Christ. It makes us one with the Christ we receive. That is why at the time of the institution of the Eucharist Christ breathed the sublime prayer for unity, "That they may be one in us . . . I in them, and thou in me." We become one with Christ.

But Christ whom we receive is the sacred Victim of Calvary, the Lamb who was slain! And here the overwhelming genius of Christ's love appears — we become *victimized*. The identity is complete, the circle is unbroken! We share in the offering and in what is offered. We offer and we are offered. We are the priest and we are the victim, for we are of Christ! We are dead and our life is hid with Christ in God. Dead! yet behold we live! His passion is ours, for we are of Christ. "I live, now not I, but Christ liveth in me."

Thus are we enabled to give ourselves in sacrifice. We offer the outward gift as a sign of our inward gift of self. The gift we offer is Christ, but because of the sacrament of the Eucharist we are so intimately incorporated into Christ that we are in truth offering ourselves, in him, with him, and through him.

No wonder the Church proclaims each morning, "O God, who hast marvelously constituted human nature, but still more marvelously hast restored it." More marvelously in very truth! Christ has restored our nature by the awful agony of his passion. In his sacred body our stubborn matter was beaten and brought into subjection to the spirit. In him were all things made new. But when the painful process was ended, when the suffering was over, then did he catch us up into that suffering and completely transfer to us his passion by enabling us to consume him who suffered, and thus by feeding upon him to become one with Him.

Here and here alone do we find the answer to man's endless quest for perfect unity in all things. The Christ upon the cross is the highpriest of all creation. But he is also the first-born of the Most High. In him does the finite meet the infinite. In him does man meet God. He has laid hold upon the human race and offered it in solemn sacrifice upon the bloody altar of the cross. And he has given himself to that same human race as food, that they might in utmost truth become one with him who offers and who is offered.

Each morning at holy Mass, as the sacred host resting upon the paten is held aloft to the Father, and as the wine blushes in the chalice, let us offer ourselves to the Father with Christ, knowing that each day binds us closer and closer to him, joining us in an ever more vital union to his passion. He has made the glory of his suffering ours. Shall not we then bring to him our trifling sorrows and trials, conscious that when united to his infinite sorrow, these trifles of ours are absorbed by the sea of his passion and are glorified by his triumph? Thus shall we make up those things that are wanting to the sufferings of Christ.

Every Christian is in truth a stigmatic, for every Christian bears in his hands and feet the glorious wounds of Christ. For every Christian is one with Christ! That is what Holy Communion does. Small wonder that St. Paul could not contain himself when dwelling upon this mystery. Small wonder that he characterized this mystery of man's complete oneness with Christ as that which "eye hath not seen, nor ear heard, neither hath it entered into the heart of man." Beside himself with awe, he could only exclaim, "I live, now not I, but Christ liveth in me."

Sponsa Regis, March, 1947

More Fruitful Confession

S.M.C.

The purpose of this article is not precisely to explain how to make a worthy confession (a subject treated in any catechism), but rather how to receive the sacrament of penance with the greatest profit and make of it a powerful instrument in our spiritual progress. This is truly to glorify God, whose wisdom and goodness have instituted the sacramental system, and to honor Christ, whose out-poured blood has merited every sacramental grace.

As a means of spiritual progress the sacrament of penance includes both a negative and a positive element. Firstly, it frees the soul from the guilt of sin and its eternal punishment and it partially remits temporal punishment. This represents the negative aspect. The essence of the supernatural life does not lie in the battle against sin, but in faith and surrender to Christ.

Secondly, penance also restores or increases sanctifying grace and merit; it augments virtue, strengthens the soul against temptation and the inclinations of corrupt nature, and by these varied blessings it unites her more intimately to Jesus, the source of our holiness. By freeing the soul from the obstacles which impede the divine action, this sacrament renders her more docile to divine inspiration and makes prayer and recollection easier and more fruitful. These, briefly, are the benefits derived from a worthy confession. The Church considers them of such necessity and consequence for religious that she requires them to receive the sacrament at least once a week.

EXPLANATION OF THE SACRAMENT

The Council of Trent teaches us: "If our gratitude towards God, who has made us his children by baptism, were equal to this ineffable gift, we should keep the grace received in this first sacrament intact and pure." But the happiness of having preserved their baptismal innocence is the privilege of comparatively few souls. Every member of Christ who has sinned, who has enfeebled or broken the vital bonds of union with his Head, has need of the sacrament of penance. In this monument of divine goodness and mercy the Lord sets the example of that precept which he gave to his followers: "Thou shalt forgive seventy times seven times."

MORTAL SIN IS SPIRITUAL DEVASTATION

Strictly speaking, then, only mortal sin constitutes the proper matter for the sacrament of penance. It is the one obstacle which defeats completely the purpose of the Mystical Body of Christ; it is the one barrier which separates man from his God. It alone severs vital communication between the Head and the members. If ever we find our horror of mortal sin diminishing, let us devote a few minutes' reflection to the disastrous result it produces in the Mystical Body of Christ. All that is good in us, grace, favor with God, virtues and merits, we possess only in Christ and through Christ. Apart from him we have no existence supernaturally, and our natural life is without purpose or value. Either we live in Christ or we become outcasts of creation; we return to that thraldom of the forces of evil from which the blood of the Savior has freed us: slavery to sin, death, concupisence, and Satan. Nor is this all. Our rupture with the divine Head is the cause of disturbance to the flow of life within the Body, and these losses must be repaired by the extra (spiritual) activity of other cells.

Concerning grievous sins, let us recall that they must be confessed clearly and honestly, stating both their number and kind, for the validity of the sacrament. But should anyone have the misfortune to commit a grave sin, let her not wait until confession before she returns to God's friendship. She should do so immediately by arousing herself to acts of perfect contrition. In this way, she will regain divine grace and favor, she will avoid the disaster of living in mortal sin and of becoming accustomed to this miserable state, and she will not expose herself to the danger of eternal damnation in case of sudden death.

VENIAL SINS ARE SPIRITUAL PARASITES

Mortal sin is an uncommon occurrence in the life of a good religious. But what of those lesser faults which, while not depriving the soul of grace, cool the fervor of charity and paralyze its vitalizing influence, which enfeeble the divine life and cripple its supernatural activity? These venial sins and deliberate imperfections, often held so lightly, are not only serious obstacles to personal sanctity, but are obstacles of grace to our community, to our country and to the whole Christian people. There is here operating one of the laws of the Mystical Body, analogous to what takes place in the human body when one organ becomes impaired.

To be frequently guilty of venial sins with the clear knowledge that we are displeasing God and setting aside his will for a selfish gratification is to stop the flow of grace into our souls and into other members of the Mystical Christ. This is a point which calls for serious consideration. Sin is more than a purely personal affair, a loss or injury to our own supernatural life. It is more than an individual revolt against God. Every offense, though personal as to its guilt and punishment, is a matter of importance to the whole Church, for the whole Body suffers when one member is wounded or severed from it.

In many cases these deliberate venial sins prove to be the cancers of the spiritual life. All our efforts towards holiness are fruitless if we are not striving to uproot such parasites. Why does so much spiritual activity, prayer, reception of the sacraments, works of charity and mercy, and exercises of mortification effect little real progress in the life of religious? Without doubt, one of the fundamental causes is that there are no consistent efforts to conquer deliberate sins of disobedience, obstinacy, self-indulgence, rash judgment, ill-feelings indulged, gossip, anger and impatience, vanity, uncontrolled emotions, inordinate affections, levity, lying, curiosity, etc.

A MORE PROFITABLE RECEPTION OF THE SACRAMENT

The sacrament of penance is the most powerful means we have for the correction of these faults, and therefore its frequent reception should be a potent factor in our sanctification. This is clearly the teaching of Pope Pius XII in his Encyclical *Mystici Corporis*. He enumerates the following precious advantages to be gained therefrom:

"We wish the practice of frequent confession to be earnestly advocated. Not without the inspiration of the Holy Spirit was this practice introduced into the Church. By it genuine self-knowledge is increased, Christian humility grows, bad habits are corrected, spiritual neglect and tepidity are countered, the conscience is purified, the will strengthened, a salutary self-control is attained and grace is increased in virtue of the sacrament itself. Let those . . . who make light of or weaken esteem of frequent confession realize that what they are doing is foreign to the Spirit of Christ, and disastrous for the Mystical Body of our Savior."

We may add that though it is not *necessary* to confess our venial sins, it is most advantageous, because we thereby obtain greater grace to avoid them in the future as well as the remission of their temporal punishment. This applies equally to the confession of sins already forgiven. We are too easily inclined to forget the element of expiation which follows on the forgiveness of sin. What is not atoned for in this world must be expiated in the next. The humble and contrite confession of past sins will considerably lessen our purgatory.

What method may be used to correct habitual venial sins through the reception of the sacrament of penance?

We should accuse ourselves of them separately according to their different kinds, and mention also the causes which provoked them. The general resolution to avoid sin in the future, which we are obliged to make, should be particularized with reference to these faults and their causes or occasions. At our next confession, we should be exact in rendering an account of how we have kept this resolution, whether for the whole time or only a part, whether in its totality or only on certain points.

As regards those faults which are semi-deliberate or which proceed from frailty, surprise, fickleness, lack of vigilance or courage, though they do not all have an equally injurious effect on our spiritual life, we should aim at least to diminish their number. In this life they can never be altogether avoided. To correct them, we may adopt the means given above: stressing some particular fault, as failing against purity of intention, want of charity, distractions in prayer.

It is equally important to mention the cause of our fault. For instance, we are often distracted in our prayer because of an inordinate attachment to a friend, an occupation or amusement, because of our curiosity, or because we are peeved over some grievance or imaginary wrong. Once we have laid bare the causes of our sins, we can more easily and efficaciously apply a remedy and persevere in our resolution.

WHY UNFRUITFUL CONFESSIONS?

The sacrament of penance was instituted to combat the deadliest enemy of our soul-life, sin, and to counteract its effects. This holy tribunal is meant to be a source of reconciliation and consolation, not of dread and anxiety. It is one of God's most merciful dispensations to humanity, a powerful help in disentangling ourselves from the meshes of sin and advancing in virtue. It is an act, performed by God and us, fraught with such supernatural energies and divine powers that we might rightly expect it to produce increasing degrees of holiness in our lives.

Yet after so many years of weekly confession, we are as we are. Why? There are several factors which may one or all contribute to the ineffectiveness of the sacrament. These do not, however, necessarily make it invalid.

1. Insincerity as regards our accusation, contrition or purpose of amendment. We live in a world that sanctions unreality at every turn, that teems with self-deceit. Small wonder if certain species of it are brought into the confessional! For instance, there is the penitent who wishes and aims to have the good opinion of her confessor, instead of accusing herself honestly and straightforwardly with no desire but to humiliate herself before God. The only sensible opinion for a confessor to have is this: this person is a sinner and as such is bent upon reformation and repentance.

Often, too, our repentance is neither deep nor lasting. Too much importance is attached to feelings and sensible emotions; too little is given to convictions and motives activated by faith. As a result, this superficial, transitory contrition produces little real amendment in our lives.

2. Routine may be another reason for retarded progress. It results from insufficient preparation and improper dispositions, weak faith and indifference to spiritual realities. Are we accustomed to run to the confessional in the same fashion that we go to the breakfast table? Do we take sufficient time and pains with our preparation, being more concerned about contrition and amendment than a meticulous examination of conscience? Are we in earnest about correcting a particular sin from now until our next confession?

3. Pride, the most subtle of sins, often masks in the garb of humility, simulating gentleness and meekness. It betrays itself in an undue esteem of one's own importance, and still more grotesquely in the disposition with which some persons accept the warnings, reproofs, or corrections of the confessor. An incalcuable amount of grace is lost when a religious resents this God-given admonition.

4. Self-pity, which leads one to seek consolation rather than forgiveness, is also detrimental to the graces of the sacrament. The primary purpose of confession is forgiveness, and with it consolation, or at least peace, will follow. It should not be primarily sought, because it gives us a false build-up: "I may not be as bad as I thought . . ." Likewise, as regards spiritual direction, we may ask for the advice that we need, assuredly; but this should not supersede the sacramental character of confession.

Suppose we have been diligent in our examination, sincere in our accusation, heartfelt in our sorrow and purpose of amendment — what may yet prevent our confessions from being more fruitful? The unsuspected factor which diminishes the potency of the sacrament is ignorance of and weak faith in its sacramental graces. It is the teaching of the Church that in every confession we receive not only the forgiveness of our sins, but sufficient grace never to commit them again.

What have we been doing with this grace? Probably we have ignored it! For our amendment, we have depended on our pious feelings, our good dispositions, our own efforts. But, though well meant, they are powerless of themselves to achieve our reformation. What we should do is to rely on the sacramental grace without discontinuing our efforts. "I can do all things in him who strengthens me." But of myself I can do nothing. Let us realize this truth and admit it practically, so that the power of Christ's Passion may be manifested in us.

How can we estimate the actual results of our hundreds of confessions? By the improvement in our character, if any; by the correction of some predominant, habitual fault; by the mastery gained over self; by the acquisition of some virtue. Indeed, from the frequent, worthy reception of the sacrament of penance we may hope for that complete victory over sin which was realized objectively on Calvary and to which we have pledged ourselves by the double vows of baptism and religious profession: death to sin and life to God in Jesus Christ our Lord.

Sponsa Regis, September, 1951

Liberty of Conscience

A Contributor

Canon 520 states that to every house of religious women there must be given only one ordinary confessor who shall hear the sacramental confessions of the whole community, unless, because of the great number of religious or for any other just reason, two or more may be found necessary. It further states that if any particular religious, for the peace of her soul and for her greater progress in the spiritual life, requests a special confessor or spiritual director, the Ordinary shall grant the request without difficulty, watchful, however, lest from this concession abuses arise; and if they do arise, he shall eliminate them carefully and prudently, while safeguarding liberty of conscience.

Canon 521 prescribes that to every community of religious women there shall be given an extraordinary confessor who at least four times a year shall go to the religious house and to whom all the religious must present themselves, at least to receive his blessing. It goes on to say that the Ordinaries of the places where religious communities of women exist shall designate for each house some priests to whom, in particular cases, the religious may easily have recourse for the sacrament of penance, without having to apply to the Ordinary on each occasion. It thereupon ordains that, when any religious asks for one of these confessors, no superioress, either personally or through others, either directly or indirectly, may seek to know the reason for the petition, or show opposition to it by word or deed, or in any way manifest displeasure at it.

Canon 522 enacts that if, notwithstanding the prescriptions of canons 520 and 521, any religious, for the peace of her conscience, has recourse to a confessor approved by the local Ordinary to hear the confessions of women, this confession, whether made in a church or oratory, even a semipublic oratory, is valid and lawful, every contrary privilege being revoked; nor may the superioress prohibit it or make any inquiry concerning it, even indirectly; and the religious is under no obligation to inform the superioress on the matter.

A bit of explanation is in order here. The expression "for the peace of her conscience" means that there is a reason for her going to confession; and there is a reason for going to confession as often as the confession is seriously made, that is to say, made with the intention of accusing sins sacramentally and receiving absolution from them. There is a reason for her going to confession if, for example, she goes to confession to solve some difficulty, in order to communicate safely, because she finds it difficult to confess to the ordinary confessor. If her thus going to confession were unreasonable, the confession would nevertheless be valid, but it would give the priest an occasion for admonition about the matter.

The expression "have recourse to a confessor" means that a religious may purposely call a confessor and the confessor may of his own accord go to her, even for the sole purpose of hearing her confession. Hence, if a confessor approved by the Ordinary of the place for hearing the confessions of women is in some religious house — either to offer Mass or for some other function, or has just dropped in, or has been called — any Sister may for her peace of conscience freely, validly and licitly go to confession to him.

Canon 523 provides that all religious women, when seriously ill, even if not in danger of death, may, as often as they wish during their serious illness, invite any priest whomever to hear their confession, provided that he be approved to hear the confessions of women, though not designated for religious women, nor may the superioress either directly or indirectly prevent them from doing so.

The very last canon of the Code of Canon Law, canon 2414, has to do with interference by superiors with the liberty of conscience of their subjects. It is as follows:

Any superioress who has violated the precepts of canons 521, section 3, 522, 523 shall be admonished by the local Ordinary. If she fails again in this matter, she shall be punished by him with the deprivation of office and the Ordinary shall at once inform the Sacred Congregation of Religious concerning the matter.

From this canon we gather how serious are the violations of the liberty of confession as regards religious women. The Ordinaries must immediately inform the Sacred Congregation of Religious. It is, therefore, the duty of the confessor and the visitator to admonish the superior of her obligation in this grave matter.

The following are some examples of the faults that can be committed in this way:

(1) It is wrong not to call the confessor whom the religious requests when he is one of those determined by the Ordinary.

(2) It is wrong to inquire as to the reason for the petition.

(3) It is wrong for the superior to show in any way whatsoever that she does not like the request of the Sister. Examples of such dislike would be: unfriendliness, coldness, resentful silence, unnecessary questions and delays, implicit accusations, impatience, revengeful discriminations or even punishment, threats and discouraging arguments.

(4) It is wrong to forbid a religious to approach a confessor approved for hearing the confessions of women, in a place in her own house designated for the confessions of women or of religious.

(5) It is wrong to forbid a religious who is legitimately away from the house to approach a confessor approved for women in any church or oratory whatsoever, even semipublic.

(6) It is wrong to inquire as to the reason why the religious approached or desires to approach a confessor approved for women in a place in her own house designated for the confessions of women or of religious.

(7) It is wrong to inquire as to the reason why the religious approached or desires to approach a confessor approved for women in any church or oratory whatsoever, even semipublic, when she is legitimately away from the house.

(8) It is wrong to demand that this matter be referred to her either by the penitent or by the penitent's companion, and to show displeasure at this way of acting.

(9) It is wrong for a superior to prevent in any way a religious, for the duration of a grave illness, from confessing to any priest approved by the Ordinary of the place for the confessions of women.

We may add that the Instruction of the Sacred Congregation of the Sacraments issued on December 8, 1938, commands that the religious superior shall have no word of reproach for those who do not receive Holy Communion, but shall rather see in this a sign of liberty and of a tender and delicate conscience. Moreover, superiors must strive "to remove all circumstances which might expose those who do not receive to astonishment from others." Again, the superior is not to give any indication that she seems to notice those who go to Communion frequently and to praise them while blaming the others.

Canon Law and the rule say that when the extraordinary confessor comes to exercise his office as such, that is, the four times a year, all the Sisters must present themselves at least to receive the blessing.

A Sister would do no wrong if she would just always ask for the blessing and not confess to the extraordinary, for Canon Law says "at least to receive the blessings." But for that she must come, even if she has no need to go to confession, even if she thinks it is not expedient for her to reveal her conscience to that confessor. It is the duty of the superior to see to it that all the Sisters observe this prescription of the law, nor may she excuse herself from its observance.

That the Sisters present themselves at least for the blessing is wisely and opportunely prescribed, for if there were no obligation, one or the other religious who probably needs his help might, out of timidity or for some other reason, not approach him to her grave spiritual harm. Because of this prescription she can without any difficulty at least go to him.

It is true that *per se* spiritual direction pertains to the ordinary confessor. But Sisters may, if they prefer, be guided spiritually by the extraordinary confessor in a constant and continuous way. But it is not expedient that spiritual direction of Sisters be continued by an exchange of letters. This gives rise to abuses, except in extraordinary circumstances.

Sister Assisi Leaves for the Ghettoes

Fret not at the convent's narrow room,
Assisi, we said; the walls are bending outward,
Giving in, and soon are going to let
The city through. But adamant is what Assisi is,
And she will go Francising among the poorest,
Will try to spread her own self like a roof
For the many unhoused. Sometimes one's own saint
Gets to be the saint beneath the skin,
What's in a name becoming what's within,
As she became vulnerable to the occasion
Of his sin of headlong goodness. Likely,
The two of them, met together
Over some needy, sick, despairing
In whatever city of God's, can share
How sainthood begins.

Nancy G. Westerfield
Sisters Today, October, 1973

Sponsa Regis, December, 1949

How Long is the Roman Office?

Sister M. Teresa Doyle, O.S.F.

How often when we read articles or books on the psalms or the Divine Office do we busy Sisters of active orders sigh and say resignedly, "Ah yes, we would love to be able to pray the official prayer of the Church, but since our time does not allow it, the Lord does not want it of us!" Thus, it is usually the *time* element which seems to us to be the great obstacle.

Some of us, to be sure, are frightened by the Latin, but we need not be, because the strong trend toward the vernacular in recent years points to the possibility of the English Office. There may be a small number of other reasons that cause some religious to shy away from the thought of the Divine Office. But perhaps the one thing that causes the most diffidence is the uncanny fear that it is very long, and that it would add something like an hour more of prayer to a program already filled. This is an absolutely false notion.

During a period of semi-invalidism I have had the pleasure of adding to my prayers the complete Roman Office in English almost daily, and it never takes more than 80 minutes on ordinary days (on some feasts, about 5 minutes more). This is at a medium rate of speed, without any rushing. Using a ratio of 4 to 5, this would be about 100 minutes in choir, or only 20 minutes longer than it takes to recite the Little Office of the Blessed Virgin Mary in Latin in choir!

It is almost staggering when for the first time one realizes that by dropping only 20 minutes of some prayers of a private nature, the complete Roman Office in English can be substituted for the Little Office of the B.V.M. *without having to add even one minute to the daily prayer time!* (It might be important to emphasize that the more important spiritual exercises, such as mental prayer, spiritual reading, particular and general exa-

mens, need not be disturbed in the least, and that the Rosary can easily be
kept also.) When once this truth is known more widely, there will undoubtedly be more and more communities that will study the possibilities of
taking up the Divine Office in place of the Little Office and some of the
private prayers that are now in use.

It takes only a short time and only a little explanation to enter into and
love the psalms in the vernacular. No one could possibly dispute the fact
that these prayers and songs of the Holy Spirit are superior in every way to
any composed prayers, and especially in the Church's arrangement of her
morning praise (Lauds), morning prayer (Prime), evening praise (Vespers)
and night prayer (Compline), that they are far more satisfactory than our
best prayer book prayers. What a simple matter it would be to drop the
substitutes and go back to the original.

Here is an example of how one community's prayer time would work
out with such a change:

Present prayer time		Possible Rearrangement	
Little Office	80 min.	English Divine Office	100 min.
Mass & thanksgiving	40 min.	Mass & thanksgiving	40 min.
Meditation	30 min.	Meditation	30 min.
Morning and night prayers and examen	15 min.	Evening examen	5 min.
		Noon examen	4 min.
Noon visit prayers and ex- amen	12 min.	Spiritual reading	15 min.
Spiritual reading	15 min.	Rosary	15 min.
Rosary	15 min.	Optional Stations and extra visit	13 min.
Optional Stations and extra visit	15 min.		
	222 min.		222 min.

It will be noted that the only prayers dropped in the above example of
rearrangement are the morning and night prayers and the noon visit
prayers (a litany, act of consecration, 12 Our Fathers; part of the Office could
be offered for the same intention).

If most active congregations would thus be able to take the complete
Roman Office in English, without any additional burden, who of us would
be satisfied with an abbreviated Office? Undoubtedly there will be a place
for a shortened breviary, especially for the laity, and perhaps for some
congregations that are not at present accustomed to 3½ hours of prayer
daily. It would be better to have a short one than nothing. But communities
that already have the Little Office and could make the transition so easily
will surely not wish to have an "ersatz" when the genuine can be so simply
procured. The complete wealth of the 150 psalms, the rich and varied
readings of Matins, especially those from Holy Scripture and the Fathers of

the Church, and the full celebration of Sundays and feast days, are treasures too precious to be shortened unnecessarily, or cut without good reason.

The next question is: but how can such a change be made when our constitutions ordain the Latin Little Office and certain other prayers? One community did it this way: the question was brought up at a regular General Chapter, voted on affirmatively, and a petition was sent to the Holy See for the change, which was granted (in this case for the Latin Day Hours). This is probably the procedure necessary for all pontifical institutes. Diocesan institutes would, no doubt, get authorization from their bishop.

Meanwhile, until Providence grants us the blessing of the Office, there is nothing to prevent us from getting acquainted with and praying some of the psalms. Good ones to start with are 22, 24, 26, 33, 83, 85, 139, 142. There are several translations of the new psalter published which make many obscure passages clear. One might use a few minutes of visit or spiritual reading time if necessary (what could be better?); it is well, also to stay with a new psalm for several days, letting it sink in deeply.

Just a word to enthusiasts: steer clear of what is called a "bitter zeal." Remember, the purpose of the Office, as of all prayer, is to glorify God and to unite us more closely to him. Do not defeat this purpose by inconsiderateness or even contempt of others' opinions. It will be wonderful if you can get the Divine Office when God wills — it would be sad to lose charity in the getting.

Sponsa Regis, September, 1962

The Religious Life and the Liturgy

Clifford Howell, S.J.

We are told in *Mediator Dei*, "The priestly life which the divine Redeemer had begun in his mortal body by his prayers and sacrifice was not finished; he willed it to continue unceasingly throughout the ages in his Mystical Body, which is the Church . . . . Accordingly the Church continues the priestly office of Jesus Christ, especially in the liturgy. She does this first and chiefly at the altar, where the sacrifice of the Cross is perpetually represented . . . . She does it secondly by means of the sacraments, special instruments for communicating supernatural life to men. She does it thirdly by the tribute of praise which is daily offered to Almighty God."

It is therefore by the Mass, the sacraments and the office — that is, by the liturgy — that Christ's life is continued among us. Hence it follows that by taking part in the liturgy we are taking part in the life of Christ. And so religious, who have bound themselves to lead the Christian life as intensely as possible, have cogent reasons for taking part in the liturgy as actively and as intelligently as possible. It is one of the chief means of attaining their end. The Pope says even more than this; for in the same encyclical he writes: "for the achievement of holiness, the worship which the Church, united with her head, offers to God is the most efficacious means possible."

As regards objective holiness — that is, sharing in the grace-life — the liturgy is obviously indispensable because it is the very source of grace. It was by baptism, our first participation in the liturgy, that we were given sanctifying grace at the beginning of our Christian life. Since then we have constantly nourished it by Holy Communion, which is itself sacramental participation in the Mass, summit and center of the liturgy.

As regards the subjective aspect — that is, conforming our minds and wills to those of Christ — the liturgy, while not the sole means to it, is beyond doubt of prime importance. For we were told by the saintly Pius X that "active participation in the liturgy is the primary and indispensable source of the true Christian spirit." Again, therefore, religious who *ex professo* are seeking the fulness of the Christian spirit have very special reasons for cultivating active and intelligent participation in the liturgy.

But, as I have just said, though this is the primary source of the true Christian spirit, it is not the only source. There is the secondary source, called private prayer, in its various forms of meditation, prayerful reading, improvisation of words not externally uttered, prayer without any words, prayer of simple regard, and so on.

Ideally each of these forms of prayer is best exercised by oneself alone, according to our Lord's recommendation: "When thou art praying, go into thy inner room and shut the door upon thyself, and so pray to thy Father in secret" (Mt 6:6). But in the circumstances of religious life this physical privacy is not always possible; members of the community may be physically together, for instance, in the chapel, yet each is praying privately in the sense that each is personally deciding both the matter and the manner of prayer.

Another source of the Christian spirit is public prayer of a type which is not liturgy. As public prayer it has an external form, including spoken or sung words in which all join; but it is not liturgy for one or both of two reasons: either its text is not that of the official Roman liturgical books, or else, even if the text accords with these books, the community praying the text is not officially deputed by the Church to be her representative in such prayer.

For example, a community saying the rosary together would not be engaged in liturgical prayer because the rosary is not part of the official liturgy. A community praying Compline together would be engaged in liturgical prayer if they were canonically ranked as *moniales* — that is, officially deputed to do so (as is the case with Benedictine or Dominican nuns). If they are not *moniales* their prayer is not liturgy in the technical sense, even if they use the Latin text, for they lack deputation. It makes no difference to the status of their community prayer whether the text is in Latin or in English. But in either case, though not official liturgy, it would be liturgical in content and style.

There does not seem to be any official and universally accepted terminology concerning these things, so I had better make clear the sense in which I am here and now using the terms "private" and "public" prayer.

By "private prayer" I mean that of which each determines the content and manner, and which is not externalized in speech or song. By "public prayer" I mean that of which the participants have not determined the content and manner; these have been predetermined, and are externalized socially in speech or song. This public prayer has two divisions: (a) that of which the content is no part of the liturgy, and (b) that of which the content is part of the liturgy. This second division is itself subdivided into (i) the

public praying of liturgical texts which ranks canonically as the performance of liturgy, and (ii) the public praying of liturgical texts which does not
rank canonically as performance of the liturgy.

No one can question the great importance of private prayer. It is
necessary for every Christian — *a fortiori* for every religious — for each soul
is a unique creation of almighty God, with its own specific needs and
inclinations, its own attractions given by God, its own propensities to evil
which must be checked, and its own spiritual life which must be developed.
Public prayer alone — whether liturgy or not — is inadequate for so specific
a task. Private prayer therefore features largely in the constitutions and way
of life of every religious order — and does so very rightly.

What has to be questioned, however, is whether this private prayer is
always of the right quality and carried out in the right way. For example,
private prayer ought truly to be private in the sense that each soul should be
left utterly free to determine its manner and content. It is against the very
nature of private prayer that one member of a community should be made to
read prayers aloud for the others. This turns it into a sort of public prayer; it
is no longer personally and uniquely the expression of each individual soul
according to specific needs, and is an intrusion into the privacy and liberty
which each ought to have in private prayer.

More serious, however, is a state of affairs all too frequently occurring
among Catholics at large, including priests and religious. But as I am at this
moment addressing Sisters, I will describe it as it occurs in them, even
though it is by no means limited to them.

Is it not a fact that many Sisters have an aversion to active participation
in public prayer, whether this be liturgy or not? They say that the attention
needed to keep in time with the others is a distraction, that they cannot pray
with sincerity words that have been put into their mouths, that they are not
moved in mind or heart by such public prayer, and that it does not help
them in their personal interior life. It is for them only a mechanical performance. When they pray, they want to be left alone to pray as the Spirit moves
them. The only real prayer for them is private prayer.

This indicates a defect in their prayer-training, and a defect in the
nature of their private prayer. They are equating the terms "private" and
"personal," and do not understand that public prayer ought to be just as
personal as private prayer, in the sense that the whole person should be
fully occupied in it with mind and heart and will. They have never learned
to express their own persons in public prayer, whether liturgical or not.
They have never made public prayer their own prayer — it is but the ritual
fulfilment of a community duty. They have made their private prayer
individualistic, that is, exclusive of the collaboration of others in praising
and thanking God.

One who feels that he or she can really pray only "on her own" is
lacking in "prayermanship." She is missing something of great value,
something intensely satisfying, uplifting, heart-warming, inspiring —

something essential to her spiritual life which cannot be obtained except in concert with other worshippers. She still has much to learn in the art of prayer; she must learn to enter fully into community prayer, making it truly her own, utterly personal as well as social. Only when she can pray with her whole person both in public prayer and in private prayer is she adequately versed in the art of prayer. If her mind and heart are moved and warmed and comforted and strengthened only by private prayer, and not also by public prayer, then she is less good at prayer than one who has mastered both forms. Her private prayer is defective.

In *Mediator Dei* Pope Pius XII says: "There can be no incompatibility between the liturgy and other acts of devotion as long as these are directed to the right end, . . . for they nourish the spiritual life of Christians and cause them to take part with greater profit in public functions, and prevent the liturgical prayers from degenerating into empty ceremonies." But the Sister whom we are describing says she gets no profit from public functions, and that liturgical prayers, because they are public, are for her but empty ceremonies. This can only be because her "other acts of devotion" are not "directed to the right ends." Her private prayer is centered on herself and on her subjective emotions; she has the "me-and-my-God" attitude, abstracting in her private prayer from the corporate nature of her union with God which, in fact, consists essentially in being *incorporated* with others into Christ, through whom alone we have access to the Father.

Now Christ's presence and activity in the Church is continued in the liturgy; and God's plans for the sanctification and salvation of mankind involve the liturgy. Hence a Sister's private prayer ought to lead her towards the liturgy instead of away from it. The Pope wrote in *Mediator Dei*: "The criterion by which spiritual exercises of any kind must be judged is the efficacy of such exercises in fostering a love for divine worship . . . . If they hinder or prevent the observance of the principles and norms of divine worship, then it may be concluded with certainty that they are not directed by right thinking and prudent counsel."

One of the principles of divine worship is that it is social by nature, since it is the worship of that society which is Christ's Church; and one of its norms is that it is designed for social performance, with active and intelligent participation of those who are engaged in it.

This confronts us with a serious question — one which Sisters of our generation must face squarely — namely, the quality of their community prayers.

A very experienced Benedictine who had attended a week of conferences in which there took part many priests, many Sisters, and not a few laity, wrote:

"One thing which struck me forcibly at this week was the gap that separates nuns from the official prayer of the Church. A number of lay men and women joined in the recitation of the Little Hours before and after the talks but, as far as we could see, the Sisters present joined only in the *Gloria*

Patri at the end of the psalms. As religious, they are by profession identified with the *Ecclesia Orans*. And yet the breviary, the prayer-book of the Church, is a closed book to them. In fact, as one Sister expressed herself, when she was a lay woman she could pray the Divine Office more readily than as a religious: the common community prayers now take all the time she can possibly spare from her other assigned tasks. Private prayers have become public; and the really public official prayer, if recited at all, must be squeezed into odd moments. Moreover, the private prayers often consume more time than would be required by the Divine Office.

"As to the quality or content of prayers commonly in use in religious houses of women, we have had occasion to contact quite a number of Sisters' communities, directly or indirectly, as retreat master or teacher, or through correspondence. There is a growing feeling among Sisters that the religious life has not offered them the opportunity it should have done of really developing their spiritual lives — of which prayer is an essential element. Much as they need new recruits, they sometimes suspect that the high-pressure campaigning for new members that is prevalent today is somehow dishonest. Candidates come with high ideals. And what do they get? They learn, it is true, how to meditate. But otherwise their spiritual fare differs only in quantity from what is ordinarily available to the laity. The same two or three litanies recited daily, the rosary, the 'acts,' the Way of the Cross, so many Our Father's and Hail Mary's for this and that intention, and perhaps strata of prayers according to the religious affiliation or enthusiasms of past retreat masters (or Reverend Mothers). And then they wonder that they are plagued by distractions."[1]

This, you must admit, is by no means an exaggerated description of the state of affairs obtaining in many convents. If only Sisters who suffer thus would boldly face up to the situation, cut away the exotic growth of unofficial and usually rather sentimental, individualistic, formless and maddeningly repetitive devotions, they would have time for that which could really nourish and enrich their prayer-life — namely, the Divine Office of the Church.

Why is it that, apart from the *moniales* whose life is centered upon office in choir, Sisters in general do not pray the Divine Office? The main obstacle to this is precisely the manifold devotions that take up as much time as a shortened office would do. Until these are eliminated or drastically curtailed the Sisters will continue to be deprived of the riches of the Church's own prayer.

Then why cling to all these devotions? Chiefly because the majority of them were prescribed by Mother Foundress when she gathered her first companions about her and shaped the details of the way of life for her Order. These many devotions are according to the rule of the Order.

[1]Godfrey Diekmann, O.S.B. *Orate Fratres*, Vol. XXII, 472-3.

The office, in Mother Foundress' day, was regarded merely as an obligation to be fulfilled by clerics and certain religious, a burdensome task to be ploughed through with meticulous exactitude and patience, but with no regard for the intrinsic purpose of the hours as sanctifying the various times of the day. It was a long and mostly unintelligible formula governed by strict rubrics.

No sensible woman of those days — and foundresses were all eminently sensible women — would have thought of imposing on her Sisters a burden such as the office then was. And so she specified those prayers which, in her own day, were most highly regarded, namely, forms of morning and night prayer, the rosary, litanies, invocations, "acts" of this and that virtue, dedications and consecrations, strings of *Paters* and *Aves* for stated intentions or the amassing of indulgences, or anything else which happened to be in vogue at the time.

But this has left a serious problem for Mother Foundress' daughters of the twentieth century. There are only certain limited hours available for prayer during a busy day; if the office, even in an abbreviated form, is to be pushed in, then something has to be pushed out. It is not surprising if some feel they would be in conflict with the mind of their Mother Foundress if they now turn to the liturgy for their prayer, because this cannot be done without severely curtailing the many devotions enshrined in the rule.

This is a dilemma which many Sisters have to face. And, in case any of you are among them, I put it to you thus: Your Mother Foundress wanted the very best for you. She was thinking with the mind of the Church of her own day — she was right up-to-date, modern in her outlook. She gave you the best then available. But if she were living today she would still want the best for you; she would be thinking with the mind of the Church of today; she would still be right up-to-date and modern in her outlook.

So you would not be going against her mind, nor betraying the spirit of your institute if you acted now according to her principles by going for the best, thinking with the Church, being modern. This means, in practice, so curtailing these devotions that you can make room for the Divine Office in shortened form. You would, in fact, be following the lead of the late Pope Pius XII, who insistently called upon Sisters to bring themselves and their institutes — even their religious habits — up to date. If this is to apply to the habits which clothe their bodies, how much more to the habits of their minds — the clothing of concepts and viewpoints and motivations wherein the mind is enveloped!

There are now numerous congregations and institutes which, in recent years, have adopted as their community prayer a condensed form of the Divine Office in their own language, and the number of these is ever growing.

Here are a few facts to think about. In 1950 an abbreviated form of the Divine Office was published in Germany — of course in the German language — for the use of religious Orders of men and women not bound to the full office in Latin. Its preface states that "the hierarchy of Germany desires, with this new office, to give to religious communities not obliged to the Roman Breviary, but who wish for a closer prayer participation in the liturgical life of the Church, a substitute for the Little Office of the Blessed Virgin — an office which is, in fact, a simplified and abbreviated version of the Roman office, and which corresponds with their needs." More than a hundred thousand religious in Germany, both men and women, are now using it with enormous appreciation; very soon it spread to Austria where some fifty thousand religious have likewise adopted it.

The same thing happened in Holland in 1954. The compiler of the Dutch office was a Redemptorist, Father Stalleart; he received a letter from the Holy See saying that "His Holiness strongly desires that the *Klein Brevier* be used by religious communities whose way of life will permit of it." In France there have appeared two adaptations of the Roman Breviary; one is by Père Henri, O.P., and the other by the Benedictines of Encalcat. The majority of French teaching Brothers and Sisters are now using one or the other.

In America the Benedictines of Saint John's Abbey, Collegeville, brought out what is called the *Short Breviary*, which is exactly the same kind of thing. They designed it in the first instance for their own lay Brothers, but it has found a wide acceptance among other Brothers and Sisters. More than 150,000 American religious now use it as their community prayer, and many articles have appeared in spiritual periodicals testifying to the great advantages they have found from its adoption. Similar short Breviaries have, more recently, been published in Italy and in Spain.

The movement for giving up multifarious, amorphus, repetitive and sometimes sentimental devotions, or the unintelligible Latin Little Office of the Blessed Virgin, in favour of an intelligible abbreviation of the Church's own office should be encouraged in every way. It will do enormous good to our Sisters, enrich their spiritual lives, help them to pray and think with the Church, and is likely to attract more and better postulants than are now presenting themselves as recruits. May God grant this blessing to any who are at present without it.

Sponsa Regis, May, 1954

Religious and the Rosary

J. G. Redmond, C.SS.R.

An ancient Grecian writer, Aristophanes, once wrote: "I should like to speak to you in roses." In the following pages I should like to speak to religious in terms of the Rosary, in those white and red and golden roses which loving souls lay gently at the feet of our Lady.

In these thoughts on religious and the Rosary we will consider how religious can give their whole lives to her. We will consider how imitation of our Lord lies at the heart of the religious life, how imitation of Christ is made easier by the spirituality of the Rosary, how the joyful mysteries illumine our birth into this divine life, how the sorrowful mysteries point out our progress in this interior life, how the first three glorious mysteries lead to a deepening of this divine life, and finally, how the last two glorious mysteries reflect the fullness of this divine life.

IMITATION OF OUR LORD

We can easily imagine our Lord lingering at the portal of heaven, looking back and saying to his followers: "I have given you an example, that as I have done, so do you also" (Jn 13:15). Our Lord is our model. We are to be copies of him. And within the circle of the Rosary — on this road of roses — living the joyful and the sorrowful mysteries of life, we may follow him to the Father and, in beholding his glory, find our own.

In painting a portrait, the artist turns from the model to the copy. His observant eyes seize upon some feature. His skillful fingers reproduce it. He compares his work with the original and retouches it till the likeness is well-nigh perfect.

In living the spiritual life we are to make a copy, to fill God's order: "Look, and make it according to the pattern shown thee on the mount," the

141

pattern of perfection found in our Lord. In the making of this masterpiece we need a brush, a chisel and a torch: a brush to splash the bright colors of joy on the canvas of our countenance, a chisel to cut deep lines of sorrow for sin into the marble of our heart, and a torch to flood the whole room of life with the gold of glory. All three are at hand in the Rosary: the brush for bright colors in the joyful mysteries, the sharp chisel of the sorrowful mysteries, and the glowing torch of the glorious mysteries.

In a very human way the Rosary brings an easy and instant vision of our Lord. With the slow movement of the beads there comes the memory of words and deeds of our Lord and our Lady that faith has garnered from the Gospel. For the Rosary is a reflection of the Gospel that bursts into flame in the heart. In the light of faith and in the fire of love the Gospel comes to life. Crib and Cross and Crown come close. The birth, life, death, and truimph of the Son of God made man are renewed in the world of my being.

In the Rosary my divine model poses for me. The Rosary is an ideal means to lead the soul to contemplation of Christ. It offers scenes that are simple, yet filled with inexhaustible spiritual riches, for under the veil of the most human events they hold all the secrets of divine life. The Rosary holds up for our contemplation the most beautiful example of virtue, the perfect example of life, the life of the Son of God made man and living thirty-three years among us to teach us to live as children of God.

However, to imitate this divine example, to copy our divine model is a task beyond our trying. Every step in the following of Christ is a grace of God. This is a truth to fill us with humility regarding our weakness, and yet to fill us with confidence in the goodness of God. It is a truth to convince us of the strategic place of prayer of petition in the spiritual life.

The Greek mathematician Archimedes once remarked: "If I had a lever long enough and a fulcrum strong enough, I could move the earth." We have a lever long enough and a fulcrum strong enough to move heaven and earth — to move the God of heaven and earth. The lever is prayer. The fulcrum is the Sacred Heart of our Lord. Now prayer offered to God through our Lady is the surest way of reaching the Heart of her Son. And the Rosary is our Lady's loving answer to the petition: "Teach us how to pray."

And so the Rosary is not only a means of grace; this devotion itself is a grace. To it apply the words of our Lord: "Father, . . . thou didst hide these things from the wise and the prudent, and didst reveal them to little ones." It is to have the precious spirit of a child, a child of Mary, a child of God. And this first grace brings another even more precious, the grace of loving intimacy with our Lady. And this brings an even more precious intimacy with our Lord.

The lives of the saints reveal that Jesus reproduced in them first his infancy, then his hidden life, then his apostolic life, and finally his life of sorrow, before he invited them to share his life of glory.

Loving meditation on the mysteries of the Rosary leads to something similar in our souls. In the midst of our joys that are often too human and sometimes dangerous, we are reminded of the nobler joys of the coming of our Lord into the world. In the midst of our sorrows, sometimes imaginary, sometimes overwhelming, and almost always badly borne, we are reminded of the sufferings which Jesus endured for love of us and to encourage us to follow on to Calvary bearing the cross he has laid on us for our purification. In the midst of too earthly hopes, we are reminded of the true goal of Christian hope, eternal life, heavenly glory. Thus our joys, sorrows, and hopes are purified, elevated, and supernaturalized. Meditating on the mysteries of the Rosary, we realize more and more that Jesus our model wishes our lives to copy something of his hidden life, something of his sorrows, that we may share his glorious life.

To come to us, Jesus chose the way of the Heart of Mary. Her Immaculate Heart was his choice! And to go to him, it must be mine! It is the surest, the shortest, the best way. In the Rosary we do not set out on a random search for Jesus. His Mother leads us by the hand to him. As we say the Rosary, meditating on the mysteries, praying for the grace to mould our lives upon them, we find ourselves walking through life in joys and sorrows and on to the glory of heaven — between Jesus and Mary.

Little Fugue

The ale sky's whistling leaves
a fall wind tunes. This frenzy
shrills cold color. Stacked

in the grate the wood's gone popcorn.
On glassed wine pale as pinions
of ice, these skaters: geese

hanging across the pane
from tattered sun-scarves. Cracking
wings, a cricket files,

saws like any prisoner.
Instead he's a prophet, cajoled
to castanet good fortune.

Geraldine Clinton Little
Sisters Today, October, 1977

Sisters Today, October, 1969

A House of Prayer

Sister Eileen Storey, S.C.

This past summer the Sisters of the Immaculate Heart of Mary implemented through their sixteen houses of prayer many of the hopes and part of the dream they and representatives of ninety-five congregations had begun to envision and to formulate at the Monroe Conference of 1968. The community deserves the deepest gratitude of the Church in America for the manner as well as the fact of implementation in our common search for God through radical authenticity. There were no structures determined in advance; each house of prayer became whatever the women involved in it shaped it to be. And the women involved shaped quietly and lovingly a contemplative life that left the Spirit free.

Before centering our attention upon the essence of a house of prayer and the reality of one or two of these sixteen houses, it seems good to recall the underlying principle that explains the essence and the existence of any house of prayer. Before we ask, "What is a house of prayer?" we must ask, "What is prayer?" For the mystery of life is here: that man can seek and find his God in prayer. The joy of this mystery prompts our unsophisticated plea, "Lord, teach us to pray!"

To pray is to open ourselves to the truth of our being. Often our prayer will highlight our multiple, almost infinite, perversions of this truth. We have such difficulty in being. To escape our Creator's challenge to be, we become and remain effective, ingenius doers of the Word spoken by God. And this is good, for we must be doers to prove to ourselves and to the world that our faith is not vain nor divorced from the world it is meant to wed.

But in our deepest heart, we know that God did not call us to be go-go people. We know that much of our activity is escape from a Presence that

144

may just as easily reduce us to silence as inspire us to action, a Presence that asks of us total abandonment to an all-penetrating love, a Presence that suggests complete detachment from values that have served us as comfortable guidelines. Insofar as our activity is an escape, it is noise that prevents our entrance into the dynamic stillness of God.

Our prayer is meant to become a joyful Alleluia. For God has made us to his own image. His indwelling Presence enables us to achieve that unique resemblance consonant with our dignity as persons. The human person, created in the likeness of the Triune God, can share in the dialogue between Father and Son in the love of the Holy Spirit. To take part in such a dialogue requires a tremendous capacity for listening — listening to the Word spoken in the silent reaches of the Godhead. This Word finds human expression in the Scriptures, in the Eucharist, in the multiple facets of its incarnation; it finds authentic personal expression when we make our own its meaning.

TWO ESSENTIAL COMPONENTS

It seems to me that the two essential components of the house of prayer, two basic elements that must be present to give birth to pure prayer, are love and silence. With our human tendency to go off balance, we sometimes find ourselves joining these two components by "or" instead of "and." In the house of prayer we try to achieve a love-silence. The hyphen must be so strong that the power generated in our love for one another runs right through into new depths of silence where each of us can be more herself than ever, while the power generated in these depths of our being spills over like a waterfall into constant manifestations of fraternal love. This love-silence recognizes the uniqueness of our personal call and the gregariousness of our human nature. It results in an atmosphere that is highly supportive as each person discovers her name and responds to that Name which is above all other names.

Love-silence finds one expression in common prayer. In a house of prayer it is surely appropriate to pray together, to let the Spirit move freely among us as we share his inspirations and our own aspirations. The spontaneity that characterized the prayer of the early Christians has somehow become fixed in beautiful but static forms over these two millenia. The house of prayer is surely a place where the Spirit can breathe warmly enough to defrost our frozen prayers, where people can feel free to formulate with a twentieth or twenty-first century vocabulary the timeless longings of the human heart.

Morning prayer and evening prayer in a house of prayer will be a thoughtful and joyful melange of Scripture, modern poetry, song and maybe dance, spontaneous prayer that will sometimes be ecstatic, sometimes deep and sure, but most often halting and terribly prosaic. We want to unblock the Spirit. For we believe that the Spirit of God dwells in us and that he is praying always in us even when we do not know how we should pray. We want him to triumph over our timidity of expression and that foolish pride that keeps us walled up in a silence that is not of the Spirit.

Because the house of prayer is one where the Spirit should move freely, many of us see it as something more than a house of love-silence. We surely see it as a house of radical witness to our community love of prayer, but we see it also as a house of ideas that can be shared with and evaluated by the people of God. If there is any human function that merits our intellectual and emotional energies, it is certainly the celebration of the Eucharist.

The house of prayer will have a particular responsibility to develop a liturgy that will speak to and of the people of God now on pilgrimage. Ideas that have come from long hours of silent prayer — if God lets us get out of these long hours with ideas — prayer patterns that the group experiences as new breathings of the Spirit, could be shared with the whole community. Theology on the move can be analyzed and incarnated here where the gift of discernment of the Spirit should be highly operative.

An ecumenical thrust will be strong in such a house, for people dedicated to prayer reach out for help to Buddhists, to Jews, to Pentecostals as well as to the mystics and men and women of prayer who form their immediate heritage. A neighborhood thrust will also be characteristic in urban houses of prayer, for to pray with the people of the neighborhood, and to invite them to pray with us is surely to share the best we have to give. Above all, the spirit of love should go out from such a center of renewal to draw us more together in our common pursuit; it can be for each of us a center filled with the presence of God making each of us, whether our prayer be vertical, horizontal, or diagonal, so many surer radii as we move within that encircling shield who is God.

THE HOUSE AT WALLED LAKE

The house of prayer found sincere but halting expressions during the summer of 1969 in the sixteen centers I have mentioned. I can describe only my own house with all that it offered us (or rather, all that we offered each other) in our pursuit of meaningful prayer.

Because of meetings in New York City, I arrived at the Walled Lake house of prayer one week after its initiation. From the moment we met at the Metropolitan Airport in Detroit, I knew that the community was living and spontaneous in its expression of love. Instead of bringing me immediately to the chapel which they had arranged in the fashion of a Zen garden, they brought me to the living room, put on a record and taught me to *Zorba*. The rhythm moved from a graceful slowness that cloaked my awkwardness to an excited beat that spoke of our enthusiasm. This was the first time I had ever danced into chapel and here the Sisters remained with me in a place I recognized as home.

What we have done here is not so important as what we have been. Indeed, before coming together we had already expressed our desire to be rather than to do. Because the young curate, Father Jim Mayworm, understood what we were about, he became, in a very real sense, a member of our house of prayer and the liaison between us and the parishioners of Walled Lake.

It was our privilege and our joy to celebrate daily Mass with neighboring families. To pass the cup of the Lord to a woman who is at that very moment giving her blood to an unborn child of God, to look into the eyes of a young boy as you ask him to discern the Body of Christ, to share your reason for praying "Lord have mercy" with the people of God for whom you have not been adequate witness to the love of Christ — this has been part of the joyful experience of the liturgies in our house of prayer.

The sharings among the eight of us as we prayed in the mornings and evenings of these six weeks further accentuate our desire to be women of prayer rather than professional women who can do a neat job of Lauds and Vespers. One week we prayed together the liturgical year, not only to celebrate the oneness of the incarnation, redemption, and apostolic commission, but also so that we, as a loving community, could celebrate together these unfoldings of the mystery of God's love.

In some ways, our common prayer evidenced an age range that goes from the early twenties to the mid-forties, and an occupational diversity that includes a student of psychology, two elementary school teachers, an artist, a CCD coordinator, a teacher of music, a nurse, and a formation directress. Thus, when one week we chose as a central prayer theme the seasons of the year, all of us were able to appreciate the hidden growth that goes on under the white earth and in a child's heart, but some of us could speak more experientially of springtime and young love while others could share more knowledgeably the summer with its harmonies and discordances, its uncomfortable dryness and its call to relax in the Lord. Rather than holding on to youth or the prime of life, the eight of us look forward to an autumn of open skies, daring colors and fruitful maturity that leads immediately into life's fifth season: God.

Aside from our meeting together for prayer and liturgy, we decided to have two meals a day in common. We met at the breakfast table and took the occasion for straightening out any knots foreseen in the day's schedule. Our evening meal gave each of us in turn a chance to demonstrate our culinary ability or our ingenuity in producing a meal without previous practice. Our dinner conversation ranged from the trivial to the profound; we never knew until one of us had prayed a spontaneous blessing whether wit or gravity would prevail. Personally, I feel we could have shared more at our dinner conversation, but we were deeply appreciative of one another and of the cook.

Sundays brought us into a larger community. All sixteen houses met for a beautifully planned liturgy, for conference with men of prayer, and for a sharing of what had been experienced during the week. We spent some very meaningful hours with Brother David Stendl-Rast, Fr. Edward Hennessy, Rabbi Gelberman, Swami Satchidananda, Lutheran Pastor Arthur Kreinheder, and several leaders of the Catholic Pentecostal group from Ann Arbor, Michigan. At Walled Lake we were able to have with us for a few days an Anglican deaconness, Agnes Hunter. The house of prayer, then, had an ecumenical as well as a parochial thrust.

PERSONAL AND COMMUNAL FRUITS

The summer house of prayer has now slipped into the past. What seeds has it nourished? At this moment, we envision a double bloom: one personal, the other, communal. For many women consecrated to God and his people through vow, the house of prayer offers the opportunity to respond to a call that they have heard for themselves and for their community. The Sisters who *begin* the house of prayer movement in their community should be chosen from among those who have asked to be members of the house of prayer. Because of the particular mission of the first house, it would seem well for the community to choose Sisters who are trying to be completely open to the Spirit as he moves through our moment in history and who have some particular strength that, through the Spirit, they could share more prayerfully with the larger community. This initial membership is what we might call the core group.

Like any group of thinking women, this prayer community will need time to interrelate; each member will need time to discover in this setting that deeper identity that she has perhaps often intuited. As a listening and responsive person, as a member of a loving prayer community, each core member will already be fulfilling a vital role in the larger community.

After the time that the core group needs together, however, it will open its doors for all members of the community who know that this moment in their lives is to be one of more intense prayer and that it will require a different atmosphere from the one they are immediately enjoying. Sisters whose work prevents their participation in a house of prayer will know that the house is there, waiting for them when they can come to share what their work has helped to build. Because the rhythm of the house has been established by the core members, those who come for short or long periods of time will hopefully find there the peace and harmony needed in their new search for personal authenticity. When people go back to their full-time professional work and different community patterns of life, they will hopefully spread the peace they have found in the house of prayer.

Sisters Today, December, 1975

Prayer and the Psychology of Women

Sister Rachel Callahan, C.S.C.

Particularly during this "Woman's Year" much has been written about the psychology of women and the importance of a woman's growing self-awareness in a world where many of the traditional and male/female stereotypes are being shattered. As women religious there is much to be said in favor of growing self-awareness of who we are and some of the implication this has for praying.

Probably when we think of self-awareness in as free and spontaneous a way as we are able, most of us come up with a unique "me-ness" that includes being a woman as a central component. "Women's liberation" has become somewhat of a loaded word in our society. The "women's liberation" that I would like to explore in this article is hopefully literally that — a freeing up by being more in touch with the feminine core of our nature and particularly as it relates to one of the central things that we do, i.e., prayer.

In addition to the physiological, biological difference and complementarity *between* man and woman, psychologically *within* each person there are masculine/feminine counterparts. Carl Jung has written extensively about this, and it is no accident that today, as some of the sexual role stereotypes are breaking down, his writings are enjoying a new popularity. Culture has tended to emphasize as qualities of maleness rational, analytical, problem-solving approaches, while females are labelled intuitive and more emotional. More serious psychological studies point out some of the feminine aspects of personality. I would like to examine briefly three of these dimensions, first psychologically and then relate them to prayer.

AN ATTITUDE OF ACCEPTANCE

Biologically, a woman gives by receiving. Each of us lives in a giving/receiving rhythm. In religious life the emphasis, at least consciously, is on giving. It is no accident that personality profiles of religious show a higher nurturance need than the population at large. Most of us are pretty much in touch with our need to give, our need to help other persons.

But the other side of this coin, and one that is less consciously alluded to, is the need to receive. Much has been written in the past decade about "search for community." If this search is stripped of a lot of its rhetoric it appears that much of the search for community is fed into this giving/receiving rhythm. Community is more than what each of us can do functionally (give). The paradox of community is that we give most when we are able to receive and accept others as they are. Each person has and is a particular gift. Community is experienced when our own giftedness is recognized and when we are able to accept the giftedness of others. When our own particular gifts are not accepted, unfortunately they can dry up and die, the end result being bitter and unhappy persons. There is awful pain and real tragedy in persons thinking that they have no gift, or are no gift. And again the paradox is that this can be avoided only by becoming more conscious of ourselves as receivers as well as givers.

AN AWARENESS OF THE UNITY OF LIFE

A woman is rooted in nature biologically in a way that a man can never experience. A woman in her very being is quite deeply committed to life. Again, perhaps because vowed celibacy means foregoing a central experience of womanhood, i.e., motherhood, we may be less conscious of this particular aspect of feminine personality than we should, although the ongoing effort to integrate rather than deny sexuality in living out celibacy helps make this more conscious.

READINESS FOR RELATIONSHIP

How does one describe relationship? The "miracle" of any genuine relationship seems to be that it is hardly ever planned, and then after it happens who can explain it? In fact, sometimes relationship suffers in the attempt to express what it is. The best explanation that I know for relationship is that somehow a bridge has been made between the separateness of myself and another. Relationship does not destroy separateness. It demands it. A relationship is strained, if not broken, as much by over-zealous attempts to possess the other as by an uncaring casualness that makes one wonder if there is any meeting with the other at all.

This meeting of another in a way that creates mutual significance is marked by the following phenomenon. In any real relationship I am a mediator to the other of his/her own truest self. There are two aspects of

relationship which are literally "wonder-full." Each person in a relationship makes a bridge between self and other, and in this gift of self to other
also paradoxically allows the other to receive and be more open to the gift of
his/her own self. The affirmation by another frees us to receive the gift of
our own selves. Self-acceptance does not happen in a vacuum. It usually
occurs when a significant other mediates my experience of me to me in a
way that I can experience myself as good.

Having briefly looked at three of the feminine dimensions of personality, I would like to examine how these might affect prayer.

PRAYER AND THE ATTITUDE OF ACCEPTANCE

Peter Von Bremen in his book *As Bread That is Broken* quotes Paul
Tillich's definition of faith. "Faith is the courage to accept acceptance." The
core of our faith is that the Lord's stance towards each of us is one of
unconditional commitment and fidelity. His love and unconditional acceptance of us is prior to and more important than any response or infidelity
of our own. Can we accept and believe in this unconditional acceptance and
experience the liberation of realizing this stance of the Lord towards us?
When we think about acceptance in prayer there are a number of attitudes
this implies, perhaps summed up by the notion of "active receptivity." We
can try to accept the Lord who has first accepted us as he reveals himself to
us in the persons and events of our lives and in his Word.

Listening to the Lord in Scripture is one of the places where we are able
at least to make the space in our lives to hear how he is revealing himself.
Theodor Reik in his classic, *Listening with the Third Ear*, talks about the
necessity of being aware not only of the content of words spoken to us but to
attend to the actions and feelings of the other *and* the feelings that this kind
of listening creates in ourselves. In this kind of participative listening I
really try to attend to the speaker and tune out other concerns to the extent
that this in itself does not become a strain.

If we apply "listening with the third ear" to praying with the Scriptures, it suggests first of all quiet presence and attention to the Lord, and
then allowing ourselves to be aware of what we are feeling. Whatever this is
becomes something to share with the Lord. He may be revealing himself in
a new experience of what it means to be healed, or simply a contentment in
his presence. Or, he may be revealing himself in absence, or very often
confusion. If we look through the gospels there are so many instances in
which the Lord revealed himself to his friends in a way that confused them,
or frightened them because they could not understand. It should not alarm
us if we experience our own human fragmentation and confusion as one of
the ways that the Lord reveals himself to us.

The Lord's presenting himself to us is not conditioned upon the quality
of our listening. If I am feeling fragmented and appear "not there" when
listening to another person, that person might go away, but never the Lord.

He receives our most hobbled attempts to accept him. All he asks is that we accept his acceptance.

When we are the givers we are "in charge." Acceptance is another story. We allow ourselves to be appropriately dependent. As Henri Nouwen points out in his *With Open Hands*, one of the real challenges of the gospel is the invitation to accept a gift for which we can give nothing in return.

PRAYER AND THE AWARENESS OF UNITY OF LIFE

Today there is a revival of interest in oriental religions and the contemplative life even from the viewpoint of natural religion, a new awareness of the need for quiet contemplation of the universe as an antidote for the frenzied pace at which we live. Taking the time to enjoy quietly the beauties of the earth, to look and see the marvels that the Lord has made can bring a new awareness of the Lord and lead us to the prayer of praise that the psalms are filled with, an enjoyment of what the Lord had made. There is a beautiful line in Psalm 104 — "May Yahweh find joy in what he creates." And may we enjoy it with him by quiet contemplation of the wonders of the earth.

Jesus used so many earth images to reveal himself and his kingdom — the seed, fruit, storms. The paradigm of his own life and gift, which is the invitation of the gospel, he explained by the image of the seed falling into the ground and dying in order that there may be new life.

PRAYER AND THE READINESS FOR RELATIONSHIP

In some sense prayer can be defined as relationship. It is in prayer that the Lord reveals the gift of himself to us and thus mediates and calls forth our own truest self. This relationship like any other is marked by separateness yet intimacy.

Do not be afraid for I have redeemed you.
I have called you by *your* name.
You are mine.

You are precious in my eyes.
You are honored and I love you (Is 43:1-6).

This relationship, like any other, probably suffers in the attempt to describe it because it is a uniquely personal and intimate experience for each person. All that the Lord asks is our own readiness for this relationship, open hands and open heart, and the realization that awesome as it seems, in our own relationship to him we also mediate his person and free him to be himself today in the place and space where each of us lives.

Sponsa Regis, November, 1939

Fostering Vocations

No doubt the most important factor for the growth and prosperity of any religious community is the recruiting of good and numerous candidates. Young shoulders must be ready to take up the burden laid down by those exhausted by work and years; young talents must be added for the extension of the community's activity. How can we attract to our doors young persons fit for the arduous requirements of convent life, new members imbued with the ideals of religion, zealous for God's cause, willing to sacrifice themselves in order to promote his kingdom in themselves and in others?

In present day conditions this question is particularly acute. The spirit of the world, of that world of which the followers of Jesus are not (see Jn 15:19), penetrates society more and more. The wish for comfort and luxury, the greed for pleasure and its increasing opportunities, the aversion for everything that demands effort and self-denial rule all the classes and are nourished, often unawares, in family, school, social gatherings, etc.

Where, then, could develop that enthusiasm for the supernatural necessary for the total surrender of self to God, that spirit of sacrifice which throws away all that the world covets? And yet, in our own days, too, God calls many to his special service. This call is like the mustard seed, like the good seed of the sower. It must be fostered, it must be protected from thorns that threaten to choke it, from a rocky subsoil if it is to bring the hundredfold of a successful religious life. What can a religious community and its individual members do in order to second God's call and to foster true vocations?

The answer to this question is very comprehensive. It has to do with the community as such and with the direct influence on aspirants to the religious life. Souls seeking to embrace this state place before themselves a high ideal; they feel called to follow Christ more closely, to imitate his life and become like unto him. Such an ideal has taken root in the soul before the young girl considers seriously the choice of a congregation. She must find the ideal realized in the community she intends to join. Its members, especially those with whom she comes in contact, must act according to this ideal. Their daily life must be based on the surrender of self in the service of God and fellowmen, on disregard for personal comfort and advantage, on contempt for worldly goods and honors.

Above all, peace and charity, these outstanding characteristics of the Christian spirit, must be felt throughout in the relations between the members of the community. The observance of religious modesty — that calm, cheerful self-control in any circumstance, that subdued, friendly way of speaking and acting without attracting attention — makes a great impression on persons of the world. A community where such a spirit reigns cannot but gain the esteem and consideration of outsiders; the well-intentioned, at least, will speak of it with respect and approval; and the young, used to rely on the judgment of their elders, will decide in its favor.

On the other hand, it happens that a community unintentionally bars the way for worthwhile candidates. When they notice that religious shun the common discomforts and privations of life, grumble under hardships endured by lay people without complaint, their esteem for the religious life receives a shock. Girls frequenting convents are keen in observing defects and are very severe in their judgments. What an impression may they receive when they hear loud, harsh voices in and outside the house, nagging and quarreling, dissatisfaction each time they come there.

A girl once changed her choice of community because she had seen two Sisters, one of them crying, talking excitedly in a corner. We with long years of experience, fully aware that human weaknesses cling to us as to all mortals, forget that aspirants seek an ideal and expect to find the ideal in the community of their choice.

In places where the Sisters go for services in the parish church, people expect that they set the example: that they are punctual in arriving, do not leave before the others, participate in the prayers said in common, give by their respectful and recollected attitude the impression that they worship God from their hearts.

With regard to religious, outsiders are particularly sensitive in two respects: truth and honesty in money matters. If they find that such fundamental duties are slighted, that untruths are told to avoid a bad impression, that lack of honesty is excused with the vow of poverty, they turn away in disgust. "Religious make the vow of poverty and we have to keep it," they say. And did not our Lord say: "You cannot serve God and mammon" (Mt 6:24)?

For the one or other community a lack of adaptation to their environment may be the cause for keeping off candidates. If a plant brought from another climate is unable to secure nourishment in its new soil or to hold out against the inclemencies of the weather, it will die. The same with a community.

There are principles of the religious life which cannot, with impunity, be tampered with. There are also certain details that have no direct bearing on perfection in themselves: customs, language, minor regulations. With regard to these the rule should be: what is likely to paralyze or to impede the great purposes of the congregation ought to be changed and replaced by what corresponds more in the given circumstances to the spirit of the gospels and of the Church.

Such changes may impose deeply felt sacrifices on the older members; but such sacrifices form an essential part of the missionary activity. A narrow nationalism is directly opposed to "catholicism"; it is mostly accompanied by extreme narrowness in other lines, too. By its unreasoned disdain for everything foreign to itself, by its inability to understand others, it imposes, in the long run, intolerable hardships which, after all, are a kind of injustice. If a congregation is not willing to grant full equality, why not make that clear and restrict membership?

Active orders must also keep pace with the requirements of their time. What was the best thirty years ago is not in every case still the best now. A word of our Lord is to the point here: "No man putteth new wine into old bottles: otherwise the new wine will break the bottles. . . . And no man drinking old, hath presently a mind to new: for he saith, The old is better" (Lk 6:37, 39).

So far we have discussed how the community as such indirectly influences young people in their choice of vocation. Now a few remarks regarding the direct influence to be exerted. A fundamental though remote preparation for religious life is a thorough instruction in religion, an instruction full of conviction and love that will impart a deep sense of God's greatness and of our dependence on him, and a firm willingness to serve him. Such instruction, together with practical training in true, everyday Christianity, embracing all the phases of life, is the sound basis for the life of perfection.

Probably nearly all the girls who have frequent contact with Sisters will some time or other wonder if they should not become a Sister, too. If this is only a passing thought with little or no effect on the girl's behavior, it is not worth much attention. The same is true of those who are eager to tell every Sister they know that they want to join the Order. Often they want, perhaps unconsciously, to make a good impression and gain favors.

The call of God in the depth of the soul is like the lover's secret. It draws to Christ, to prayer; it begets joy and happiness that in some is calm and interior, in others overbubbling, yet is silent as to its cause, except to a chosen friend or advisor. If one receives confidences of that kind, it is good to give to such a girl some spiritual reading, showing the ideal as well as the difficulty of a life of perfection, to encourage her to receive the sacraments frequently, to practice self-denial.

It is advisable, however, not to show too much concern about her aspirations. The girl should learn, in spite of all kindness shown to her, that such confidences do not purchase divers little privileges, such as impunity in breaking school regulations, special indulgence as to school work, etc. Especially should there not be made any promises of privileges or the like regarding her future religious life. Those who make them will perhaps not be in a position to fulfil them; besides, it is doubtful whether it would be wise to fulfil them.

At any rate, such inducements appeal only to weak characters. There is a possibility that in time the true spirit of religion will gain the predominance in their heart; the greater probability is that they will be found wanting and either leave or become a cause of trouble for all concerned. If a sincere attraction for the convent life persists, the girl should be told to make it known to her confessor who is the competent judge and guide in this matter.

It must not be forgotten that to such means of fostering vocations must be added prayer and an intense inner life. God alone has access to the innermost heart; vocations come from him. "Pray the Lord of the harvest that he send laborers into his harvest" (Lk 10:2). God is the sower of the good seed. In order to bring fruit a hundredfold it must fall on good soil, i.e., a community wherein the spirit of Christ reigns in full vigor, wherein the members make easy for one another the intimate union with Jesus, the ascent to the holy mountain of perfection; a community that is in truth the reproduction of the Holy Family. Now we may help to prepare the soil, but "God giveth the increase" (1 Cor 3:7).

PART FOUR

QUESTIONS AND ANSWERS:

What Sisters Always Wanted to Know and Were Not Afraid to Ask

Asking questions and receiving answers is as ancient an exercise as it is an essential one. No sooner are man and woman created than they are asked by the serpent, "Did God really tell you not to eat from any of the trees in the garden?" (Gen 3:1). A little later God begins his dialog with his creatures by asking, "Where are you?" (Gen 3:9). On the next page the creature gets into the asking act with that burning question, "Am I my brother's keeper?" (Gen 4:9). Since then the process has never ceased.

Questions provide a clear clue to the concerns and needs of those who ask them. That is why a careful combing of the gospels for the questions asked by and of Jesus gives us a picture of some of the matters uppermost in the minds and hearts of the early Christian community. For example, "Who can forgive sins except God above?" (Mk 2:7); "Why does he eat with such as these (tax collectors)?" (Mk 2:16); "Good Teacher, what must I do to share in everlasting life?" (Mk 10:17); "Who can be saved?" (Mk 10:26). Such samples show that the catechism technique was not invented by the Councils of Baltimore.

During the first three decades of publication, *Sponsa Regis* periodically provided a forum for Sisters to ask some of the questions that concerned them. A question and answer column dealing with matters related to the liturgy and Gregorian chant began appearing in 1933 and continued through mid-1936. Father Gregory Huegle, O.S.B., of Conception Abbey in Missouri, answered such questions as "Why should the Divine Office be recited on elevated pitch?" and "How may Sisters acquire a correct and beautiful pronunciation of Latin?"

From mid-1934 to early 1937 questions relating to a variety of topics appeared in the magazine. Queries that may now seem like exercises in trivia were made concerning the wax content of candles, the correct color for ciborium cover lining, and the neglect of the sanctuary lamp. Answers that reflect the certainty, solemnity, and occasional arrogance of yesteryears were provided by experts who only initialled their comments — R.R.S., J.K., and B.M.

After a lapse of sixteen years, a rather regular feature called "Convent Queries" began to appear in *Sponsa Regis* and continued from early 1953 to late 1959. Questions ran the gamut from "Is it against the spirit of poverty for a religious to travel by airplane?" to "Are hair shirts made of horse hair or camel's hair or what?" The wisdom and occasional wit of Father Winfrid Herbst, S.D.S., provided the answers to these questions. The author eventually found it necessary to assure his readers that the queries were really asked and not made up.

It may also be necessary for the present reader to be reminded that even though the questions that apparently agitated Sisters yesterday now seem insignificant and irrelevant, so do most questions have a way of losing their edge as time goes by. After all, can't we suppose that the serpent really knew the answer to his own questions about Adam and Eve being told not to eat from any of the trees in the garden? And surely the Lord God Almighty knew perfectly well where Adam was before he asked, "Where are you?" And Cain was only swallowing hard and buying time when his insolence prompted him to inquire, "Am I my brother's keeper?"

Questions, however, are a part of life, for God made us curious. Questions, moreover, are necessary for the continuing creative process. And to get to the really essential issues we do have to clear the air by asking questions that later may sound silly or stupid. But then who of us hasn't asked, "How are you?" without expecting a medical diagnosis?

Sponsa Regis, 1935

Questions on Reciting the Office

Gregory Huegle, O.S.B.

Are any musical priniciples involved in the recitation of the Divine Office in communities?

Religious that live in communities and perform the Divine Office in common are exhorted by the rule or constitution to lay the greatest possible stress on a worthy performance of the *Opus Dei* — the divine work. For this purpose the rule or constitution generally uses terms such as the following: "Let the Divine Office be recited with a clear and distinct voice, on elevated (i.e., musical) pitch, in reverent manner, without haste."

*

Why should the Divine Office be recited on elevated pitch?

Out of reverence for the divine majesty. The official praise of God Most High should *not* be performed in the tone of common parlance. When men converse with each other, the ordinary tone of conversation is in place, but mere natural reason seems to point to the employment of a solemn, elevated pitch of voice when the community in a body, at stated hours, offers up the divine praises.

*

Is there any tradition with regard to the musical pitch to be employed?

An ancient tradition in the Benedictine Order points to G as "the golden medium." It is said that all voices can do good work on that pitch:

159

the high voices can come down and the low voices can come up and meet them in friendly manner. G is called a truly democratic tone because it deals out equal justice to high and low.

*

But what about those religious that begin the Divine Office on a low pitch (C below the staff) and soon find themselves lost in A (below the staff)? Is low pitch a desirable expression of lowliness of spirit?

We have never come across any tradition pointing towards the choice of low pitch for the Divine Office as an expression of a penitential spirit and a lowly heart. Prayer is always an elevation of the heart to God. Holy Mother Church from the very beginning declaimed her prayers, not in an ordinary speaking voice, but on a musical tone, so that the words might be clothed with an added beauty and solemnity.

*

But what about the other extreme, viz., of reciting the Divine Office on high B or higher still?

The advantages of high pitch are said to lie in the lightness and freedom of tone; the heavy element of chest resonance no longer pulls down (it is said); like a balloon, the voice soars triumphantly above the depression of the lower atmosphere. This ideal attainment seems to be a by-product of the more recent voice pedagogy. It certainly is astonishing to hear a crowd of four hundred children raise their voices to any tone above the staff with ease and brilliancy! In choir work of religious communities, due regard must be had for all voices: high and low, trained and untrained. Justice and charity demand that a *democratic* tone gain the upper hand over an *aristocratic* note. Impartial observers have given this verdict: "the extremely high pitch in choir is unnatural, and therefore painful to the listener."

*

What helps are there to get started on a musical pitch?

Practical experience has shown that the use of a reed organ is an excellent help to establish the sense of pitch and to unify the voices. A few sustained cadences will do the work. At the end of the psalm quickly strike the note, so that the antiphon or the new psalm may be properly intoned. Another help will be to direct all the syllables into the forepart of the mouth and establish them there by sufficient practice. Remember the motto of the great singers: "Upward and forward" with the voice. Finally, avoid all strain. The right way is an easy way; do not aim at a loud voice; let it be round, mellow, and sweet.

*

How may Sisters acquire a correct and beautiful pronunciation of Latin?

To attain the best results the pronunciation of Latin must be approached as that of any foreign language. To speak Latin like English is to spoil its charm.

*

On what foundation must the rules be based to acquire a correct and beautiful pronunciation of Latin?

The rules must be based on the Italian manner of pronouncing Latin. Latin is not a dead language in the Catholic Church, and we cannot expect to find a more correct pronunciation than that of Italy, its natural home.

Sponsa Regis, 1934-37

Questions and Answers

R. R. S., J. K., B. M.

May 51 per cent wax candles be used for Holy Mass and Benediction, or must they be 75 per cent wax?

The Holy See has prescribed that the large Easter candle as also the candle used for blessing baptismal water and the candles for Holy Mass should for the most part be of wax. "For the most part — *in maxima parte*" means that candles should at the very least be 75 per cent wax, but preferably 80 per cent or more. However, the actual percentage of wax is a matter for the bishop of the diocese to decide, for it is the wish of the Holy See that private individuals need not anxiously inquire into the quality of the candles used on the altar. As to the other candles which are placed on the altar, for Benediction and other services, these candles should contain a considerable quantity of wax. Again, the actual percentage has not been determined, but it is the common opinion of authors that they should be at least 25 per cent wax. Less than this could hardly be considered a notable quantity.

*

Why do some monsignors wear red and others purple, and what is the difference between Rt. Rev. Monsignor and Very Rev. Monsignor?

The observer may possibly be mistaken in calling red that which is really purple. All monsignors wear purple at all functions, even at funerals. The only time they wear black is when the Holy See is vacant. The difference in color noted by the inquirer may likely be due to the fact that prelates do not all procure their prelatial dress from the same tailor or manufacturer.

This therefore explains the different shades and tints of purple. The Holy See has recently decreed just what quality of purple is to be used henceforth. Hence, in the future, there will be less variety of tinges in this matter.

The reason why some monsignors are called Right Reverend and others Very Reverend is that the former are slightly higher in rank and have a few more ecclesiastical privileges than the latter.

*

May the ciborium cover be lined inside with red or yellow silk or satin, or must it be white?

There are no special prescriptions concerning the lining of the ciborium cover, although it is more proper to exclude such a color as purple or other colors than red, yellow, or white. It need not, however, be white.

*

Is it proper to have candles burning on the side altars for the sake of greater solemnity while Mass or some other service is going on at the main altar?

The rubrics allow candles to burn only at the altar or altars where Mass is being celebrated or some other religious function is actually taking place.

The only case in which it is allowed to have the candles burning at a side altar, with no special function taking place there, is during Vespers if the Blessed Sacrament is reserved at the side altar and not at the main altar. In this case, then, both the main altar in choir and the side altar where the Blessed Sacrament is reserved are incensed during the *Magnificat*. There is, of course, another time when candles are kept burning during Vespers on all the solemnly consecrated altars of a consecrated church. This is on the feast of the dedication of a consecrated church at Vespers when all the consecrated altars are incensed during the *Magnificat*.

*

In some places the children are taught to say aloud and in unison the indulgenced words, "My Lord and my God" during the elevation of the Sacred Host at Mass. We were always under the impression that these words are not to be said in a loud tone of voice. Your opinion on this matter would therefore be much appreciated.

On November 6, 1925, the Sacred Congregation of Rites issued a decree which expressly states that the faithful may not say the ejaculation, "My Lord and my God," in a loud tone of voice, since such a practice is contrary to the traditional silence which is to be observed during the Canon of the Mass. They should say it privately and secretly. This, along with glancing at the Sacred Host when it is elevated is sufficient to gain the indulgences attached to these words, provided one is otherwise properly disposed.

*

When preparing the altar for Benediction of the Blessed Sacrament, is it proper for the sacristan to place the Benediction burse upright and in front of the tabernacle door?

Strictly speaking, the officiating priest should himself carry out the burse when he goes to the altar. In any case, the burse should never be placed upright in front of the tabernacle door. This door should remain free from anything in front of it except for the veil which surrounds the tabernacle. It is only by exception that the "Gloria" card may be placed there. The burse for Benediction should be laid flat in the middle of the altar (with the tabernacle key nearby) before and after Benediction of the Blessed Sacrament, unless the priest, as he strictly should, carries the burse and key out and back. During Benediction service the burse should, if possible, be placed upright at the left side of the tabernacle.

*

How many lighted candles are prescribed for exposition of the Blessed Sacrament and at Benediction?

It is prescribed that, outside of Forty Hours' Exposition, at least twelve wax candles be kept burning on the altar while the Blessed Sacrament is exposed in the monstrance. During Forty Hours' Exposition, however, at least twenty wax candles should be kept burning on the altar. For private exposition and Benediction of the Blessed Sacrament, that is, with the pyx or ciborium, when the tabernacle is merely opened so that the ciborium may be seen, at least six wax candles must be burning on the altar, although more may be lighted if desired.

*

How should the burse and monstrance be placed on the altar before Benediction of the Blessed Sacrament? As sacristan, I usually place the burse upright in front of the tabernacle, but the chaplain at the end of Benediction merely lays the burse flat upon the altar. Which is the correct thing to do? I fear to ask the chaplain since he is perhaps not aware of the difference.

The monstrance should be covered with a white linen or silk cloth and placed slightly to the left of the center of the altar, so that when the corporal is extended, it will be at the edge of the corporal for the convenience of the priest. The edge of the monstrance, not the flat surface, should be towards the people. Sacristans might also note that the back of the monstrance should therefore be facing the Epistle side of the altar, so that when the priest uncovers the monstrance he will not be obliged to turn it around first.

As to the burse, this should be laid flat in the center of the altar and should not be placed in an upright position in front of the tabernacle door. This direction is based on the principle that nothing is to be placed before the tabernacle doors which might hide the front of the tabernacle, except of course the veil around the tabernacle and the altar-cards at Mass. Only when the corporal is extended is the burse placed upright to the left of the tabernacle.

*

May a ciborium veil made of linen instead of silk be used?

If you are at present using one and the church is poor, then you might continue to use it until it is worn out. But we can hardly recommend the use of a linen veil for covering the ciborium, even though Wapelhorst's manual of rubrics and ceremonies does say that nothing definite is prescribed as to the material out of which the ciborium veil is to be made, adding, however, that it is more proper that it be made of silk. The reviser of that manual evidently overlooked, as sometimes happens, a rubric in the Roman Ritual (Tit. IV, Ch. 1, 5) which says that the vessel in which the consecrated hosts are reserved should be covered with a "white silk veil." Other eminent authors also quote the Roman Ritual to this effect. That the veil may and should also be appropriately ornamented is to be taken for granted, although plain white silk will do.

*

Is it permissible to set plants or votive lights on the altar stone when decorating a side altar containing an altar stone?

There are no specific laws of the Church which govern a case of this kind. We know of nothing to forbid such decoration directly. It might, however, be better to leave the center of the altar table free from plants and the like. As for the rest, good taste and simplicity must guide us in matters of decoration and ornamentation in church.

*

Permit me to ask another question about the burse. Is is proper for the burse to be placed 1) so that the opening is at the right near the tabernacle, or 2) so that the opening is at the top, facing upward?

The burse should regularly, according to common custom, be placed upright to the left of the tabernacle, with the opening facing the tabernacle. This, of course, presupposes that the monogram or other ornamentation on the burse will appear in its normal position if the burse is placed as above. If, however, the ornamentation of the burse demand that the burse be placed so that the opening faces upright, then it should be so placed. Benediction burses are usually so ornamented that they must be placed with opening upwards. While there does not seem to be any definite rule regarding this matter, it seems better to ornament the burse in such a manner that the burse may be placed with the opening facing the tabernacle.

*

Are tabernacle veils prescribed by Church laws? I was taught that this veil is the only exclusive sign of the presence of the Blessed Sacrament, yet few comply with the regulation, saying that it was not prescribed in former days and old customs may prevail. Is not this reasoning false? If such negligence be the abuse of Church law, why such indifference on the part of those in charge? People will seek in this negligence reasons for disobeying other precepts too. Should not all the laws of the Church be important to us and not only those that please us? Many concern themselves much about flowers and lace, but when Church laws direct that a veil should cover the tabernacle, they merely smile. What is your attitude about this? Is the veil as necessary as the sanctuary lamp?

Practically every ecclesistical magazine we know of has so often answered and discussed the question about the tabernacle veil that one wonders how any ignorance or doubt should still exist about the matter. Those who still fail to cover the tabernacle on the outside with a veil are perhaps mainly such as find the present structure of their tabernacle a real problem when they come to fitting a veil over it. The words of the Roman Ritual are clear insofar as they take it for granted that the tabernacle be covered with a veil or *conopaeum* (Tit. IV, 1, 6). If anyone doubts the preceptive force of this rubric in the Ritual she may consult any approved author. The decrees usually quoted are nos. 3520 and 4137. These decrees say explicitly that the Roman Ritual must be followed in this matter of a tabernacle veil and that the custom of not having such a veil may not be retained. And that is therefore our attitude. One seeks in vain for any authority to uphold that such a veil is not obligatory. Whether the veil is as necessary as the sanctuary lamp is hardly a fair question for discussion.

*

A Sister was told that it would be a mortal sin for her or any woman to enter the sanctuary for the purpose of arranging candles or flowers on the altar where the Blessed Sacrament is exposed. Is this correct?

It is not correct. Such an action would not even be a venial sin. It is, of course, proper that a woman refrain from working around the altar while the faithful are assembled in church, unless necessity demands otherwise, as often happens in convents, or in smaller parish churches, whether the

Blessed Sacrament is exposed or not. On the other hand, when it is necessary to replace or light candles while the people are present, as usually happens during Forty Hours' Exposition, or to rearrange flowers, then such tasks should be performed with due reverence and, if possible, by the altar boys dressed in cassock and surplice. But, we also know how difficult this is for smaller boys. Hence, the need for older persons to lend a hand. In all cases, care should be taken not to give offense to the faithful. We know of no specific Church legislation which forbids women from doing this work when necessity demands. Oftentimes, in fact, our altars would remain quite bare, or poorly decorated, and sputtering candles would become a great fire hazard were it not for the skill, the zeal, and watchfulness of the Sisters and the ladies of the parish.

*

How many hours may the sanctuary lamp be left extinguished until this neglect is a mortal sin?

While mortal sin is ordinarily not calculated on the basis of hours, still it is the general opinion of authors that to neglect the lighting of the sanctuary lamp for more than a day would constitute a grave matter.

Sponsa Regis, 1953-59

Convent Queries

Winfrid Herbst, S.D.S.

What do you think about the use of radio and television by religious?

I think with the Church. To think with the Church — *Sentire cum Ecclesia* — should be the motto of every Catholic. In August, 1957, the Congregation for the Affairs of Religious sent to the Superiors General a letter containing new instructions concerning the use of radio and television. Superiors are, by virtue of these instructions, put under grave obligation to exercise a strict control over the use of radio and television. The following instructions are emphasized to the Superiors:

"1) There is no justification whatever for the introduction of a television set into a contemplative community, whether of men or women; a radio can be tolerated for the sole purpose of allowing the religious to hear the words of the Holy Father spoken to the whole world and to receive his blessing, or for some exceptional celebration of a religious character.

"2) In active Orders

"a) it can never be allowed to anyone to have a radio, and much less a television set, for free individual use and outside the control of the Superior;

"b) radio and television must be always and exclusively in a community room, in an unconcealed position, and under the control of the Superior or his delegate;

"c) the Superiors must regulate the time given to television or to radio, so that there shall be no interference with occupations and duties of the religious state or of the office entrusted to anyone, or with the care of souls, the exercises of piety, community exercises, time assigned to rest, according to the horarium of the community;

"d) Superiors must forbid television or radio when, from the point of view of morality or worldliness, they are not conducive to religious life; except for news transmissions or programs of instructive or religious character, all other transmissions must, or at least can be so considered with regard to religious life and, therefore, must be prohibited, if they are sought only as a means of recreation for the religious;

"e) if considerations of the apostolate clearly demand, for individual religious and in particular cases, reasonable exceptions, the decision is to rest with the Superior alone, who must, *graviter onerata conscientia*, see that any danger is made remote by choosing religious who are sound in religious spirit and have a wise experience of life, who are capable of judging not only what can be harmful to religious, but also what can be harmful for those for whom the program is intended."

*

Is it against the spirit of poverty for a religious to travel by airplane?

Traveling by plane nowadays by a religious who can thus save time is not in any way against the spirit of poverty. In the first place, it is not much more expensive than a train, especially if you count the meals, the tips, perhaps the taxis, the hotel, etc., while waiting for connections.

In the second place, the saving of wear and tear on the system, with the consequent ability to do more for the Church, is a justification for this modern mode of travel, even apart from the matter of expense.

In the third place (and I should think this would apply especially to Sisters, though the same may be said of all religious), one is not away from the convent and community life so long, but is quickly within the sheltering walls of some religious house again. So religious need not hesitate to use this mode of travel, with due permission, when it is advantageous, when there is some advantage in the saving of time, health, etc.

*

Our rule says that no Sister shall enter the room of another. May I, as Superior, inspect the rooms of the Sisters? Must I do so?

You certainly may do so in the interests of religious discipline. Whether or not you must do so depends upon the constitutions. Some rules prescribe that from time to time the Superior shall inspect the individual rooms to see whether everything is consistent with holy poverty and religious simplicity. As Superior you should not hesitate to do this from time to time. But you should do it in all charity. Simply drop in casually sometime when the Sister is in, and say with a smile that you'll have to make a little inspection of the room. Look it over, and then ask whether she would mind showing you what she has in the clothes closet, in the bureau drawers, etc.

But do not be like a customs official and ransack dressers, trunks, satchels, etc., leaving everything in a mess. What bitter feelings you could thus create! You are not looking for things to report to the motherhouse; indeed, you are not looking for trouble at all. Show that what you really want to do, in addition to your distasteful duty, is to find out whether Sister has everything she needs for her health and comfort, especially in the way of clothing. Ask her sincerely whether there is anything that she feels she needs in the line of wearing apparel, or whether there is anything that does not suit her which she would like to exchange.

In this particular matter be very, very considerate and delicate. Remember that so many of your Sisters are simply modern girls, who have become religious and who are used to this and that, and who can be deeply humiliated and keenly hurt by indelicacy or lack of understanding in this matter. And rudeness will only embitter them. Be sure they will pass the news along, good or bad. They will love you dearly for your charity and thoughtfulness. On the other hand, they will be repelled by lack of consideration and will hesitate about inviting girls to join your community. Remember that adaptation to modern conditions does not necessarily mean mitigation.

*

I am not complaining, but it does seem to me that the Sisters of our community are all overworked. Can anything be done about this?

It seems to be a common thing in our day and in all religious congregations of women that many Sisters are sadly overworked. They are not complaining, but in a spirit of self-abnegation and devotion to duty toil on at their assigned tasks until they are physically and mentally exhausted. Some go on until they actually collapse and have to be hospitalized. True, many Sisters live to a ripe old age, and of them it can even be said that it was their hard work which kept them in trim. But it is also true that many have died prematurely. Just how many, it would be hard to say, since various communities have the practice of not putting the dates of birth and death on the tombstones or markers.

When we look about to see who is to be blamed for this condition of overwork, we find a variety of probabilities. It seems that sometimes the blame is to be attached to the superiors of the Sisters. Not that they, both higher and local superiors, are fully conscious of how they are overburdening the Sisters, for the Sisters themselves in their great zeal are always ready to add yet another burden to a load already too heavy, and the superiors find the demand for taking more and more places ever more pressing. But we wonder whether, if they realized what they are doing when they drive the Sisters to the breaking point, the superiors would not be guilty of serious sin against charity and prudence. Here another Sister has a nervous breakdown; there one has to go into isolation with TB. Who is to blame? And does the one who is to blame suffer any qualms of conscience?

Among other things, such as more periods of real leisure during each day, Sisters should have a reasonable vacation every year. Here is a Sister who teaches school all year, then is sent to summer school, then has to make her annual retreat, then has to help clean up the convent, then assist at registration, then begin to teach school again. Is this prudent, fair, considerate, redolent of Christian charity, even in the best interests of the community?

*

Do we all have to go to purgatory before we reach heaven?

It seems to be a common attitude among religious as well as among the laity (which latter is more understandable) that a delay in purgatory before reaching heaven is inevitable. It is taken for granted, it seems, that "Who am I to aspire to immediate admission into heaven?" is the correct, humble attitude; that it is too difficult, even impossible, to escape some delay in purgatory; that purgatory is not greatly to be dreaded, because there we will be secure and happy in the knowledge that we are saved.

We do not think that is the correct attitude to take. The uncommon but correct attitude towards purgatory is that it is a sacred duty to strive so to live as not to need purgatory; that my heavenly Father wills it that I come directly home — and I have no right to choose a delay; that in view of the powerful and superabundant means at my disposal, it is possible to avoid purgatory; that purgatory is a very terrible punishment, inflicted by a just God who hates the slightest sin.

If a religious, a Sister let us say, were released from purgatory and permitted to return to the earth for another trial, to live her life over again, how observant she would be! She would live a detached and holy life, crucified to the world and separated from it in spirit, daily giving all honor and glory to God through the Mass, and sanctifying herself more and more through Communion. Then, at the end, God willing, she would get that other key of heaven, Extreme Unction, received with perfect dispositions, and that double assurance which is the plenary indulgence, connected with the apostolic blessing after the last Sacraments, to take effect only at the moment of death, and she would go straight to heaven.

When God made us and set us forth on the journey of life, it was his will that we should so conduct ourselves along the way that, when the journey is ended, we should be found worthy to be admitted immediately into his presence. He is our loving Father; he wants us, his children, to be with him as soon as possible. Indeed, he could not have willed otherwise. To have done so would have been to will an imperfect work, which is an impossibility for an infinitely perfect God.

*

In our community there are two religious who never speak to each other. This has been going on for a number of years. One is greatly grieved and has tried repeatedly to be friendly, but the other hardens all the more. So, finally, the grieving one has found that it makes more for peace not to speak either. What can be done?

We would threaten the guilty one with hell fire in view of the Savior's assurance that unless we forgive we shall not be forgiven; but that would not help either. So we can only commit such to the mercy of God.

We were reading of a husband and wife who lived together in the same house, even taking their meals together, without saying a word to each other for twenty years. Thereupon, considering that their marriage was not a success, one of them took action to get a separation from the court. In view of the fact that they were living together and yet paradoxically not living together, the separation was granted. The decision was interesting. The court said: "What makes a separation is not separate roofs but separate lives. These two have been separated as effectively as though they were living in different homes. Men and women may live as strangers, even as enemies, more separately, more contentiously, more violently, under a single roof than under two."

We wish all religious would meditate on the last sentence of that decision. What can be more contentious, more violent than silence such as that mentioned in the question above!

*

I regret to say that I am proud. Can you give me a cure for this?

What are you proud of anyway? We will ask you a series of questions, taking it for granted that your answer to each one is "No." What are you proud of — are you a descendant of an ancient and noble family? Are you exceptionally learned, or gifted in some special way, a genius as a singer, or speaker, or writer, or adminstrator, or something else? Do you think that you are exceptionally good and pious, and that all your goodness comes from yourself and not from God? Do you think that there is nobody just as excellent as you are? Things being so, be at peace. You are not proud, but only stupid. And stupidity is no sin.

*

When a visit to the chapel is prescribed for gaining a plenary indulgence, I know that one has to make an extra visit for each indulgence. One has to leave the chapel and come back again. Is it enough to step out into the corridor and then come right back again? Or must one go out of the convent, or even down the steps to the sidewalk?

It is sufficient to step outside the door. If then you turn around and go in again, you make another visit. "He is considered to go out of the church who goes into the sacristy or who goes out into the atrium of the church itself," says Ferreres (*Compendium Moralis*, ed. 16, 1940, vol. 2, no. 795). The atrium is what you would call the vestibule, a room into which other doors open, from which other rooms open, an entry.

*

I want to do lots of penance and become a great saint. Please help me. What should I do?

Suppose you do the following penances to begin with: (1) Keep the rules and customs conscientiously and as perfectly as possible. (2) Rise promptly in the morning. (3) Kneel sometimes without or with only partial support. (4) Conceal involuntary discontent. (5) Do not show pain caused by humiliation. (6) Conceal dissatisfaction at a task imposed. (7) Never complain to others. (8) Do not talk about your successes. (9) Never tell news during silence. (10) Tell some good points about a person disliked. (11) Defer reading letters received. (12) Give in. (13) Beg pardon. (14) Delay taking that drink of water. (15) Keep order. (16) Let duty come first. (17) Let others talk. (18) Keep silent when blamed.

*

I wish I had a hair shirt, just in case I want to use one, with due permission according to the constitutions. Are hair shirts made of horse hair or camel's hair or what?

The vast majority of religious in this country, and no doubt in other countries too, have never even seen a hair shirt. Neither this nor other penitential instruments are necessary in order to attain perfection, though there are communities where their use is prescribed by rule. In all religious orders, of course, bodily mortification of some kind is highly recommended. But one can practice all kinds of bodily mortification without the use of penitential instruments. Our convents are full of saintly religious who never saw any of the penitential instruments soon to be mentioned. They live in ignorance of them, will die without having used them, and will get a high place in heaven for their most meritorious lives of prayer and mortification.

But some do want these additional aids. There seems to be an increasing demand for them. We have been corresponding with a Carmelite monastery and find that you can get the following penitential instruments at the following prices, subject to change without notice, if their supply is not exhausted: Full size regular hair shirt: $13.50; hair shirt, large size: $4.50; hair shirt, medium size: $4.00; hair shirt, small size: $3.50; hair cincture: $1.50; hemp discipline, heavy: $1.50; hemp discipline, lighter:

$1.00; metal discipline: $1.10; chain cincture: $2.00; chain armlet: 75 cents; leg chain: $1.00. The hair shirts, for your information, are made of sterilized, chemically cleaned horse hair; the hemp disciplines are made of imported Italian flax; and the best quality of stainless steel wire is used for the chains.

The hair cincture is a band of hair cloth about three inches wide to be put around the waist. We think this item should become the most popular (!) of penitential instruments. The nuns say it would be a great help if folks would tell them what length they wish their cinctures. It is pretty hard to guess whether a Thomas of Aquin is sending the order, or a Peter of Alcantara.

*

May I ask whether the questions asked in a former issue of Sponsa Regis "Convent Queries" were really asked, or whether you made them up, being sadly in need of material? They are not much of a recommendation of the intelligence of Sisters as I know them. I wonder what others think when they read such queries.

Yes, the questions were really asked. I must admit, though, that I do sometimes edit the questions a bit, the better to express the questioner's thought, for brevity's sake or, as in the case of the one now being answered, to take the sting out of them.

I am thinking now of Cardinal Newman's sense of humor. Having gravely dissatisfied the superior of a celebrated convent by his address to the school, he was taken to the parlor and given a glass of raspberry vinegar. "Sweet acid," Newman remarked later, "like a nun's anger."

Shortly after your query arrived, I received the following note from another Sister: "Dear Reverend Father, This is a tribute for the wonderful understanding, but above all, Christ-likeness, that 'Convent Queries' brings from your pen. Many of my questions were solved through reading them. May our divine Savior let you continue in this wonderful charity that ought to draw us closer to himself." I might have edited this note a bit also, eliminating the repetition of the word "wonderful," but I decided to quote verbatim.

PART FIVE

THE VOWS:

Developments in Poverty, Chastity, and Obedience

If any of the pillars in the Lord's temple have been shaken in recent years by would-be Samsons, it would be that trio of towers that give shape and support to religious life — poverty, chastity, obedience. But for all the rattlings and rumblings, the pillars are still standing, and no one has succeeded in convincing religious that Jesus prefers them to be filthy rich, sexually promiscuous, and stubbornly self-willed.

This is not to say, however, that our present understanding, appreciation, and practice of these three basic vows have remained static and unchanging. The articles in this section sample the insights gained during the last fifty years of reflection and renewal. Father Karl Rahner, S.J., is therefore able to discern "entirely new problems" regarding poverty that could not have been considered almost twenty years previously. "A Contemporary View of Obedience" sees that particular vow and virtue from a somewhat different perspective than the earlier article that compares a religious community in which obedience flourishes to "a great symphony orchestra under the skillful direction of a master musician." The contemporary situation at times seems to turn that metaphor around and give all the instruments to the conductor and a baton to each player! Pity the superior who has only had a couple of lessons on the triangle.

Regarding the vow of chastity and the concomitant area of interpersonal relations, the changes in attitudes and actions are most pronounced. Compare, as you will, the rasping rhetoric of this remark in "Religious Friendship" — "At the miasmic breath of particular friendships, the fair and lovely garden of religious community life withers into a sere and blackened waste" — with this comment in "Overcoming Problems in Friendship" — "The most mature person is the person most capable of deep, intimate, faithful relating. Problems which develop in relating are solved only by developing the ability to relate more intimately rather than by backing away from relationship.''

We have come a long way, haven't we?

Hospitality

"Who makes the meal shouldn't have to clean it up,
is what I always say."
And Martha threw her tired heart into a chair.
"The meat was just a little tough,
but they don't give us better parts
where we buy our fare."
She chuckled at the joke she made
and toed the footstool to her feet.
She knew he liked her best.
Why make a point at every meal to eat
it all and bread the gravy off the plate?
She smiled at her own knowing, and caught him in a doze.
It was comforting, just the two of them,
with daylight winding down outside
and Mary contemplating dishes in the sink.
It was comforting, after all her work was done,
to get a piece of better parts:
to sit, to doze, to think. . .
sharing satisfied hearts.

Sister Carolyn Martin, R.S.M.
Sisters Today, May, 1977

Sponsa Regis, July, 1943

Poverty

V.S.

> *"Blessed are the poor in spirit, for theirs is the kingdom of heaven"* (Mt 5:3).

Christ's famous Sermon on the Mount began with the eight beatitudes, and the first of these is an exhortation to the practice of poverty. "Blessed are the poor in spirit, for theirs is the kingdom of heaven." In these words, our Blessed Savior virtually proclaimed the priority of poverty over the other virtues as an indispensable means of attaining perfection.

Of the rich young man, otherwise perfect, Christ demanded poverty as a condition for discipleship and a requisite for higher sanctity. "If thou wilt be perfect, go sell all that thou hast and give to the poor and then come and follow me." When the rich young man turned away, Jesus was sad, but he did not compromise, he offered no substitute. "Give up all," he persisted. There is no other way — then "come follow me." Renunciation must stand. Poverty of spirit must be the characteristic mark of the follower of Christ, the passport to his kingdom.

Peter must leave his nets, Matthew his tax-roll, James and John their father, Jude his little home in Nazareth. Human and earthly ties must be broken if these aspiring disciples will throw in their lot with Christ and become fishers of men. The apostles understood the requirements. They knew that Jesus had no earthly riches to offer them. They saw where he abode. As he himself had told them, he had not "whereon to lay his head." Nevertheless, they gladly renounced their simple possessions. "Leaving all things, they followed him."

Animated by the same teaching and example, the first Christians "lay down their goods at the feet of the apostles. Neither did anyone say that aught of the things he possessed was his own." Yet, as St. Paul says, "Having nothing, they possessed all things."

So has it ever been in the history of the Church. In every age, in every clime, the poverty of Christ has lured people on to holiness. Hermits, missionaries, martyrs have stripped themselves of all earthly encumbrances that, naked, they might follow the lowly Savior and preach Christ crucified to all nations.

Religious founders have never failed to lay down poverty as the foundation stone upon which to build their religious institutes. St. Alphonsus calls poverty the citadel, the bulwark of religious life, the custodian of all the other virtues. "Poverty," he maintained, "is the thermometer by which the fervor of a congregation may be estimated, for fervor of spirit thrives only in those institutes wherein poverty flourishes. On the contrary, once poverty declines, relaxation creeps in."

For this reason he regarded violations of poverty as grievous faults; and he required superiors before assuming office to promise with an oath to safeguard the observance of poverty. "When poverty leaves a convent," he declared, "the world enters — then goodbye recollection, obedience, and humility; goodbye silence, charity and peace."

As wealth, with the power, luxury and dangerous pleasures it procures, draws men on to perdition, so poverty, by removing the temptations of pride and worldly ambition, guides them on to the acquisition of true wealth — God and his blessed kingdom.

The spirit of the world is diametrically opposed to the poverty and simplicity of Jesus. "Blessed are the rich," the world cries out. "Blessed are the powerful. Therefore, get rich. It is the big business of life."

In marked contradiction to this doctrine the voice of the lowly Savior rings down through the ages: "Blessed are the poor in spirit." "Woe to you rich, for you have your consolation here." "Seek ye first the kingdom of God and his justice, and all these things shall be added unto you." "Everyone that hath left home and brethren, or father or mother, or lands for my name's sake shall receive a hundredfold in this life, and in the next, life everlasting."

Who is right? Christ or the world?

You and I gave the answer long ago when, with St. Peter, falling down at the feet of Jesus, we declared, "Lord, I believe. Thou hast the words of eternal life." Divine Truth had spoken. Infinite Wisdom had revealed the mind of God.

With simple faith and abandonment, strong in our trust in God's goodness, providence and justice, we joined the ranks of his chosen poor. We bound ourselves to share the destitution of our humble Savior and the folly of his cross. But oh, sublime paradox! No sooner had we despoiled ourselves of earthly vanities than we began to participate in divine riches. We began to share in the provident love of the master, receiving even here in our exile a portion of the hundred-fold of the blessed, who in the possession of God would prefer annihilation to possessing the universe without him.

In professing poverty, we gave up the false liberty of earthly wealth and glory, only to find true joy, lasting peace, and liberty of spirit in the company of a tender spouse and all-powerful bridegroom.

The merry world went on its way feasting, dancing, but what cared we? What could the world give us in exchange for Jesus? "Foolish and vain is he who desires aught but Jesus. To live without Jesus is the height of indigence — to live with Jesus is supreme riches." "Better is one day in thy courts, O Lord, above thousands. I have chosen to be an abject in the house of my God rather than to dwell in the tabernacles of sinners."

Though the selfish world pitied us and disdained the call to renunciation, yet it paused to admire the courage and heroic love of those wise virgins who, heeding the voice of the bridegroom, "went forth to meet him." So true it is that Lady Poverty always commands respect, evokes admiration, and elicits confidence. Her queenly simplicity never fails to attract hearts, to elevate minds, to convert souls.

Having triumphed over the wiles and allurements of Satan by removal from worldly seductions and pleasures, we could now freely devote our minds and hearts to the exclusive love of the master. Untrammeled by earthly cares and worries, we could engage with all our powers in the service of Christ for his glory, our own perfection, and the salvation of souls.

By our religious profession we entered into a sacred contract with our beloved bridegroom. We gave him our all, and he gave us himself. We stripped ourselves of earthly riches, and he clothed us with the bridal robes of his spouses. We left our homes, and he admitted us into his royal palace. We relinquished our worldly name, and he gave us a new religious title — as a member of his court. Instead of an earthly mother, he gave us his own immaculate mother to be our own spiritual mother in the heart-fold of her love. God would be a kind Father to his adopted children, more tender and solicitous than any human father ever could hope to be. For sisters and brothers, Christ gave us in religion new ties of relationship in our Sisters who, sharing the same poverty, animated by the same hopes and ambitions, would go with us side by side through life, encouraging, comforting, uplifting as we struggled on in the footprints of our sacrificial leader.

As a further pledge of love and fidelity, Jesus placed upon our finger the ring of holy espousals. For our guidance, he furnished a rule book to show us the way to the homeland of our eternal dwelling. He established us in the very heart of his Mystical Body with a commission to an apostolate in his kingdom.

Moreover, he enriched our souls with a profusion of gifts and graces, himself remaining among us as food and companion, as victim in daily Mass.

In view of such divine liberality, who could hesitate to love and embrace holy poverty? Who would not cry out with St. Francis of Assisi, "My God and my all," or with St. Ignatius, "Let me possess only thyself, O Lord, and I shall be rich enough and have no more to desire."

It is not sufficient to have made the vow of poverty, however; it remains for us to keep it if we would not be numbered among those whom St. Alphonsus describes as longing to be poor and to resemble Christ as long as they have nothing to suffer; who covet the honor of poverty, but will have nothing to do with its discomforts; or like that fictitious character who is represented as saying to God, "I give you all I have and am, O Lord, but please do not take from me this leg of mutton." It is possible for us to offer everything to God with our right hand, while with the left, we still cling to at least a slice of bacon in the form of a book, a picture, a box, or some trifling article in our charge or classroom.

Privileges bring responsibilities. The privilege of being a spouse of Jesus demands that we share the rank of Jesus and be like him in poverty, humility, and sacrifice. Freely have we received, freely must we give.

For the better understanding of our obligations, it is well for us from time to time to reflect seriously upon the responsibilities of the vow and virtue of poverty, how we can make practical our theoretical knowledge of poverty and closer resemble Christ. Such considerations will reanimate our fervor and keep us from slipping into easy, selfish habits which might tarnish the luster of our obligation and prevent the full merit of our sacrifice.

We are well aware that by the vow of poverty we renounced the right of proprietorship; that is, the right of disposing of temporal goods of money value, except with the permission of lawful superiors. We understand that this right of proprietorship includes such acts as that of giving, receiving for personal use, lending, borrowing, selling, exchanging, destroying, or disposing of articles in any way contrary to the rule or the wishes or orders of superiors.

The numerous regulations of Canon Law and the prescriptions of the rule pertaining to the vow and virtues of poverty have been amply explained to us in the novitiate, in our study of the catechism of the vows, in our meditations, spiritual reading, and in retreats. We have been reminded frequently by superiors of the various applications of poverty in our daily lives. To these sources of information or to our confessor we can refer for the solution of particular doubts or problems which may arise.

Sponsa Regis, July, 1962

The Problem of Poverty[1]

Karl Rahner, S.J.

The history of religious life for the two millennia of its existence has been, without much exaggeration, a history of various explanations of poverty. Today entirely new problems have been added to those that existed previously concerning the true character of poverty. We live in the midst of an emerging economy which in a forceful manner changes the material content of religious poverty.

It would be utopian to think it possible to carry out exactly what an Anthony, Pachomius, Benedict, Francis or, at the beginning of the modern era, an Ignatius conceived concretely as poverty. Such a concept would surely overlook reality and would bypass the real task, namely, to grasp anew and to realize the essence of what has been traditionally understood by poverty in the changed economic circumstances which are inescapably ours. In the realm of material goods and values more than in any other field, man is a function dependent on the social, collective form of this entire realm, whose formation is almost entirely independent of him: a reality which pre-exists and is withdrawn from his decision.

To wear a shirt or not to possess one, to go barefoot or shod is at various times and under various economic systems something very different, almost wholly determined in its concrete content by prevailing circumstances. Hence it happens that the early religious rules regarding poverty — which are intended to describe and determine the material content of poverty in the various Orders — either are no longer in force to a large extent or no longer reflect present reality at all. We shall return to these points later.

---

[1] "Die Armut des Ordenslebens in einer veränderten Welt." *Geist und Leben*, v. 33, heft 4 (September, 1960), 262-267. Translated by Rev. Gregory J. Roettger, O.S.B.

In this place we wish merely to call attention to the situation in order to make clear that we cannot expect a satisfying answer, which is strictly theological, regarding the religious meaning and the theological essence of poverty. A concept of poverty in its concrete application is not at all clear and cannot be clear, and we do not sufficiently understand the larger picture of the concrete economy of today, of which the concept of poverty forms only a part. Were we to try to give an exact theological formulation of poverty, this formulation could only be created by withdrawing into the realm of the abstract and the formalistic, where everything would be true, beautiful and marvelous, but where one might wonder whether the subject of the discussion is the poverty with which we have to deal in everyday life.

It may be comforting to stress the point that theoretical uncertainty and theoretical problems do not necessarily affect the practical activity of reasonable and wise persons. In man's concrete life there exist thousands of things which the experience of millennia has proved meaningful and valid, but which lend themselves to a clear theoretical explanation only with the greatest difficulty. The simple experience of life always teaches us more than theoretical discussion, which can never grasp life adequately. We know that religious life is meaningful and good as regards poverty, because it has been lived for centuries according to the venerable wisdom of experience, in the Church animated by the Spirit. And we know, even before we possess certainty, what we are observing and why it is good. This does not mean that reflection loses its meaning and its necessity, but merely suggests the uncertainty and the destructive power which it might have if it remained entirely abstract.

SOME TRADITIONAL PROBLEMS

1. The distinction between the poverty of the individual in an Order and that of the Order as such is well known. Such a distinction has its value. Without doubt the poverty of the individual contains an element of dependence on the community in the disposition of material goods. But dependence in the disposition of material goods cannot be identified with poverty (even if this temptation often assails ascetics and canonists).

If the poverty of the community were not presupposed, it would be impossible to speak of the poverty of the individual. The absolutely dependent member of a truly wealthy society could not seriously be considered poor, if words are to retain any meaning. From this it follows that the problem of religious poverty is primarily a problem of the poverty of the community, insofar as it exists in the Order and insofar as it presupposes that the individual's manner of life is determined by that of the community. This truth should be obvious.

I have the impression, however, that modern religious communities, even if they wished to accommodate the regulations concerning poverty in their rules to present-day conditions, are always tempted to think first of the individual, and to let the questions of poverty, as it affects the community as a whole, recede into the background. This can be understood. Nowadays the problem of the poverty of the community is much more difficult to solve than that of the poverty of the individual.

But it must be solved. Otherwise legislation concerning the poverty of the individual necessarily becomes formal casuistry, and we try to decide how the *juridical dependence* of the individual on the permission of the superior regarding the disposition of material goods can be maintained, simplified, or made stricter under present circumstances, without regard to the concrete poverty which is involved.

Such things easily turn into external formalities which do not necessarily possess supernatural meaning or exert any formative influence on the personality. Dependence and poverty, as we have said, are not identical. This is an old problem that must be re-thought anew today. To put it in another way: a rich Order cannot have poor members. Its great wealth may be strictly withdrawn from the arbitrary will of the individuals; it may have members who do not own property in a legal sense. But a really wealthy Order cannot have poor members. At most they will be completely dependent members with regard to the common ownership of material goods absolutely vested in the community.

Someone might say that such assertions already presuppose a fundamentally Franciscan concept of poverty, which was not verified, for example, in a rich medieval community (a royal monastery). Over against this objection it may be asserted that this concept of poverty — Franciscan, if you will — is the biblical concept, the early ascetical concept, the "evangelical" concept, which is presupposed also in the mentality of the modern Church and of the laity when the demand is made that religious should be poor. It must likewise be presupposed theologically. Otherwise poverty shrinks together and becomes a mere modality. (No wonder that the old Orders had no vow of poverty in the strict sense of the word!) It forms no proper evangelical counsel nor a real vow nor a strictly theological problem.

In a word, poverty of the individual and poverty of the community are, in the last analysis, the same problem. If the community is poor, and insofar as it is so, the individual participates in the poverty of the community, because he is a member of it and therefore shares in its manner of living; and since he is poor, he unites with a community that lives this poverty. What degree and what character the poverty of the community has or should have remains very much another and an open question.

2. In saying this, the second point to be treated has already been anticipated. Neither dependence on the disposition of material goods nor the juridical concept of lack of private property makes a person "poor" in the sense in which the word "poverty" is used in a theological and ascetical discussion. A person who has no private property cannot, indeed, dispose of material values at his own good pleasure, or even do so validly from a juridical point of view. But if he belongs to a community which is willing to

supply him with such economic goods as are possessed by a person who is termed "rich" in relation to the common economic standard, then such a member of such a community cannot be regarded as poor.

At the most it may be said that such a person is economically completely dependent. Such a dependence may indeed be felt as unpleasant. It may make the person in question "powerless" (at least as far as the outside world is concerned), and this dependence and powerlessness in comparison to others may also be acceptable from a Christian and ascetical point of view, within the meaning of religious ideals. But it cannot be called poverty.

If offenses against the vow of poverty were seen only in those cases in which the juridical dependence regarding ownership is violated, this would constitute a legalistic distortion of the genuine concept of poverty. And correspondingly, in circumstances where the superior acts juridically and canonically only as the legitimate administrator of the community property, he may be acting very much contrary to the spirit of religious poverty.

If, for example, the superior seeks to increase the wealth of the Order endlessly, in a capitalistic and ruthless manner like a clever businessman, he may offend against the spirit of poverty even though privately he lives in the same ascetical manner as many modern managers of great industrial enterprises. In such a case he has not offended against the principle of dependence, because as superior he legitimately performed these acts of administration; but he has sinned against poverty. If a superioress of a Sisters' congregation exploits the individual Sisters through overwork in order to make the congregation rich and powerful through the addition of new houses, she has offended against poverty, even though, because of it, the individual Sisters have to live very poorly.

3. Religious poverty and *forms* of poverty must not be confused. Certainly poverty may not be theoretically sublimated to the point where it is incompatible with any kind of use of material goods. Yet poverty demands a certain degree of deprivation of material goods, though we may leave aside the questions as to *which* goods fall under the deprivation of poverty (and under what circumstances).

Poverty has a very material content. Poverty in religion cannot be simply "poverty in spirit." The relationship to the world of material goods must be made concrete, and separation from it must be concretely realized. Still, a clear distinction must be made between poverty and determined forms of poverty. This has always been recognized. And for this reason, even in those cases which presuppose the common Franciscan concept, poverty has differed very much in various times and places.

This is not the place to analyze the various historical forms of poverty, to describe their physiognomies and to differentiate among them. In earlier days, possibly, the attempt was made to express this distinction too facilely, by use of the categories of "stricter" and "less strict" poverty, and therefore of "most perfect" and "less perfect" poverty.

Greater caution will be observed in this regard today. More attention will be given to the difference in form than immediately and directly to "strictness." It will have to be granted that, as in so many other matters, the difference in the "strictness" of the various Orders has tended to level off, and that at present it tends still more toward a rather uniform style in all Orders. This possibly is unavoidable because of the common economic situation and the modern common manner of life.

If this difference between the essence of poverty and the form of poverty is admitted as an historical datum, then it is impossible to close one's eyes to the fact that today, both in general and in every individual Order, thought must be given to a form of poverty that is really convincing and liveable at the present time. It simply does not do to assume a rigidly conservative attitude that tries to preserve the ancient form inherited from the Fathers and thus considers all problems solved.

In the face of the modern economic picture such a solution cannot be accepted. If it is still attempted, there results a turbid mixture of purely external concessions to the new age, perhaps made in haste and without clarity, together with remnants of the old traditions, which *de facto* are no longer ascetically significant, but only survive as a kind of religious folk-lore.

4. It cannot be denied that both in the tradition of poverty and in the tradition of the theology of poverty various motivations and definitions of poverty have existed. The poverty of the ascetics of apostolic times and of early Christianity was different from that of the cenobites, both in fact and in motivation. The poverty of pure contemplatives and of persons engaged in the apostolate simply cannot be identical in fact, and consequently cannot be identical in motivation.

The poverty of the religious life, leaving intact its essential identity, receives a peculiar character from the varying totalities of the individual Orders and, as a result, has a variously specified motivation. Hence history, which reveals these very different motivations in the many movements and struggles concerning poverty, justifies the conclusion that no absolutely univocal meaning should be attempted in the theological definition and the motivations of poverty. It must be assumed that poverty in the Orders presents a comparatively complex picture, which cannot be reduced to one theological root.

Sponsa Regis, March, 1949

What is the Vow of Chastity?

Bruno M. Hagspiel, S.V.D.

Not only those who have entered the cloister, but the men and women who are able to see below the surface of things can detect the triteness and, what is more, the injustice of the frequent comment that the religious state is an escape from life. Those who view at closer range the three vows that give the religious life its essential quality may easily discern that they imply, on the contrary, a coming to grips with life, and with life at its roots.

As in all things that bear the stamp of the Trinity, there is a basic union but, at the same time a fundamental separateness in the three religious vows. From the point of view of difficulty, poverty takes its place as the easiest in practice. To be rich in worldly goods means to carry heavy baggage through life, and baggage is an encumbrance to the traveller. He who would reach his goal with greatest speed must be stripped of all that is superfluous.

The religious, stripped of earthly possessions, loses likewise the care for all material needs and wins freedom from the daily battle for bread. Paradoxical as it may seem, the vow of poverty brings security. There is no room for worry about a home, a bed, or even a coffin and a sheltered plot of ground at the end.

The vow of obedience is another matter. Obedience grapples with the will and reaches the ego in its most deeply embedded hiding place. For this reason it is regarded as the most difficult of the vows.

Chastity is at the middle point, neither the most nor the least difficult in practice. It partakes of the renunciation that belongs to poverty and borrows the toughened fibre of obedience; but its peculiar beauty is its own. Strong yet delicate, simple while complex, it is the flowering of the tree of the religious life; or better still, the lily unadorned with the rainbow colors of the open fields, yet including them all in a garment of woven light.

Since the religious life is not a static thing resting fixedly upon the props of the three vows taken at profession, there is need, as with all growing things, to clear away entangling weeds, to take means to deepen the roots and to improve the soul. Fulton Sheen has spoken of the thrill of monotony. This would imply the presence of some stimulating concept that has the power of enlivening the pedestrian pace of everyday existence. According to a similar line of thought, it becomes evident that there is constant need on the part of religious to deepen old convictions, to light them with new fire, to find in them some new experience of beauty.

To this experience, for which a sense of joy and freedom is essential, the vow of chastity often presents the most serious obstacles. Because of its delicacy and complexity it often becomes a source of uneasiness, even torture, to the religious. Things imperfectly understood are apt to be disquieting. Lest after years of effort one miss the essential point of the whole undertaking, it seems imperative to examine closely, but without strain, this important duty of the religious state.

The following question is the first to present itself: What does it really mean to take the vow of chastity? What does it mean to renounce the privileges of family life in order to work without restraint for our dear Lord, for heaven, for the salvation of souls? St. Paul indicates the ideal of virginity in the spiritual state of life: "He who is unmarried is concerned about the things of the Lord, how he may please God. Whereas he who is married is concerned about the things of the world, how he may please his wife; and he is divided. And the unmarried woman and the virgin thinks about the things of the Lord, that she may be holy in body and in spirit. Whereas she who is married thinks about the things of the world, how she may please her husband" (1 Cor 7:32).

These are strong words. We must bear in mind, however, that this division of heart to which the apostle alludes is not a criticism against people living in the world, whose vocation compels them to carry a burden on each shoulder. They must, on the one hand, not lose sight of God and eternal life; on the other, they have the obligation to provide for the welfare of the family. Those who do not marry, in order to unite their virginity to the eternal beauty, are in an entirely different position. They must be concerned only with the things of God, with that which will please him to whom they have devoted themselves with a fulness of consecration.

St. Paul continues: "Now this I say for your benefit, not to put a halter upon you, but to promote what is proper and to make it possible for you to pray to the Lord without distraction," i.e., without any division of the heart.

Those who enter the religious state, therefore, must in a special manner tend to a wholeness of being, concentrating their full strength of soul and fervor of heart not upon earthly love or worldly possessions, but upon God as the supreme good. Instead of dissipating their resources as many do, spending them too lavishly upon human beings, they must direct all their most loving thoughts, the noblest and tenderest emotions of which they are capable, to one alone, the bridegroom of the soul, to Christ the eternal lover and to his blessed mother.

This includes the great concern that St. Paul lays upon the dedicated woman, "that she may be holy in body and in spirit." Hers is the love of a bride directed toward the highest good with undivided affection, as Solomon expresses it in the Book of Wisdom (8:2), and as the Divine Office of St. Agnes describes it: "I am espoused to him whom the angels serve, whose beauty the sun and the moon admire. . . . I am utterly faithful to him; to him I give myself with complete devotion."

This is the selfless, interior love that animated the spiritual life of the saints. In this devotion to Jesus, in the love for his mother, in the joyous expectation of eternal beatitude, they sought and found in abundant measure the satisfaction and the delight that people of the world seek in a well-ordered family life. This attitude of the saints is eminently reasonable, since it is only in God that the human being can find complete and lasting satisfaction. God alone never changes. God alone is Lord of all. Sooner or later all earthly things must be relinquished, and even while one possesses them, they do not yield complete satisfaction, nor can one depend upon them. The "tribulation of the flesh" (1 Cor 7:28) is never entirely absent from the life of husband and wife. Those whom God calls to the state of virginity are, if faithful to the ideals of their state, more fortunate in every way.

It is obvious, of course, that this undivided devotion of the heart to the highest good is a lofty ideal and can, therefore, be maintained only at the cost of patience and many a struggle. In its realization it manifests itself in countless gradations, revealing itself in differing ways in childhood, in adolescence, in old age. For those who choose celibacy as their state of life, the two following considerations are imperative.

First of all, since the complete surrender of the heart to God is the special goal of the vow of chastity, particular solicitude should from early youth be given to this point. Why is this vow demanded of us, and why does one recommend that young people who wish to dedicate themselves to the religious life take the vow privately, some time in advance? Is this idea meaningless, or is its principal purpose to safeguard the modesty of the young person, to provide added protection against sins contrary to chastity? Definitely no! To achieve this end does not require a vow. The natural law as expressed in the sixth commandment gives the latter so impressive a sanction that nothing more is necessary. If God's holy prohibition does not restrain one from sins against chastity, any number of vows would not suffice to do so.

Furthermore, one is not justified in permitting anyone to take this vow, unless he or she has proved himself or herself strong enough through a long and spotless period of probation to guard this virtue faithfully. Therefore, when the vow is actually taken, it must be presupposed that the person in question is practically never guilty of a deliberate, serious sin of impurity. To bind oneself by so solemn an obligation with the idea of not observing it would be nothing short of criminal.

The conclusion that those who wish to take this vow must have higher ideals in mind than the mere avoidance of impurity is inevitable. The virtue of purity in its full beauty and significance does not consist in a turning away from, but rather in a turning toward something, and chastity as a complete ideal demands an absolute bestowal of the heart upon God. For this ideal we must strive with all the vigor that is in us. Without this, celibacy remains a negative thing even though it be not marred by sins against purity. As such it will contribute little toward God's honor and the integration of the inner man. Our lives will be poverty stricken if not unhappy, and we shall be in constant danger of falling victim to the lure of impurity. It is precisely the assiduous striving for virginal purity as a positive ideal that constitutes the most effective protection for the virtue of chastity.

This leads us to the second consideration concerning candidates for the religious life. They must be made aware of this essential demand of the spiritual state, the giving of the whole heart to Christ. This ideal must be set before them despite their otherwise youthful unpreparedness. Its beauty, its drawing power will have a positive appeal for the spirit of youth and will act as a corrective for those whose first fervor has cooled. For those who have grown old in its pursuit it will be a panacea for the burdens and the fatigue of the journey.

For us the division of heart, which is the duty of married people, would be a betrayal, one similar to that of a married woman who did not center her love upon her husband and children but sought satisfaction outside the family circle. A person who cannot come to terms with herself interiorly and give her complete devotion to God, one who cannot suppress her longing to pour out her heart in an earthly love, one who believes that she needs some palpable human being, be it a husband, a home or a sentimental friendship, is not destined for the religious life.

If she positively requires these things in order to be happy or to find the proper expansion of her own life she will be an excellent exemplar, perhaps, for any worldly calling, but she should not enter a convent. She may have an excellent character, she may never have committed a sin against chastity nor have suffered a grievous temptation against it; nevertheless, she is not in a position to satisfy the essential duty of the religious state, the duty of celibacy.

Celibacy must be regarded as Niederberger depicts it in his *Life of Blessed Vincent Pallotti*. The latter in his old age was conducting the spiritual exercises for the scholastics of the Roman seminary and repeated again and again that the preservation of chastity is the most essential virtue for those preparing for the priesthood, — and *the same applies to any religious!* "To be a priest," he said, "three things are necessary: 1) Chastity, 2) Chastity, 3) Chastity."

When accepted in this sense, chastity is the honor of the Church. The holy Fathers are eloquent in its praise and regretted that they did not have the voices of the seraphim to exalt it adequately. They characterize the pure of heart as the true heroes of humanity, as Christ's legion of honor and his intimate friends.

If our Catholic people are willing to reveal the secrets of their souls to the priest as the guardian of morals and the judge of conscience, or if they entrust so often matters of conscience even to a Sister in religion, it is due less to the sacred ordination of the former or to the religious profession of the latter than to their life of celibacy. They have the underlying conviction that since the one and the other has conquered the most dangerous evil spirit in himself, they may readily regard them as above every other evil doing.

Sisters Today, November, 1978

Becoming a Celibate Lover

L. Patrick Carroll, S.J.

We never know how we are doing at something unless we are quite sure what it is we are trying to do. That seems obvious, but for a long time in religious life we have not been very clear on what it is we aim at, what our project, outlined by the vows, proposed; and so our evaluation of progress individually and corporately has been similarly muddled.

So often the project of poverty appeared to be to become poorer and poorer, have less and less, flee from any use of, much less dependency on material things. We have spoken recently of simplicity of life.[1] But our education, tastes, mobility, and security leave us looking, if not being, richer than most around us. If we re-direct our aim to the Lukan concept of stewardship and see ourselves as keepers, rather than owners, and our vow as one that commits us to sharing life and service, our project changes. It becomes possible and, in fact, more Christian. Poverty that aims at sharing everything, rather than possessing nothing or little, becomes a gospel virtue and not just a discouraging task.

THE SAME WITH CELIBACY

Something akin to this happens in the vow of chastity or celibacy. Consciously or not, many religious seem to be trying harder and harder to love God more and more, seem to strive to be less and less involved with, responsible towards human beings. We seem in fact, sometimes, to hold an angelic rather than human ideal. With no yardstick to measure our prog-

---

[1] L. Patrick Carroll, S.J., "Poverty: Open-Handed Love and Open-Hearted Sharing," *Sisters Today*, October, 1978 (Vol. 50, No. 2), 105-110.

ress, we create a false one, or give in to discouragement at the inability to achieve this angelic state.

I want to suggest a way of looking at the project of celibacy, or, more precisely, the project of becoming what I would call a celibate lover. For that is what we are called to be: not just lovers, and not just celibate, but both. There is no virtue in being simply celibate, unmarried, unsexed as it were. There is deep virtue in loving, or even trying to love, as God loves us: freely, deeply, broadly, unpossessively.

When we look at our religious project, we need honestly to admit that failures can come from two directions, not just one. We can be, in a sense, too loving, or too celibate (though obviously "too loving" is a contradiction in terms). We can be too careful, too distant, too cold, . . . too celibate. Or we can love unwisely, insensitively, possessively, manipulatively, . . . too (falsely) loving. But we *can* fail on either side. The religious who has three pampered dogs and no friends fails to live his vow as much as the religious with a mistress, for both fail to live out the call they professed to answer. We can, then, fail in either of two directions. Just as importantly, we will fail! Only Jesus did not.

If we see our lives as aiming at becoming more and more loving, more and more celibate, and hope to become an integrated combination of both by the time of death, we see, schematically, our project. Every human being will wander from that line, being at times either too careful or too free, too intimate or too distant, too involved or too uncaring. We can manipulate the feelings of people, dominating their emotions to our own selfish or needy ends. We can also manipulate the minds of people in a feelingless insensitivity to the freedom that is theirs to be. Both are failures.

LOVING PEOPLE

Please note: I am not talking about loving only God in a celibate way. I am talking about loving real skin and bones, body and soul, flesh and spirit, human people. The kind Jesus asks us to love. This needs some clarification.

Many religious seem to think that they are called to love God alone, despite what the gospels always and everywhere say. A vow to love God exclusively would be un-Christian, inhuman, and impossible. Jesus tells us, "I demand that you love each other as much as I love you" (Jn 15:12). Saint John writes, "Since God has first loved us, we ought to love one another" (1 Jn 4:11). In fact, we search the New Testament in vain to find somewhere where we are asked to love God directly. Jesus and his followers continually indicate that the movement of grace is from God to us, and from us to others (not back to God).

LET GOD LOVE US

How many try to live out their vow of celibacy by spending more and more time in prayer (not a bad thing in itself, if right-headed), trying to show God how much they love him, and that they are totally his. But a Christian actually goes (or should go) to prayer *to let God love him or her*.

Read that last phrase over again; it is an important and neglected concept. We go to prayer to deepen our sense and conviction that God loves us, from which we can move, in his Spirit, towards a world that needs to experience that love incarnated in people like ourselves. Nothing in scripture says that we show God our love for him by how often, or how deeply we pray, how frequently we participate at Mass, the vigils we keep. All kinds of things indicate that we are sent to show his love for others, having first received it ourselves. So we go to prayer to know God's love for us, and we must go there honestly, deeply, often. But whether or not that prayer has been fruitful is not measured by how good it feels at the time, or by the great insights we derived, unless that feeling, that insight leads us to be a more loving presence of Jesus towards his people.

So the project of our vow of celibacy is not just to love God, and not just to stay celibate, i.e., unmarried, without intercourse. The project is to love, and yet remain honest, free, mobile, able to carry the Lord's love where it is needed next and most.

A VOW TO LOVE

Perhaps we need to be convinced that celibacy is a vow to love. Well, it is a vow of Christian women and men, after all, and Christianity itself is a baptismally based vow to love, whether celibate or not. It is, I am presuming, more important to be Christian than to be celibate. Celibacy must be a vow to love, a way, a style of loving, of witnessing to God's love.

Every Christian continues the mission of Christ, to bring liberty to captives, sight to the blind, hearing to the deaf, good news to the poor (Lk 4:18 ff.). Every Christian is invited to love her enemies, to do good to those who hate her (Lk 6:27), and to take the injunction that ends that passage seriously: "Be compassionate, as your Father is compassionate." We are all called to be ready to forgive, and hence to be vulnerable to the failures of others, not just once or twice, or seven times, but seventy times seven times (Mt 18:21-22).

In Matthew's twenty-fifth chapter the entire basis on which our life will be evaluated is in terms of love: did you feed, visit, clothe, love me? We know that, but somehow we fail to connect it with our life of the vows. At the end of our lives, Jesus, our judge, will not (if Matthew is correct) ask whether we had sexual relations with anyone, or how many hours we prayed, or how many vows we took (though, hopefully, our answers to these questions will help us to answer positively the really important question). He will ask us whether we loved anyone.

So the vows we take, and celibacy in particular, are as valid as they free us to love, broadly, deeply, honestly those the Lord sends us.

LOVING SPECIFIC PEOPLE

Now it would be easier if it were true that we can love in general, but it is not, and we cannot. We could, perhaps, say with Lucy in the Peanuts cartoon, "I love mankind; it's people I can't stand." But to love really means to choose to care about specific individual people, men and women, good and bad, nice and not so nice. It means being vulnerable to them, able to hurt them, and to be hurt by them, and, more importantly, to call them to life. It means not being afraid: "Perfect love casts out fear" (1 Jn 4:18). It does not mean that our perfect love takes away our fear, but that God's love for us makes us less and less afraid to love concrete, specific human beings.

Jesus in the gospels is portrayed as saving all people, but specifically by loving John and Martha, Mary and Lazarus, and Zaccheus, and you and me. He was able to change lives because he cared about people. To do so he was able to be deeply hurt by them: "Could you not watch one hour with me?" (Mt 26:40), or "Will you betray the Son of Man with a kiss?" (Lk 22:48).

NOT NAIVE

As I write these lines I do believe deeply in what I say, but I do not want to appear to be naive. I realize that the religious who try to live this out, to love as God loves them, will encounter problems. They will need to become extremely prayerful (i.e., aware of God's deep personal love for them) if they are to truly love human beings and not try to hold on, to control, to possess, or be possessed by them. The longings of their human, sexual natures will arise, confusing good and healthy relationships. This will happen when least wanted, least expected. Because they are not Jesus, they will fail, as they try to learn to be celibate lovers. But these failures can at least be Christian failures, in the right direction, a falling forward rather than a falling back, and we can learn from them and go on.

Too often the Church, or a community within the Church, has judged and punished those human frailities occurring in the person honestly trying to learn to love, and not even noticed those failures of distance, coldness, and aloofness that destroy the Church and Christ's call to union so that the world can believe. We decide to expel the very apostolic young man admitting to homosexual tendencies, generally under control, and ordain men with no close friends, who, in fact, fear intimacy.

In every generation of religious life there have been too many crusty bachelors and mean old maids masquerading as celibates, going to their graves without once letting sex rear its head. Too often love was squelched in the process, and they witnessed to nothing but will power. What the world needs, the witness we are called to place alongside the sacramental witness of committed married love, is that there is a human possibility of loving and not having to possess or be possessed, a human possibility of loving and not holding on or being held on to. We are called to witness to a love that is one facet of the love of God for his people, a love that moves over rich and poor alike, over the beautiful people and the not so beautiful, over the alive and the not so alive.

I do not want to minimize the risk involved in living such a project. We risk involvement and pain, risk even sin and separation from our community, risk, in myriad ways, the cross. But I would emphasize that the risk involved in any other project is perhaps more grave. For it is the risk to fail to be a Christian, to fail to love at all. As John Courtney Murray pointed out many years ago, in choosing not to love anyone particularly, personally, uniquely, we risk never loving at all, never being alive at all, never letting Jesus be alive in us.

THE NEED FOR PRAYER

Let me emphasize a point already made. No one can fulfill in any successful way the project of becoming a celibate lover without a deep, enduring life of prayer. No one can reach out in an effort to really care for other human beings unless they know day in and day out how cared for they are themselves. It is only since God first loved us that we are able to try to love one another in his fashion. We cannot become celibate lovers if we are trying to make up for the absence of this love of God for us by the multiplicity or depth of our relationships with others. We cannot give what we do not have.

THE NEED FOR COMMUNITY

Finally, this vow of celibacy is a vow that only becomes Christian, only ultimately is possible within a community. A religious promises to support others in their project, and to accept, even to demand support herself. How often it is sadly the case that a religious struggling to love and yet be integrated within one's overall commitments finds herself or himself isolated from or judged by the community. How often we fail to reach out a hand to someone hurting, believing it to be none of our business. How frequently has every community talked of other things at meetings.

We talk, for example, endlessly about poverty: simplicity of life, personal budget, personal or communal lifestyle concerning clothes, travel, or recreation. And we easily and often discuss and debate the obedience involved in a discernment process, in corporate versus personal apostolate, our mission from Church and community. And these are good things to discuss. But how rarely we talk about our corporate struggle to become celibate lovers.

This struggle rarely surfaces except between intimate friends. Generally we bury our fears of temptations, failures and successes, and struggle on alone. Too often we seem to be the only ones struggling while the dimming vision seems unique. We search out a director to do what our next door neighbor could better accomplish if only she were not afraid, or he were more sensitive, if only they would listen, care, share their own bent or broken dreams. In fact, it seems to me that the possibility of living out a loving celibacy is in direct proportion to a community's ability to talk openly about the subject. How few communities provide such support.

My point in all of this is simply to insist that the vow of celibacy is a part of the overall communal commitment and communal project. Our convents, rectories, religious houses must be homes where brothers and sisters challenge each other to laughter and to love, where failures are accepted and hope is nourished. The witness we give is given together, founded on the great love God has, not just for me, but for us, from which we turn together from a deeply shared life to a work of service together.

I began by saying that we can never know how we are doing unless we are clear on what it is we are trying to do. I suggest that this essay indicates a neglected part of that project. If we agreed and helped each other along the path, all of us who seriously try to be religious people could distinguish how we are progressing better than we have been able to do in a long time.

Sponsa Regis, April, 1944

Religious Friendship

C.O.

In considering the matter of religious perfection, we must not overlook the problem created by our normal human capacity and desire for affection. We give much time and thought to the curbing of our tongue, to the discipline of our eyes, to the mortification of our inconsidered actions, to the restraining of our impetuosity of hand and foot; but what about our hearts?

We do not leave those outside the cloister as the Orientals leave their shoes before the doors of their houses. Our hearts are always with us, even though we be religious, and if we fail to understand them, if we have no principles to guide us in the important matter of our affections, we are in for a great deal of suffering and even, possibly, tragedy. To make the topic I am treating very clear, we shall try to answer the question, "What about friendships within the religious community?"

Let us first get an idea of what we mean by love and affection. Love in its strictly philosophical, purely spiritual sense means the will to do another good, to be benevolent, well-willing towards another. Thus does God love his creatures. Thus the saint, repelled and sickened by the leprosy of a dying outcast, loves that poor individual for God's sake and tries to alleviate his sufferings.

Ordinarily, however, we do not think of love in that purely spiritual sense. Our usual concept of love is of something warmer, something more vital: in other words, physical love or affection. Of course, as long as the emotion we are considering is true love, there will be that desire in the lover to do good to the object of his affection, although the desire to benefit the other may be mixed up with motives of self-interest.

Love, as sung by poets and experienced by humans, is a more complicated affair than that clear, calm, philosophical love. The affections and

197

their attachments are often hard to understand. Usually our affections are won by some excellence, real or imagined, in the person beloved such as grace of form or figure, beauty of countenance, sprightliness of conversation, wit or sympathy.

In this matter of physical love, the important thing to understand is the innate power and activity of the affections. Except in the case where age or experience or voluntary training has made a person master of his affections, not a great deal is needed to awaken and attach them. The ancients represented Cupid, the god of love, as a blind boy; they thought him blind because oftentimes people show the poorest taste in picking objects for their affections; they thought him a boy because sensible or physical love is inconstant — flaming up and burning out overnight.

The affections are not bad in themselves; they are evil only when they make us act unreasonably. God planted affections in our hearts, gave us this ability to love sensibly for a very good purpose. The purpose of this faculty is to cement society together. It is God's will that man perfect himself through association with his fellows. Family groups and larger communities are kept united chiefly through the mutual affections of the members. God wants us to use our affections — but sanely, according to the dictates of common sense.

Let us get clearly in mind that we have in our personality a power that drives us on to attach ourselves to others who in some way appeal to us; it is a power that seeks also to attract others to ourselves. As long as we are alive and conscious, our affections will seek objects to fasten upon, will rejoice at manifestations of affections shown us, will be hurt by the coldness and hostility of others. Now we can repress our affections with such a strong hand that they may seem to be deadened. Certainly that is possible, but that way lies abnormality. The crabbed, eccentric, caustic, sour, critical individual is he who through the tricks of fortune or because of a mistaken idea has starved his capacity to love and be loved. Excessive repression of the affectionate side of our nature is an extreme to be avoided.

The other extreme, which is just as vicious, is undue, irrational cultivation of our affections. This is where the problem chiefly touches the religious life. We have said that the affections were implanted in the human frame by God to assure the well-being and continuance of society through which the human race would achieve its development. Now the foundation of society is the family, and therefore it is principally towards the creation of this basic unit that the affections, especially in the young, are directed.

If people had to reason themselves into marriage, how many weddings would there be annually? Not many, we may confidently suppose. The young person of marriageable age and tendencies, that is, the individual who through lack of age, experience, or voluntary training is emotionally immature and unstable, is so constituted that he is practically swept along on the tide of his affections. It doesn't take much to set the youngster mooning. Blond tresses, blue eyes, a tilting laugh, a big yellow tulip pinned against a pastel-shaded bodice — and he feels that the world can't go on without the object of his affections. He is driven on by sentimentality and feeling to attach the loved one to himself by gifts and speeches; he becomes possessive and restrictive, jealous and demanding.

The affections, especially of young men and women, but of older people too, in varying degrees according to their emotional maturity, normally act in the manner just described. Physical or sensible love is of its nature disposed so as to bind two individuals into the closest possible association.

Now when a young man or woman decides to surrender the right to marry and for the love of God takes the vow of chastity, such a one does not by that act shake off the affections and their normal way of acting. Therefore, every religious starting out on the path of perfection must under pain of spiritual distress and mental turmoil recognize the absolute necessity of securing control of his affections. Our hearts will reach out with importunate, demanding hands for affection. We have to understand that our affections must be directed, dominated, harnessed to our new supernatural state of life.

Unless we face this task of supernaturalizing our affections — and are willing to pay the price asked — there is a very real possibility that we will develop attachments which are supernatural neither in their motive nor their manner of expression. The classic name, as you know, for such an unreligious love affair, an attachment due to inordinate sentimentality and uncontrolled emotion, is "particular friendship."

Would that particular friendships were less frequent than they are or were less disastrous in their effects on both the individual religious and the community in which they occur. As regards the individual, particular friendships at their best result in inquietude of mind, irritability of temper, and spiritual stagnation; at their worst, they are the cause of perversion and unnatural sin. As regards the community cursed with particular friendships, they sow uncharitableness, quarrelsomeness, and even open enmity and dissension. At the miasmic breath of particular friendships, the fair and lovely garden of religious community life withers into a sere and blackened waste.

A particular friendship is something that cannot be concealed in the community; sometimes it is betrayed even to outsiders to the scandal of all concerned. I remember being told how quite a number of years ago a group of novices visited a community of teaching Sisters. One of the Sisters took the novices through the school and convent. She paused at one room to speak at length about the young Sister who taught there; she went into detail on the virtues, ability, etc., etc., of the Sister concerned. Later she brought this Sister down to introduce her to the visitors, and as she made the introduction, stood with one hand resting on her friend's arm. The visitors were just innocent novices, who aren't supposed to notice things, but all of them noticed that!

The mild and gentle St. Francis of Sales, who was always sweetness and light, has some very harsh words in regard to particular friendships, words you would hardly expect to hear from so kind a counsellor: "Cut them off," he says, "break them, rip them out; don't stop to unravel these foolish love affairs, but crush them; you must not undo these knots, you must tear and hack them." It would be difficult to find more forceful language in the whole range of ascetic theology.

But why must we resort to such force, to such painful methods? Why get ourselves in a condition where such terrible measures are necessary? After all, the religious is master of his religious destiny to a very great extent. He came freely to embrace the life of perfection; certainly it should be his sincere wish to understand the principles of the religious life and to put them voluntarily into practice. Of course, if the superior detects the existence of particular friendships in the community, he must try to eradicate them. Otherwise he would fail in his duty to both the community and the individuals involved. But why should pressure be necessary? Why call for the pound of cure when the logical thing is the easily grasped ounce of prevention?

The religious is an intelligent person — usually above the average — a person, moreover, endowed with supernatural faith, sanctifying grace, and common sense. Mortification of our sensibility and training of our affections is a necessity if we would achieve that degree of emotional stability required for our vocation. Control of the affectionate part of our nature should be as normal an objective for us as is mastery of our senses and of our unruly imagination.

But there is a price to be paid for this emotional stability, and generosity is demanded. Our affections, as I have pointed out, are insistent in their seeking for an object upon which to fasten. One of the implications of the vow of chastity is that we cannot allow them to focus with restrictive, exclusive, possessive force upon any one individual — that is part of the sacrifice for being a spouse of Christ.

Thus each one of us has a job cut out for us. Have you ever observed how grape vines grow in a vineyard? The poor vines seek support and so send out tendrils, pale green, slender, frail hands, which curl around anything they find. If they chance on the framework provided for this purpose, all is well, and the vine reaches up. But sometimes the vine touches the ground and the groping tendrils clasp dry sticks and futile stones, things that serve as obstacles to the vine's growth up into the sun. Our hearts are like those vines; our affections are like the tendrils of the grape, always reaching out, always searching. That is the nature of human affections. We religious must be the vine-dressers of our hearts, not cutting off the tendrils of our affections — that would be folly — but seeing that they clasp the true supports of the supernatural life.

The question now is: how are we to go about it? Discipline of the heart consists in a two-fold activity: First, we must keep our affections free from exclusive attachments. Whenever we see ourselves growing too fond of any one individual, desiring that person's company inordinately, having our thoughts taken up by that person almost entirely, it is time to grip the reins of our run-away affections and bring them into control. No creature must be able so to play with the heart of a spouse of Christ. Since our affections are so active, it is to be expected that a certain amount of repression would be necessary. Thus, we must avoid any sentimental expression of our likes, any manifestation that shows an exclusive, absorbing devotion to a certain person. We may long to have tete-a-tetes, to exchange confidential messages, to see that our affection is returned in a special way; but we must not give way to such promptings of sentimentality.

This discipline of the heart is hard; for some it is a crucifixion; others are happily spared its intenser agony. The repression of our affections may be as painful as pulling barbs out of our flesh, but believe me, it is necessary. At this point of our spiritual development the shadows of loneliness close down upon the soul. Sometimes the novice in the way of perfection grows panicky: "Will I always have to be tearing my heart, will I always be racked by this terrible loneliness?" Patience; be of good cheer! This is but a passing phase of your development into a saint of God; this is the travail that must accompany the spiritualization of the affections.

The second phase of the discipline of the heart is the directing of our affections to objects worthy of our high calling. I said, it is as foolish to try to repress our affections entirely as it would be to cut off the tendrils of the grape-vine. If the blind tendrils are reaching out to clasp things that will keep the vine weighted on the ground and thus ultimately spoil the fruit, disengage them gently, patiently, and place them about their proper support.

Our affections will exist as long as we do; they must spend themselves; the reasonable thing to do is to direct them to objects that will be helps to the soul. The first and pre-eminent object of the affections of religious is our Lord and master, the Word Incarnate, our divine friend, our lover, our spouse, Jesus Christ. It may be that we shall have to cling to him in the darkness of faith, without any light of consolation. But his Sacred Heart is a true human heart, understanding, tender. It will not always be easy, but we can pour out our affections upon Jesus unstintingly, and he in turn will draw us ever nearer to himself.

In the next place, we must try to direct our affections toward the members of our community indiscriminately. Each one of us has a capacity for friendship if we but choose to exercise it. There is a wealth of joy and deep happiness to be found by cultivating the friendship of those wonderful persons who have left the world to follow Christ even as ourselves. We should like to be with our associates; we should be sincerely happy in their company. When a religious tells me that he finds community life a cross to carry, I immediately think not that his community is at fault, but that that religious has some personality problem that he is hedging himself about with — a fence of self-pity, of uncooperativeness, of gruffness, of gloom and criticism. In this matter of directing our affections towards the members of our community, let us never forget this principle: "Make your friendships extensive rather than intensive."

If the problem of educating the affections with its two phases, namely, repression of undue manifestation of special, exclusive liking for any certain individual, and direction of our affections towards our Lord and towards our associates in general — if that seems difficult, remember that there is a goal to be won well worth the effort. With the help of God's grace and the exercise of a little common sense we can become personalities of balanced, controlled emotions.

We may have our periods of loneliness, our temptations; but usually peace will reign in the little kingdom of our heart. Certainly from the practical angle, the effort required to attain a certain religious detachment, a measure of general amiability, is greatly preferable to the hell one goes through by giving free rein to the promptings of sensibility and to the bitter restlessness of irregulated emotions.

With all this in mind, can we, will we, have special friends? We can, we will. I have been hammering at the necessity of restraining the natural development of exclusive, absorbing, sentimental attachments. They are a plague, a cancer, a revocation of our absolute dedication to Christ; they must be avoided; they must be warded off by repression of the little ingratiating acts, the gifts, looks, conversations that become lovers rather than religious with a vow of chastity; they must be torn out of our lives if they have mushroomed into being.

But once we have learned to control our affections and are master of our emotions, we shall find that the blessing of sincere friendships will be ours. There will always be certain persons who are more in sympathy with us, whose likes are similar, with whom we can talk and feel that we are understood, to whom we can go for impartial advice, who will ever be interested in what concerns us. And certainly we shall enjoy their company and rejoice in thinking of them as friends. But this friendship, as Fr. Tanquerey points out, "instead of being passionate, absorbing and exclusive like particular friendships, is characterized by calmness, reticence, and mutual confidence."

True religious friendships are God's own special gift to those who for love of him have sacrificed false attachments. But most of all, the reward for discipline of the heart is greater love of God, greater holiness.

Sisters Today, May, 1978

Overcoming Problems in Friendship

Sister Jane F. Becker, O.S.B.

Among the many liberations that religious women have experienced in the years since Vatican II, one of our healthiest changes has been our acceptance of friendship. Close friendships between one Sister and another or between one Sister and a lay woman have become basic values in our way of life. They are so established that they are even taken for granted where they once were regarded as suspect.

This growth, however, has not come about without problems, as friendships often develop in which one or both individuals are frequently preoccupied, worried, jealous or otherwise upset with the relationship. Sometimes friendships are apparently quite satisfactory and meaningful to the individuals involved, but are a source of aggravation to other community members. These tensions can give friendship a bad name, even in the midst of a general willingness to accept the positive value of relationships.

THREE TROUBLE SPOTS

My intent in this article is to deal directly with troubled relationships. In no way do I want to undermine friendship; rather, I hope that by facing and working through problems we can free ourselves for even more meaningful relationships.

There are three trouble spots which I will consider: first, the confusion of friendship with dependency; second, the fear of homosexuality; and third, the conflict between the friendship pair and their community. As a clinical psychologist serving other religious women, I have seen these concerns surface frequently. Whether an individual Sister contacts me for therapy or a whole house meets with me for community building, the desire to build better friendships is a common goal.

I will also limit my comments to friendship with other women since heterosexual relationships already receive their fair share of attention in the literature. Almost everything said here, of course, would apply to heterosexual friendships, but a special discussion of the bond that two women can share will bring a needed perspective absent in current literature.

FRIENDSHIP IS GOOD

Let us start with the basic axiom that friendship is a good, a basic value to be sought. In fact, intimacy is one of the most life-giving experiences a person can have; through relationships one becomes fully human, fully a social reflective being. The most mature person is the person most capable of deep, intimate, faithful relating. Problems which develop in relating are solved only by developing the ability to relate more intimately rather than by backing away from relationship. I reject the position that starts out, "Relationships are good, but. . ." Even in celibate life one should be able to say "Relationships are good, and. . . " and proceed to explain how the development of intimacy can bring one to a more profound and meaningful living of celibacy.

Although it may sound trite to say that friendship is good, in practice we do not seem to believe it. Our first thought when we encounter a problem in a relationship is to assume that the friendship has gone "too far," that the couple are in "too deep," spending too much time together, etc. While elements of this position may be true, let us consider what amounts to the opposite position. Suppose we begin by examining problem relationships as friendships that have not gone far enough or deep enough. What would that mean?

When a relationship starts to create trouble for a Sister or for her community, we might ask whether the relationship is stuck at some early stage of relating. For instance, ambivalence about one's feelings, questioning of the other's motives, and testing of the other's fidelity are all problems that crop up to create trouble in relationships. These tensions all belong quite appropriately to the initial stages of a relationship when the pair are getting to know each other and are first deciding to take each other seriously.

When this ambivalence or this lack of trust shows up repeatedly in a relationship of some duration, when there is jealously, fighting and preoccupation with the friendship, then we might suspect that one or both of them is not yet capable of sustaining the trust (or trustworthiness) that true and lasting friendship requires. Basic deficiencies in one or the other individual — liabilities such as a poor self-concept, the inability to trust oneself or others, the inability to commit oneself, or the inability to communicate feelings — all can hinder the relationship from moving to more authentic depths of trust and mature interdependence. Of course, no one can be totally, consistently trusting or trustworthy all the time, but a growing relationship will be characterized by a series of recommitments at newer and deeper levels, a series of moves forward, while a stagnated relationship will crash repeatedly on the same rocky issues and at the same level.

THE FEARS OF FRIENDSHIP

One approach to understanding friendship problems is to examine the various fears that intimacy evokes. Fear is a common enough experience for all of us. Whenever we worry or become preoccupied about a relationship (or about any situation in our life) the underlying emotion is usually fear, a fear even of some catastrophic outcome looming on the horizon. Worry is in fact a cue that one is afraid of something, even if the feared object is not consciously known. When a client or friend is obsessed with some vague worry, I like to surface the hidden fear by asking, "Well, what is the worst, most outlandish thing that could possibly happen here?" Once the fear is recognized and verbalized, then steps can be taken to deal with it.

What are the fears which arise in friendship? The first fear worth considering is the fear of intimacy itself, the fear to trust. This is the most common fear but the one on which I will say the least. I am more concerned with two fears that surface when love becomes confused with dependency. The dependent-prone individual finds intimacy painful because she is preoccupied with the fear of the loss of love. Her more independent friend may be troubled with the fear of being smothered by the relationship. A fourth fear is one common in our society, the fear of homosexuality. And finally one finds a very legitimate concern in religious communities, the fear that community may hurt friendship or vice versa.

THE FEAR OF INTIMACY ITSELF: DARE I CARE?

To trust or not to trust is a universal conflict. Erik Erickson made Trust versus Mistrust the very first development crisis of infancy, but I believe the real test of one's willingness to trust comes in adult friendship and love. Many people must consciously struggle between whether or not to give themselves over to a developing relationship. In spite of the universality of this tension, many individuals go through the experience wondering if they are the only ones who have ever been afraid to love, thinking they are the only ones who have ever been unable to trust. John Powell reflects this concern in the titles of his popular works, *Why Am I Afraid to Love?* and *Why Am I Afraid to Tell You Who I Am?*

This fear of trust haunts a person in the repetitious phrases that keep running through her head. She might worry, "Dare I care about someone that much? What will happen to me if I get too close?" Or another worry would be, "If she really knew me, would she still like me?" Underlying the first question is the fear that the other will let me down, that trust never pays. She will lose interest in me, leaving me high and dry with my wounded feelings. She may make fun of me, telling others my secrets. I may end up caring for someone who doesn't care for me or trusting someone who is not trustworthy.

Such fear may be based on past experience. Most of us have experienced some disappointing relationships, and some people have been let down more often than was their fair share. In the face of such past hurts, a new relationship demands taking risks, giving people a second chance, gambling with the possibility of being hurt again. This is a call to trust others in spite of fear.

The second worry, the worry that she could not like me if she really knew me, has the fear behind it that *I* will let her down. I will disappoint her. I am not worth her care. She will see in time that there is nothing to me after all. She will discover that underneath I am an evil (selfish/angry/incompetent) person. Or she will discover that I am weak and need her very much, and this pressure will scare her away.

This concern may again be based on rejection experiences. Here, however, the individual has concluded that the "breakup" was her own fault. She has put the blame on her own personality. Entering new relationships demands the same risks and gambles mentioned above, but for this individual it also demands revising her self-concept. This is a call to love oneself more, in spite of past opinions.

I mention these fears to indicate clearly that worry about a relationship does not automatically mean that something is amiss. Rather, risk is part of the price that one pays for love. Obviously some relationships do end up in pain and disappointment, and risk is definitely involved in any choice to be open to another. Because the risk is real, hesitancy about trusting others is quite common and normal. Of course, one hopefully learns to choose risk over fear, but some hesitancy can be expected. The individual who recognizes the risk involved has an accurate perspective on what intimacy entails. I can accept that view in contrast to another person who may falsely assume that true love will take away all risk and insecurity. In this latter case the individual may be confusing love with dependency.

DEPENDENCY: TRYING TO CAPTURE LOVE

When a relationship between two women has gone "too far," it has usually gone too far in the direction of dependency and not far enough toward a supportive but respectful interdependence. The confusion of intimacy with dependency is a particularly female problem because much of our socialization has taught us that some day we would find our true love who would love us and take care of us. While little boys were being taught that they would eventually have a wife and children to take care of, we were being told the reverse, that we would have a husband to take care of *us*. Entering the convent did not blot out those assumptions that one of the joys in life is finding a way to hand over all worries and responsibilities to someone else and to return to childhood dependence.

"Caring about" another is not the same as "taking care of" the other. "Caring about" can happen between any two people who are attuned to each other's needs and actually do help each other in various ways. This caring involves neither taking over responsibility for the other nor forsaking one's own integrity to keep the other secure. When either of these two conditions is present, one has a case of "taking care of."

This can happen between a stronger and a weaker person, for example, between a parent and child. The stronger person must assume responsibility for the other's welfare because the weaker person, the child, is not capable of taking care of himself or herself. The child is too inexperienced, too imprudent, too stupid to survive alone. The stronger will also make sacrifices. A parent might forego the opportunity of a career advancement for the sake of the child. Some marriages are kept intact only "for the sake of the children." The child's welfare is the primary commitment, as the parent's life becomes adapted to meet the child's needs.

When an adult becomes dependent on another adult, she is often not aware of all that is happening. She may unconsciously be expecting the other to take care of her, to pay close unfailing attention to her needs (take responsibility for them) and to meet her needs (sacrifice self) at all times. This expectation is often quite unconscious. When the friend does not live up to these expectations of total commitment, what emerges is a pattern of worry, jealousy, doubts and fear of the loss of the relationship.

While the relationship might have begun as true friendship, a compulsive need has entered in. She feels jealous and resentful. She feels totally dependent on the other's love, yet she finds herself doubting whether the other cares. She watches for little signs that the relationship is still on solid ground; but, of course, no evidence is forthcoming to "prove" once and for all that the other cares. Her expectations that the friend should take better care of her come through in disappointments: "She should have spent my birthday with me; how could she consider her house meeting more important than me? (I need her more than her house does.)" "She should have been more sensitive to me (in spite of her headache; I am weak and need an understanding ear more than she does)." Because the friend does not take care of her in particular instances, the friend does not seem to care at all. This preoccupation is painful and can be destructive to the individual's peace of mind and ultimately to the relationship.

UNREQUITED LOVE

Oftentimes a person will feel that she loves her friend more than the friend cares about her. This perception ought to be explored. Is it accurate or is there another explanation? If one's friend does care less about one, then the individual is in a situation of authentic but relatively unrequited love. She can strive to be honest with the other when the other hurts her by stating how disappointed she feels, but she is really in no position to demand that the other care more. This realization is hard medicine for anyone to take. It goes back to the simple fact that love is a gift and cannot be demanded of anyone. It can be invited but not forced. If one is repeatedly disappointed by a certain "friend," she may have to admit that she has a false image of the other's care which is simply not founded in reality.

Suppose now that the other *does* care. Suppose B does care about A but A experiences B as not caring. How can one explain this discrepancy? Two possibilities come to mind.

First, it is possible that both friends care about one another but A expresses love differently than B. Different personality types speak in different languages. Some people remember their friends' birthdays; other people do not even remember their own. Some people write letters; others pick up the relationship where they left off six months ago. This communication problem is common in male-female relations, as the sexes tend to have different ways of showing love. When opposites attract within a community, the same dynamic is certain to occur. Learning to speak (or at least understand) another's language naturally clears up much confusion about how the other feels.

A second explanation might be that my friend cares about me but I have a more dependent form of love. She might care for me but have no interest in depending on me to fulfill all her needs; she does not seem to "need" me because she asks no great sacrifices of me, nor does she want me to worry over her. "I'd do anything for her. I really try to please her. But I don't think she really cares." Sometimes she chooses other people over me; sometimes she seems too absorbed in her own concerns to notice mine. She does not want to be dependent on me, nor does she want me dependent on her.

"She needs me" or "I need her" is a statement of dependence, not of love. Maybe I also love her, maybe not. Need often leads to resentment, as in the case of the teenager who still needs his parents but resents them for it. The degree to which two people are dependent on each other is not a good measure of the degree of their care and concern for each other.

SOLUTIONS FOR A DEPENDENT RELATIONSHIP

A frequently proposed solution for the dependent relationship is to get out of the relation completely. Usually this is a poor solution. The individual may experience even more pain over the separation, she will probably fail to resolve her confusion of dependency with love, and she could end up with neither support nor love. Quitting the relationship can be a way of running away from one's dependency needs rather than trying to work through them. When one finds oneself repeatedly pained by this pattern of jealousy, fear and unfulfilled need, then one ought not blame a particular relationship for all the trouble. Rather, the individual may have a deeper dependence/independence problem which calls for help from a knowing counselor or friend.

One route that a person can take to overcome dependency is to attempt to broaden one's social contacts while still keeping up the older, closer relationship. The person who is overly dependent on one friend often gives evidence that she is fearful of reaching out to new less-than-totally-secure relationships. She may not know how to initiate and develop other friendships. Perhaps she has come to prefer the safety and ease of remaining with the best friend. After awhile other relationships shrink to nothing, and expectations for the first friend escalate to superlative heights. Her friend is now pressured to satisfy all her intimacy needs. Her friend becomes community, colleague, counselor, sister and mother. Obviously the development of alternative sources of support would take the extra pressure off the overloaded relationship and allow it to develop more naturally, with less dependency involved. Development of such social skills and social "guts" is possible only through painful risk-taking, through coaching from a counselor, or even through classes in assertiveness training.

A second line of action concerns the relationship itself. Frequently the boiling point in this relationship is reached when A begins to doubt B. She wonders whether B really wants her along, so she stays home and waits to be asked. Or she becomes jealous of B's relationship with C and starts to complain. These feelings indicate difficulty in trusting. These feelings are hard to squelch and cannot be attacked directly.

Sometimes, however, one can *act* in trust in spite of one's *feelings* of distrust. Doing so is not always possible because one is acting counter to one's feelings and this demands risk, self-discipline and coaching again from a perceptive third-party friend or counselor. Sometimes one does have the courage to join B without being asked — and this results in a delightful, affirming evening in spite of one's prior feelings of distrust. Usually acting in trust results in experiences that validate a relationship, while acting in distrust results in arguments, the withholding of positive feelings, and a decrease in good times together.

One obstacle to this line of action is that acting in trust, without proofs of the other's care, takes considerable independence and maturity. To act in a trusting manner is to act independently. To do so is to "take care of" oneself while caring for the other but no longer demanding that the other take care of me. The decision to operate this way is never made easily because it obviously means letting go of older, more secure ways of relating. However, to take such action is to say that one values the relationship too much to let dependency destroy it. And the individual who is willing to make such changes in her own behavior certainly shows authentic love for her friend and herself.

THE OTHER SIDE OF THE STORY: SHE'S SMOTHERING ME

The counterpart to a jealous friend is the individual who has been told that she does not love enough. She thought she cared about her friend, but her friend wants more. "I think I care about her, but I don't want to spend so much time with her. I like her but I have other friends, too. I like her but I don't want to have to 'prove it.'" A variety of bad feelings and fears can emerge depending upon how the individual interprets this difference of opinion between the pair. The person who wants a less encompassing relationship may feel angry with her friend for all the pressures and demands being placed on the relationship. She may feel guilty knowing that she cares about her friend but finding herself reluctant to give as her friend demands. Her anger may be accompanied by the fear of being smothered. Or she may simply wonder whether she is in the wrong, fearing she is selfish or incapable of true caring.

Let us assume that she is actually a caring person but that she is feeling pressured because her friend has confused love with dependency. She is being asked to enter a dependent relationship and to take care of all her friend's needs, but she is resisting the pull of dependency and asking for a different kind of friendship. In a community setting she will have other friends who have a place in her life as well. Other friends may relate to aspects of her personality which she cannot share with her one troubled friend. Her friend may find it difficult to believe that they can have a good relationship without ever fully knowing or possessing each other.

RESTRUCTURING THE RELATIONSHIP

Again, backing out of such a relationship is not always the best decision. Ending the friendship may be necessary if the friend's demands are simply too strong to cope with, but often one is able to restructure the relationship into a more mature, less dependent relation if one has a clear idea of her preferred kind of friendship and some ideas of how to get there.

The "how to" is chiefly a matter of holding one's ground, communicating clearly why one is being so insistent, and also communicating clearly that one does really care for the friend in spite of a refusal to give in to her requests. Anger will subside if one is confident that she cannot be manipulated into a relationship she does not want. If she has a clear understanding of the difference between "caring" and "taking care of" she can avoid feeling guilty when her friend begs for a more exclusive or possessive bond. For example, she will have to cope with her own irrational guilt when she says "no" to a demanding schedule of visits or when she refuses to apologize for other relationships that make her friend jealous.

Although women may be more inclined to dependency, the pull toward an overly demanding relationship is not unique to female friendships. Stanton Peele elaborates on this same kind of relationship while confining his examples to dating and married couples. In *Love and Addiction* he gives several stories of couples who, once they found each other, cut off all other social contacts, spent every free hour together, and relied totally on each other for their social needs. One student, for example, had his girlfriend sit close by while he studied so that she would be available to rub his back, listen to his groans and bring his meals as needed.

Stanton's theory is that dependent individuals become addicted to relation-ships the same way one might become hooked on liquor or other drugs. These addict relationships are distinguishable from true love, however, on the basis of many behaviors already mentioned above.

Throughout this discussion I have used the terms "love" and "friendship" interchangeably. Some readers may find this annoying or confusing since most of us have quite different meanings for the two words. However, in both long-lasting true friendships and in troubled depen-dency relationships the feelings are often more intense than mere friendli-ness. In real friendship the friends do care about or love each other. In dependent relationships the dependency pull is also often erroneously labeled love. One feeling which I do not mean to imply in the term "love" is sexual attraction. Sexual feelings are another area and need to be treated separately. They demand consideration, nevertheless, because fear of homosexuality is an emerging concern for many in our society and may be an emerging fear for religious women as well.

HOMOSEXUALITY: I THINK I'M GAY

In some same-sex friendships the fear arises of whether the relation-ship has "gone too far" in the direction of evoking sexual feelings. I fear that if I express how much I care for her then "She'll think I'm homosexual." In an alternate form, this is the fear that if I face how much I really care for her then "I think I'm homosexual." This question may surface without either person having the faintest desire for physical sex — yet the fear of homosexuality occurs. How come?

A current cultural development is inducing many people to suspect homosexuality in situations where they would never have considered it before. In recent years the public media have made a concerted effort to surface our attitudes toward the topic, to acquaint the public with the fact that homosexuality exists and that homosexuals are real, ordinary indi-viduals.

This move in the media reflects a development in our society at large, in that people are becoming more knowledgeable about homosexuality and less resistant to thinking and talking about it. What we observe in counsel-ing situations is that as people think about it more, many raise the question of whether they themselves are potentially homosexual. This question can surface even in the midst of no evidence. Counselors will often conclude that the person is not homosexual at all, but to tell a person "don't worry about it" is simply to submerge a deep concern, one that will continue until the individual examines it honestly. And, of course, in some instances true homosexuality will be present.

BACKGROUND THEORY

Some background theory can help us understand this better. Although there is much controversy over definitions of homosexuality, I prefer to use one from the social learning psychologists. According to this school we are born with diffuse sexual energies which are focused, early in life, on the other sex. This focusing occurs by subtle sex-role training which inhibits all our attractions toward the same sex and emphasizes all our attractions toward the other sex. By this definition we are all capable of same-sex attractions but we have repressed them and failed to develop them. A homosexual or a lesbian was not born that way but developed, through early conditioning, in a different direction.

Strictly speaking, we should not even call one person a heterosexual and another a lesbian since we all have a degree of capacity for both feelings; but practically speaking most people have strong preference one way or the other. In other words, while only a minority of women may be lesbian, homosexual feelings are possible in all of us; homosexual feelings are not "queer." Most of us have so strongly repressed these feelings that we never become aware of them, but as the larger culture encourages more acceptance along these lines, then consciousness of these feelings is more likely to arise.

Several factors increase the probability of a celibate having questions about her own sexual orientation. For one, it is not unusual for a woman having troubles with sex (e.g., a girl frightened by intercourse or a wife disappointed in her husband's style) to ask herself whether she is homosexual. Homosexuality may have absolutely nothing to do with her situation, but when she is not aroused in her current (hetero-) sexual life, she begins to wonder about herself.

A celibate may ask the same question because she may similarly have no clear evidence that she is heterosexual. She may have never found the sexual area particularly appealing. She perhaps has limited social contacts with men, and certainly has never "tested" her responsiveness in a physically sexual situation. When she finds herself strongly caring about and "loving" another woman, a friend, the issue becomes stronger.

SEXUAL FEELINGS

Sexual feelings tend to make themselves felt when we care deeply about someone; their arousal seems to be a natural part of intimacy. Women especially are able to blend love and sex to the point where they often feel no sexual attraction for someone they do not love. Although we have been conditioned from early childhood to let those sexual feelings surface into consciousness only when the loved one is of the opposite sex (and of an appropriate age), nevertheless sometimes the feelings break through anyway. So it is possible that on occasion a person feels sexually toward someone whom she loves deeply, even if sex is not a dominant theme in the relationship and even if the sexual feelings are never acted upon.

In the celibate, whose regular sexual outlets are limited, sexual tension may build up. Also, physical sexual responsivity apparently increases in females over the years, rather than diminishing as it does in males; it should not be surprising when a religious woman has sexual feelings for the first time many years after novitiate. (The total homosexual life-style, on the other hand, is usually entered into in late adolescence or early adulthood.)

Once a woman becomes concerned about her sexual orientation, a number of reflections feed her fears. She remembers "playing doctor" with other girls as a small child or having crushes on other girls in high school or novitiate. She may reflect that she feels indifferent to sex (with a man) or has a repugnance for thinking about (male) genitals. She may note that she was once a tomboy, has more masculine interests than other women, has always tried to imitate her father, or even wishes she herself were born male.

She is correct in recognizing that any one of these characteristics may be significant in a particular lesbian's history, but she is wrong in assuming that any of these prove homosexuality. These are quite common experiences, frequent in the lives of both homosexual and heterosexual women. For example, the high school same-sex crush is a normal stage in the adolescent girl's development. Also, a significant number of women feel inhibited about sex and sexual parts of the body. Finally, a majority of women say they were tomboys as children.

EXAMINING THE EVIDENCE

When a religious woman is plagued with questions about her own sexuality she would probably fare best by facing her thoughts directly and examining the evidence thoroughly. She is most likely to find her questioning unfounded in the end, but she will not know this until she has thought the issue through carefully. A spiritual director or friend who is too quick to reassure may only expose his own fear of the subject and fail to give her the supportive environment that she needs to examine these concerns. Reassurance is certainly in order, but the message should be one of "Let's explore these questions together and get to the root of why you are worried; let's get to the truth together."

Homophobia, the fear of homosexuality, is a far more damaging feeling than homosexual desires. Homophobia is reflected in the feeling of repugnance one experiences in talking (or reading) about homosexuality. Homophobia is the feeling that causes one to shrink from ministering to a lesbian or from listening calmly to a counselee who wants to discuss homosexual concerns. Homophobia can also make one hold back from ordinary friendship when the feelings get intense, as mentioned above. This condition needs to be overcome.

Sometimes a woman, in questioning this area, may come to realize that while she is basically heterosexual, she still has some sexual feelings for one or more same-sex friends. If she is homophobic, hating and fearing homosexuality, she will hate herself for these feelings and have a very difficult time accepting them. Yet these feelings are hardly cause for self-condemnation. The first task of her counselor or director is to help her acknowledge her fear and repugnance toward such matters.

AN IMPEDIMENT TO COMMUNITY?

Community personnel argue about whether a homosexual orientation is an impediment to community living. I tend to believe that a homosexual orientation need not interfere. Homosexual desires in a homosexual are no stronger than heterosexual desires in a heterosexual; both individuals can be celibate.

The celibate lesbian is in a situation analogous to her heterosexual Sister working with males. The latter may have colleagues whom she finds sexually attractive; she may have to sort out feelings in the midst of turbulent (but growthful) relationships. But if she is committed to community and celibacy, she remains so committed in the midst of temptation. In fact, the preservation of celibacy is a poor excuse for avoiding contacts with the other sex; one's value of celibacy should be more solid and internalized than that. The homosexually oriented Sister may find the same challenges within her own community. Yet like her mature heterosexual Sisters, she should also be able to handle relationships in a mature way.

The critical variables here are not one's sexual orientation but one's ability to maintain mature celibate friendships and one's commitment to this lifestyle. Research with lesbians suggests that this choice of celibacy is even more possible for females than males since even active lesbians are less interested in the physical aspects of their relationships (and more interested in psychological intimacy) than are their male counterparts.

RELATIONSHIPS THAT TROUBLE COMMUNITY

To treat another's friendship as a problem seems almost blasphemous today. When I hear someone criticizing friendships my first reaction is suspicion of her. I suspect that she is the last of the great witchhunters of pre-Vatican days, still out stalking the infamous "particular friendship."

When many of us entered religious life, special friendships among Sisters (or worse, with lay women!) were discouraged and sometimes forbidden. Many of us have at least one traumatic instance burned into our memories, an instance of a fellow novice publicly censored for secret meetings with a professed Sister, or an elder Sister reassigned for unexplained reasons and amidst assorted rumors and tensions. There was the feeling that something sinful and abnormal had taken place. Occasionally homosexuality was hinted at, but more likely this suspicion was not necessary; the friendship alone was enough to cloud the atmosphere.

Then as other aspects of religious life were being renewed, our attitude toward friendship shifted considerably. We breathed a sigh of relief and friendship came out in the open. Sisters renounced their years of self-sufficiency and acknowledged their very natural desires to form meaningful bonds with one another. The witchhunt was over.

It is out of this context that Sisters have developed another problem, their reluctance to define *any* relationship as unhealthy and their hesitancy to call another Sister to accountability when her friendships are creating tension in the community. Probably because we have seen how harmful the negativity of the past was, we find it quite difficult to be negative about any friendships today. Witness the guilt you feel over your dislike of some friendship of a fellow Sister — and your reluctance to confront her about what it is doing to you (or to her or to the house).

I suspect that this guilt and reluctance stem back to the old days, the days when we first discovered that friendship was not evil anymore. I suspect that we each made an unconscious vow back then that "Never again will I criticize another's friendship; never again will I witchhunt. Forgive me, Lord, for I have sinned." The only problem with such an unrecognized vow is that it now confuses us when we have to admit that friendships do indeed have their problems. I have no intention of starting a second witch-hunt, but perhaps it is time to face the fact that others are capable of both healthy and unhealthy relationships, and that a caring person has the right and obligation to say something when she sees a Sister harming herself or the group.

TENSION STARTS TO BUILD

Concretely, the tension starts to build when a Sister (or a whole house) begins feeling guilty for thinking badly of another Sister who seems to have something special going with a third Sister (or a lay woman). She has a friend and friendship is good; yet I find myself constantly tense about their relationship. When they get on the phone I think, "Not again!" When we plan a house meeting or community outing, I unfairly expect her to have an interfering engagement with her friend. When her friend is visiting, I feel awkward. I compare my feelings with the feelings I have for other friends in the community, other Sisters' phone calls, other interfering engagements, and I chastize myself for being so uncontrollably negative toward her. I wonder what has happened to my charity, and I blame myself. I remind myself that I, too, have had some immature friendships in the past and "nobody's perfect."

As with the other fears we have already considered, there can be various reasons for this negative feeling toward the friendship pair. Perhaps this is *my* problem; perhaps I am jealous of the two individuals or have a personality conflict with one of them. Perhaps I still disapprove of any friendships that are formed outside community boundaries. But it would be shortsighted to assume that the friendship is always in the right and the onlookers are always in the wrong. There are friendships that are harmful to the local community or to the couple involved.

APPROACHING THE PROBLEM

How do we approach the Sister whose friendship we find trouble-some? Mixed in with our annoyance over someone's relationship, we often make judgments about the Sister's motivations and maturity level. We may accuse her (in our hearts) of dependency, rejection of us, rejection of community, even homosexuality. I hope I have been clear so far in indicating that dependency takes a big share of the blame for problem friendships among women; homosexuality is a much more remote possibility. However, even the accusation of dependency can be unfair.

Before jumping to confront a Sister on motivations which we have merely inferred from her behavior, it is probably better to be clear first on the specicfic behaviors that actually upset us. These behaviors can be annoying in themselves. They might be signs of dependency but they also might be simple results of insensitivity or poor judgment. Let us consider the behaviors first.

FREQUENCY OF CONTACT

When communities describe the kinds of relationships that have created house problems, two behaviors are mentioned. The first is easy to guess — frequency of contact between the two friends. "She's always with so-and-so." Punching time cards on a relationship is of course dangerous business. Why should her happiness annoy me anyway: am I just jealous of her free time? Or judgmental about her dedication to the apostolate?

While one needs to move carefully in making judgments, I believe frequency of contact *is* suspect under certain conditions, namely, when it becomes either inordinate or harmful to the house. By harmful I mean that it becomes very difficult to share community with Sister A because she is always out of the house or off in another room with B. Community events become difficult to plan because Wednesday night A is going over to B's house, Thursday they teach CCD together, and this weekend B is spending the night(s) here. And A is very reluctant to cancel out some engagements for the sake of the group.

By "inordinate" I mean the kinds of contacts that would lead me as a psychologist to suspect that the two were almost "courting" each other — with daily phone calls, letters every other day, or every weekend spent together. I do not mean courting in a sexual sense but with reference to the initial stages of some relationships when two people are inclined to play games with each other; they are trying to entice each other into a more intense relationship. A healthy friendship does not need that much reassurance. In many cases this amount of time devoted to one friend would also limit one's ability to share community, carry on one's job, pray, keep up creative outlets, and be responsible to other friends all at the same time. At this point the individual is limiting herself and shifting her priorities. Friendship always takes time, but this amount of time is unusual.

SECRETS

The second behavior that upsets communities is secrets. "When I am with them I miss a lot of the conversations because they keep using words with private meanings, making side remarks or facial expressions that only the two of them understand." This is the language of lovers — secret nicknames, a repertoire of special meanings because of intimate times they have shared together. (Again I do not speak in a sexual sense.)

One needs to be cautious of accusing another of secretism if one is really feeling jealous. In any healthy relationship there will be levels of intimacy that are not shared with others. However, most friendship pairs do not make us uncomfortable about their closeness. Perhaps the couples who annoy us are somehow flaunting their secrets or putting more stress on them than what we do in our own relationships. Or we may be upset because this exclusiveness, like the time factor, makes the Sister inaccessible to us. We do not like to be left out; we want to get to know our Sisters better. But "when they talk like that they leave me out. I can't get to know either one of them as a friend if they always come attached to each other."

SORTING OUT MOTIVES

In confronting a Sister about my reactions to her relationship, it is of ultimate importance to sort out my own motives. What *aspect* of her behavior actually concerns me? If I approach her about the time she spends away from community and she reminds me that I spend an equal amount of time away at a second, part-time apostolate, then I have not been clear on what really bothers me. Maybe I approve of people sacrificing community for apostolic reasons but not for recreation (another whole issue on which to examine oneself). Or perhaps my concern is deeper, an uneasy feeling that she no longer cares about the group or that she is losing interest in religious life or that she is in some vague way "in trouble."

If my doubts are that vague, I have the choice of clarifying them further with my own director or close friend, or of being very honest with her about my vagueness. "A, I feel uneasy about your relationship. I worry for you, that you are somehow drifting away or heading for trouble. I can't say it any clearer; it's intuition, but can you help me understand this feeling any better? I worry about you." At this point I have communicated worry rather than resentment, and she may be more open to responding. Also, if I am able to be clearer about my data, then I can point out to her the particular behaviors that concern me.

Underlying our rather intense reactions to these relationships may be a concern over whether the Sister is homosexual. I do not mean that we consciously, willingly suspect sexual interest between the two friends, but our strong gut reaction sometimes suggests that we have stronger unconscious fears about the relationship than what our reason admits to. We are, after all, able to trace seeds of homophobia in the old prescriptions against touching one another or visiting another Sister's bedroom (although no one ever told us the reasons for these rules).

While a counselor or very close friend can be helpful in opening this question with the Sister, I do not think it is the business of a local community to make judgments on whether the Sister's feelings for her friend are sexually based. That area is too sensitive for a productive confrontation. One would do better to deal privately with one's own sensitivities around sex and to limit confrontations to observable behaviors such as time priorities and exclusiveness. After all, behavior is the level on which another community member is accountable to us. Feelings are neither right nor wrong in themselves; any reservation we have about another Sister's feelings may be based on our own homophobia, not on valid judgments about her morality.

DIFFERENT DYNAMICS

I believe that most friendship problems in religious life can be accounted for by dynamics other than sexual motivation. Dependency is one factor already discussed at length. Also, the joy of a new friendship can be enough in itself to sweep one away with enthusiasm. And why not enjoy the relation to the full for a while so long as one is able to recognize when she is beginning to neglect community?

At particular times in our life we may also be more inclined to get overly absorbed in one relationship at the expense of community. Something so simple as shyness on one's first assignment can cause the timid soul to withdraw into the comfort of a single close friendship. Depressions can also cause us to turn more to our most intimate relationships. Depression can result from an intolerable apostolic situation, a major failure in one's profession or studies, loss of a sense of purpose in life (the existential crisis or the mid-life crisis), loss of a parent, or the first awareness of aging and death.

One may not even be conscious of the depression if it is a slowly developing one, yet one begins to act differently as one's need for support and consolation increases. There are also years in community when one's living situation is so hopeless that the only means of survival is to get out of the house more frequently. This situation is understandable if one recognizes that she is not really living community that year, if that year is an exception to her general life pattern, and if she is taking steps to "reenter" community eventually.

THE RESPONSIBILITY TO CONFRONT

If we are serious about building community and caring for each Sister's welfare, then the responsibility falls to us to say something when we see a Sister harming herself or the group. When we see a Sister drifting from community, limiting her personal and professional growth, causing herself undue tensions, or causing the group undue tensions, it is time to speak. Hopefully we care enough to accept the pain and risk involved in doing so.

Confronting another Sister is difficult, especially since we usually wait so long to say something that by the time we go to her we are already experiencing considerable annoyance and resentment toward her. In order to approach her in a truly caring manner it is important to back off and reflect on her position first. We can assume that as a committed religious she feels some responsibility to share community with us and to care about our feelings. There is the foundation — her commitment and concern — for our letting her know if something bothers us. Hopefully she does feel concern for us even when she misreads our feelings. Possibly she is totally unaware of how her choices affect community. Even if she does sense the tension, she is unlikely to be the one to open the topic for discussion. After all, such openness takes real courage and few of us are strong enough to invite confrontation when we suspect that we are at the center of the problem.

The confrontation can and should be supportive. That is, we need to speak out of concern as much as resentment. Our responsibility is to share our perceptions and insights, to be of objective assistance if she is fooling herself. We also need to offer support by inviting dialogue or being a listening ear. A Sister who feels that others do not approve of her friendships, which are a very significant part of her life, is likely to withdraw more and more from the group unless community members directly and verbally offer their support.

We read psychological literature to understand ourselves better or to "psyche out" others. If the other individual is someone we care about, then we hope the new-found clarity will help us help her, for insight does often bring new solutions. If the individual is someone who annoys us, then we gain a superior feeling in being able to label her "deviancy" or "pathology." A certain satisfaction is gained in being able to describe someone else's problems in correct psychological jargon. Although the temptation is ever present, this latter use of psychological insight is not particularly charitable. The purpose of this article was to bring insights to human relationships, particularly as they effect community life. Hopefully these insights will be used to help rather than to condemn others.

Sponsa Regis, September, 1945

Obedience

V.S.

*"You are my friends if you
do the things that I command
you"* (Jn 14:15).

The things that God commands us are things that he enjoins upon us or forbids, either personally, as in the decalogue, or through his representatives, that is, through men invested with his authority.

The principle, the model, and end of all authority is God. Created or delegated authority but reflects the power received from the divine generator. "There is no power," says St. Paul, "but from God, and those that are, are ordained of God." All authority, therefore, is of divine origin. God alone can confer it. "We have many superiors, but only one master, Christ."

God could give all his commands personally, if he so willed, but normally he prefers to govern men through men. He would have St. Paul receive instruction from Ananias, the wise men from Herod, St. Joseph from an angel. He himself submitted to this arrangement in his incarnational life from his birth to his passion and death. Divine wisdom decreed this representative government, since man as a social being must live in continual relationship with his fellowman.

In the natural order of human society there exist three types of delegated authority: domestic, that exercised in the family; professional, the authority of employers; and civic authority, that vested in the state.

In the supernatural order, we have ecclesiastical authority, that established by God in his Church. This authority is exercised by the hierarchy and all duly elected or appointed superiors in sacred orders, or in religious congregations approved by the Church. As religious, consecrated by vow to a life of obedience, we are chiefly concerned with this latter type.

The Sovereign Pontiff is the head of all religious orders. He is their first and highest superior. Through him, as Christ's vicar on earth, the divine will is transmitted to religious, sometimes directly, more often indirectly through the bishops and legitimate superiors.

Every superior is entrusted by God with something of his own authority. To the superior, as to the apostles, Christ says, "He who hears you, hears me."

Monsignor Gay calls this human investment with divine authority a sort of sacrament wherein the outward appearances of man remain poor, weak, mortal, but contain God. This substitution of human agency for the divine personality he likens to the transubstantiation of the host in the holy Sacrifice of the Mass.

Such a comparison does not seem overdrawn when we consider the sacramental system which God has established in the universe, wherein he uses material things as means of reaching the soul through the senses: creatures as signs, symbols, and channels of invisible grace. Christ himself was the living sacrament of God, for behind the outward appearances of his human form, he concealed the splendor of divinity.

Obedience unites us to God like a perpetual spiritual communion, causing God to abide in us and us in God. "He that keepeth my commandments, abideth in me and I in him."

It is clear, then, that by submitting our wills to divinely constituted authority, our actions assume a supernatural character. They become acts of the virtue of obedience, for obedience is defined as a supernatural virtue which inclines us to submit our will to that of lawful superiors in as far as they represent God.

Obedience, being founded upon divine authority and directed to our sovereign creator and last end, must be honorable, ennobling, and sanctifying. It is supernatural, for by faith it is from God-in-her that we receive orders of our superiors. It is God-in-her to whom we submit our will and judgement. It is God-in-her whom we see behind the human accidents of her command, whom we recognize in her government as the principle of authority, and whose arrangements we accept as the will of God.

This supernatural obedience, this faith in obedience, like a needle, draws after it the thread of divine love. Love becomes the mainspring, the motivating principle of our acts — love founded not upon feelings but upon reason which urges us to immolate our self-will and to fulfill to the best of our ability the will of God.

It has been said that God is where his will is. If this is true, then the obedient soul must walk hand-in-hand with God. In each prescription of obedience she can grasp the outstretched hand of Christ and say, "It is the Lord." This hand may be the hand of Jesus crucified and may leave upon her palm the stain of blood, yet it is the hand of a loving Father extended to support and bless.

Faith and love make obedience sweet and easy. Without them, obedience may become but a galling yoke. Without faith we see in superiors only human beings, with human faults and frailties. With faith, we see Jesus Christ hidden behind a human personality as once he walked the earth, disguised beneath the garb of poverty and contempt.

With faith, all that is little and insignificant in our daily routine becomes sublime and worthy of God. Eating, sleeping, recreating, manual labor, all become meritorious for heaven, even as do those actions, holy in themselves, as assisting at Mass or teaching Christian doctrine. In fact, we may please God more by washing dishes in the kitchen through obedience than being rapt in ecstacy in the chapel through our own will.

Blessed Claude de la Columbiere, writing to his sister, a religious, once said to her: "It should not be more difficult for a good religious to obey a child in the office of superior than the founder of the Order, were he living, or our divine Lord himself, were he to undertake the government of the house."

Out in the world there is little supernatural obedience. Among the people of the world obedience can scarcely be styled a virtue. It is usually force, mercenary, performed through necessity, diplomacy, or as a matter of fact. Look at the submission of factory workers, men in the armed service, government employees, women in society who are slaves to style. All of them must practice some sort of obedience, but what place has the supernatural in their lives? Only selfish motives drive them on to submission to the yoke of authority. They must cater to the will of higher officers, to the whims of their clientele; but their obedience is slavish, revolting, without merit.

The obedience of faith and love, however, elevates man to the state of the blessed, for it is given to a divine King. It establishes man in the security of divine wisdom. It frees him from evil passions and the perverse influence of human nature, destroying that baneful evil, self-love, which St. Thomas claims is the chief obstacle to union with God.

Obedience admits man to intimacy and family relationship with Christ and his blessed mother, as he promised when he said, "Whosoever shall do the will of my Father, he is my mother, and sister, and brother."

Obedience enriches man with merit, restores to him the grace and dignity lost by the disobedience of the first man in Paradise, and entitles him to the eternal reward of the children of God. "Not every one that says to me, 'Lord, Lord' shall enter into the kingdom of heaven, but he that doth the will of my Father who is in heaven, he shall enter into the kingdom of heaven."

Obedience advances man in perfection by making his will one with Christ's, which union is the essence of sanctity. It enables him to give to

God the most pleasing sacrifice, the oblation of that master faculty, his own will.

Obedience is a guarantee of sainthood. "Whoever obeys is sufficiently prayerful; whoever obeys does enough penance; whoever obeys practices union with God, for one is a thousand times more united with God in the midst of a crowd where he is through obedience, than hidden away in his cell through self-will." Such was the teaching of Dom Marmion, that great lover of obedience, who esteemed this virtue so highly that he left the ranks of the secular clergy and entered a monastery in order the better to practice obedience and submit his will to the guidance of a superior. "To do nothing when so commanded," he said, "is to do one's whole duty, while to do much through one's own will is to do nothing towards one's spiritual progress."

The soul shielded by obedience has nothing to fear: nothing to fear from God, whom she obeys in his representative; nor from the devil because all hell together is powerless to injure the soul that clings to authority; nor need she fear her fellowman since they, too, are creatures of the great King who sooner or later will take the part of the obedient. Neither need she fear her own weakness, because she leans on divine strength; nor death, for the obedient religious already has one foot in paradise.

Obedience, like a high-priest, consecrates all our actions and transforms them into Christ-deeds, stamped with the seal of eternal life. Whether we be given work in the classroom, the kitchen, the laundry, the garden, or the chapel — it is all the same, if in every place we give to God the sacrifice of our own will.

Obedience does not imply a lack of initiative but requires that all be submitted to obedience. Neither does it hinder individuality. Rather it tames the soul's wilfulness, chastens its pride, purges its motives, enriches it with wise counsels, hinders its precipitancy as well as its tardiness, checks its self-conceit, and adorns strong natures with the supreme merit of humility.

A religious community in which obedience flourishes is like a great symphony orchestra under the skilful direction of a master musician. Each player executes the part assigned upon his particular instrument with eyes intent upon every movement of the director, that he may be always in tune and may contribute his part to the harmony of the whole orchestra. Each instrument is important and necessary, whether it be the harp, the flute, or only the bass drum or tinkling cymbal.

Obedience in the religious life is the music of souls, chiming the harmonies of the Holy Spirit. As the strings combine with the wind and percussion instruments in the orchestra, so the religious unite in one harmonious canticle of praise to God. Each contributes her individual notes to the grand symphony. Each is bound up in the rapturous unity of divine concord. From this mystic orchestra, whose composer and director is Christ, celestial music rises to the throne of God. Through the vaults of heaven rings out the glad melody of obedient souls who have caught the hallowed vibrations of the Holy Spirit. And so the heavenly Father hears, coming up from earth, the same harmony as in heaven — the created echo of the eternal symphony of God.

To these happy troubadors, how applicable are the admonitions of St. Paul: "Be ye filled with the Holy Spirit, speaking to yourselves in psalms and hymns and spiritual canticles, singing and making melody in your hearts to the Lord."

Obedience is the essence of religious life, just as the obedience of Christ to his minister in the consecration of the Mass is the essence of the holy Sacrifice.

The vow of obedience is the most fundamental, the most important, the most meritorious, although the most difficult of the three vows of religion. It demands faith and requires greater sacrifices, but brings greater peace, order, and security than poverty or chastity. By obedience we practice greater humility and trust toward God, greater charity toward superiors, and greater loyalty to our community.

From the motherhouse all the provinces and missions draw their religious spirit, their unity, vitality, and strength. Like dutiful children, they turn to this fountainhead for counsel, encouragement, and guidance. The branches never cease to be nurtured by the sap of the mother tree. United in love and obedience, they go on safe and secure, doing the work of God in the vineyard of the Church.

Like a formidable army they march shoulder to shoulder in the ranks of Christ's advance-guard, seeking the conquest of souls for their leader and the conquest of heaven for themselves. Would we know how victory invariably crowns the works of religious, let us listen to St. Ignatius when he tells us that divine Providence is bound by contract to those who have vowed obedience and is no longer free. God *must* show love and solicitude for those who have entrusted themselves to his keeping and thrown themselves trustfully into his arms.

The fervent community is characterized by regularity, loyalty, and childlike obedience. The subjects are united with their superiors in filial confidence, cheerful obedience, and devoted love. Criticism, fault-finding, murmuring find no place in such a community; much less signs of insubordination, so hateful even in the world and so detestable in the house of God.

Sisters Today, March, 1970

A Contemporary View of Obedience

John P. Keating, S.J.

Vatican II is acclaimed as the Council that rediscovered the laity. By stressing the fact that the People of God *is* the Church, the Council reminded
every baptized person of a personal call to holiness, of an individual
initiation into the priesthood that every Christian shares, of a responsibility to work with the community to plan and direct the progress of the
Pilgrim Church. In a word, the Vatican Council proclaimed that lay
Catholics are first-class citizens of the Catholic Church. It did not simply
parrot this truth, but enunciated a conciliar theology of the laity that was
previously unavailable.[1]

It is an obvious rule of rhetoric that emphasis on one truth overlooks
the development of other important considerations. While the Council
reasserted the important birthrights of the laity, critics observe that the
Council Fathers failed to provide contemporary, progressive, logical insights into consecrated religious life. Religious communities were exhorted
to initiate a program of renewal by the decree *Perfectae Caritatis* and the
directive for its implementation, *Ecclesiae Sanctae*. Religious greeted the
prospect of renewal with enthusiasm. But newborn insights about the
vows, so characteristic of the Council's approach to the laity, were lacking.

Religious life is not lived in isolation from the whole life of the Church.
Renewal of any segment of the Church is related to renewal of the life of the
Church in all its dimensions. Theological considerations the Council of-
fered on the life of the laity are easily translatable to religious life. While the
laity are reminded of their responsibility for the well-being of the People of
God, religious recall their personal responsibility for the health of their own

---

[1] Martin H. Work, "Introduction to Decree on the Laity," *The Documents of Vatican II*,
Walter M. Abbot, S.J., ed. (Guild Press, New York, 1966) 487.

religious congregation; when the laity are told to assume active responsibility with their pastors in directing the Church, religious correspond with this exhortation by actively cooperating with superiors in renewal of their institutes; and when pastors are instructed to seek and heed the advice of their people, religious superiors cannot overlook the application of this counsel to the government of religious communities.

Since the Council clearly underscored the concept of active participation by all Christians in shaping the destiny of the Church, it was not surprising that religious began to rethink the role of authority in the life of the vows. As theorists swung the pendulum from paternalistic rules to government by the will of the community, most discussions on obedience focused on the obligation of superiors to seek and discern the will of the community. Everything was discussed and, by and large, superiors tried to take the pulse of their communities through these discussions.

Religious knew that they were consecrated to work for the People of God, to bring Christ back to the world he saved. The goal was simple. It was not new. But the most effective way to Christianize a contemporary world became the topic of endless debate and discussion. As gross anachronisms disappeared from their lives, religious grew optimistic in the effectiveness of their renewal. But as obvious issues became resolved, more subtle topics demanded examination. Progress slowed, patience diminished, and temporarily veiled frustrations reappeared.

Before the initial renewal of religious life it was relatively easy to single out the deficiencies of a congregation. With obvious targets gone, it became difficult to articulate meaningful criticism. Critics assumed a scatter-gun technique and all phases of the life came under attack. Without viable, pinpointed goals to seek, such criticism could and did become corroding.

First in the line of fire stood obedience. Superiors seemed to put up stop-signs that frustrated progress. Obedience itself became an anachronism. But, rather than ramble in generalities, ideas must be concretized. Obedience had to become personalized. Was it the vow of obedience in general or the vow as personally lived that deserved criticism? Was the spirit of the vow practiced, or was easy conformity over-valued? Were injustices, attempted under the guise of the vow of obedience, winked at or conscientiously represented? These are questions that focus on areas of religious obedience that must be considered.

ONE CAUTION: THE VOWS ARE MYSTERIES

When examining the evangelical vows, one caution must be offered. Ladislas Orsy rightly observes that discussions on the vows, including obedience, are necessarily about mysteries.[2] The vows are mysteries. Obviously everything about obedience cannot be exhaustively explained. Neither can anyone fully explain poverty or chastity. Each of the vows is a

---

[2]Ladislas M. Orsy, *Open to the Spirit* (Corpus Books, New York, 1968) 131.

personal invitation of Christ which forms the mystery of religious life. When obedience is vowed, the religious vows to live a mystery. Unfortunately, the word "mystery" elicits the tendency to check discussion: it is something not talked about; it seems classified theology like "Trinity" or "transubstantiation." Discussions about mysteries only foster confusion.

A negative understanding of the concept of mystery, whether the Trinity or vowed obedience, can stifle investigation and deaden insight. When positively understood, a mystery is so pregnant with content that it invites study and demands reflection. Thus a growing insight into the vow of obedience must take place.

Religious are historical people with questions about religious obedience in the present setting. Religious life is developed from the tradition of the early Church, with most congregations articulating this tradition through a 12th or 16th century religious genius. The history of religious life has offered various insights into obedience. These insights must not become a stagnant, frozen awareness. Contemporary religious must contribute freshness to the meaning of obedience if they are to live their responsibility to the historical progress of the Pilgrim Church and its institutions. If any period of time does not rethink tradition in its own terms, it is unfaithful to tradition itself.

This is not a question of throwing out everything that has preceded the present time. Such a consideration would be nonsense, a foolish denial of historical process and progress. To build on and progress from former insights to a new awareness of obedience is the vocation of every religious community. The letter on obedience that St. Ignatius wrote in 1553 is a monumental document. But he would be the first to deny that it was intended to be the embodiment of the ultimate thought on obedience.

DOES OBEDIENCE HELP OR HINDER ME?

Christians know they have a vocation to sanctify the world. This is the vocation of every Christian, and certainly of consecrated religious. The baptismal commitment of a religious to this task is deepened through the vows, not changed. Consequently, the religious vocation is meant to consecrate the world to Christ. The one question that a religious must always ask himself is, "How does obedience, vowed in religion, help me sanctify and save the world with Christ?"

If a religious has to respond that it does not help at all, that in fact it might even slow down the process, but that it is "better" to be a religious, he is only fooling himself. If religious life is going against anyone's prime Christian vocation, it is meaningless for that individual. But if someone can say that he can more effectively work for this People of God, that he can more effectively bring Christ to the world through the vow of obedience, in a particular community, then he is talking about deepening and fulfilling his Christian vocation.

There are numerous places to begin an examination of the tradition of obedience in the Church, but none could be safer than a return to the New Testament. A difficulty that this approach presents is that vowed obedience is not found in the New Testament.[3] The vow of chastity can be seen as recorded in the New Testament through the personal invitations that Christ extends during his personal life, as well as through the elaborate reasoning of Paul on the subject. The Suffering Servant, Christ's personal invitations to sell all, the practice of the early Christian community recorded in Acts, all point to a New Testament foundation for vowed poverty. These are ways to imitate Christ.

But the question of vowed obedience, obedience to a superior in the Church and not directly to God, is a different matter. Christ's obedience was to do the will of the Father, as Mary's obedience was directly to do the will of God. But obedience to another human as a way to evangelical perfection cannot claim the New Testament as the source of its validity. How then was such a vow concocted as an essential for religious life?

To say that vowed religious obedience is not found in the New Testament is not to say that Christian obedience is not found in the gospel, nor that Christian obedience is not *the* lesson of the New Testament: to follow the Father's will. Mary's prerogatives were contingent on her "fiat": let God's will be done. The very act of salvation was done in obedience, even to death on the cross. Obedience to the will of God is the essential of Christian living.

When we look at the Christian community in the New Testament, the basis for vowed religious obedience emerges. Christ lived, died, and rose to send his Spirit to the community of believers. It was the community, gathered together, that discerned the direction and development of the gospel message. The Acts of the Apostles is simply a recording of the community's reliance on and guidance by the Spirit. The inspiration for every move the community made, whether the sending of Paul on a journey, or that the religious purifications of the Jews were not binding on convert gentiles, is attributed to the work of the Holy Spirit. The community was conscious of this guidance. They were confident in their activity because they were confident that it was Spirit-directed.

DISCERNING THE SPIRIT

How was this direction discerned? The community gathered together — not just individually climbing a pillar and deciding, "I got this light, you got that light, this is the way the Spirit is directly guiding me" — they came together, prayed together, and then the community decided: "So it was that after fasting and prayer they laid their hands on them and sent them off" (Acts 13:3). Paul traveled in the context of community. This is the very

[3]Karl Rahner, *Theological Dictionary*, Herder and Herder, New York, 1965, 155 and 320. August Brunner, "Religious Obedience Today," *Theology Digest* 14 (1966), 107.

important development that Christianity brought to the world: the will of God is discerned through the Spirit-filled community.

Vowed religious communities should be a paradigm for the larger Christian community. A community of Christian religious must decide in community through discernment how to operate to best accomplish the Father's will.

A simple contrasting of the individualistic aspects of Eastern religions with Christianity will highlight this added dimension of Christianity. Christianity does not simply lead towards personal union with God. Its focus is on the Pauline, living, visible body that we call "mystical," the one body of Christ operating effectively in the world. To find the will of God together through prayer that blossoms into perfect charity is the basis for all Christian religious communities. Obedience to the Spirit is the only obedience that religious vow, even though they vow it in a unique way: to pray and work in a particular community to discern and correspond with the direction of the Spirit.

The earliest form of religious life in the Church appeared with the fathers in the desert. Religious obedience that considered the superior in an authoritative type of role was foreign to these early communities. The fathers could properly be called "spiritual fathers," helping the people gathered around them to discern the direction of the Spirit. It was in the communitarian type of religious life that obedience, as we know it today, developed. It was not obedience simply to make the community function-able. The communities were established as ends in themselves. It was important to have a group of people trying to live to perfection the Christian life, and doing this together.

The need to work out the direction in which the Spirit was leading a community was evident. When considering the role of superior in such communities, the admonition of Saint Matthew becomes most pertinent: superiors should be servants, not like the pagans who lorded it over their subjects (Mt 20:25,26). The superior's task was, as Acts would suggest, to find and cooperate with the direction the Spirit was leading a community. Discovery of this direction demands that superiors look, listen, and actively consult the community of good people who have individually received the Spirit.

RESPONSIBLE MEMBERSHIP

The context is now set for an understanding of the vow of obedience. The individual freely chooses to enter a distinct religious community. The vow binds religious to work out in community a particular role in the life of the Church. Consequently, a major responsibility to the Spirit rests, not just with superiors, but with the members of a congregation. The individual must assume responsibility for the direction that a community moves. This is not to deny that the Church has approved a community, or has given the superior authority to make decisions for the community. This is precisely to affirm such thinking. Religious are in one community, trying to come together with one mind, articulated through superiors. But it is important to emphasize that the membership must be responsible for that articulation. The members and the superior equally possess the Holy Spirit.

This emphasis has caused most discussions of obedience today to focus on the role of superior. The insights of Vatican II concerning the individual person and his place in the Church has dictated such considerations. But beyond a simple personalism, when people have decided and vowed to come together in a community, they cannot talk simply of *my* guidance by the Spirit but have to look for the Spirit guiding a community. The role of the superior is one of discernment of spirits. In such a context religious obedience makes good Christian sense.

The only way the Church challenges the world to respond is through the concrete expressions that manifest it to the world. Michael Novak is quoted as saying, "Don't worry about preaching the gospels any more, because, after all, you can dial the radio on a Sunday morning and hear the entire gospel message." Students study biblical literature at the most sophisticated secular schools. The world "knows" what the message is. *The essential present need of Christian evangelization is concrete witness to what Christianity means.* Religious communities form a vital part of this witness. The various communities mirror the works and concerns of the whole Church. Each community makes a unique contribution by accomplishing the goals for which the individual community had been founded.

The direction of the Spirit should guide the communities to accomplish their unique roles; to witness to Christ in a particular way, whether by teaching, nursing, work with the poor, etc. Each community must be faithful to its role so that as a corporate unity the whole Church can witness to the multiform aspects of the gospel message and Christ's concern for man.

An individual community is intended to be a keen witness to one or other aspects of the gospel. What emphasis this would be personally each religious decided when he chose a particular community: "How do I live out my religious conviction? How do I best express myself as a Christian?" To choose a religious community is to choose the vehicle to best express a personal Christian commitment. Obedience is an attempt to assure that this community will faithfully follow the direction that the Spirit as leader and guide is setting. This direction is articulated through the superior so that the community can most effectively fulfill the unique role that it must play in the world.

A DISTINCTION: ORGANIC OR PERSONAL COMMUNITY

Such considerations naturally lead to a distinction that must be made in this area of obedience. In Robert Johann's terms, a community can be viewed as an "organic," functional, or operating community and as a "personal" community, or the type meant when discussing the value of a group of religious people simply living together.[5]

To confuse the organic with the personal community can lead to confused notions about obedience. An efficient school demands a principal, a boss to assign teachers to individual classrooms at particular times, to assure fulfillment of certain dictates of school boards and state regulations. In this functional situation the religious principal of a school, like the principal of a public school, is managing that school. He must ask his co-workers to supervise here, to teach first-year math, and to accomplish all the other minutiae of running a modern school.

Such requests should not be considered in the context of obediential commands. When a principal decides to throw out sociology or introduce Sewing II, the mistaken judgment can be made that such a stupid decision proves the inoperancy of obedience. The obedience structure has proved that it cannot work. A more realistic judgment of this situation is simply that the principal of this school made a stupid, functional mistake. It is true that a religious is working in a school through his vow of obedience and may well be somewhere else if he had not vowed obedience. Where a religious works, and the general directions of his life, are most frequently dictated by superiors cooperating with their communities. But to let the trivia of life blacken the total picture of obedience would be tragic. The functional thrust of a community should never usurp the values of the personal community.

The personal community highlights the importance of obedience. This community states that the Christian community is a value in itself; people united together trying to live the fullness of charity is good. The direction this type of community should follow falls under the competence of the superior discerning the guidance of the Spirit in his community.

The important questions for the religious are: How is this personal community growing in charity? How am I fulfilling the perfection of charity by living in this community? How is this community helping me fulfill the aim and goal of life as a committed Christian?

In asking questions like the above, we are immediately reminded that in such a community people cannot be considered simple pawns on a chessboard. This personal dimension in religious life makes it impossible for a community to function like General Motors. The personal dimension must be kept in the forefront of discussions on obedience if religious are even to pretend to form a religious community.

In such personal religious communities the basic responsibility of the superior is to make the individual members of the community as responsible as they can become. There are many insignificant things in the religious life that the superior should not meddle in through the name of obedience.[6]

[5]Robert Johann, "Authority and Fellowship," America 114 (1966), 591.

[6] Orsy, op. cit., 161: "Regulations may be necessary, but many of them are simply irrelevant for the kingdom."

Unlike the parent who should guide his children to maturity, the religious superior hopefully inherits mature people as his community. Canon Law cannot be the ultimate, iron-bound norm in such communities. Personal, prayerful decision made in individual cases must be the rule.

OUR FREE CHOICE

Religious have the responsibility to recognize the free choice they made when entering religion. Usually no one is put on a treadmill, automatically propelled into this or that novitiate and told, "Here is your institution and this is where the Spirit has led you; stay here." Entrance into religious life is an exercise of freedom. Real freedom is not simply to say that all the options are open. To talk negatively about freedom, the dozens of options that were denied in order to say "Yes" to one could be considered. In order to be free there has to be more than one option. Many things had to be denied in order that one thing could be done and done well.[7]

You can sit and dream about being a bird, a kite, or preaching like John Henry Newman. You can dream about it, but you cannot do it because you are not a bird or a kite or Cardinal Newman. A mature person learns to accept the present situation, the situation that he himself has created. A religious came to religion with a unique background, family, educational experience, and social contacts. All these things have built him into who he is. The biggest task to become mature is to accept this and then decide what to do. When someone entered a religious community, he did it because he thought that the direction a particular community was going was important. With this belief, he made a commitment to live in the unity of this community. He made a commitment to be obedient within the structure that he chose. To be a subject in a community means that one is very interested in the direction of his community, in his own life, but also has made a choice to live as a subject in a certain community.

Occasionally the extreme happens, when someone can honestly say that this particular community is violating the whole direction of the Spirit. In its renewal and progress a particular community can refuse to recognize the inspiration of the Holy Spirit present in it. If such a consideration is not a rationalization occasioned by a decision that went against a pet project, then the religious must conclude that he can no longer continue to live in such a community. To live in a community not in touch with the direction of the Spirit would be a violation of the prime obligation on which the vow of obedience is based. A direction contrary to the will of God can never be obeyed.

If, on the other hand, the community is trying to follow the Spirit, while there is a responsibility to tell the superior particular disagreements to ensure that he knows the total picture, in the long run, since the Spirit

---

[7] Cf. William Lynch, "The Problems of Freedom," *Cross Currents* 10 (1960), 97-114.

was freely followed in accepting a particular community, personal fallibility must be recognized and the possibility that a superior is correct accepted. St. Peter was not happy declaring the alteration of Jewish ritualism for gentile Christians. But he went along with the consensus of the people. Nobody likes to lose an argument or give up a cherished idea. But openness to the Spirit may demand such a course of action.

INTERIORITY AND MATURITY

If obedience is living in accordance with regulations due to an abiding fear of being caught in violation of the rule, it cannot really be called a virtue. Psychologists agree with St. Ignatius by saying that until motivation becomes interiorized, a person is not mature. Interiority is an essential of maturity. Obedience for the mature is not constituted by exteriors. If it were, at best it would be an amoral way of acting. Obedience is a most interiorized state — the state of fundamental conformity to the will of God in an individual life.

To place the emphasis in obedience on the action of the Spirit would be most dangerous without equal emphasis on a prayerful way of life that invites the Spirit to be heard. St. Paul must be taken seriously. To emphasize this point, a sharp dichotomy might be drawn: either follow the Law or follow the Spirit. If emphasis is on a pneumatological type of theology in religious life, then personal openness to the Spirit must be demanded. Otherwise it would be better to live according to the Law. The Law is discernible to the most opaque. The direction of the Spirit must be illumined by clarity that only comes through intimate openness and dialogue with him. This is prayerful awareness of the Spirit, or simply prayer.

In his letter on obedience, St. Ignatius urged all in a community to be of one mind with the superior. This would obviously imply that the superior has a tremendous obligation to be open to his community. Subjects must be equally open with superiors, even when it hurts, to accomplish such unanimity. If this is done in a prayerful spirit, the unanimity is not an artificial effect of an efficiently functioning corporation. It is rather the mind and will of Christ articulated in the community. Obedience is then not optional, but must evoke free assent from men dedicated to the life of perfect charity.

If this is how obedience is lived, how can it be irrelevant? How can religious life be irrelevant if its only purpose is to discern and accomplish the will of the Father? No one can program this will, nor can it be predicted where this discernment will lead religious in their renewal. The only thing that can be affirmed is that Christ will always work through his Spirit in truly Christian communities. The task of contemporary religious is to assure that their individual community is Christian, and that when the will of the Father is discerned, the community can gladly reply as a community, "Fiat."

Circus Godman

We're looking for you, Godman,
searching everywhere because we need you
to mend our Big Tent.
It's collapsing,
holes in it the size of lions.
We're thinking big,
expecting you'll show up soon
in the center ring.
We hope you'll be higher
than a skyscraper
and wider than a superhighway.
Or maybe you'll stretch over the earth
like a prairieland
and rise taller than Kansas corn.

We're scanning the skyway, Godman,
hoping to sight your large white finger
as you speed toward us like a jet.
Or maybe you'll be leading a long motorcade,
waving to everyone with your top hat.
Or spin like an acrobat
on a cathedral spire.
Or cut through the waves,
gleaming like a ship.
Or thunder out of the cannon
which sit like crows around Fort Niagara.
Or glide in
on the wind,
your robes billowing like sails.
Or maybe you'll ride over the Rockies,
you and your horse flashing in the sun
like foil.

Where are you, Circus Godman?

Sister Mary Lucina, R.S.M.
Sisters Today, December, 1972

PART SIX

WHOLENESS AND HOLINESS:

Helps for Health and Happiness

The emphasis on the vocation of suffering and the promotion of the Victim Soul apostolate in the early issues of *Sponsa Regis* did not imply that the journal was unconcerned with the spiritual, mental, and physical health of its readers. Far from teaching that sickness equals sanctity or that the answer to every ailment is to "offer it up," the editors and authors have shown a balanced approach to wholeness and holiness. The healthy, hearty religious who is able to count on her vitality in the often strenuous and demanding routine of prayer and work has always been the rule, not the exception. Convents have never come close to being identified with convalescent homes.

Excerpts from "Letters to a Scrupulous Person" by Father Roger Schoenbechler, O.S.B., contain the practical advice given for overcoming this all-too-common condition that plagued so many conscientious and sensitive religious. The prevalence of this "perfection syndrome" is indicated by the fact that the letters numbered eleven in the 1937–38 issues of the magazine.

Recognizing that his readers were living in "the age of nervousness," the founding editor treats of nervous disorders in his article on "Sin or 'Nerves'?" The Catholic chaplain of a Minnesota state hospital for emotional and mental disorders adds his own experience and expertise to the discussion of "Mental Health and Holiness." The need to screen candidates in order to better assess their basic mental health is considered in "Psychological Testing and the Religious Life."

Religious share the common condition of not growing younger. The importance of establishing and maintaining a healthy attitude towards aging is considered in "Planning for Retirement." Communities of Sisters pioneered in the planning and implementation of pre-retirement and retirement programs during the last several decades when removed veils revealed the quantity and quality of those "silver threads among the gold." Amid the how-to suggestions offered the aging, "How to Survive the Generation Gap" is good proof that good humor is a welcome asset for every age.

Since the proverbial ounce of prevention is still worth a pound of cure even in our inflationary times, a study of "Life Changes and Subsequent Illness in Women Religious" should help Sisters to remain healthy.

Beyond Tether*

There have been books so deep they would drown rivers
And pages green enough to grow leaves;
There are still words beyond history—beyond tether.

In the beginning, *logos;* the great hawk's hunger
Crying for a lost prize. Eden grieves.
There have been books so deep they would drown rivers.

We have only regrets, who are not carvers
In stone, whose lines the furtive spider weaves:
There are still words beyond history—beyond tether—

Where the eight-toed secret silk-spinning spider
Draws tongues in the stink of deeds.
There have been books so deep they would drown rivers

Of men; carrying epilogues like divers
To the rocks that bear the marks of our creeds.
There are still words beyond history—beyond tether.

The stones stand passive: chanted to icons, weathered
In the reign of ice, read by blind reeves.
There have been books so deep they would drown rivers.
There are still words beyond history—beyond tether.

Judith Neeld
Sisters Today, June–July, 1977

*Title poem of the New Jersey Poetry Society's 1975 Anthology.

Sponsa Regis, 1937–38 *passim*

Letters to a Scrupulous Person

Roger Schoenbechler, O.S.B.

Dear V,

For some time I have been thinking over the troubles of soul that you have been experiencing. You have frequently come to me and to others. You are cured for the moment, but are soon again face to face with the same or added difficulties. Readings have been given to you, and not a few words of advice and oral instructions.

SYSTEM NECESSARY. However, the whole treatment has not been so very systematic, and this is probably the reason why the effects have not been so lasting. Besides, the spoken word is quickly forgotten, For these reasons, I thought it might be well if I put down on paper just exactly what I want to say to you, and then you can ponder on my words as long as necessary to clear up your difficulties.

Furthermore, I thought it might be better if this were done by means of short letters which I shall send to you one at a time. Problems in the spiritual life must usually be solved step by step. We cannot expect a solution to come overnight nor in an instant, ordinarily speaking. Your case seems to be just such a one that requires the ordinary procedure, step by step. If you were to receive all of these instructions at once, they would fail to make the necessary impression. I therefore ask you to follow me in all patience and calmness from one letter to another.

CHILDLIKE CONFIDENCE. All that you need to do is to place a childlike confidence in me and render yourself docile and obedient from the very beginning, starting with the reading of this first letter. Your confidence will lead you to obedience, and obedience will lead you to cure.

It should not be necessary for me to add that I am on your side; I am working for you, with God's help to support us both. Remember this well. But

237

in return, you must surrender yourself completely to my advice in this matter of solving your problem. If you do this, I guarantee you that even in a brief course of time your obedience in this matter will be rewarded a hundredfold, and you will once more be able to raise your eyes to an all-loving God with the greatest childlike simplicity and confidence, so that the love and the goodness of God will once more, as of yore, thrill you with wonder and fill your soul with peace.

PATIENCE. Let us, therefore, embark upon this voyage together, trusting in the help of God and our own fervent prayers, both of us resolving to be patient no matter how stormy the voyage may prove to be. Because it may be a bit stormy, you must summon up all your courage, not for any special ordeal, but for the sake of the sweet peace and charity of Christ.

BE NORMAL. I do not want you to be thinking of this matter all the time. Especially should you guard against letting these letters or your problems interfere with your studies. Read the letters and reflect on them when you are more or less free from studies and work. As for the rest, continue to go about your daily life and work and prayer in the regular and usual manner. There is no necessity for you to take all this any more seriously than you would any other ordinary duty or detail of life. Let these letters simply be part of your regular means for attaining the goal you have set out to attain.

* * *

OTHERS HAVE SUFFERED AS YOU. You should know that the troubles you face quite regularly from time to time are not something unusual, nor are you the only one so afflicted. They may seem very serious to you at present or when they come upon you, and thus you may at times think that you are alone in the matter. But, you are not. Perhaps there are others around you suffering in a similar manner.

If this is not the case, then let me remind you that great and learned theologians as well as many of the saints of God, learned and unlearned, have had similar difficulties, especially in their younger years. You are therefore in some very good company.

YOU HAVE MY SYMPATHY. At times you may experience that others have little or no sympathy for your difficulties; perhaps you have thought this of some to whom you have gone, even of me, especially when I would lay down some stern alternative. You have perhaps also thought of times that others therefore do not properly understand you because they fail to appreciate the difficulty under which you are laboring.

I do wish to assure you, however, that no matter how stern I may be at times, I sympathize with you heartily. By this I mean that I fully appreciate and quite understand the heartaches you have been going through and from which I hope to be of some help in relieving you.

DON'T GROW WEARY! You may be tempted to grow weary of all this, and to think that I am not getting to the real heart of the subject soon enough. No, I am not stalling for time. I am merely trying to solve your problems step by step, and build from the bottom up. Firm foundations must first be laid.

BUILD COURAGEOUSLY, OBEDIENTLY, CHEERFULLY. To build from the bottom up, you must now prepare yourself for a short series of instructions. The subject matter which we shall begin to take up the next time may not be immediately to your taste. It is, however, very important. Accept it, therefore, courageously, obediently, and cheerfully.

* * *

You will no doubt have noticed by now that there is one word which I have not yet used in the foregoing talks. Yes, you have guessed it — scruples. I am not going to ask you for the present to accept my judgment immediately when I say that your trouble is mainly a somewhat mild attack of scruples that occasionally becomes very vexing for you and again disappears for a while, only to return repeatedly. The following will help you to see for yourself.

NOTHING SINFUL IN BEING SCRUPULOUS. It is not a sin to be scrupulous or worried. Scrupulosity is a spiritual indisposition of the soul, just as a headache or toothache is a physical indisposition of the body. Indispositions of soul or body last until the causes of them have been removed. In any event, we cannot ordinarily avoid all such indispositions. In the case of the soul, some people simply cannot help being worried or scrupulous, especially in their younger years. It is not your fault that you are worried and afflicted. Hence, there is nothing sinful in that fact, unless, of course, you had purposely brought about this state, which you did not.

NO NECESSITY TO BE WORRIED OR SCRUPULOUS. On the other hand, it is not necessary to be scrupulous or worried. Worry never brings us happiness but is rather an obstacle to true happiness and joy in the Lord. It is, indeed, an unfortunate state of mind and conscience. Common sense tells us that we should make use of the available means to get rid of our scruples.

WHAT IS A SCRUPLE? The Latin word *scrupulus* means a small stone, a pebble, which was used in ancient times to designate a small weight for use on very sensitive and delicate scales so that very small quantities could be weighed out.

In the moral or spiritual sense, the word scruple means something similar, a small trifling matter which only a very delicate conscience would notice.

In common usage, therefore, the word scruple signifies "the anxiety about having offended God, which certain souls feel for little or no reason." Be sure to read those last words.

A scruple may also be described as "a groundless fear of having sinned grievously in an action which is perfectly lawful and permissible and praiseworthy," or at least a groundless fear of having sinned grievously when there was no sin at all.

* * *

We must be very careful to distinguish well between a scrupulous conscience and a tender or delicate conscience.

A SCRUPULOUS CONSCIENCE IS NOT THE SAME AS A TENDER CONSCIENCE. In order to understand this, let me quote you a number of statements of writers on this subject.

"Whilst scruples are a real evil (i.e., something disagreeable and to be avoided, but not sinful in this case) to be carefully avoided, there is nothing more precious than a delicate conscience."

Having carefully thought through this statement, look at yourself in the light of the following.

"The *delicate* conscience loves God ardently and, in order to please him, wants to avoid the least fault, the slightest imperfection. The *scrupulous* conscience is led on by a certain egoism (self-seeking) which causes an inordinate eagerness for absolute certainty of one's state of grace.

"The *delicate* conscience, while hating sin, has a rational (reasonable) yet quiet fear of displeasing God. The *scrupulous* conscience harbors vain fears of sinning in every circumstance.

"The *delicate* conscience knows the difference between mortal and venial sin, and, in case of doubt, abides by the judgment and decision of the spiritual director and confessor. The *scrupulous* conscience peevishly questions the decisions of the spiritual director and submits to them only with difficulty."

SIGNS OF SCRUPULOSITY. In order to help you to see how much or how little you are scrupulous, I am going to ask you to look at yourself in the light of the following. The signs of scrupulosity are more or less as follows:

1. If you persist in maintaining that something is a mortal sin, in spite of the fact that the confessor has declared and assured you that it is *not* a mortal sin, but only a venial sin, or no sin at all.

2. If, after seeking advice on some doubt of conscience, or worry, the answers have left you as disturbed as you were before seeking the advice, and perhaps even more disturbed.

3. If, after thinking over past confessions, or over your past life, you have a burning desire to make a general confession for no greater reason than merely to relieve yourself of the anxiety caused by looking over the past.

4. If, after having made a general confession, you wish to make another, or repeat the former, not being satisfied with the one made (or not being satisfied with past confessions), despite the fact that the confessor has told you that there is no further necessity to make another or to repeat the former.

5. If you firmly believe that your present confessor or chosen counsellor does not understand the condition of your soul.

6. If you are of the opinion that you are deceiving your confessor or any other chosen adviser, and that he does not really know how bad you are or were, even after you have sufficiently explained, this, finally, is another sign of scrupulosity.

* * *

You have no doubt often wondered just why you should be having any troubles of conscience at all. Where do they come from? Where do yours come from? These are big questions. Before answering the second, before bothering about the origin of your own troubles in particular, let us first make a list of the various sources of scruples and worries of conscience.

THE SOURCES OF SCRUPLES. 1. Sometimes God withdraws that divine light by which we see clearly what is good and what is sinful, what is mortal sin, what is venial, and what is not sin at all. The result is that we are disconsolate, become confused, and can no longer tell good acts from bad; or in our confusion we start thinking that we are sinning when we are actually performing even good acts. This is scrupulosity.

But why should God allow this? For various reasons: sometimes to punish our pride, our vanity, our self-complacency, our inordinate attachment to self or things around us. Sometimes he permits scruples as a trial, so as to give us plenty of opportunity to suffer and atone for the sins of the world and our own sins, or in order to make us less and less attached to spiritual consolation, or to test our fidelity. He often does all this in order to prepare us for greater holiness.

Rule to follow: Accept these things humbly, suffer them patiently and cheerfully and as courageously as you would any other suffering.

2. Sometimes the evil one stirs up our imagination, makes us believe that we are in mortal sin (when we are not) in order thereby to keep us away from Holy Communion; or in order to keep us from performing our daily duties of our state in life as we ought; or in order to keep us from entering religious life; or in order to make us sin; or in order to make us disgusted with ourselves, with others, to make us weary of life, and thus bring on indifference and laxness.

Rule to follow: Completely ignore these wicked temptations of the evil one.

3. Scruples are sometimes caused by bad nerves, nervous depression. If this be the case—and generally a good physician can tell you whether your nerves are bad—then you had better follow the doctor's orders. You ought to assure yourself, through a physician who knows you, that your state of physical health is what it ought to be.

4. Another cause of scruples for some persons is a meticulous mind, a mind that becomes confused and clouded amid the most trifling details and wants to reach absolute certainty in all things. Not being able to find that certainty, they become scrupulous, troubled, and worried.

Principle to follow: In matters of moral good and moral evil, absolute certainty is ordinarily not possible for any of us. Therefore, give up trying to reach absolute certainty in the matter of sin, in the matter of right and wrong, or the state of grace. Leave that to God for he knows best how much to let us know about ourselves.

We can, however, have moral certainty, probable certainty, in these matters, and this should suffice because moral certainty is all that is necessary and sufficient and because we have faith and hope to sustain and strengthen us.

Rule to follow: Be satisfied with moral or probable certainty. When really in doubt, ask your confessor or someone in whom you have confidence and who is reliable, and let his decision be final to clear up the doubt.

* * *

We treated several sources of scruples in the last letter. We shall now continue with the others.

FURTHER SOURCES OF SCRUPLES. 1. Sometimes scruples come from a mind that is beclouded and pessimistic or cynical or prejudiced. If this is the case, then one begins to look upon God not as an all-loving and just being but as a merciless master. This quickly brings on scruples at times and even nourishes a tendency to despair, to give up trying.

Rule to follow: Meditate more on God's goodness, mercy, and love for us; pray to the Sacred Heart of Jesus, burning furnace of divine love.

2. A person sometimes becomes scrupulous because he confuses feeling with consent in human acts. He thinks because he feels something which is evil in itself, he therefore also has consented and sinned. This, of course, is a mistaken notion. He supposes that because the imagination has been very much alive, even for a long time, to all sorts of bad thoughts and desires, sin has been committed. But also this is a mistake not to be repeated.

Principle to follow: There is no sin without full, free, and deliberate consent. This holds true of all feelings and emotions and imaginations, no matter how evil they may be. As long as you doubt whether you consented, then you can be sure and morally certain that you did not consent.

Rule to follow: Say often with St. Anthony of Egypt whenever bad thoughts or desires or bad feelings come upon you: "I see you, but I do not look at you." That is to say, "I see you, but I do not want you, I do not give my consent, I turn away from you, I will have nothing to do with you."

3. A final source of scruples is one that few people like to admit. Some people become and remain scrupulous because they obstinately prefer their

own judgment and opinion to that of their confessor or adviser, and they do not follow the confessor's advice in matters of conscience. They do not wish to submit their own will to the judgment and decisions of the confessor or adviser. Such persons think that they know better than the confessor, and are guided by their own feelings and impressions rather than by reason.

Rule to follow: The confessor is guiding you by the laws of reason and faith, in which he has been professionally trained. If your judgment does not square with his, then your judgment over yourself in matters of conscience must be wrong; at least, this is ordinarily the only sensible conclusion to draw. Therefore, humbly and even blindly submit your mind and will to his opinion and decision.

Meeting in Snow-time

I touch you
    delicately, like Braille;
read you in negatives . . .
    skeletons of winter leaves,
    open spaces of snowflakes.

I listen to your silence:
    pause between the sough of bending trees,
    space where shore waits for a wave to crash,
know my winter joy will flower,
    finding you, come Spring,
    between two blossoms on a cherry branch.

Sister Helena Brand
Sisters Today, January, 1976

Sponsa Regis, August, 1944

Sin or "Nerves"?

Joseph Kreuter, O.S.B.

It is a known fact that many good and devout souls of our day lack that interior peace and quiet which are so indispensable to real spiritual progress. They are full of unrest, fear, and doubt, and given to constant worrying and introspection. A heavy load seems to press down upon their spirits and to deprive them of real cheer and interior joy. How happy they would be if they were able to rid themselves of this burden. They search through books hoping to find a cure for their trouble. Above all they expect their confessor and spiritual guide to be able to free them from the yoke under which they are groaning.

In such cases "nerves" frequently play a role. One is unable to judge one's own condition and mistakes a morbid inhibition or fear, caused by irritated or exhausted nerves, for pangs of conscience and guilt, the more so, of course, when there is question of matters which would really be sins if responsibility would enter into them.

Religious should not be ignorant of such mental disturbances, for in their work they may often encounter persons (especially teaching and nursing Sisters) who are victims of these afflictions. It may also be that they are obliged to live together with other fellow religious who, on account of such sufferings, are unable to live the community life as they are expected to do. Then too, a religious may herself be afflicted with some nervous ailment. All reasons for us to deal with this problem of "soul sufferings."

I.

How to recognize a morbid condition of soul.

We are living in "the age of nervousness" and, no doubt, there will be a considerable increase in the number of "nerve cases" as an aftermath of this

World War. Yet we would err were we to look upon every difficult and ill-adjusted character as a sick person. On the other hand, it might entail fatal consequences if we were to neglect a real nerve disturbance. It is highly important to discern nerve trouble in ourselves or in others from its early beginnings and to judge and treat it accordingly.

Sufferers from nerve ailments are, as it were, bundles of contradictions. They may be divided into two large groups. One comprises all those who are afflicted with inhibitions which impair their health in a greater or lesser degree. They must be freed of these inhibitions if their lives are to be made bearable. Then there are those persons who have no inhibitions. They are sorely in need of inhibitions if their existence is to be tolerable for themselves as well as for their fellow-religious.

Among those beset by inhibitions must be reckoned sufferers from compulsion neuroses. They usually are clever in concealing their condition before others. However, this very ingenuity adds to their sufferings, for they live in constant fear because their outward conduct does not seem to correspond to their interior condition and they imagine themselves to be outright hypocrites.

In religious matters they are forced to undergo a great many privations and renunciations. What gives light and consolation, joy and happiness to others brings them nothing but fear and doubt. Many of these sufferers are even harassed by the idea that they have lost their faith altogether, and they find themselves doubting almost everything. At the same time they cannot rid themselves of the thought of death and eternity, which forever terrorizes them, making them dread the lot that awaits them in the other world.

Others again are constantly molested by temptations against holy purity that seem to follow them wherever they may go. They greatly suffer because of these temptations, even more so as they abhor all that is contrary to the holy virtue.

Compulsion neuroses cause their victims to see everywhere near occasions to sin, responsibility, the obligation of repairing scandals, the duty of warning and correcting others, etc. They are constantly uneasy and tortured by the fear to commit sin. They dare not use their senses or open their mouth. When doing some work, they find themselves forever in perplexity. When there is question of an obligation, they give themselves over to endless repetitions (of prayers, penances, etc.). They see nothing but obligations, vows, promises. Horrible thoughts and imaginings follow one another, especially when the holiest and the vilest things combine in their mind.

The fear of having made bad confessions and unworthy communions in the past adds to the misery of these souls. Although their confessor has often and solemnly reassured them that they may lay aside their fears and abstain from making repetitions or general confessions, the reception of the sacraments remains a veritable torture.

To this group of sufferers must also be reckoned all victims of melancholy and mental depression. Every happening from within or without has a crushing effect on these and causes them great suffering. They seem paralyzed in soul and body; they are unable to work, to sleep, and to pray. Because they find it difficult to unbosom themselves to others they are not understood by their companions. This brings them much misery, the more as they feel the need of consulting with and leaning on others. They find great relief when they are able to weep to their heart's content or else give vent to their feelings by a sudden outburst or explosion of emotions.

Sufferers from nervous exhaustion must also be placed in this group. Their strength simply breaks down under the weight of the burden that presses upon them. This condition may be brought on by an exaggerated sense of responsibility which causes them to overwork in their daily tasks. They have developed a so-called vocational neurosis. Theirs is a grave irritability of nerves which makes association with them very difficult.

Superiors and all religious should learn to discern such morbid conditions and disturbances wherever they may appear. They will then be able to judge correctly and benefit souls who are in great need of help.

II.

How to judge and treat morbid soul-ailments.

1) The rule is: It must be left to the all-knowing God and his representative, the confessor, to pass judgment on the moral guilt of such persons. All these afflicted souls need an enlightened confessor who understands them and knows the condition of their conscience. If in an individual case the confessor advises it, a physician is to be consulted, at least in order to ascertain the particular character and extent of the ailment. Should the confessor make light of the trouble, the penitent must abandon his own judgment and permit himself blindly to be led by the confessor even if he be unable to understand the latter's decision and direction. In such cases only unconditional subjection and complete childlike obedience will be of any avail.

It may happen in these circumstances that certain souls will find it impossible for the one or the other reason to cooperate with their confessor. In their misery and perplexity they wish to seek out another priest. In such cases, permission should not be withheld from them; on the contrary, they may be encouraged to find another confessor, provided there is hope that such a change will help them to overcome their difficulties and no abuse is to be feared. A holy reverence for man's conscience is ever in place. Has the Church not in our time greatly facilitated the confession of religious in cases where a change of confessor might be deemed expedient? No doubt the Church had good reasons for such a policy.

2) It is also to our own advantage if we are able to form a correct notion concerning the various psychic conditions man may be heir to, for such knowledge will enable us to treat persons thus afflicted justly and charitably. Inconsiderate or harsh conduct toward these ailing souls is doubly painful and renders their already difficult existence still more unbearable. For these souls are often enough condemned to lead a lonely and solitary existence.

One cannot easily be too kind and charitable to those who suffer from compulsion complexes and whose life is one of constant fear and doubt. The same may be said of those who are victims of mental depression and nervous exhaustion. They will never abuse our kindness and love. They are most eager to unbosom themselves to the one or the other of their co-religious in whom they have confidence. Many religious in such instances have benefited patients more than even a nerve specialist would have been able to do. Every capable and devoted nurse, every intelligent teacher and educator in religion has had experience in this regard. They justly delight in recalling how much good they have been able to do to such afflicted souls.

Souls suffering from compulsory notions above all must be quieted down. One should not permit himself to be confounded and upset by their complaints. As they are forever agitated by fear and doubt, it is necessary to free them of these handicaps. They are to be taught to overcome their inhibition and regain the use of their free will. They will never misuse such liberty. If you demand energy and force of will on their part, you are apt to increase their difficulties. Yet a certain resoluteness is needed, but one that brings understanding and peace of mind.

Souls suffering from mental depression must be induced to unbosom themselves. They are forever busy with themselves and find no end of their thoughts and imaginings. They therefore need our special sympathy and attention. To ignore their misery would be cruelty to them. A change of place and occupation may have most beneficial effects on such persons, for they, above all, need distraction and diversion in order to turn their thoughts into different channels and to help them once more to the use of their senses. Light work may distract them, likewise everything that arouses their interest and holds their attention. Blessed the religious who knows how to relieve the depressed soul of her care and to bring much sunshine and joy into her life!

Sufferers from nervous exhaustion need rest and new strength. They must have good care and recreation. In their case there will frequently be a noticeable improvement as soon as the body gains in weight. Above all, it is very important to bring about a restful, dreamless sleep. What nourishment is to the body, sleep is to the nerves. As soon as these have been strengthened, many a trouble of the soul vanishes as by magic, whereas exhausted nerves lead to ever greater irritability which eventually may become unbearable.

Sponsa Regis, December, 1953

Mental Health and Holiness

Joseph J. Quinlan

Sisters often come into contact with varying degrees and types of emotional and mental disorders as they fulfill their duties in the hospital, in the classroom, and in the social services. Your editor is keenly aware of this. In an attempt to be of service to you, he has asked me to contribute to *Sponsa Regis* a few of my impressions and thoughts concerning this very important but greatly misunderstood and, sad to say, feared type of human affliction.

Let me introduce myself to you. I am a Catholic chaplain in a hospital which specializes in the care and treatment of patients who suffer from emotional and mental disorders. I have had training in the basic principles of psychiatry — that specialized branch of medical science which deals with the causes, the prevention, the care, and the treatment of persons who suffer from emotional and mental disorders.

However, I do not pretend to assume the role of a psychiatrist, nor do I have any ambitions in that area. My one and only interest is the same as that of any other Catholic priest and religious, i.e., the spiritual welfare of those souls which are entrusted to my care. My training in the basic principles of psychiatry enables me to recognize, evaluate, and cope with the various types and degrees of emotional and mental disorders. My training enables me to become an active member of the hospital staff in dealing with these illnesses. This training enables me to appreciate and recognize my obligations and limitations as I strive for the spiritual welfare of the patients entrusted to my care.

The area of emotional and mental disorders is a broad one. The resistance and fear which exists in relation to these disorders is largely due to a very superficial and inaccurate knowledge and appreciation of them. Very often this resistance and fear are found to be without an intelligent foundation, because the person having such an attitude is completely ignorant concerning emotional and mental disorders.

In passing, let me say that I sometimes gain the impression that we priests and Sisters who take an interest in and devote ourselves to those who are suffering from emotional and mental disorders are secretly suspect of being "a bit abnormal" by our "normal" brothers and sisters. While in this trend of thought, the remark of one of our chaplains comes to my mind. On being asked by a sympathetic friend to compare his feelings towards the patients in his hospital with his feelings towards his former parishioners, the chaplain somewhat facetiously replied: "I now seem to experience a certain peace of mind, because I know and understand my present parishioners whereas some of my former parishioners used to confuse me."

Until comparatively recently, due to ignorance of the nature and causes of emotional and mental disorders and the fear engendered by that ignorance, very little progress was made in understanding, preventing, arresting, and overcoming these illnesses. The same is true of other forms of illness such as heart disease, tuberculosis, and cancer. Just as there are various types and kinds of heart disease, tuberculosis, and cancer, so there are various types and kinds of emotional and mental disorders.

If we are to make the same progress in arresting and overcoming emotional and mental illness as has been done in regard to these other forms of illness, we must begin at once to banish our ignorance and fear that have hindered progress in the prevention and control of the various types of emotional and mental disorders. Ignorance in regard to a person or thing inclines us to be cautious and reserved, if not suspicious of that person or thing. If we were to examine our ignorance a bit more closely, we would find seeds of fear — we are inclined to fear the unknown. In respect to emotional and mental disorders, this blind and unreasoning fear, engendered by ignorance, paralyzes us mentally and emotionally. This is not a healthy state of mind. Meanwhile, due to our passive and permissive attitude, emotional and mental disorders continue and multiply.

Emotional and mental illness is not a malady of recent origin. Plato and Aristotle make mention of it in their writings. Down through the ages we have written accounts of these illnesses and the very crude and brutal methods which were employed to treat and cure them. These methods were begotten of ignorance, fear and superstition by the "normal" people of those times.

Emotional and mental disorders are not rare or uncommon among the afflictions of the human race. Because of the unintelligent stigma or shame attached to this type of illness and the great lengths to which families and relatives of the patient will go to conceal or hide this illness, the general public is misled into believing that this type of illness is quite rare. This is far from the truth.

Carefully made and validly established statistics tell us that about one out of every twenty persons of our population suffers in varying degrees and duration from some form of emotional or mental disorder at some time during their life. Or if we are to consider families as a whole, about one out of every five families has one or more of their members afflicted by this illness. When we consider the state of Minnesota, a very average state insofar as the incidence of this illness is concerned, we discover that there are ten state hospitals with a total population of fourteen thousand patients. This census does not take into consideration the Veterans Administration and the many privately owned hospitals that receive and care for those suffering from these illnesses. Need I say more to shake us from our complacency on the widespread frequency of this illness?

Modern psychiatry is making progress in that it is systematizing and categorizing the many and often complex human emotions and drives. An attempt is being made to establish a scientific method for the study, the understanding, and evaluation of the emotional and mental make-up of the human being. As in other branches of human science, mistakes and erroneous statements and claims have been made. The sincere scientist is quick to admit his error and to correct his mistake. The entire branch of a science is not to be condemned and cast aside because of an error or mistake. The good and the true are to be salvaged and progress is to be encouraged.

Much of the suspicion of and resistance to the science of psychiatry is due to unfamiliarity with the many technical terms it has created and, of necessity, must employ. Technical terminology is used in religious as well as other sciences. Such terminology is essential to every branch of science, so that there may be a minute and clear understanding of the matter under study by the scientist. This terminology avoids confusion and repetition of the efforts by those scientists who follow in the footsteps of their predecessors.

Because psychiatry is the science which deals with the emotional and mental health of man, it might be said that this science is of major importance to all scientific progress. Without emotional and mental health, all progress, whether it be spiritual, material or scientific, is hindered if not made impossible, depending on the degree and kind of mental and emotional illness.

As religious who seek to know, love, and serve God and our fellow men, we have a serious obligation to protect, strengthen, and improve our emotional and mental health. Let us not be numbered among those whom sinful pride and culpable ignorance keep from accepting and recognizing that, although they are now children of God due to the sacrament of baptism, they still bear within them the remains of original sin and are still subject to the frailties and disorders of human nature.

Sponsa Regis, October, 1959

Psychological Testing and the Religious Life

Aubrey Zellner, O.S.B.

Screening of candidates for religious life has been going on for a long time, and no one will question the necessity of screening. However, the methods used to evaluate the suitability of candidates for religious life have been sometimes questioned, and with good reason. If the judgment of superiors and commit-tees and chapters has seemed haphazard at times, perhaps it has been because insufficient objective evidence has been available for making that judgment. Mistakes have been made. Infallability in this area will always be an impossi-ble objective, but it is only reasonable to make constant effort to improve.

If psychological tests are to be used to help screen candidates, two ex-tremes must be avoided. First of all, psychological tests will never be a substitute for the experienced observation of candidates and prudent decisions made by responsible people. Thus it follows that if anyone is looking for a pat answer to the question of choosing vocations by screening, she will be doomed to disappointment. Psychological tests should be used most properly as aids. One uses glasses as an aid to impaired eyesight. In many cases perfect 20-20 vi-sion does not result even with the use of glasses. One uses aids for impaired hearing. Even with the best of hearing aids a person with impaired hearing may not achieve perfect hearing. Thus to formulate the principle: if anyone tries to use psychological tests as a complete substitute for experience and observation, she is misusing the tests.

The other extreme is this: if anyone makes a judgment on a given candi-date and considers the psychological test valid only if it corroborates her judg-ment and considers the test invalid if it does not agree with her judgment, then most likely such a person is over-rating her private judgment. She really has no trust in the psychological test results, and it can be considered a waste of time for her to go through the motions of administering the tests.

Somewhere between the two extreme views described we must look for a balanced mean if we want to make legitimate use of psychological tests for screening candidates for religious life.

Just as the admission practices of the various agencies of educational and occupational fields have been affected by the contributions of psychological testing, so it seems but natural that if superiors of religious groups are alert they will see to it that their admissions policies will involve the use of techniques developed as the result of contemporary advances in the understanding of personality.

To this point Cardinal Tisserant has been quoted as saying that the mere fact that recent developments in the psychological and social sciences are entirely new to the thinking of people in religion does not give them a right to neglect these developments and shunt them aside.[1]

The acceptance of the contributions of psychological testing in screening is but an initial step. In the application of the test results we have to consider the competence of the psychologist who makes the interpretations. It is not difficult to master the mechanics of administering and scoring most of the psychological tests on the market. Interpretation is the phase that demands experience and training.

The psychologist must have a solid formation in her chosen field and she must have familiarity with related fields of study such as sociology, physiology, anthropology, philosophy and theology. Training in the use of psychological testing is never really complete. Considering current developments there is always more that can be learned. Training which is adequate to qualify for membership in the American Psychological Association and membership in the American Catholic Psychological Association should be a minimum.

In the field of psychological testing one finds a wealth of literature each month in periodicals and books. An interesting book on the subject has been released under the joint authorship of Antoine Benko and Joseph Nuttin published by the University of Louvain in French.[2] The main part of the book is concerned with the presentation of an experiment with the use of the Minnesota Multiphasic Personality Inventory. The test items were translated into French and the test was given to 181 young religious who were studying philosophy or theology. It was also given to 79 novices in religion. Selection was not determined by this testing. The test was just administered and the results kept for use in the experiment. The novices were observed carefully for two years after taking the test.

Out of the original 79 the number who had left the novitiate was ten. Of these, seven had shown abnormal peaks on several scales of the personality test. The other three left the novitiate for reasons of their own. Twenty-five

---

[1] Benko, Antoine and Joseph Nuttin, *Examen De La Personnalité Chez La Candidates A La Pretrise*, Louvain, Belgium, Publications Universitaires De Louvain, 1956, 109.

[2] *Ibid.*, 1–138.

novice masters and other competent spiritual directors prepared a questionnaire which they administered to the 181 young religious mentioned above. The questionnaire, together with an interview, was used to gain an insight into the degree of the subjects' adaptation to their vocation and to religious life. The symptoms of maladjustment thus obtained were compared with the profiles which resulted from the Minnesota Personality Test Profiles of the same person. The results were conclusive. Those who had abnormal peaks on two or more of the scales in the personality test — there were eight in this group — also showed themselves maladjusted in the special questionnaire concerning their vocation and the records of the interviews that accompanied the questionnaire. Although the authors of the book say that there is room for more study and continued research, the Minnesota Personality Test has proved that it has considerable value as a device in screening candidates for religious life.

It seems to the writer that screening with psychological tests can be employed on three general levels. Some religious superiors will demand of each candidate not only a personality test like the Minnesota Multiphasic Personality Inventory but also deep-probing tests like the Rorschach and Thematic Apperceptive Test (TAT) besides an interview by a psychiatrist. This seems to the writer to be asking too much in the way of testing of the candidate. The principle of the more tests the better is not valid for the screening of candidates. To test too much may put the whole testing program in jeopardy.

The second general level of screening involves a procedure where the superior demands the Minnesota Personality Test and screens with deeper type tests all candidates who score outside one standard deviation from the mean. That means about thirty percent of the applicants will be subject to the more probing tests such as Rorschach and TAT.

The third general level might be described as one in which the Minnesota Personality Test or another such test is administered; applicants who score outside two standard deviations from the mean will be given additional testing of the more probing type. This means that about two percent of applicants will be subjected to the more extensive tests. In all levels an interview should be demanded at least by directors of vocations or the mistress of postulants.

There are different kinds of tests that have been perfected and that can be used in psychological screening. These will be considered very briefly and then something will be said about the moral problems involved in testing.

First of all, there are intelligence tests — tests of ability to do academic work. For any kind of religious life, a good average intelligence is necessary. We must have some assurance that the candidate understands instruction and the obligations of the life she intends to embrace. She must take vows and she must understand what the vows imply. There is evidence to show that when a person is limited intellectually and therefore struggles to keep up with training demands, she tends to develop serious emotional conflicts because of constant frustrations.

After intelligence testing we must consider achievement testing. We have national achievement tests which have been standardized over the whole country, or at least standardized for certain specific areas. In addition to testing in individual schools it is worthwhile to know how a candidate can perform on standardized tests of achievement.

Another type of test is the interest test. There are many types, but perhaps the most commonly used are the Kuder Interest and the Strong Interest Tests. Much research has been done on both these tests. A priest of St. Bonaventure's University in New York has worked out a priest scale for the Strong Test.[3] He validated the scale by administering the test to priests over the country, so that it is possible to compare the interests of a candidate with the typical interests of priests.

There is a Strong Interest Test Profile for women. There is a form for women on the Kuder Test also. It would be most desirable if a Sister searching for a dissertation topic would work out a scale on the Strong Test to determine if there is a typical interest pattern for Sisters. Candidates for the convent could be evaluated in terms of their interests and the typical pattern for women religious. Perhaps the same could be done with the Kuder Interest Test.

A final type of test that can be used in screening candidates is the personality test. This is perhaps the area in which most people have been critical and anxious. One test which is commonly used has been referred to before, namely, the Minnesota Multiphasic Personality Inventory.[4] It has been used extensively and has been subjected to careful research with practically all types of people. It consists of 566 items which are answered as true or false. The Minnesota Test is valuable in that it has a lie detecting scale. It even measures unconscious falsification and exaggerated defense against being evaluated by the test.

Briefly, the Minnesota Test will bring out evidence of hypochondriasis or over-concern about health, depression or feelings of uselessness, nervousness or tension, hostility and aggression, effeminacy or masculinity, suspiciousness, compulsiveness about details and indecisiveness, grasp of reality or extremely bizarre thinking, hypomania or exaggerated drive often coupled with a tendency to want to reform others, and finally, sociability. A test of this kind is not sufficient to evaluate the personality of a given individual. An autobiography is desirable together with interviews by a spiritual director and in some cases by a psychiatrist to supplement test results.

If personality tests are to be used it is most important that definite rules and objectives be formulated and a confidential method of filing results be determined before the testing program is initiated.

[3] Lahota, Brian, *Vocational Interests of Catholic Priests*, Washington, D.C., Catholic University Press, 1948.

[4] Hathaway, S. R. and J. C. McKinley, *Minnesota Multiphasic Personality Inventory*, New York, The Psychological Corporation, 1951.

When a community has to decide on the acceptance of candidates, it does not seem desirable that professional psychological information be presented in technical terms. Technically expressed test results are either meaningless to the non-psychologist or they are easily misinterpreted. They tend to be threatening sometimes to those who have to decide on acceptance of candidates because practically everyone must admit some degree of emotional instability some time or other. Perhaps it would be desirable for a committee to screen the candidates and then one qualified individual present the findings of the committee on an individual candidate to the chapter. The physical examination of candidates for the novitiate is important, and it seems desirable that it be done by a doctor who is psychologically oriented or at least has had some training in psychology and has some knowledge of the pattern of living that will be demanded by the religious group. If we are realistic we must admit that recommendations from pastors and others acquainted with the prospective candidate are often vague or have little meaning and sometimes are very misleading.

What are some of the indices to consider in a candidate? One writer says that the candidate should have maturity, balance, stability, good control and adjustment.[5] More specifically, another says that he would rule out candidates who are the shut-in type, unsociable, irritable, violent and uncontrollable in their temper.[6] Another says the paranoid suspiciousness and definite deviant sexuality tendencies should rule out a candidate.[7] Certain neurotic types seem unsuitable for religious life. These include hypochondriacs who have a very abnormal concern about health, the obsessive-compulsive type whose problem shows up in severe scrupulosity and extreme indecisiveness. We do not refer to a casual or intermittent type of scrupulosity but one that is persistent and does not ever really seem to clear up.

As far as doubtful cases are concerned, most writers seem to agree that we should be severe rather than lenient, especially when it comes to application for vows or even the novitiate. The Church and religious groups have rights. The common good should prevail over the demands of the individual candidate, even if she has relatives in religion. It is mistaken charity to accept doubtfully mature and questionably stable individuals into religion. We are unrealistic if we look for a miraculous change in an individual through training in religious life. The chances are not good that there will be basic changes in psychological functioning. There is definite evidence, carefully compiled, which shows that the effect of religious life is to extend and to deepen the pre-

[5] Bier, William, "Psychological Testing of Candidates and the Theology of Vocation," *Review for Religious*, Volume 12 (November 15, 1953), 296.

[6] Moore, Verner Thomas, "Insanity in Priests and Religious," *American Ecclesiastical Review*, 95, 601–614.

[7] Vaughan, Richard, "Moral Issues in Psychological Screening," *Review for Religious*, Volume 16 (March 15, 1957), 68.

existing psychological tendencies and thus produce a quantitative rather than a qualitative change in the psychological functioning of the individual religious.[8]

What if a candidate absolutely refuses to submit to psychological testing before the postulancy or the novitiate? It seems to the writer, in agreement with responsible authorities, that the superior can refuse such a person entrance. The very fact of refusal seems to indicate that something is wrong. The testing and its results are to the individual's advantage as well as to that of the community. The superior is within her rights in asking for both physical and psychological tests. If the testing program detects the grossly abnormal applicant and screens this person out, then it seems to the writer a very fundamental good is accomplished.

Abnormal individuals are not easily recognized even by persons with good intuition and experience. Sometimes the grossly abnormal individual masks her abnormality. There are some individuals who are so perceptive that they can present a false front in an interview even with a carefully prepared questionnaire administered by a vocational director with a tremendous amount of experience. There is objective evidence that trained individuals have a hard time determining the intellectual functioning level of an individual, much less her psychological and emotional functioning level, merely by an interview. Few authorities would dispute the fact that intelligence testing is easier than personality testing.

To accept a candidate conditionally is a very questionable procedure. In most cases she will not leave voluntarily. A delayed decision becomes more and more difficult to make. Furthermore, after a candidate is in religion for a time she tends to devise defenses to hide serious weaknesses. There are cases on record where individuals held themselves together with tremendous effort until final acceptance and then a complete breakdown or disintegration occurred. The individual then becomes the expensive charge of the religious community.

When a candidate is refused admission even to postulancy, it is not the obligation of the superior to tell the individual just why in specific detail she was refused. A general statement is sufficient. If a candidate seems to need psychiatric help, the superior can recommend it, and perhaps she should do so.

As to persons who are already in vows, there is dispute as to whether the superior can demand psychological testing. Certainly the superior is free to urge testing and point out its benefits. Church law does not allow the superior to demand a manifestation of conscience. The law does not forbid voluntary manifestation of conscience. Taking a personality test does not involve a manifestation of conscience. Furthermore, the writer has examined almost all recent pronouncements of the Holy See on psychological testing and listened

---

[8] Mastej, Sister Martina, *A Study of Influence of Religious Life on the Personality Adjustment of Religious Women as Measured by the Modified Form of the MMPI*, New York, Fordham University, unpublished doctoral dissertation, 1957.

to discussions of these pronouncements by conscientious and competent Catholic authorities and finds there is no evidence in these pronouncements on which to base disapproval of such testing.

It has been said that in God's providence we will always have difficult members in religious groups to help make life a source of virtue and sanctification for others. It seems unreasonable to knowingly contribute to the difficulty of others in religious life or the problems of the faithful in parishes by admitting psychologically unsuitable persons to religion. Psychological testing has a function to perform in the evaluation of candidates for religious life. Such a program is in keeping with the spirit of religious vocation as understood by the Church.

Paul, Utterly Out of Himself

Nights come when the slow swirl of leaves
and the lilt of clouds across, around, across the moon
so settles into me
that I sink onto a huge stone,
squat beneath a terebinth tree,
and see, or think I see,
my finished supper plate on my lap in front of me,
a fly sauntering about, savoring the olive pits,
the crazy crumbs of bread,
the bits of crust
and a fish bone or two,
and, oh, I do not really know
whether I am in pain or not
or awake or dazed
or insane or in love with a dream
or just so terribly tired out
or anything but the shimmer and unearthly breath
of wine in a cup
and the blood beating somewhere behind my eyes:
I am who am, I am who am.

Sister M. Pamela Smith, SS.C.M.
Sisters Today, February, 1976

Sisters Today, May, 1970

Planning for Retirement

Sister M. Pauline Drewniak, O.S.F.

Among Sisters there is a growing awareness that each period of life from infancy to old age is a provident, necessary, and integral part of the whole human person. In this production-oriented and materialistic society, we must give time to some positive thinking upon the values of aging, to explore what the aging process has to say to each of us in the light of faith and our own experience. We cannot understand the meaning of age unless we explore the meaning of hope.

I think too frequently we rate the contributing years of adulthood as of prime importance. We look at infancy and early youth as a promise of future contributions, and we view aging as a time of uselessness and perhaps helplessness. This influence is so subtle that we find ourselves devoting more time, planning and effort to the needs of the young than to the aging members of our communities. It is becoming increasingly obvious that major adjustments *must* be made. We have to examine the role of the older Sister.

This reminds me of reading some time ago a newspaper article which told the story of a reporter who stopped to watch a new building being erected. He spoke to a man wearing a steel helmet and looking over some blueprints of the construction. He asked what his job was, and the man replied that he did not work for the construction firm. He worked for a wrecking company. This company had someone assigned to every major construction project in the city. Their task was to maintain extensive records of the manner in which the building was being erected so that when it was declared obsolete, their company could submit the lowest bid for tearing down the structure.

I tell this story because it sharply depicts one of the phenomena of our times — that of planned obsolescence. We not only accept, we plan generations ahead for the destruction and replacement of those things which seem so absolute and so permanent. But in dealing with human lives we have not quite reached this level of sophistication. Perhaps it is because we have accepted the inevitable of the short span of anyone's time on earth. This acceptance may explain why we have placed the halo on youth in our society.

For too many older religious, the later years still mean loneliness, lack of purpose, and meaning. Today we have the tools to change this. We have the power to enrich the lives of older religious and to benefit from their skills, their wisdom and their experience. These older people have earned the right to participate in more dynamic activities than televison, golf, movies, chess, and crocheting, and they want to exercise that right. We need these dedicated women who have the vision of their great task as women who can help restore the social equilibrium by creating a vital current of the great womanly virtues: the spirit of love, of compassion for the suffering, and generous self-sacrifice.

True, age robs us. But on the other hand, it enriches us. It offers many compensations, many insights, often much peace, and certain fruits of wisdom. It brings new contributions, new hopes, fulfillments and perspectives. Delights of memory are often keen — discovery of new and deeper interpretations of matters which long have puzzled one come into clearer focus. Aging must be recognized as a natural phase of our life; it enjoys its own dignity, its own privileges and character. If then, we accept aging as a normal phase of our life, it would seem only natural to integrate it into our whole scheme of life and to search for its deeper meanings.

A BASIC QUESTION

The question arises, "How do we help an older Sister to give up her work?" For example, I am thinking of the Sister who has worked for about fifty years in the laundry or in the kitchen, and then it is decided to phase out these operations and to contract with special firms for laundry and food services. How do we help these Sisters who are suddenly displaced continue to feel useful to their community?

This is the sort of question that led to the establishment of a department within my community to study the retirement needs of Sisters. It was apparent that the functions of this department had to be guided by the needs of the Sisters whom the program was to serve — a need to create an awareness of and an interest in the realities of the aging Sisters on the part of themselves, their fellow Sisters, superiors and administrators; a need to establish plans for community education in developing proper attitudes toward retirement; a need to see retirement as a time of wholesome and constructive activity rather than a barren and unproductive interlude between employment and death; a need to develop a conviction that one retires to something and not from something; a need to plan and organize a program to facilitate the transition from an active apostolate to an equally important, though perhaps radically different phase of her life in keeping with the Sisters' abilities, health, and interests; and a need to conduct research in all phases of pre-retirement and retirement in and out of the community, in other religious orders, and in industry, research which would provide a springboard of action for retired Sisters into new phases of the apostolate.

A complete concept of the retired Sister's nature must take into account all the levels of reality, not only the physical but the riches of her intelligence, her intuition for mystery, her tendency to inwardness and contemplation, her capacity for selfless love, and the hunger of her being for total dedication. Each Sister must be recognized as an individual, unique and distinct, identified by her past, in the present and the future, respected as a member of a total community, a person who continues to contribute *to* and participate *in* community life and work in the role Providence has designed for her.

Considerable ego support must be given at this time of retirement because it is at this time that attitudes and self-esteem are extremely important. The lives of the Sisters must be made challenging, not merely bearable; life must be exciting, not merely safe; it must be rewarding and not merely pleasant. A quality life includes a sense of accomplishment and the knowledge that someone cares. Many Sisters will want the opportunity of pursuing the vital issues of the day and the social activities that lend vitality to life.

It is imperative that we develop programs to use the skills and energies of our aging religious who have the ability, the desire, and the need to play a constructive role in our society. Equally important are the more refined skills represented in our senior age group, skills which are in short supply in our society such as the skills of retired teachers, nurses, medical technicians, office aides, and tutors.

The religious community must recognize that whatever feelings of usefulness and purpose, of worth and creative satisfaction the Sister derived from her works as a teacher, a nurse, a homemaker, or an administrator have now been displaced, and she is faced with the necessity of finding new sources of satisfaction in the different life that retirement requires her to make for herself. The degree to which we preserve the dignity and self-esteem of the retiring Sister by helping her accept limitations as a natural human phenomenon, which need not destroy her usefulness, is a more potent factor for successful adjustment to retirement than we realize.

When we come to the full knowledge of these levels of reality, our overall problem of retirement will narrow tremendously. Compulsory retirement will become normal retirement, looked forward to and accepted as an open door to new vistas, to a richer and fuller life, a capstone to life. I am convinced that our older people want continued commitment, not enforced idleness. It appears fairly obvious that they do not much like the role of relative inactivity to which we oftentimes relegate them, a role which neither permits them to participate in nor contribute very much to the work of the Church.

Contrary to many fables which are repeated about the aging, the facts are increasingly evident that it is the improved health, the longevity, the mobility, the freedom, and the desire for involvement in the mainstream of life that has created some of the major issues with which we are coping today. Never before in history has practically everyone who reaches the age of sixty-five been assured that he can retire and that he will have an average of 30,000 hours of free time to do with as he chooses.

THE ISSUE OF ATTITUDE

One of the most fundamental issues which confront us today is attitude. If we can achieve no more than changing the attitude people have of aging — both as it affects themselves and their image of others — we will have done much to solve one of the most critical problems. Our role is *not* to do *for* the aging. Certainly when one cannot meet his own needs for survival, then someone must step in to assist.

But what about the other needs, the psychological needs which we have at any age and which give meaning to one's life? It is difficult to give fulfillment to these psychological needs. Yet we are obligated to find the means or we will become overwhelmed with the problems when needs go unmet. We have to be community catalysts as well as individual therapists. We must engage the community in establishing a basic design for upgrading the lives of our old members — we must respond to this "new society" of ours.

As we extend the life span and act to relieve our senior citizens of debilitating ailments, we must provide outlets for the energies we are preserving. Not only does this enhance the lives of many senior members, but their service to the religious and civic community enhances the quality of the community which can so well utilize the skills and knowledge of these people. My contention is that opportunities for useful and meaningful lives for older persons exist, not primarily in continued employment in the regular work force but in the whole new and vast areas of services which will use their accumulated skills and wisdom. Until we discover what we really want from the older members of our communities we have no right to cut them off from occupational activity.

A successful retirement does not just happen. It requires planning and specific goals. The question of proper retirement age is not settled and probably will never be to the satisfaction of everyone. That arbitrary age of sixty-five is considered by some to be a waste of manpower and by others as being unfair to younger people. No one grows old by living a number of years. People grow old only by deserting their ideals. Age should be measured by attributes and attitudes rather than by years.

It is a challenge to those of us who are involved in trying to make life meaningful for the aging to examine our progress and to bring both the breadth of vision and depth of commitment to our programs. The two ingredients, I feel, most essential to insure a quality life for our older Sisters, priests or Brothers are freedom and respect. Freedom from fear and isolation from people. A freedom of choice — to choose where to live and the activities to be engaged in. Respect for older people is much more than the obligation of an "honor thy father and thy mother" philosophy. It is the recognition of the essential value of every human being and the right of older people, along with all other community members, to have access to community resources.

Can we establish goals for older members of our religious families without establishing goals for all members of our communities? One cannot create a dynamic way of life for older persons unless there has been emphasis on such a way of life during the early and continued years of formation. The problems of the elderly are the problems of the young.

THE LA FARGE PROGRAM

The retirement program in my own community is known as the La Farge Program. One of the essential goals of the La Farge Program is to reinforce a true climate of community that says more by action than by deed: a person who is truly loved and responds to love never grows old. The world we live in is essentially the world we are.

The La Farge Program has a credo that says life is what we make it, what we bring to it. It aims to reaffirm that strength of the will, that quality of the imagination, that vigor of the emotions, that predominance of courage over timidity and the desire of genuine effort over a complacent love of ease.

The program has a director in each Province with a coordinating community director. These directors meet monthly to formulate, discuss and evaluate plans to meet the immediate and future needs of the Sisters, using information obtained from personal interviews with the Sisters, from the data obtained from the age distribution tabulation, and from the work and location preferences indicated on the Sisters' Survey of 1967, as it applies to our specific community.

Old age is a time of hidden charity and of the awareness that love is life. It is a time for courage that comes from a sense of destiny, from a sense of strength that can flow to others from the example of others, a time of going forth to meet people. There is nothing nobler in the aging process than the courage to accept in our natural life its length of circumstances and to accept the life of the resurrection, which is love.

This courage of age has helped the Sisters in the La Farge Program to think more of other people rather than less, to go out of themselves to the younger child at Day Care Center in Milwaukee's inner core, to tutor the older child and adult who needs assistance in academic work, to visit the aged and infirm at five units of the Milwaukee County Institutions and in private homes, to perform clerical work in offices and libraries, to sew for the poor, to counsel and teach the emotionally disturbed adolescent, and to participate in in-service workshops in order to better extend themselves to the people of God. It is imperative to have an orientation into the specific area so that the aging Sister is at ease with what she does and feels security in her work.

Research shows that a good judgment to retirement is more likely to occur when retirement has been anticipated and planned. Happiness in retirement depends upon the possession of inner security and some kind of satisfying activity. These findings have led to study and discussion with resource people from every Province of our community, and a program which provided for an enriched future resulted.

In order to meet the needs of the individual Sister, as expressed in questionnaires and interviews, courses in theology, library science, typing, reading (preparation for tutoring) and home economics were offered during a month-long Institute. The Sisters were invited to share in art and music appreciation studies, in film, tape and record evaluations, in basic understandings in current areas related to political science, in lectures, concerts, tours and art exhibits.

One hundred and fixty-six Sisters above the age of fifty-five accepted the invitation to attend this first Inter Provincial La Farge Institute at the mother-house during the month of July, 1968. These Sisters had the courage of vision to take a short look back and a long look ahead, planning for the needs of pre-retirement, semi-retirement and the eventuality of complete retirement. The second such Institute had a pre-registration of 275 Sisters.

Responsibility toward the aging cannot ignore the responsibility of the aged themselves. It is a lifelong responsibility that each one of us has to prepare onself for the time when one becomes the repository of all the memories of self and one's forebears. Quality life in later years is one of the positive results that can be created only by the deep convictions of those who visualize it as a positive personal goal. Only the dignity of self and its realization can demand the respect of others.

Our older Sisters do have great potentialities for social good and for personal achievement, and the individual Sister must develop the vision to bring these potentialities into play. The aging Sister, then, can accept this period of growth, through diminishment, by thanksgiving, by faith, hope and love and can be led to see the reward of old age as a time to give her new and varied opportunities for the experience of this new life of love for God and man. The more meaning one has found in life, the clearer will be the meaning of old age.

Sisters Today, May, 1970

How to Survive the Generation Gap

Sister Rita McGuire, G.S.I.C.

"I really don't think that way, but I can understand *your* thinking like that." If you have heard something similar lately, my dear, you are on the decline; perhaps not in your own eyes but certainly as viewed by a certain segment of the population. It would appear that this is the time for some personal stock-taking.

In breaching the barrier of today's zeitgeist you must never be obvious, you are simply to absorb and exude the nouveau vogue by some specialized type of social osmosis. Try to develop an awareness of, or cultivate the new *in* and *out* terminology. One of the inconveniences of creeping senility that you will have to cope with is the fact that by the time you have mastered what is *in*, it is by then *out*. This is when the gap shows.

If you have resolved to do something about this situation, play it cool. Being shocked is out, understanding is in, but never deteriorate to the tres gai mentality. Studied casualness is what is called for here; deadpan it and learn to deliver a steady, opaque look. Total immersion into the society of the under-thirty devotees is too self-destructive and is recommended only for suicide types. Involvement, the classicists tell us, means wrapped up in or turned in upon, so perhaps participation is a better word, but there is no point to be gained in being sticky about philology.

The vocabulary department seems also to be a red alert area. I am constantly intrigued with the young's use of words like *commitment, involvement, meaningful* and *dialogue,* to mention only a few. Certainly there is little evidence of those four-letter words we were raised with: work, dust, wipe, push, pull, rush. But is there a message here? Are they trying to tell us there should be some beer and skittles in our lives, that all work and no play brings the inevitable result? When the hurricane years have spent themselves will there be reason to recall with mixed emotions poet Sandburg's comment that, "Yesterday is a wind gone down"?

Just for starters, you might open a conversation with a compliment, preferably a sincere one; the penchant of the young for the authentic has already been established. There is room for disagreement among women of good will, but to enter into debate could prove there is an intelligence gap as well. Regardless of how much expertise you bring to bear on a topic you might end up being treated as if you had an I.Q. of nine. Lung power is way out: they can outshout you anytime, gathering a class cohesion we could never muster. Whether this form of togetherness, when they get together to fight for their individual rights, is born of conviction or desperation is, as the writers of academe are wont to say, beyond the scope of this paper. In the nitty-gritty pattern of everyday living take cognizance of these spurts of intolerance and regard them as on-the-job hazards.

EPIGRAMS OF AN EARLIER AGE

Like the rest of us the young are the product of their age. To what extent a people are molded by the slogans of their times could be a question of the first order, for even a quick look at the verbal fodder of Madison Avenue will assure you the human mind reacts to aphorisms like ducks to you-know-what. Now when you consider the type of epigrams that brainwashed us, there is small wonder the youngsters find us dull.

Remember the work-oriented ones that were enough to drive you into hippiedom? "No great deed is done by falterers who ask for security"; along with, "The indolent man values rest; but the industrious man labor." And then we were cautioned that, "The man who rolls up his sleeves seldom loses his shirt." A bleaker outlook for the non-achiever of any generation could hardly be imagined than, "Applause is the spur of noble minds, the end and aim of weak ones."

There were gloomier ones: "A gem is not polished except by rubbing nor a man perfected without trials." Couple this with, "It is too bad success makes failures of so many men." Lest you forget: "It takes a pretty evenly balanced man to be as strong in prosperity as in adversity." We were reminded that we never hear a hen cackle until she has finished her job—this was before the media with its nuts and bolts took over. Then there were those sticklers with the internal rhyme scheme: "A man of words and not of deeds, is like a garden full of weeds." And yet one more: "You may be as orthodox as the devil, and as wicked." Think about that for a while.

Sometimes I think a great swath of the spectrum in the current psychedelic dilemma can be delineated by two of the modern aphorisms which bulge with thrill and thrust content. First, there is the overly-exposed, "Sock-it-to-me" and the other: "God is the answer; what was the question?"

In your re-evaluation of life and living, a good rule to follow is simply to keep to the middle of the road. Age factors and interests should be considered in this climate of moderation. Some things have to be learned while you are young and that's that. The fancy footing called for by the Charleston escapes me; I was too young for it in the twenties and missed its revival in the fifties, though I used to be and still am a veritable whirling dervish at things like Flora MacDonald's Fancy. At community get-togethers there is no need to be socially embarrassed if some of the modern dance steps give you pause or stall you outright. The dances of the day are given more to gymnastics than to grace, and if you have been neglecting your XBX exercises lately, I would suggest you call the whole thing off, plead Hong Kong flu or something. Replacement-personnel our age is difficult to come by.

Becoming hysterical about this aspect of social life within the walls is a trap or pitfall that even the wary should be counselled about. A friend of mine, same vintage, told me about one determined hoofer from another community who climaxed her pas de deux with a rousing rendition of some verses from Don Marquis' Archie. Just when she got to that part where the indomitable Mehitabel hurls her challenge:

> freeze you bloody december
> i never could stay a pet
> but i am a lady in spite of hell
> and there's life in the old dame yet. . .

they carried her off the floor in a state of collapse.

Little can be so damaging to the psyche as that knowing look passed around among those still in their salad days which asks so eloquently, "What is she trying to prove?" The realignment of your private aggiornamento might be helped by setting for yourself some of the following trendy targets:

1. Above all learn to play a musical instrument. Forget about guitars, they are for the very young; a bongo drum is ideal for the tone deaf. At the next happening, come prepared to do your thing with a syncopated blast of boom-a-la, boom-a-la, boom-a-layee! If your memory for the modern boggles at "Only the Lonely" or the saga of Harper Valley, learn a gaggle of parody songs. Here again the gap will yawn abysmally, for an oldie like "Seven Beers With the Wrong Kind of Man" could be lost on this Pepsi generation. In fact they may even think the lunatic fringe has taken over.

2. Let it be known that you plan to invite a non-denominational minister to be one of the judges at the annual Snow Queen Festival or the Spring Prom. Then shop around until you find one with a beard.

3. Appear at odd-hour snacks and bring along your matching coffee mugs, the ones stencilled boldly: OPIUM and HEROIN. Scrap the diet for now, you can always go back to it. Nowadays the shape of things to come depends largely on image.

4. Be lenient with attacks on pop culture. Especially offensive in this area is the use of puns. Some people are swift enough to manufacture their own but most of us have to be content with borrowing others. Indiscriminate comments about "rot an' role singers" or "plop art" leave the young unamused. This is unfortunate. Not their inability to appreciate puns (for that genre of humor

has long been low on the totem pole), but it is their apparent lack of capacity for being amused that causes me no little chagrin. Someone pointed out that they are not exactly devoid of humor, they just don't seem to have the time for it. Admittedly, meaningful dialogue and personal involvement in their commitments is time-consuming.

5. Show up at all sing-alongs. You may overcome the problem of having to sit on the floor by bringing a Snoopy cushion, the one that says: "Security is having someone to lean on." If the occasion arises, share it.

6. Avoid like the devil what is commonly known as the 19th century syndrome — the 19th century having begun for this generation any time prior to 1959. When in conversation, never give a black and white answer. I have known a knowledgeable reference to Nietzche regarding the God-is-dead theory to set up a communications block that would be the envy of a Red envoy in the General Assembly at the U.N. Always demur with something like, "Of course, you have probably taken the long view, while I was taking the short." (Whatever that means.)

7. Nomenclature clamors for attention but it can easily degenerate into name-dropping. The once starchy Sister Elizabeth of the Rosary who was reduced to Betty of the Beads behind her back, now primly tells you that "Betts will do nicely." Nicknames are taboo, especially the overly cute ones like Pokey and Snooky. Take heart, family names are rapidly emerging.

8. When you invite two or three to your room for a chat (I mean dialogue), see that a beer stein containing a miscellany of pens, pencils, paper clips, used stamps and sunglasses, has a prominent place on your desk. I never realized those things have glass bottoms until I was dusting mine the other night in preparation for la grande rapprochement. Dust off also your copies of Teilhard, *Journey of a Soul*, and Dag Hammarskjold's *Markings*, and neglect not to display a few pencilled notes on the detached jacket of a Schillebeeckx volume. But sit on your copy of *The Power of Positive Hell-Raising*.

9. Never stay home from an outing, be it a protest march, a peace rally or one of those hunger walks. Should the time conflict with Mass or one of those other religious exercises which were formerly considered essential to give some spine to the Mystical Body, ignore it. Stuff a copy of *The Gospel According to Peanuts* into your purse and be off. Make sure the title shows.

10. Overcome the temptation to reminisce. You are wasting your time recalling the good old days when you kept fit with the help of Scott's Emulsion, Minard's Liniment and mustard plasters. If your audience is under two score or less, you may be sure these shot-riddled youngsters have long been immunized against any appreciation for a good rub down with a mixture of goose oil plus a dollop of sewing machine lubricant. Alas, grafitti tells us, nostalgia is not what it used to be.

11. Be on guard for an enemy within the camp. To me nothing is so phony as someone fiftyish declaring that she thinks these young adults are stupendous. Check for vocabulary clues; if she substitutes the word *children* for *adults*, this calls for drastic action: spread the rumor that she is about to be

named a *superior*. Now a person sixty-six making this remark is something altogether different. She is sociologically past the acquisitive stage and, what is more, she already has one year compulsory retirement tucked under her cincture.

COMES THE CONFRONTATION

In spite of all this, the inevitable confrontation is bound to come. Not by happenstance will you be simply overwhelmed with the fact that no matter how you strive, your efforts lack, whatever it is you wish to call it — oomph, carisma, pizazz. You can't give the Charleston a fair shake; after the last hot dog blast you were up half the night with acute indigestion, to say nothing of shortness of breath and palpitations. Yet you still have the urge to be numbered among the quick. So you face yourself in the mirror and try to discover the real *you*. This, girl, is called identity crisis. Have nothing to do with the daemons who will suggest that although time heals all, it is sure no beautician.

Take a piece of paper and write down all the things you have going for you apart from longevity. After an hour or two, staring at you from the sheet should be some comments about the experience of things past, notably how you have survived the roaring twenties, the dirty thirties, and even the sizzling sixties. Having emerged from this endurance test, you, as a true modern, have the right to reject the past and dislike the present simultaneously. But for goodness sake refuse to fall into fashionable despair.

Below both hope and hopelessness, reach a bedrock conclusion: you can survive all the new-old styles of frustration. Possibly your most important asset right now is a sense of humor which seems to be missing from so many of this much-splendored generation. This humor which is neither sick nor black nor shaggy dog will allow you to keep things in their proper perspective and not take yourself so seriously that you reject the fact that change is king and life goes on, some days good, others bad, but always endlessly fascinating.

Before you leave the mirror of your mind, here are a few reflections to consider. Competition with the young Sister who is a cross between a Joan of Arc and a lunar-minded astronaut is not realistic. An alternative is integration, but integration brings with it the problems of the tightrope artist: you either move on or fall off. Recently a retired observer of the scene summed it up like this: while the private lives of the religious are clannish, perhaps their real power lies in being able to stimulate the over-thirty group.

Sisters Today, October, 1978

Life Changes and
Subsequent Illness in Women Religious

Sister Joan Therese Anderson, R.S.M.

Recent research studies document the association between a person's life stress and change in ongoing adjustment with subsequent illness in the individual.[1] It was not known how the relation between stress or ongoing adjustment and subsequent illness applied to women in religious life. The author conducted a study[2] to investigate whether a positive relationship existed between the total adjustment necessary in one year of a Sister's life and her likelihood of developing subsequent illness in the next year. It is the intent of this article to share with the reader the purpose and results of this study and suggest possible ramifications of the study results for women in religious life and their communities.

The life change events found to be associated with illness onset can be socially undesirable, negative and stressful, such as death of a loved one or being fired. The events can also be socially acceptable or desirable, such as success or achievement. The theme common to all life events is that occurrence of each is associated with some adaptive or coping behavior on the part of the individual involved.[3]

---

[1] Allen Wyler, M.D., Minoru Masuda, Ph.D. and Thomas Holmes, M.D., "Magnitude of Life Events and Seriousness of Illness," *Psychosomatic Medicine*, Vol. 33, #2 (Mar.–Apr. 1971), 115–122.

[2] Sister Joan Therese Anderson, R.S.M., "Life Change Units and Subsequent Illness in Women in Religious Life," Unpublished Masters Project, State U. of NY at Buffalo, 1975.

[3] Thomas Holmes & Richard Rathe, "The Social Adjustment Rating Scale," *Journal of Psychosomatic Research*, XI (1967), 213–218.

MAJOR CHANGES AND ADJUSTMENTS

Religious life today is a setting of significant environmental alterations requiring a major change in ongoing adjustment for individual Sisters. Due to the increasing variety of apostolic commitments of a religious community, such as CCD teams, parish ministries, home care of the elderly, social justice centers, spiritual direction and many others, as well as the problems of closing schools, opening new works, serious illness, retirement or death, and the continuing numbers of Sisters leaving religious life, much change is necessary in religious communities to meet the ongoing commitments.

Movement of Sisters from one assignment to another to meet the above needs requires tremendous adjustment for individual Sisters. The Sister must adjust to from three to fifteen new members in her local community, a new pastor, a new parish, a new superior, a new principal or administrator, a new horarium, a new job and possibly a whole new lifestyle depending upon the consensus of the small community she joins. In addition to the above, individual Sisters have been adjusting to the changes in religious life brought about in response to the call for renewal by the Second Vatican Council. This entailed major adjustments in life style, prayer forms, recreation, freedom to choose or request apostolates, shared authority, and greater involvement with the laity.

LIFE CHANGE UNITS

Holmes and Rathe[4] have described a method of qualifying the significance of various life events as they occur in the adult population. They succeeded in rank ordering a series of forty-three life events, including changes in family structure, occupation, income, education, health and peer relationships, and in assigning scores estimating the magnitude of stress experienced. These scores were called *life change units.* They found that the higher an individual's life change unit score for a given year, the greater one's chances of experiencing a major health change within the near future.[5]

The magnitude of stress experienced was the basis for the life change unit score. Stress is the wear and tear of living every day. Persons worrying, straining muscles, enjoying a basketball game, fighting an infection, losing a loved one or object, and experiencing changes in their everyday life are all undergoing stress. Stress consists not only of damage to the body but the adaptation and adjustment to the damage, irrespective of the cause. Stress is also evoked by putting up resistance to arguments, by boredom and by fatigue. Stress produces different diseases of adaptation in different individuals. The same kind

[4] Holmes and Rathe, *op. cit.,* 216.

[5] Stephenson Holmes and Thomas Holmes, "Short-term Intrusion into the Life Style Routine," *Journal of Psychosomatic Research,* XIV (1970), 121–132.

of stressful life experience can cause a duodenal ulcer, hypertension, migraine headaches or a heart attack in different people.[6]

A positive relationship between the occurrence of stressful events and the onset of illness has been appearing in the last two decades in psychological and medical literature.[7] Research studies have been cited which indicate a direct relationship between the number and intensity of life changes experienced by individuals and their likelihood of developing physical and psychological illness in the near future. If a positive correlation exists between stressful events and illness onset in religious life, the identification of stresses can be used to plan a program of prevention.

Since it was not known how illness in religious life correlated with the amount of previous adjustment, the problem investigated was whether a positive relationship existed between the total amount of life change experienced in one year by women in religious life and their likelihood of developing subsequent illness within the next year. If there was a correlation, significantly lowering life change events, for example by gauging the placement of Sisters with reference to their current life change totals, might become a means of decreasing vulnerability to disease in religious women.

THE MEASURING INSTRUMENT

The existing instrument for measuring the intensity of life changes developed by Holmes and Rathe was modified by the author to measure the intensity of life changes experienced by religious women today. The "Social Readjustment Rating Scale for Women in Religious Life" is the final modified form with each item assigned its numerical rank for the average magnitude of stress experienced by the 360 Sisters in the randomly selected research population. This scale is contained in Table 1. It was devised by totaling the numerical figures given by each of the 210 religious tested for each event and calculating the arithmetic mean score for each event and then dividing by ten. This method was the one used by Holmes in the original scale.

[6] Hans Selye, "The Stress of Life," (New York: McGraw Hill Book Company, 1956).

[7] D. T. Graham and I. Stevenson, "Disease Response to Life Stress," Psychological Basis of Medical Practice, H. I. Leif and V. F. Leif, eds. (New York: Harper and Row, 1963), 115–136.

Jerome Meyers et al., "Life Events and Psychiatric Impairment," Journal of Nervous and Mental Diseases, CLII (March, 1971), 149–157.

Richard Rathe et al., "A Longitudinal Study of Life Change and Illness Patterns," Journal of Psychosomatic Research, X (1967), 335–366.

TABLE 1

SOCIAL READJUSTMENT RATING SCALE
FOR WOMEN IN RELIGIOUS LIFE

RANK	LIFE EVENTS	LIFE CHANGE UNITS
1.	Decision to leave community	84
2.	Decision to take a leave of absence	79
3.	Death of a close family member	75
4.	Stay in a psychiatric unit or other institution	71
5.	Crisis in faith	70
6.	Death of a close friend	66
7.	Major personal illness or injury	59
8.	Being reassigned with consent	57
9.	Friend leaving the community	54
10.	Retirement from work	53
11.	Final profession of vows	50
12.	Changing to a different line of work	49
13.	Major change in number of arguments/disagreements with Sisters in the local community	48
14.	Closing of an institution in which you are living/working	47
15.	Reconciliation (with God, friend, Sister in community)	45
16.	Major change in involvement with family	45
17.	Decision to seek counseling help	44
18.	Major change in amount of freedom permitted by rule/custom	44
19.	Major change in religious rule or constitutions	44
20.	Major change in form of local government	44
21.	Change in a line of work outside community commitment	43
22.	Troubles with the boss	43
23.	Sexual difficulties	42
24.	Major change in responsibilities in the community	42
25.	Major change in responsibilities at work	42
26.	Major change in the involvement of seculars in local community	41
27.	Change of residence	40
28.	Trouble between convents or convent and larger community	40
29.	Troubles with local church (parish) over renewal	40
30.	Becoming responsible for community finances	40
31.	Revision of personal habits	39
32.	Menopause	39
33.	Outstanding personal achievement	36

RANK	LIFE EVENTS	LIFE CHANGE UNITS
34.	Major change in working hours or outside commitment	35
35.	Major change in prayer forms	34
36.	Major change in social activities or recreation	33
37.	Being assigned with consent	32
38.	Major change in financial state (money available in community)	31
39.	Beginning or closing formal schooling	30
40.	Change of a member of your local community	30
41.	Major change in local community get-togethers	27
42.	Change in independent use of money	26
43.	Contact with individuals who have left the community	26
44.	Major change in number of family get-togethers	25
45.	Major change in eating habits	24
46.	Major change in sleeping habits	22

A QUESTIONNAIRE OF EVENTS AND ILLNESSES

A self-administered questionnaire containing the events of the "Social Readjustment Rating Scale for Women in Religious Life" and a list of ninety-two illnesses was mailed to 982 women in three religious communities. Each Sister was asked to check the life events she experienced in one year and the illnesses she experienced the following year. The list of illnesses ranged in severity. They included the common cold, headaches, acne, sinus infection, pneumonia, psoriasis, bursitis, gout, depression, asthma, hepatitis, peptic ulcer, heart attack and cancer. The numerical rank for the severity of each disease developed by Wyler[8] was utilized and the correlation between the events and the illnesses was computed for the 380 questionnaires returned.

The religious women returning the questionnaire ranged from twenty to ninety-one in age. They spent from one to seventy-three years in religious life. The scores were 0 to 6188 with a mean of 1153.

THE RESULTS

The results of the study indicated a highly positive relationship between the magnitude of life change units for one year and the likelihood of experiencing a major health change within the following year. As the life change units totals increased so did the percentage of illnesses. The findings suggest the possibility that the higher the life change unit total, the greater will be the vulnerability to subsequent illness, as can be seen in Table 2.

[8] Alen Wyler et al., "The Seriousness of Illness Rating Scales," *Journal of Psychosomatic Research*, XI (1968), 363–374.

TABLE 2

SERIOUSNESS OF ILLNESS SCORES IN RELATION TO
CATEGORY OF THEIR LIFE CHANGE UNIT SCORES

Life Change Unit Score	Mean Illness Scores	Number in Sample
Under 150	500	126
150 - 199	1066	44
200 - 299	1250	79
Over 300	1773	131

Twenty religious had zero illness totals and sixteen of these were related to zero life change unit scores. The remaining four had life change unit scores of 44, 58, 141, and 169. Only twenty Sisters reported no illness, which is a significantly lower no-illness rate than other studies reported. The studies explored showed an absence of illness in one-third of their sample, while only five per cent of this study reported absence of illness. This cannot be accounted for solely by high life change scores as these appear very similar to mean life change unit scores in other studies. This would indicate further study is needed. It is possible illness may be more useful than other measures in forcing needed changes or eliciting needed help for a particular milieu in coping with stress.

THE PACE OF RENEWAL

Each Sister in the study was also asked to evaluate the pace or renewal in her community as 1) too slow 2) slow 3) just right 4) fast 5) too fast. A Sister who perceived the pace of renewal in her community to be fast was more likely to have a lower illness score than those who perceived the pace of renewal as slow. A Sister who perceived the pace of renewal in her community as slow was likely to have a higher illness score than those who perceived the pace of renewal as fast. It would appear that both a perceived slow and fast pace of renewal would be stressful.

It is possible, however, that a perceived slow pace of renewal may be more stressful as there is little one can do as an individual to change the pace, and this can daily become more frustrating depending upon a person's individual need for increasing freedom, shared authority and liturgical renewal. However, if a Sister perceived the pace of renewal as too fast, she could remain in a local community which is traditional and the changes might not have affected her personally. No matter how frustrated she may be with the fast pace of renewal in her total community, she might be able to control her own exposure to and acceptance of the renewal objectives. This difference in the ability to control and adopt a lifestyle acceptable to the individual may be the cause of the greater illness totals in those perceiving a slow pace of renewal.

THE YOUNG AND THE OLD

The greater the age and years in religious life, the greater the likelihood of a lower life change unit total and illness total. The study, however, did not document the accuracy of recall, and recall may well decline as age increased. Also, as age increases a religious woman may be more settled in residence, education and occupation than her younger counterpart and less vulnerable to illness from adjustment to recent life events.

Younger religious are in many cases changing their philosophical stance which renders them more vulnerable as they expose themselves to change, whereas older religious may tend more to hold on to tradition and risk exposure to changes in the Church and in religious life at a much slower pace. Many may also be retired from active work and are not as affected by the changes occuring within the school systems and through greater exposure to the lay world.

IMPLICATIONS OF THE STUDY

The implications of the study are many. Considering the higher probability of vulnerability to illness with increased life change, religious superiors and individual Sisters may wish to take into more serious consideration elective decisions to initiate further change in the life of an individual who is already experiencing a high life events total for a given year.

As illness scores were higher in women perceiving the pace of renewal as too slow, efforts should be made to assist Sisters who do perceive the pace of renewal in their community to be slow in adjusting to this pace or in coping with the stress in their own lives. Women in religious life could be assisted in understanding the correlation between adjustment and illness so they may elect new coping mechanisms or more effectively seek assistance in dealing with stress in their own lives.

Since a positive correlation exists between stressful life events and illness onset in religious life, the identification of stresses can be used to plan a program of prevention. The program could consist of elimination of unnecessary changes or the planning of community needs around the intensity of potential stress assignments would necessitate for individual Sisters.

A system of assistance could also be developed to aid an individual Sister who is coping with a high life change total which is unavoidable. As illness may reflect stress, religious superiors and individual Sisters could be alert to identify stresses in community life and then work to reduce or eliminate the identified stresses, thereby decreasing illness. Life events high on the scale in correlation with illness could be identified and preventive intervention planned on a community-wide scale.

Out of Blindness Into Your
Glorious Light

That soft pause
falling like a rose
petal and then your eyes
wordless, still and deeper
than all sound; I have
it all here behind my open
eyes. It lies behind
them opening blindness out into
sight. And always I see you.
If I live to see my God
I know he will look just that
way. Delicate as a petal,
eyes deep as the deepest part
of love. My heart fondles
the memory of your tears, your smile,
like a sudden light down a chill
and darkening hall, warms
me, suns me. And always I
die again over the memory of my
blindness. Until the glancing
sun shines again upon your
deep and sun dark eyes.
        I lie down in the sunset
        and with your glorious sun
                    I rise.

Sister Galen Martini, O.S.B.
Sisters Today, August–September, 1972

PART SEVEN

ADAPTATION AND RENEWAL:

Meeting the Challenge of Change

The renewal of religious life was well on its way before the Second Vatican Council came along in 1965 and spoke of the two-fold process of appropriate renewal involving "1) a continuous return to the sources of all Christian life and to the original inspiration behind a given community, and 2) an adjustment of the community to the changed conditions of the times." Father Kilian McDonnell, O.S.B., third editor of *Sponsa Regis*, in his "The Pope on Adaptation" gathers quotations from papal documents that plainly point to the beginnings of *aggiornamento*. Significantly, the dates on these documents are 1950, 1951, and 1952. The author was Pope Pius XII.

The stereotype of "the good Sister" whose simplicity, humility, and overflowing charity were meant to cover a multitude of intellectual omissions continued to come apart. There surfaced the agonizing awareness that a year or two of novitiate training in how to polish floors and make a meditation were not an adequate preparation for professional performance in any apostolate. "The Evolution of the Idea of Sister Formation, 1952–1960" describes the phenomenal progress in what might be better termed not an evolution but a revolution. Formation became the new name in convent vocabulary, and the name became the movement described as "the most important single activity in the Catholic Church in the United States during this quarter century."

A renewed challenge came to women religious when Cardinal Suenens' *The Nun in the World* appeared in 1962 and quickly became a kind of new testament for Sisters. This new call for Sisters to take their proper place in a Church that had removed its "Dead End" signs and was willing and able to move back into the modern world produced the term "the new breed." Seven distinguishing characteristics of this class that had received its diploma from the halls of Vatican II are discussed in an important essay entitled "The

277

Psychology of the 'New Breed' of Religious." "Attitudes of Sisters Toward Renewal" is one measurement of what was happening between community discussion and the implementation of ideas.

Renewal did not stay in community confines but soon became a diocesan and a national phenomenon. A Sisters' Congress was convened in the state of Georgia in 1966. Not long afterwards national organizations of Sisters began to emerge in a tangle of letters like NAWR, NCAN, ACS, SFCC, and NSFC. Sisters Uniting seeks to offer some unity to this diversity. Sisters' Network aims at "channeling information to Sisters throughout the United States and encouraging active concern in political issues related to social justice." The article "Contemplative Renewal" witnesses to the Spirit's blowing through the grilles of strict enclosures.

Two aspects that have served as indicators of *aggiornamento* are the religious habit and community living. Lest the quantity of serge be identified with the quality of the renewal surge, essays such as "Religious Habits and the Psychology of Dress" appeared.

The concept of community that had seldom been considered in earlier years now comes in for full and frequent scrutiny. "Community by Objectives" gives a practical, five-fold process for community goal setting. The trend from quantity of community to its quality is demonstrated by "Small-Group Communal Living." How small is small is considered in "Sisters Who Live Alone."

But along and/or together, women religious have accepted and accomplished a renewal of life that hopefully will prove to be as deep and lasting interiorly as that renewal has been exteriorly extensive.

Sponsa Regis, July, 1957

The Pope on Adaptation

Kilian McDonnell, O.S.B.

The General Congress on the State of Perfection held in Rome in 1950 had as its theme: *accommodata renovatio,* that is, the renewal of the primitive spirit of religious institutes adapted to the needs of the present day. To attain this end the Congress urged changes on two levels.

First, a return to the spirit which animated the founder. This is the most essential part of the program. Without this spiritual return, without a return to the sources of spiritual greatness, the renewal would be mere externalism, mere shifting of props and scenery.

Secondly, the adaptations and accommodations must be made with regard to the apostolate of each religious institute. Without this accommodation to the times, the institute or order will lose its effectiveness. What the Congress advocated, with the approval of the Holy Father, was accommodation in accidentals, externals, not in the essentials or the distinctive spirit of the various institutes.

A word of warning. Adaptation in the papal sense can never mean relaxation of the essential discipline. It does not mean a less strict way of life. Adaptation does mean change, and because of these changes it may mean being strict in a different way, using different means.

The quotations from papal documents printed here stress the second level more than the first. It goes without saying that the Holy Father considers spiritual renewal more intrinsic and more necessary than external adaptation to the times. But if the Holy Father uses forceful words in urging accommodation to the times, it can only mean that to neglect this accommodation is to compromise the spiritual effectiveness of the institute. Accommodation in non-essentials is always a means to a spiritual end, either of the Church as a whole or of the institute and its individual members.

"When the young people hear the statements: 'We must keep up to date,' and 'Our efforts must be commensurate with the times,' they are fired with an extraordinary ardor of soul; and, if they are serving under the standard of the religious militia, they keenly desire to direct the efforts of their future religious undertakings according to this principle. And, to a certain extent, this is proper. For it has often happened that the founding fathers of religious institutes conceived new projects in order to meet the challenge which newly emerging needs were urgently presenting to the Church and her work: and in this way they harmonized their enterprises with their age. Hence, if you wish to walk in the footsteps of your predecessors, act as they acted. Examine thoroughly the beliefs, convictions, and conduct of our own contemporaries; and, if you discover in them elements that are good, proper, make these worthwhile features your own; otherwise you will never be able to enlighten, assist, sustain, and guide the men of your own time" (Pius XII, Address to the General Congress of Religious Orders, Convocations, Societies, and Secular Institutes, December 8, 1950).

Keeping up to date is often looked upon with suspicion, and, to a certain extent, this suspicion is justifiable. In what sense can a religious institute accommodate itself to the world without betraying the very ideals which distinguish the institute from the world?

In Sacred Scripture the term "world" is used in two senses. When our Lord said, "I do not pray for the world," he used the term in the broad sense of "all that is evil and opposed to God." Then there is the second sense in St. John's exclamation, "God so loved the world that he gave his only begotten Son." Here the term is used in a generic sense to designate mankind, the people of the earth capable of receiving salvation. There can be no question of accommodation to the world in the first sense. An attempt at accommodation to the world in this sense would be apostasy. But there must be accommodation to the world in the second sense.

In this Christ is the example to be followed. Christ did not become a member of mankind in some super-temporal, super-terrestrial sphere of existence. When the Second Person of the Trinity took on human form, he did not become part of mankind in some universal abstract form. "The Word became flesh" is a concrete, individual way, determined by time and space. The Christ of time is a concrete human being. The Word became incarnate at a determined moment of history. The divine life was particularized in human form in a given thirty years of time. What the Godhead assumed was not only flesh, blood and bone, but country, nationality, language, accent, and all that makes the creature belong to this particular segment of time in his particular country.

"Follow in letter and spirit your constitutions; too, facilitate and bring the Sister all she needs and must do in our time to be a good teacher and educator. This applies to purely mechanical matters. In many countries today, for example, even Sisters use bicycles when their work demands it. At first this was something entirely new, though not against the rule. It is possible that some

details of the school schedules, certain regulations — simple applications of the rule — certain customs which were, perhaps, in harmony with past conditions, but which today merely hinder educational work, must be adapted to new circumstances. . . . You wish to serve the cause of Jesus Christ and of his Church in the way the world of today demands. Therefore, it would not be reasonable to persist in customs and forms that hinder this service or perhaps render it impossible. Sisters who are teachers and educators must be so well versed in all with which young people are in contact, in all which influences them, that their pupils will not hesitate to say: 'We can approach the Sister with our problems and difficulties, she understands and helps us'" (Pius XII, Advice to Teachers, September 15, 1951).

For the Church and for religious institutes to be of their time, for them to be incarnate in the world of today is the law of the Incarnation. To refuse this accommodation to the world would be to be more spiritual than Christ. It would be to neglect the commandment of Christ. Speaking of this Pope Pius XII said, "The work of extending God's Kingdom that every age carries out in its own way, using its own means and at the cost of much hard struggle, is a commandment binding on all."

What the Holy Father says of Catholic Action is true also of religious life: "To accomplish this task of regeneration by adapting her message to the changing conditions to the times and to the new needs of the human race is the essential office of our Holy Mother the Church." This adaptation is the price of effectiveness in the apostolate.

As the Holy Father points out, the young will go to the Sisters if they find them deeply religious, aware of the problems of their times, and unencumbered by accidental "customs and forms" which make the religious strangers in their own time and country. Unless the religious institute is of its time, the Holy Father warns, "you will never be able to enlighten, assist, sustain and guide men of your own time."

There is here the problem of respect for tradition. What the founders or foundresses have ordained are not lightly to be set aside, even in non-essential matters. But the Holy Father points out that one of the reasons why the foundresses were successful was their readiness to harmonize "their enterprises with their age." To expect foundresses, even canonized foundresses, to legislate the externals of religious life which would be valid for all times and for all ages would be to impose upon them a burden not even God expects them to bear.

The Holy Father asks the religious institutes to go back and study the lives of their foundresses. This means studying their lives in the context of their foundresses' age. If the foundresses are studied without reference to their historic, cultural, and religious background, if their lives are torn out of the context of the time in which they gave their unique contribution, the result will be a type of historic and religious violence done to what is most sacred.

Again we have the law of Incarnation. The saintly foundresses incarnated Christ in their times. There must be an understanding of how they incarnated Christ in their times, to understand how they would effect such an incarnation in our age. In short, the principle of the Holy Father is: not so much do as they did centuries ago as do what they would do were they alive today. Those religious institutes which follow this principle will be the truest followers of tradition. Those religious who are content to adhere to customs and practices which were valid "in another cultural framework," that of their foundresses, but no longer valid today, may well be reproached on the day of judgment by their very foundresses for a respect that was more human than divine.

Occasionally it will happen that in studying the life of a foundress in the context of her historic and religious background, it will be found that there was not in her day the same liturgical understanding as generally prevails today. Since the liturgical revival in Europe in the last century and in America in this century, there has been a greater appreciation of the role the Mass, sacraments, and the Divine Office play in the spiritual life.

The basic papal text, the charter of the liturgical movement, is the following sentence from the *Motu Proprio* of St. Pius X: "Our deepest wish is that the true Christian spirit should once again flourish in every way and establish itself among the faithful; and to that end it is necessary, first of all, to provide for the sanctity and the dignity of the temple where the faithful meet together, precisely in order to find that spirit at its primary and indispensable source, that is, . . .the active participation in the most holy and sacred mysteries and the solemn and common prayer of the Church."

That which St. Pius X promulgated and promoted, Pope Pius XII expanded in his historic encyclical on the liturgy, *Mediator Dei*. Pope St. Pius X and Pope Pius XII never tired of encouraging the faithful to go to the purest source of spirituality, the sacred liturgy. How much more this applies to a religious institute!

The liturgical movement did not become of age in Europe until the end of the Second World War, and therefore foundresses cannot be expected to have that full appreciation of the Church's official worship which the Church as a whole now enjoys. This full appreciation is seen in such papal legislation as the Decree on Frequent Communion by St. Pius X, Pius XII's restoration of the Easter Vigil, the privilege of evening Mass, the use of vernacular in the liturgy, the vernacular ritual, and the new eucharistic regulations for fasting.

Religious institutes would only be following the lead of Pius XII, whom both Cardinal Cicognani and Cardinal Maguigan have called "the Pope of the Liturgy," in extending adaptation of religious life to things liturgical. In this regard Father Creusen writes, "The liturgical movement, for instance, will prompt the taking of a more intimate and active part while assisting at the holy Sacrifice. All members of the community will be provided with a missal so they can follow the prayers of the priest. On certain days, perhaps, the dialogue Mass will be held. Some of the set prayers recited in common might be preferably replaced by others borrowed from the liturgy. One community, for example, has introduced the custom of reciting Compline as its evening prayer."

"As for yourselves (Mothers General of Religious Institutes for Women), here are our recommendations: in this crisis of vocations, take care that the customs, kind of life, or the growth of your religious families does not constitute a barrier or cause of failure. We refer to certain usages which, if at one time they had meaning in another cultural frame, no longer have it today and in which a truly good and courageous girl could find nothing but obstacles to her vocation. We gave various examples of this in our discourse last year. To return, in a word, to the question of clothing: the religious habit must always express consecration to Christ; it is this which everyone expects and wants. For the rest, let the habit be appropriate, and correspond to the needs of hygiene. We were able to see that one or two congregations had already arrived at some practical conclusions in this matter. In synthesis, in these things which are not essential, adapt yourselves to the extent that reason and well ordered charity counsel" (Pius XII, Address to 700 religious at the First International Congress of Superiors General of Orders and Congregations of Women, December 15, 1952).

One of the marks of psychological maturity is the ability to evaluate dispassionately the structure and elements of one's personality. A child does not ordinarily tend toward an analysis of what it is or has become. Only with age does it recognize the need for evaluating the components of its personality, and only with age does it attain that degree of objectivity which makes such an evaluation possible. If a person cannot bring herself to self-evaluation, if she is so enclosed within the confines of self that she cannot, with calm assurance, subject herself to any critical evaluation, then it must be said that psychologically she is immature. Her chronological age may be fifty, but in this psychological area she is still a child.

What is true of a person is to some degree true of institutions made up of persons. It is not at all impossible for a religious institute to be able to glory in a century or more of existence and yet lack the specific type of maturity we are talking about. The religious of the institute should be able, without suspicion of distrust for custom, to question custom. It was Pope Gregory VII and Pope Urban II who reminded us, "The Lord did not say, 'I am custom,' but 'I am Truth!' Very ancient and very widespread custom should be able to give way to Truth." If this freedom of evaluation is not allowed, then there would be sufficient grounds for holding the maturity of the institute suspect.

There should be no doubt as to what is valid material for such an evaluation. The specific end of the order has been determined by the foundress and the Holy See. Obviously, this is not, in the ordinary course of events, matter for adaptation. There are some means which are essential for the attainment of the end of the institute. These, too, are not matters for adaptation. There are other means which are not essential to the institute. These accidental means, determined by the foundress and found suitable in her cultural framework, might be quite unsuitable in another framework, our own. What is the means to an end in one age may well be an obstacle to the same end in another age.

In the above quotation from the Holy Father, he is speaking of one means, the religious habit. Generally, though not in every institute, the religious habit is considered an essential means. Though the habit may be an essential means, the style or cut of the habit is not. The style of the habit can be changed without changing the institute.

This may seem like belaboring the obvious. Theoretically, the argument is all too obvious. But in the practical order the line of reasoning is not so easily seen. There is good reason for this. "Clothes," it is said, "make the man," or the woman, or the Sister. We tend to identify the person with what one wears. If I want to imitate a man, to be taken for him, I put on his clothes. In this way I assume his identity. The identification between person and clothes carries over, and there is an identification between institution and habit.

In the realm of theory, all will admit that the habit can be changed without changing the institute. The difficulty is not theoretical, but practical. In the practical order or, if you like, in the psychological order, the one who suggests the modification of the habit is sometimes thought to be touching or tampering with the essence of the institute, and this because of the mentioned tendency to identify institute with habit.

Sisters are to be commended for the great reverence they show their habits. They are truly holy garments. But some clarification is needed as to what is holy in a habit. What does Sister mean, or what should she mean, when she speaks about "the holy habit" of the institute? The Holy Father says, "The religious habit must always express consecration to Christ." The person, the Sister, is the subject of consecration. This personal consecration is expressed, externalized in the covering of the body. The garments achieve the expression of this consecration by their penitential and symbolical character.

But what is to be noted here is that the consecration is to be found first in the person, and secondarily in the habit. This is not said to lessen the respect for the habit. Indeed, the Church blesses the habit with a liturgical blessing in order to impress upon religious that they not only put on the grace of Christ, interior transformation, but even put on material garments sanctified with his blessing, exterior transformation.

Speaking to teaching religious in September, 1951, the Holy Father said: "The religious habit: choose it in such a way that it becomes an expression of inward naturalness, of simplicity and spiritual modesty." Father Victor D. Vierge, O.C.D., reduces this principal to some practical suggestions. He writes, "When the different religious habits were adopted by the founders, they resembled the dress of the poor people of the period. Today a habit is required that helps the body, not one that embarrasses it: it should be practical, simple, and have pockets. . . . In order that in our day the religious habit may keep its esthetic appeal and its character of poverty, together with the attractive symbolism of consecration, it would suffice to simplify it. It would thus become more practical: fewer pleats, narrower sleeves, less pretentious coifs and coronettes."

Returning for the moment to relate the question of religious habit to the question of tradition, there comes to mind a certain Sisterhood which in the common estimation of the bishops, priests and laity could well profit by a modification in their habit. Perhaps quite proper in the cultural framework of the foundress, the habit is a continual source of amazement to the people of our age. "Amazement" is used here as a synonym for the technical ecclesiastical term *admiratio*, which denotes mild shock or unhealthy wonder. When politely asked if they were contemplating a modification, the superior answered, "No, we have decided to remain true to tradition."

The Sisters, in all sincerity, had conceived of tradition as a static thing, something that is received from the past, which must be handed down to succeeding generations just as it was received. Whatever justification the Sisters may have had for their concept of tradition, it is not the papal definition of tradition. In the mind of the Pope tradition is a dynamic concept, vital with relevance not only for the past, but also for the present and future.

Pope Pius XII makes tradition synonymous with progress. These are his words: "Tradition is something entirely different from mere attachment to an irretrievable past. It is exactly the opposite of reaction against all healthy progress. Even etymologically the word is synonymous with progress; although synonym does not mean that the words are identical. While progress means the mere act of marching forward step by step, looking into an uncertain future, tradition conveys the idea of an uninterrupted march forward, which progresses both serenely and in a vital manner in accordance with the laws of life, and which solves the agonizing dilemma between youth and old age."

It was Pius IX who is reported to have said, "We are so fond of traditions, that we do not hesitate to make new ones." To invoke tradition has lost none of its validity. But care must be taken that such invocation is not the conjuring up of the dead past. Tradition should still be held in veneration, guarded with that fierce jealousy with which we guard life and sacredness, but not enshrined like a dead relic. Tradition is related to life. It lives.

The Holy Father, surely by reason of his office the greatest respecter of tradition and custom, is greatly concerned lest traditions become obstacles to religious perfection, rather than means. And he refers in a special way to the effect which out-dated customs and out-dated religious habits can have upon girls aspiring to the religious life. He goes so far as to say that a "truly good and courageous girl" will be discouraged from entering religious life. There is in this girl no lack of generosity; though generous, she is not attracted to an exalted vocation which is overlaid with anachronisms in observance and in habit. The Holy Father leaves no doubt as to where the fault lies.

The Pope's words about the "crisis of vocations" and customs constituting a "barrier or a cause of failure" brings to mind a religious Sisterhood who have been teaching in a certain parish for nearly a hundred years. In these one hundred years the Sisterhood has received only a handful of recruits for its novitiate. The parish itself is thoroughly Catholic, the people are fervent. This particular Sisterhood had a European origin, and they never adapted themselves in custom or in habit to their new home. They are good religious, but both their customs and their strange habit have been obstacles to their growth. Their institute has suffered from one long "crisis of vocations." As an institute and as individuals they have had neither the maturity nor the courage to re-evaluate those accidental means which keep them from being better religious and attracting more vocations.

Strange

At night
the trees wail
and the wind
mourns
in my blood. Sin hides
near my soul
as the world sings
for me, and a strange air
it is.
            My hands
are a cracked heart aloft.
            I ache
            for God.

Brother Patrick Ryan, O.C.S.O.
Sisters Today, January, 1978

Sponsa Regis, April, 1962

The Evolution of the Idea of Sister Formation, 1952–1960[1]

Sister Mary Richardine, B.V.M.

When Sister Bertrande, D.C., wrote her doctoral dissertation on *The Education of Sisters* in 1941, she was dreaming of the day when Sisters would enter the apostolate of the works of mercy fully equipped for the tasks at hand. Did she dream then that Marillac College, of which she is president, would be the extraordinary reality that it is—with Sister specialists from fifteen different religious congregations on its staff?

When Sister Madeleva, C.S.C., startled a National Catholic Educational Association audience in 1948 with her paper on "The Education of Sister Lucy," did she envision what has actually been happening in Sister Formation from coast to coast during the past ten years?

Even secular educators are amazed at the development of Providence Heights, Seattle University's College of Sister Formation, whose administration is co-shared by the University and four participating religious congregations.

The evolution of the idea of Sister Formation shows growth taking place silently and almost imperceptibly at one time; at other times the whole world has seemed aware of what was happening within this microcosmic movement. Whenever obstacles seemed insurmountable, humanly speaking, some special mark of divine condescension would give reassurance that this work must be pleasing to God. From the very beginning those interested in the movement were deeply convinced of the present and future good to be accomplished for the Church, for the Sisterhoods, and for individual souls if the objectives of this movement were achieved.

---

[1] This paper has been adapted for publication from a talk given at the Marquette University workshop on the Role of the Faculty in the Sister Formation Program, August 5, 1960. It covers the period up to the end of Sister Mary Emil's work.

At the 1952 N.C.E.A. convention, concern to have adequate preparation for Sister-teachers reached a high point when a panel on teacher education discussed Pope Pius XII's Directive to the International Congress of Teaching Sisters. "See to it, therefore, that they are well trained and that their education corresponds in quality and academic degree to that demanded by the State." More than an exhortation, these words of our Holy Father were truly a command, and they were recognized as such. It was decided that we religious would do well to assess our strengths and weaknesses.

Immediately a volunteer committee was set up to study the preparation of teaching Sisters. The movement which we have frequently heard described as the most important single activity in the Catholic Church in the United States during this quarter century came into being at that moment. Those who have watched it grow and spread can best corroborate Cardinal McIntyre's observation that it must have been needed or it never would have taken hold so rapidly.

In 1952 the first and primary objective of the movement — if it could even have been called a movement then — was to secure an accurate picture of the education of Sister-teachers, to disseminate the information to Mothers General and to ecclesiastical and educational authorities, and to propose some solutions to the problems which the survey would undoubtedly bring to light. Along with statistical data of the survey itself, the findings of a very pertinent related study on cost of living and education, and a valuable summary of comments of major religious superiors on besetting problems hindering their efforts to educate their Sisters, were incorporated into the Survey Report. The task of making the survey, compiling and disseminating the information was the major accomplishment of the Survey Committee during that year.

(Since the impetus for the survey came from the N.C.E.A. Teacher Education Section, it was natural that attention was focused on Sister-teachers, and not on nurses and social workers. This special emphasis on teacher education continued through the first two or three years of the movement. While this was advantageous in many respects, it also created misunderstandings which delayed the involvement in the Sister Formation Movement of religious communities engaged in other apostolic works.)

Even though reactions to the Survey Report varied, by and large it was recognized as an important document, embodying facts never before assembled yet vitally significant to the future of Catholic education. As might be expected, the findings of the report pointed up many problems. The members of the Survey Committee were keenly aware that the Teacher Education Section alone could not solve these problems or even propose adequate solutions. Every effort was made to channel the data of the Survey Report to the competent ecclesiastical and religious authorities as quickly as possible.

A highlight of the 1953 N.C.E.A. convention in Atlantic City was a joint meeting of the Superintendents' Department and the Teacher Education Section of the College and University Department, featuring a panel of superintendents and members of the Survey Committee who discussed the findings and implications of the Survey Report. Of even greater importance for the future of the Sister Formation Movement was the support expressed at this meeting for Sister Mary Emil's proposal of Sisters' Educational and Professional Standards Commissions, similar to N.E.A.'s Teacher Education and Professional Standards Commissions. The College and University Department's Midwest Regional Unit had already placed its stamp of approval on the proposal. Yet S.E.P.S. still had a long road to travel before gaining final approbation from the National Catholic Educational Association. Nevertheless, progress was being made.

The first phase in the evolution of the idea of Sister Formation was almost over. The Survey Report was completed; its findings disseminated. The *Directory of Catholic Women's Colleges with Facilities for Sisters*, and its *Graduate Supplement*, outgrowths of the original survey, were proving their worth both to Sisters and to educational institutions. A capable editor, in the person of Sister Ritamary, C.H.M., was promised for the intercommunity publication which was part of the Sister Formation dream for the future. The proposal to establish Sisters' Educational and Professional Standards Commissions was being carefully scrutinized, yet sympathetically and with evident enthusiasm.

Between the 1953 and 1954 conventions those who believed in the movement worked hard to win support and understanding of the objectives of the S.E.P.S. Commissions. The idea was new. Some feared it. Others were confused about the goals. Still others recognized the need for such activity as the commissions would generate, but they hesitated to become involved. Yet there was a healthy nucleus of Catholic educational leaders, more alert perhaps to present problems or with greater vision of the challenges of the coming decade, who eagerly espoused the cause. Outstanding Catholic educators served on a national consultative committee to assist in guiding the initial activities of the S.E.P.S. Commissions.

The movement could count among its ardent supporters members of the hierarchy, major superiors and subjects in religious communities of both men and women, school superintendents, college personnel and officers of several lay organizations. Leaders came to the fore in all parts of the country, glad to assume the burdens inseparable from a monumental project such as was envisioned. It seemed to them eminently worthwhile to expend their energies to set in motion any authorized machinery through which the Sisterhoods of the United States could help one another find answers to mutual contemporary problems. Generous assurance of cooperation from many members of the hierarchy gave impetus to even greater efforts.

By January, 1954, all necessary authorizations had been obtained from the N.C.E.A. General Executive Board and the Executive Committee of the College and University Department for enlarging the Committee on the Survey into an integrating group which would "sponsor exploratory regional conferences with a view to the ultimate establishment of Sisters' Educational and Professional Standards Commissions." At this time the name of the organization was changed to Sister Formation Conference, as more expressive of the integration of the spiritual and intellectual elements in the formation of a Sister for her apostolic work. Even the new name was a proof that the concept itself was truly evolving.

As more people became active in Sister Formation work, greater precautions were needed to direct the evolution of the idea. Some had to be disabused of the notion that the conference was a panacea for all ills in Catholic education. It was imperative that there be a statement of purpose. The one determined upon was: "The Sister Formation Conference seeks the advancement of the religious, cultural, and professional formation of Sisters, on pre-service and in-service levels." Adhering to this stated purpose has been one of the major strengths of the movement. It has furthered the proper evolution of the Sister Formation idea and ideals.

The National Catholic Educational Association tabled the motion to establish a Sister Formation Section in 1954; however, a Committee on Sister Formation was authorized, with Sister Mary Emil as chairman. Major superiors of many teaching communities responded to an invitation to participate in the movement at this time. Personally or through delegated representatives at the N.C.E.A. convention, these religious superiors cooperated in the preliminary planning for the first series of regional conferences.

Every caution was being exercised at this stage of activity so that the tremendous potentialities of the proposed conferences might not be lost through imprudent or inadequate planning. Sister Mary Emil, I.H.M., accompanied by Sister Ritamary journeyed to every region to insure the correct development of the growing movement in all parts of the country. Meetings of local planning and consultative committees during the summer of 1954 had the benefit of wise counsel as tentative agendas were drawn up for the first regional conferences. Their successful outcome is one of the most glorious chapters in Sister Formation history. But it was no chance happening. The groundwork was laid with meticulous care.

With a wisdom born of prudence, the theme selected for the 1954 Regional Sister Formation Conferences was "The Mind of the Church in the Formation of Sisters." The very theme itself reiterated the papal directives and answered the questions in some minds about the direction this new movement might be expected to take. As national and regional officers assessed the results of the first conference series they decided that a study of "The Integration of the Spiritual and Intellectual Elements in the Formation of Sisters" was a vital second step. It seemed important to make this desired goal of integration very explicit from the beginning.

Participants in the second conference series clarified their own thinking on the type of formation which we should be envisioning for our young Sisters, as one which will be deeper and richer from the very fact that a solid philosophical and theological foundation will insure an intellectual grasp of the spiritual life. Sister Formation personnel from all communities were brought to realize that there need be no dichotomy between intellectual and spiritual formation;

but rather that each is essential if we are to give a Sister the best preparation for her apostolic work.

Since the curriculum is one of the most dynamic forces in educational formation, it followed almost naturally in the sequence of conference themes. The third regional conference series explored the content of the Everett Report, which summarized a three-month cooperative study to plan an ideal curriculum for pre-service formation for Sisters. This study, financed by a grant from the Fund for the Advancement of Education, was the work of a committee of outstanding Sister-educators during the summer of 1956. The College of Saint Teresa in Winona, Minnesota, and the Seattle University College of Sister Formation assumed the burden and now share the distinction of being demonstration centers for the Everett Curriculum, which was the end-product of the study.

With the understandings which the first three conference series developed, delegates to the fourth Regional Sister Formation Conferences were ready for consideration of "The Juniorate in the Mind and Directives of the Holy See." The Apostolic Constitution, "Sedes Sapientiae," promulgated shortly before this conference series, provided basic resource material on the mind of the Church in the formation of male religious which could be applied analogously to the formation of Sisters.

Although the first four regional conference series were directed to pre-service formation, this was not the sole concern of the Sister Formation Movement. The statement of purpose indicates that the needs of in-service Sisters is an equally important objective. Mindful that the vast majority of the 168,000 Sisters in the United States have not had pre-service formation in a juniorate, the delegates to the fifth Sister Formation Conference series considered the problems of "The In-Service Sister," so appropriately described as "our greatest resource" by the Sister Formation Committee's first National Chairman, Mother Mary Philothea, F.C.S.P.

From 1954 until the present time the Sister Formation message has been reaching religious superiors, mistresses, and administrators through the regional conferences. The influence of these conferences has been extended to the rank and file within religious communities and to a general readership through four published volumes of Conference Proceedings.

A quarterly bulletin with a mailing list of 6,000 also effectively communicates the story of Sister Formation both within and beyond the United States. The first issue of this *Sister Formation Bulletin* was sent out in October, 1954, to more than eight hundred subscribers, thus putting into circulation what is thought to be the first, and as far as we know "the only English language periodical in the world devoted to the literature of the pre-service and in-service formation of Sisters." From its first appearance the bulletin won whole contingents of enthusiastic supporters for the movement, not alone on this continent but in the age-old centers of spiritual and educational influence in Rome and other parts of Europe.

Originally the *Sister Formation Bulletin* was planned as a publication exclusively for religious superiors. Popular demand altered this purpose before more than one or two issues had come from the press. As a result the scope of materials was enlarged to carry the story of Sister Formation to a more general readership. Since December, 1957, the *Sister Formation Newsletter for Higher Superiors* has been accomplishing the more limited objective of the original bulletin. Through this newsletter major superiors can keep abreast of current developments, issues and trends of importance in today's apostolate. The *Newsletter for Higher Superiors* is one of many services to the Sisterhoods of the United States emanating from the Sister Formation Secretariat of the National Catholic Educational Association.

Thanks to the vision of Monsignor Hochwalt and the apostolic spirit of Sister Mary Emil's superiors, a secretariat was set up at N.C.E.A. headquarters in Washington in 1957 with Sister Mary Emil as executive secretary. Mother Rose Elizabeth, C.S.C., first National Vice-Chairman of the Sister Formation Committee, welcomed Sister to residence at Dunbarton College of Holy Cross in Washington.

The National Sister Formation Conference Leadership Group decided that the executive secretary should give priority to the following activities:

1. Travel for evaluation of the Everett Report;
2. Attendance at all regional conferences;
3. Study of helps available from Catholic and national agencies;
4. Investigation of available scholarships and fellowships;
5. Sending of information concerning Sister Formation to higher superiors and to the NSFC Leadership Group;
6. Efforts to secure from some foundation the necessary funds for training of SF personnel.

As Sister Mary Emil set about achieving these objectives, other needs of the Sisterhoods also became more evident. On that account travel to regional conferences or for evaluation of the Everett Report always allowed time for visits to religious communities, especially to those small communities in isolated areas, whose superiors still turn with confidence to the Sister Formation Secretariat for assistance with their formation programs. Long and arduous lecture tours became a part of the treks across the United States and into Canada, helping thousands of religious better to understand and appreciate the Sister's role in today's apostolate. Pastors have grown more sympathetic with Sister Foundation ideals, and more eager to share the financial burdens inseparable from prolonged pre-service formation, after listening to Sister Mary Emil's cogent arguments. Seminarians have been charged with zeal for the Sister Formation cause after even one short lecture on the movement. Lay people have responded to Sister's inspirational challenge with a thrillingly Catholic participation in the educational enterprise of the Church.

Designed as a "clearing house of Sister Formation information and assistance," the secretariat has realized the almost limitless possibilities which such service may embrace. The Director of Notre Dame's Institute of Spirituality for Religious seeks the fertile resources of the Sister Formation Conference when planning programs and securing speakers. Officers of the non-sectarian Religious Education Association turn to the Sister Formation Conference Executive Secretary for assistance in selecting scholars to present Catholic views on today's religious education problems.

As one of its commitments the Sister Formation Secretariat has ceaselessly tracked down information on helps available for the Sisterhoods from Catholic and national agencies. Information on grants, scholarships, and fellowships has been relayed to higher superiors as quickly as possible. As a result many Sisters have enjoyed extraordinary educational opportunities which financial limitations might otherwise have placed beyond their reach.

Using a Raskob Foundation grant for expenses, Sister Mary Emil represented the Sister Formation Conference in its approach to educational foundations, industry, and individuals to interest them in financing the education of Sister college teachers, who will in turn train the young Sisters now being prepared for elementary and secondary Catholic schools, and for hospitals and social agencies. The 150 or more juniorates which have sprung into existence must have an adequately prepared faculty or the whole purpose of the formation program will be defeated. Progress to date on the Raskob Foundation project justifies high hopes for its success in providing funds for the preparation of Sister Formation personnel.

Many other activities clamor for expression as we think about the evolution of the idea of Sister Formation. We try to share the feelings of the native Sisters from Kerala, India, who journeyed to America recently. Two by two they went to various parts of the United States to colleges conducted by the Sisters of Mercy. Next year, and every year thereafter, another group will come. After four years the first Sister-students will return to Kerala, and their number will grow from year to year. Back in their own country, these native Sisters will carry on their apostolate, equipped spiritually, intellectually, and professionally with the same excellent formation which the Sisters of Mercy are providing for their own junior Sisters. This "Mercy Plan" under the Sister Formation Conference seems to be the first organized program for educational adoption, although many Sisterhoods in the United States have shared in the apostolic work in other countries through the education of Sisters.

Today in cloistered convents across the United States contemplative nuns are listening to tape recordings of the Institute on Mental Health, conducted at the College of St. Catherine in St. Paul, Minnesota, under Sister Annette, C.S.J.'s efficient direction. Again on tape, these religious are sharing the benefits of the Sister Formation Conference Workshops on Instructional Programs in Spirituality. These lecture series, conducted by Father Elio Gambari, M.M., of the Sacred Congregation of Religious, are making a tremendous impact on formation programs in religious congregations throughout the United States and Canada.

Together with Father Gambari's lecture, novice, postulant and junior mistresses have added opportunity for college courses in ascetical theology, planned as part of the Sister Formation effort. Carefully structured to fulfill the most exacting educational requirements, these courses are offered in four weekly units at spaced intervals throughout the year, thus successfully meeting the mistresses' problem of time. The Sister Formation message is now reaching college personnel, who likewise share formation responsibility, through special sessions at N.C.E.A. conventions and through workshops at colleges and universities. Through each of these new programs the Sister Formation Movement continues to evolve.

September, 1960, marked a new phase in the evolution of the idea of Sister Formation when Sister Annette, C.S.J., assumed the duties of executive secretary. "Far from representing any break in the continuity of our effort," wrote Sister Mary Emil, "this change, we truly feel, can mean an enhancement and a solidifying of every good thing for which the movement has stood, so that in ten years from now we will look back upon this time as representing a step up to a distinctly higher level of activity."

This sentence from the *Newsletter for Higher Superiors* epitomizes the Sister Formation spirit. It is the spirit which has earned recognition for the movement from our Sovereign Pontiffs and the Sacred Congregation of Religious; the spirit which motivates Sister Formation activities as a joint apostolic effort of the National Catholic Educational Association and the Conference of Religious Superiors of Women of the United States. This is the spirit which Cardinal Larraona surely had in mind when he told Sister Catherine, D.C., National Chairman of the Sister Formation Conference, that he believes the Sisters of the United States will play a "directive role" in the formation of women religious throughout the world. This is the spirit, clearly discernible now, which was pulsating without our realizing it through every line of the six-page agenda for the first meeting of the Committee on the Survey in 1952, a truly startling record of Sister Mary Emil's vision of the potential of the Sister Formation Movement.

Sponsa Regis, April, 1964

Cardinal Suenens and American Sisters

Francis MacNutt, O.P.

Almost as soon as *The Nun in the World*[1] appeared in the book stores, it disappeared—sold out. At the NCEA convention in St. Louis, the Newman Press booth was caught short by a surprising demand for copies. Soon after, the whole printing was exhausted, and for several weeks Sisters thought themselves lucky to borrow a battered copy that had passed from hand to hand. Everywhere Sisters were discussing Cardinal Suenens and his proposals.

In some communities unrest was built up when Sisters suddenly experienced a desire for apostolic action but felt they were not living up to the Cardinal's ideal. Implementation of his ideas could only be carried out by authority and under obedience (as he himself clearly pointed out); yet the younger members of some communities were restless for action.

Some superiors who agreed with the Cardinal's apostolic suggestions made whatever adaptations they could. Others waited to watch and weigh the reactions of the majority of U.S. communities before making their own decisions.

Amidst the burst of favorable reviews there also appeared a few unfavorable notices, while the privately expressed opinions of Sister-superiors seemed to vary as widely as the reviews.

In general, the critics of *The Nun in the World* made two objections:

a) Cardinal Suenens' ideas are not practical;

b) He is speaking about European Sisters, not about Americans.

Now that surprise at his proposals has had time to dissipate, superiors are calmly considering whether the Suenens challenge applies to American Sisters. Still more concretely, they must wisely decide how the Cardinal's suggestions bear upon their own particular communities.

---

[1] Newman Press: Westminster, 1962.

This article will try to point out the main questions raised by *The Nun in the World* for American Sisters — the questions that American communities will have to ask themselves and answer in the immediate future.

THE CARDINAL'S BASIC PREMISE

Before considering practical questions, we must first be clear about Cardinal Suenens' starting point, for once this has been agreed upon, most of his conclusions follow with inescapable logic. Moreover, some critics, failing to take issue with the Cardinal's basic premise, attack him on peripheral issues ("Obviously our nuns cannot hobble about in tight, knee-length skirts and slinky sweaters; nor would it be feasible to try chasing the elusive hemline from year to year"[2] — as if the Cardinal had suggested this!). This dodging of the main issue is perhaps unconscious, so it is important to emphasize the major assumption underlying *The Nun in the World*. It is simply this: *All Sisters* (excluding the strictly contemplative) *have an obligation to exercise the direct apostolate.*

This idea, once it is fully grasped, is a startling concept not only to Sisters but to clergy and laity as well. The Cardinal is saying that it is not enough for Sisters to exercise the apostolate of good example (indirect apostolate) but they must also exercise a real, personal, missionary apostolate among the people. This direct apostolate involves:

a) a *spoken*, doctrinal apostolate, so that Sisters can take an active part in spreading the faith, rather than merely being content to give good example as consecrated women carrying out their professional duties;

b) a *person to person* apostolate, requiring private, conversational contact in order to inspire, console, and enlighten;

c) an *active seeking of contact* with women and girls, students and parents, patients and families, rather than waiting within the convent in hopes that stray individuals will knock on the door of their own accord.

In schools this would mean that Sisters should take a non-academic, personal interest in their students (without, of course, unduly interfering), so that they can turn out committed, apostolic women whose entire lives are Christianized by the school. Unless Sisters can do more than teach individual courses, they cannot fully exercise the apostolate to which the Church today calls them.[3]

---

[2] "The Nun in the World," *Doctrine and Life*, September, 1963, 446.

[3] Students themselves feel this need. As one girl wrote after an unfortunate school episode: "This tragedy prompts the question: could the Sisters have done something to prevent it? Now, I realize something most of my friends would be *surprised* to hear: that their teachers do have a strong personal interest in each of them. But most girls shrug their shoulders and think the teacher regards them only as a slot in the grade book and a locker number. As a result, the average student is content to keep school impersonal. Since most of us are unaware that our verb-conscious French teacher is concerned about more than memory, we back away from any contact in our after-school life."

To get a complete understanding of what the Cardinal means by a "direct apostolate" we must read *The Gospel to Every Creature*,[4] for *The Nun in the World* is merely an expansion of Chapter V of the earlier and, perhaps, far more important book. Yet some reviewers of *The Nun in the World*, the sequel, seem unaware of *The Gospel to Every Creature*, and do not even bother to comment on the central thesis underlying both books (that all Christians have an obligation to exercise the direct apostolate).[5]

In any serious evaluation of the ideas contained in *The Nun in the World*, we must first read *The Gospel to Every Creature* and understand why the Cardinal says that every Christian (with the exception of the strict contemplative) has an obligation to exercise the direct apostolate. Jesus said, "Go, preach the gospel," and this order leaves no room for evasion; it must be obeyed by all — not just bishops, not just priests, but by all religious — and by the laity as well.

In this book he is thus attacking the widely held view that the laity do their apostolic part simply by giving good example. Most laymen react with great surprise (and sometimes with disbelief) at first hearing that they have a serious obligation to be direct apostles; they have never heard of such an idea. So it is little wonder that some Sisters, too, are surprised to hear that they are especially included in the great command to preach the gospel.

Despite the dynamite within its pages, however, *The Gospel to Every Creature* passed almost unnoticed into our libraries, even when it contained statements such as:

> Our duty as baptized Christians is as compelling for religious as for the laity and takes precedence over our professional duty. No one has the right to limit his obligations to the organizing of a hospital or school, and to confine his efforts to working for the success of his institution (p. 94).
>
> Why has one come to spend one's life in a particular spot, unless in the hope of spreading the Gospel message and acting as a radiant center of love? The specific end, the education of children or the care of the sick, is not the final objective, but a door of communication, . . .the justification of our claim to be members of Christ. . . . This does not in any sense mean that one is bound to reserve for the final objective the same amount of time as for the specific end: a few hours given up to the organization of the laity may have incalculable repercussions. . . .
>
> Religious should continually resist the temptation to restrict their mental vision. . . (p. 95).

Consequently, the first thing we must consider in evaluating Cardinal Suenens' proposals is the gospel basis on which he builds: "Sisters, like all

---

[4] Newman Press: Westminster, 1957 (reprinted most recently in 1963).

[5] Symptomatic of the lack of attention paid to the more basic *The Gospel to Every Creature* is the footnote on p. 68 of *The Nun in the World* (first printing) in which the Cardinal's reference to his earlier work is given as "Cf. L'Eglise en état de mission." Apparently not even the editors of Newman Press recognized that this referred to *The Gospel to Every Creature*, which they themselves had published five years previously!

Christians, have a strict obligation to exercise a direct apostolate." Once it is granted that this obligation exists, then it follows that Sisters must act to fulfill their missionary vocation.

Incidently, while some may not have noticed the first appearance of *The Gospel to Every Creature*, there was one who did: Pope Paul VI, then Cardinal Montini, who wrote the Preface and endorsed the Suenens theme as follows:

> The theme of this book is so important that it cannot leave unaffected anyone who has at heart a love of the Church, or is conscious of the spiritual crisis in the world. . . . This is a disturbing and a courageous book, because it springs from a close observation of the existing weaknesses of the Christian community: but fundamentally it is an optimistic book. . . . With a clear vision and a vigorous style, the writer marshalls all his arguments to one conclusion, namely, the necessity, the possibility of that energy which, springing from love, can alone bring forth within the Church a new spirit of the missionary apostolate and thus save the world. This is a book to be read (p. viii).[6]

With the approval of the Pope, it then seems that the first question Cardinal Suenens proposes is:

"*Are all American communities of Sisters* (aside from the strictly contemplative) *fully aware that they have a strict obligation to exercise the direct apostolate* (as distinct from the apostolate of good example)?"

As reviewers have pointed out, one of Cardinal Suenens' basic proposals — that Sisters have a part in the formation of adult women in Catholic Action — depends upon the attitude and initiative of the bishop and priests of any given diocese. In many places, therefore, it is not immediately possible for Sisters to engage in Catholic Action.

Nevertheless, there are questions which communities can now ask themselves and can now act upon, once they realize the validity of the basic premise of *The Gospel to Every Creature*. These questions, posed by *The Nun in the World*, which are of immediate practical importance to American communities, can be directed to teaching communities and to nursing communities.

QUESTIONS PROPOSED TO TEACHING COMMUNITIES

Once a teaching community sees that it has an obligation to exercise the direct apostolate, then it is clear that, within the context of the school situation, the Sisters are called to influence the entire lives of their students, out of

---

[6] Compare these statements with one criticism of *The Nun in the World:* "His words would have more force did they not convey the unfortunate impression of one living in an ivory tower, whose strictures are often unrealistic and sometimes unnecessarily severe. . . . His expression is often old-fashioned, at times obscuring his own meaning" (*Doctrine and Life*, September, 1963, 448, 446). Might this not be the fault of the translator rather than the author?

school as well as in class. Moreover, this implies an apostolate to the parents and to the alumnae as well.

The following is the primary question proposed by *The Nun in the World* to American teaching communities:

Is there any way of improving the Sisters' direct personal apostolate among their students?

Are Sisters in this community given the opportunity to talk to their students about non-academic matters outside of class? Does the rule make it possible for Sisters to talk to girls who come to them with problems? If the rule forbids such conversation or contact, then the rule must be changed (see ch. 8, "The Wider View"). Not only should the rule make it possible for Sisters to exercise a direct apostolate among their students, but it should encourage such action. "One wants to give one's life, not to become a supervisor or a grammarian but to bring Christ to souls" (p. 88).

Is the schedule arranged to give time for the students to approach the Sisters outside of class, or, on the contrary, is the schedule so filled that it is physically impossible for the Sister to do anything but teach class and correct papers? Is the Sister encouraged, within the bounds of prudence, to have personal, non-academic contact with her students, so that the girls can talk to her privately if they wish?

Are the rules of enclosure so strict that the Sister cannot see a student except in the convent or in class? Can the Sister participate with the students in appropriate outside activities when her presence would help and is desired by the students (e.g., the class picnic)?

These are questions posed to *American* teaching Sisters, not only by Cardinal Suenens but by the girls themselves in some parochial schools who feel that their teachers are unapproachable, "out of it." As one girl wrote about the Sisters at her school: "They seem to be above everybody else, having no interests in common with us. They seem to have been Sisters all their lives, never having shared the experiences we are now having."

Moreover, since direct contact with parents is necessary to solve many individual and social problems (dating and drinking, for example), the Sisters should have some kind of apostolate to their parents. Are teaching Sisters, then, encouraged to meet with parents for a mutual solving of student or school problems? Are Sisters allowed to visit homes where the family is relaxed and more ready to talk than in an office?

Furthermore, are Sisters encouraged to keep in touch with alumnae on a personal basis (as distinct from keeping in touch with alumnae only on a fund-raising and strictly institutional basis)? Are alumnae organized on a spiritual, apostolic basis, or merely in order to help support the school's finances?

These are pertinent, practical, and immediate questions that are addressed to Sisters all over the world — not just to those in Belgium.

Wherever the rules against visiting, the rules against going out at night, the rules against letter writing, the rules against contact with seculars seem to oppose the good of the apostolate, Cardinal Suenens advocates a re-examination of the rules. "To isolate the yeast from the dough for fear of contagion is to miss the whole point. By its very nature the apostolate implies a risk" (p. 124).

He advocates changing any customs or garb that reinforce in a modern girl's mind the impression that Sisters are out of touch, and quotes Pope Pius XII's Allocution of September 15, 1952, to Mothers General that warns them against certain "customs which, though they formerly had some meaning in a different cultural context, no longer have any and in which a young, fervent and courageous girl would find nothing but fetters inhibiting her vocation and her apostolate" (p. 133).

These, then, seem to be the basic questions with which *The Nun in the World* confronts American teaching communities.

QUESTIONS PROPOSED TO HOSPITAL COMMUNITIES

The direct apostolate for a nursing Sister consists mainly in her talking with patients to console them spiritually, and to help them see the meaning of suffering and death. The nurse can also help the patient and his family solve the other questions that perplex a person when he is forced to lie in bed and think.

> A great many moral problems are confided to nuns who come to the sick with Christ in their hearts.
> Nuns know and feel that devotion and evangelization are not synonymous. Their unselfish devotion to the sick rouses everyone's admiration and often paves the way for more intimate contact, but devotion as such is not the apostolate. . . (pp. 90, 89).

Therefore, the primary question Cardinal Suenens would seem to ask of American nursing communities is:

Is there any way of increasing the nursing Sisters' direct, apostolic contact with their patients?

Are nursing administrators so tied up with desk work that they have no time for direct contact with patients or with the patients' families on a non-professional basis? "The danger of officialism is perhaps even greater for nursing nuns (than for teaching nuns), for medical care does not produce the same directly apostolic opportunities as teaching does" (p. 89).

Do nursing Sisters in the wards have time to visit their patients, or is their schedule so crowded that there is no time to spend talking with the sick? Are the Sisters' hours so long that they are too tired to visit the sick after their working hours are over? (In some hospitals the Sisters fall asleep during Mass from sheer exhaustion.)

The Cardinal also advocates keeping in touch with ex-patients and, in addition, exercising an apostolate to the families of patients; yet the basic problem is whether nursing Sisters have adequate time to talk to their patients. Do they have a chance to heal souls as well as bodies?

CONCLUSION

In summation, it seems that Cardinal Suenens very definitely has something to say to American Sisters. The main questions proposed by his writings are:

1) Are American Sisters fully aware that they have a strict obligation to exercise the direct apostolate?

2) Is there any way of improving the teaching Sisters' direct apostolate among their students, alumnae, and parents?

3) Is there any way of increasing the nursing Sisters' direct, apostolic contact with their patients?

These, it seems, are practical questions that should be investigated immediately. Ultimately, only Sister-superiors can give appropriate answers to these questions raised by the Cardinal. But, confident of their wise and prudent resolution of the apostolic problem, he predicts:

> The consequences of this change in religious customs would be incalculable, not only for the world outside the convent, but for the nuns themselves, who would be the first to benefit by it.
>
> This apostolic fervor would give to daily action a new range and a supernatural character even more marked than before. . . . That sense too common among them of being. . . enclosed in a sealed-off world will disappear like a mist in the bright sunshine of radiant spiritual charity through which they will be "all things to all men," and will feel themselves, in the words of St. Paul, to owe a debt to their brothers in the world. . . . The very consciousness of having the responsibility to guide others will here as everywhere work marvels of transformation. . . . We must believe in the power of humble and little ones in the Kingdom of God. Let us beware of hesitation.[8]

---

[8] *The Gospel to Every Creature,* 108–109 passim.

Sisters Today, December, 1965

The Psychology of the
"New Breed" of Religious

John R. McCall, S.J.

In the last five to ten years, some major changes in attitude and behavior have been noted in men and women religious currently designated by the term "new breed." The term itself may have objectionable overtones for those so characterized and for their older counterparts. However, we shall use the term, implying nothing more by it than a simple designation of the age-group we have mentioned: the religious who have joined Congregations and Orders in the past five to ten years. Precisely during this period, the author has been engaged in extensive counselling of male and female religious of many Congregations and Orders; hence he feels that while some of his observations may be debatable, they are worthy of consideration.

The "new breed" may be described as possessing seven distinguishing characteristics. These marks are not hermetically sealed from one another. Perhaps one could find another set of characteristics equally descriptive; but these seven will do as a basis for discussion. The "new breed" seeks Fulfillment, Authenticity, Change, Encounter, Freedom, Equality and Dialogue. Freshly minted yesterday, some of these words have already become clichés.

FULFILLMENT

The young religious woman has grown up in a world of psychology — perhaps too much psychology. For this reason, she is preoccupied with her developing personality. The Sisters of an older generation were "task-oriented." They were told that a certain work had to be done by the community and they would be assigned a part of it. The younger Sister is "person-oriented." She says, "I will not be good at any kind of work unless it is fulfilling. Unless my personality can grow in it, I shall not be doing any good for myself or for others."

In an age of specialization, where guidance counsellors are trying to fit square pegs into square holes and round pegs into round holes, this attitude should not surprise us. The young religious is affected by our age of specialization. She has become extremely self-conscious. She is searching for fulfillment. When those in charge of the formation of the young religious try to make them all come off an assembly line, molded and matched, the "new breed" is frightened and annoyed. Each member of the "new breed" wants to maintain her individuality and be fulfilled as a unique human being.

Here is a real area of conflict. Superiors and older religious want the younger ones to develop mature personalities and use their talents in fulfilling work. No community, however, has the ideal position for each subject. If we over-emphasize the work, the younger religious say we are depersonalizing them. If we over-stress development of their personalities, seeking the ideal position for each subject, will the work get done? What of those works which by their nature are not very rewarding? Who will do them?

The request of the younger religious is not altogether absurd. If they do not find fulfillment in religious life and in some work within the community, they do not grow. They do not accomplish much for God, themselves, or others. Shall we tell the younger Sister, "Forget yourself; forget about becoming a person; get the job done"? The Sister will reply that if she is unhappy, she cannot become a full person and grow in holiness, which she feels is little other than wholeness.

We may point out Sisters who have spent full lives in tasks which were depersonalizing. By the grace of God and a deep commitment to the purpose of their institute, they grew into full human beings, fully developed, with all the human qualities praised by God and man. Unfortunately, the younger Sister will find it much easier to point out a larger number of religious whose later years find them cold, cynical, and unhappy.

It *is* possible for a person who is totally committed to the work of an institute to find fulfillment even in tasks which are rather meaningless in themselves, tasks that could easily be performed by a lay person. Witness the fulfillment attained by generations of lay Sisters who spend lifetimes sweeping, laundering, cooking for a community of teaching Sisters. Today, it is extremely difficult to get a young Sister to give her life to the kitchen, the most fulfilling of all the household duties. Part of this difficulty is due to cultural change. A Sister who entered religion forty years ago, if she lacked education, expected to be in religion what she would have been outside — a domestic.

This is not true today. If we accept an aspirant with a high school education, she does not envision herself as a domestic. Even if she lacks the requisite intelligence to do college work, graduate, and teach, many self-fulfilling roles are open to her outside of religion. She may be a secretary, do practical nursing, perform many roles in modern merchandising. Any of these roles involves dealing with persons in helping relationships. Reflect for a minute on the role of the Sister alone in the kitchen.

There is a real area of conflict here, and facile solutions are not available. Older religious, certainly, should not underestimate the cultural changes that have taken place. It would be easy for them to see spiritual heroism in one generation and cowardice in another, when they are really only looking at products of totally different cultures.

What shall we tell the young religious, then? "Abandon yourself; ignore your personality; forget the quest for identity." Are these fair demands? Will not a young religious be a better religious insofar as she becomes a more fully developed person?

There is certainly a supernatural answer. The revelation of the most blessed Trinity shows us that the solitary person is a contradiction in terms. Personality growth is possible only in terms of relations with others. The Father in the Trinity is so because of his relationship to the Son. To put it more poetically, God the Father is "I" by saying "Thou!"

The Catholic Church mirrors this Trinitarian life. The mystery of being a Catholic is this: I find *myself*, my own individual personality, by being in a society. The society which is the Church is a community. In it I attain my true individuality. "Outside the Church there is not salvation." This could be interpreted to mean that outside it one would be the already mentioned contradiction, a solitary person. As such, he would be stunted, stranded, and lost.

Each Catholic must learn that he cannot fulfill himself unless he is a member of the Church, since salvation flows through the Church and the channels of her sacraments. In the cells of the Church which are the religious Orders, each Sister fulfills herself as an individual only if she surrenders herself fully to the life of the community. Young religious must try to learn that they can never fulfill themselves in a religious Order unless they abandon themselves totally to the goals of the community. Superiors have the obligation to make the ends of the community worth such abandonment.

Moreover, local superiors have to make sure that the work of the community members is not trivial or dehumanizing. Many of the tasks which irk the "new breed" are those which had meaning in the eighteenth century, but lack any meaning now. Among these we might cite pressing thirty-six pleats into a habit skirt, counting the Sunday collection in a rectory, or wasting time as a "companion" while another Sister visits the dentist.

We must insist: the "new breed" has a *right* to fulfillment in religious life. Religious life is capable of affording such fulfillment. The young religious, however, who has little or no interest in the community in which she lives is doomed to emotional and religious failure. As in the Trinity and in Christ's Church, so in religious Orders, one becomes oneself only by relationship to others. Even today, some young Sisters must be assigned to tasks which are not very self-fulfilling. If, with the grace of God, they can learn totally to commit themselves to the ends of the institute and to sacrifice themselves for those ends, they can find fulfillment in the tasks assigned.

The subject must keep the above in mind. The superior, on her part, must ask herself why a Sister is assigned to tasks such as working in the convent kitchen. If the honest answer is, "To save money," a further question is in order. Do we have the right to ask a girl to give herself to the community for that reason? In the twentieth century, is it possible for a "domestic" to live happily in a community of teaching Sisters? Should the community only accept girls who are capable of college training and a teaching career?

AUTHENTICITY

Sisters of the "new breed" want to develop into really genuine persons. They do not wish to do anything or avoid anything "for appearances' sake." They strive to be honest themselves and they demand honesty from others, especially from superiors. Members of the "new breed" must speak the truth. Frequently they do not reflect that speaking the truth may do little good, cause hurt or even harm. As individuals, they are incapable of being devious, opportunistic, or even diplomatic. Many of them feel that diplomacy has no place in the religious life. They feel they must tell their superiors frankly what they think of them.

Prudence has never been a characteristic virtue of the young. The "new breed" seems at times almost to delight in lack of prudence. Prudence, they feel, causes one frequently to "avoid the issue," to "seek peace at any price." For them, this is being less than authentic. When instructed by prudent superiors to avoid this or that because "it would not look good," they are extremely annoyed. They consider this hypocrisy.

This tendency sometimes reaches extremes. They scorn any formality or protocol. Politeness is considered to be "phoney," and "phoniness" is the vice they abhor above all others. The young religious woman may rebel when it is suggested that she be lady-like, refined, gracious. Sometimes she considers this a surrender to bourgeois convention. For those of us who have worked with young religious, this is their most refreshing trait. It is at times their most exasperating one. They have great difficulty in distinguishing between legitimate prudence and excessive caution.

The older a person gets, the greater the investment he has in his own personality. He has developed it over the years in a certain manner, and it becomes hard for the older person to accept even honest negative criticism. Younger religious do not understand, even when it is harsh, how difficult it is for older ones to accept their criticism. The younger religious view the criticism they offer as honest and well-intentioned. If the "new breed" is able to take criticism in middle years as calmly as it offers the criticism now, the Church will certainly enter a golden age!

CHANGE

The "new breed" wants change in the Church and desires the change to come immediately. Members of the "new breed" are not gradualists. This should not surprise us when we reflect on the age in which these young religious grew up. Its chief characteristic has been change. Older people lived through periods of up to fifty years in which the Church changed not a whit. Reflect for a moment on the changes of the past fifteen years. The "new breed" is used to picking up the diocesan paper each week and reading of another change in the Church and her institutions.

They tell us that they want change because they want the Church to be relevant to the needs of the day. They love Christ and his Church. They are not thinking of leaving the Church, but they are thinking of reforming it. They wish to abolish many of its archaic forms. They want their reforms implemented *now*, not next week.

This is one more source of conflict. Superiors by their office are preservers of tradition. They are of the establishment. All older religious find change hard, after investing more than half their lives in a particular religious vocation. Moreover, superiors and older religious have a convincing argument for their posture. Younger religious are frequently asking them to surrender a presently real and positive good for an ideal future one. Older religious have seen too many such quests end in failure. They tend to cling to the real present.

A parable might make the situation clearer to the "new breed." Two Sisters are engaged in carving marble statues. One of them is sixty and has been working daily for forty years, making a statue of our Lady. She is almost finished. The other Sister is twenty. She has yet to lay a chisel to the marble assigned to her and has not yet finished her preliminary sketching. Now a prophet arises and announces that henceforth only group statuary will be significant. Solitary statues must go! The younger Sister turns to the older and says: "Sister, abandon your project, which is now passé. Come; assist me and together we will carve statues of the Holy Family from my untouched piece of marble." Imagine the feelings of the older Sister! Perhaps the prophet is correct; perhaps the "new breed" must follow him. How gentle the "new breed" must be in dealing with the "old" in such situations!

The conflict between generations here calls for a good deal of compromise and much charity. Edmund Burke once remarked, "A disposition to preserve and an ability to improve taken together would be my standard of a statesman." This could serve to describe what is required of all religious, young, middle-aged, and old, in our lifetime. Each religious must maintain a disposition to preserve and an ability to improve.

We know the defects of the "new breed" all too well. Superiors are aware that change causes themselves and the older generation much more inconvenience than it does the "new breed." What they must be more aware of is this: ought it not be the presumption that the longer one has lived in the tents of God, the more capable he is of leading a life of faith? Change is always a call on faith; it involves a surrender of what we have for what we have not. The "new breed" finds change naturally attractive. If they wish to be taken seriously by superiors and older religious, they must cultivate the aforementioned quality: the disposition to preserve what is best in the past, while they seek to improve, looking to the future.

ENCOUNTER

The "new breed" talks constantly about encounter. There is a fierce personalism among them. They will tolerate nothing that is non-human. They feel that they can help others only if they can relate to them as persons. They feel that they cannot relate unless there is a possibility of fulfillment in this relationship. They are not attracted by any type of work that will not admit the possibility of an "I—Thou" relationship. (Most young male religious go through a phase in which they all want to be psychologists or guidance counsellors.) They all seek out the type of apostolic work which places them in a helping relationship.

As they go through their period of formation, searching for self, they are terribly anxious about their ability to love and be loved. Young religious spend hours discussing Buber and his now famous "I—Thou" relationship. This is not a case of their confusing love with sexual romance. They have been brought up in a world in which sex and romance have been so exploited that they are a bit inured to the sexual side of things. Rather, they are looking for something deeper than romance. They refer to it as encounter. They worry whether they are capable of real friendships and deep relationships. This too is part of the psychological age in which they live. Persons no longer assume that they are capable of giving and receiving love. They keep reflecting and testing themselves in this area.

Our old solutions to the problem of "particular friendships" infuriate the "new breed." If we caution them against telling each other details of their personal lives, they rebel, saying, "How can I become fulfilled? How can I be a mature, authentic person unless I have deep friendships?" They spend hours with one another in discussing their most intimate anxieties, ambitions, and desires. Thus they hope to equip themselves for apostolic encounter with other persons.

At this point, they find much fault with their superiors. They feel that superiors and older religious frequently treat the "new breed" impersonally. "Why," they keep asking, "is a religious community so unlike a family? Where is the warmth, the tenderness and love that should be manifest between persons who call one another father, brother, sister?"

This area of conflict is most important. If a religious woman does not grow to the point where she is capable of deep relationships in her community, with the students she teaches, and with others with whom she deals, how can she be Christ-like? How can she develop into a full human being? On the other hand, many of these young religious have not yet found themselves. Can such young religious strengthen one another by these early efforts at deep relationships? As a matter of fact, one of the detriments to deep relationships among religious is premature efforts at such relationships. These fail because the young religious are seeking from them what they cannot give. Disappointed in these early efforts, they withdraw. They do not make efforts later when their chances of success would be much greater.

Some older readers may say, "We did not think about all that nonsense!" For some reason, perhaps the difference in psychological climate of which we have already spoken, the older religious were not so self-conscious. They were not so unsure of themselves, so anxious about their personality development. They had more toughness. By toughness we mean the ability to set sight on some distant goal and to pursue it relentlessly, letting nothing interfere with the goal.

We must be very careful in praising this quality of toughness. Unaccompanied by a corresponding tenderness, it makes for a very poor religious indeed. Toughness without tenderness accounts for the sadly large number of older religious to whom the "new breed" can point with just accusation that they lack the essentials of the religious life. Toughness without tenderness has made them cold and inhuman. Can such religious lead others to Christ? How often a Sister of the "new breed" tells us, "I do not wish to grow into a religious like this one or that one."

Perhaps we should make it easier for the "new breed" to develop the ability of forming friendships and relating to each other more deeply. They will make mistakes; it is inevitable. If they do become warm human beings, they will do the work of Christ much better.

It is important in community life that the relationship between any two Sisters be closely aligned with their relationship to God. No two young Sisters in training can give to each other what they need. But if they go to God for what they need, they can share with each other what God has given them. Older religious who are capable of warm personal relationships count these as great blessings and realize that they are an overflow of the good God who is helping us live the Trinitarian life, giving us of his grace.

FREEDOM

The desire for freedom causes conflict in the area of obedience. The "new breed" does not refuse to obey, but wishes to discuss reasons for the orders. The "new breed" is confused when those in authority feel threatened and become unreasonably anxious about this desire for discussion. All superiors find the "new breed" a trial. The superior who is very unsure of herself is terribly threatened by these brash young Sisters. Since she is threatened, she demands much blinder obedience than she would otherwise.

Members of the "new breed" are not intentionally disobedient or disre-spectful of authority. They are shocked when we interpret their honesty as a sign of disrespect or their desire for discussion as a sign of disobedience. They tell superiors that theirs is a much better obedience than the obedience of those who manifest external docility, but complain bitterly in the absence of the superior. Such views are not without merit.

Again, they contend that their desire for understanding the superior's reasons is motivated by their desire to do the work better. Literal obedience, they point out, can sabotage the goals of the superior. They tell superiors, "You are much better off with the consent of free men than with the compli-ance of automata." They are surprised that superiors frequently do not view the situation this way.

Much of the above difficulty comes about because superiors and the "new breed" alike do not fully understand either freedom or obedience. It takes much patience and listening, but eventually the "new breed" comes to grasp the essence and spirit of obedience. They then realize that if they comply freely, obedience takes nothing from their essential freedom; it enhances it.

In this area, as in most others, the role of the superior is more difficult to-day. It is easy to crush the spirit of a member of the "new breed," but, broken in spirit, the young religious is not worth much as a person. Dealing with the "new breed" in the sensitive areas of freedom and obedience demands much time and patience on the part of the superior. The superior who is charitable enough to grant this time and use patience will produce a generation of religious who obey in a better way than many of us did in the past.

EQUALITY

Their need for equality is patent. It is most obvious in their difficulty in dealing with titles of honor. They call bishops and cardinals by their last names. His Holiness becomes simply "Paul." They are inclined as students to call teachers by their first names.

Even as they dislike formality and protocol, they wish to remove any hierarchy among persons. Much of this is good. It motivates them to work for the poor. They love the ecumenical movement, seeing it as reaching toward religious equality among all. Some of their reaching for equality is not good. It sometimes overreaches the non-essentials and strikes at the core of the struc-ture of authority. Then it has gone too far; the "new breed," in franker moments, will admit this, too.

DIALOGUE

This is the unsilent generation. They have an insatiable need for dialogue. For the "new breed," silence in the community is suspect whenever it interferes with dialogue. In retreats they want discussion groups. In class, they wish to have lectures replaced by discussion. Perhaps they despise form for form's sake. They love talk for talk's sake. Frankly, one may suspect, they are afraid of silence and afraid to be alone. Why? Silence and solitude cause them to be introspective. When, alone, they search within themselves, they become frightened and insecure. In a group discussion they seem to supply the strength for one another that each needs to face himself.

Listen to these words: "Every man is a potential adversary, even those whom we love. Only through dialogue are we saved from one another. Dialogue is to love what blood is to the body. When the flow of blood stops, the body dies. When dialogue stops, love dies and resentment and hate are born. But dialogue can restore a dead relationship. Indeed, this is the miracle of dialogue; it can bring relationship into being and it can bring into being once again a relationship that has died." These words are taken from a book published in 1962, *The Miracle of Dialogue*. Its author is Reuel L. Howe. This may be exaggerated, but it states perfectly the feeling of the "new breed." Everything they want — fulfillment, authenticity, change, encounter, freedom, and equality — all these depend on dialogue.

The "new breed" insist on being heard. They wish to be taken seriously. They will be heard; the age in which the superior could simply refuse to listen is coming to an end. One solution is this: they should be encouraged to dialogue without ceasing until they have learned the technique well. Until they learn to discuss without becoming shrill, until they learn not to point and shout *j' accuse* at all who disagree with them, they must persist in dialogue. They must learn the difference between raising a question, even an unsettling one, and demanding a change in established thought and practice. Dialogue is necessary for the "new breed," perhaps more so than for the old. Without it, they will never learn that discussion does not presume that the matter is already settled and that nothing is left but implementation of their decision.

In the past, one of the great obstacles to growth in charity in a community was lack of open communication. The "new breed" has discovered a means to remove this obstacle — dialogue. As with all new discoveries, its discoverers are tending to see it as the solution to all ills. They are using dialogue to excess. The excess must not delude us into thinking that the discovery is not a good one.

Young religious should spend many hours in dialogue. This should be done on their own time after the assigned work is done. If they do much more, they will learn that dialogue is necessary but not sufficient. Perhaps from their discussions will come the conclusions that silence, solitude, prayer, and study are also real goods. Among other achievements, these goods serve to make dialogue more worthwhile.

There are some puzzling things about the "new breed," but God has chosen them to be the religious of the late twentieth century. A distinguished Jesuit, former major superior and current tertian instructor, recently remarked to the author: "My tertians wish to do many things whose intrinsic merit I do not see. When there is a consensus among the tertians that these things should be done, I permit them. I cannot believe that the Holy Spirit has attracted to the Society of Jesus men who *en masse* totally lack an appreciation of that Society and what it should be doing in their lifetime."

"Old breed" and "new" can look to the future with confidence that their highest aspirations will be fulfilled. God is with us.

My Kind of Music

Music uncurls
from the church bells,
the peace of
white horses.
Music sits in the blue eye
of God.
It sings in rusty hills,
and when the moon
cleans out its shell
music is
a lamb chewing
shadows of afternoon,
restless boats
and velvet figures
in the river's
ripples.

Marion Schoeberlein
Sisters Today, October, 1976

Sisters Today, September, 1966

Attitudes of Sisters Toward Renewal

Robert Y. O'Brien, S.J.
Sister Mary Edith Laing, S.S.J.

Three hundred and forty-five Sisters of all ages, representing eighteen religious congregations, participated by personal choice in six Institutes of Renewal for Women Religious. Sponsored by INTERCOM, the Sisters' Vocation Committee of the Diocese of Wheeling, these Institutes were conducted in various cities of that diocese during October and November, 1965.

Each Sister was given a one-page questionnaire relevant to renewal for Sisters. Each Sister was free to record her views, assured that no individual names or communities or congregations would be associated with the results. The responses to these surveys indicate current attitudes of these Sisters toward renewal programs. Among the participants were teachers, nurses, catechists, administrators, major and local superiors, directors of formation, Sister-students, and novices.

The questionnaire was composed of two parts: 1) a listing of sixteen items to be checked (a) change not needed, (b) change needed, (c) change urgently needed; and 2) six questions: two pertaining to elements of Christian spiritual life neglected or exaggerated in a Sister's life; two asking for descriptive qualities for the ideal Sister and the Sister who terminated her vocation; and two relating to the virtue of trust.

CHART A

(reproduced from the questionnaire, with tabulated data inserted)

Directions: Please put an x in the column you think correct, judging from your
personal experience and from observation in your particular
religious family:

In regard to	Change not needed	Change needed	Change urgently needed	(Total for change)[1]
Retreat program	128	85	22	(107)
Garb or habit	67	149+	30	(179)
Horarium	113	102	22	(124)
Vocal prayer requirements	177+	47−	11	(58)−
Education-formation program	86	121	32	(153)
Rules on travel	114	106	24	(130)
Community recreation; custom	68	139	41	(180)+
Attitude toward poverty	82	132	21	(153)
Attitude toward chastity	113	100	8−	(108)
Attitude toward obedience	81	114	27	(141)
Attitude toward Christian friendship	57−	123	56+	(179)
Government structure	122	92	24	(116)
Liturgical formation	124	100	9	(109)
Provisions for spiritual direction	93	99	48	(147)
Spiritual reading program	146	70	15	(85)
Concept of local superior's authority	104	98	35	(133)
Totals	1675	1677	425	

Conclusions from Chart A

The distribution of responses hardly justifies any concept of a monolithic
viewpoint among Sisters. Nor may one conclude that women religious are

[1]Figures in parentheses are obtained by adding the figure under *Change needed* to the figure under *Change urgently needed* to give an overall indication of desire for some modification. In each vertical column the most frequently occurring response is indicated by a + beside the figure; the least frequently occurring response is indicated by a − beside the figure.

generally desperately anxious for renewal in many areas, for the ratio of "not needed" to "urgently needed" responses is approximately 4:1.

Strong satisfaction with *vocal prayer requirements* and with *spiritual reading programs* is indicated. But Sisters singled out the *attitude toward Christian friendship* as a neuralgic problem. General sentiment favors action concerning the *garb or habit* and concerning revisions in *community recreation and customs*, but these two items are not regarded as urgent problems by more than one of every six Sisters replying to the questionnaire.

A wide divergence in attitudes toward *provisions for spiritual direction* is indicated, with many regarding this as an area calling for urgent change. Sisters differ in judgments on the adequacy of *liturgical formation*, with very few deeming the formation in liturgy in need of urgent revision. However, their attitudes toward the *education-formation program* intimate a desire for some modification.

Chart A suggests Sisters are more satisfied with *government structure* than with the existential *concept of local superior's authority*, and the data suggests that the *attitude toward obedience* may be the crucial factor. Perhaps changing the attitude toward obedience seems called for first, rather than changes in constitutions or in authority of local superiors.

OPENNESS IN ATTITUDE TOWARD AUTHORITY

To check the outlook on confidence in communications between subjects and superiors, the two questions comprising Chart B were inserted in the questionnaire, but not in direct sequence.

CHART B

1. In general do you feel that superiors trust you as they should?
    Yes *174*   No 72

2. In general do you feel that you trust superiors as you should?
    Yes *166*   No 73

Conclusions from Chart B

Approximately 70 percent of the Sisters registered satisfaction with the mutual trust existing between superiors and themselves. This reinforces the rather general satisfaction with government structure found in replies recorded in Chart A.

MISEVALUATIONS OF ELEMENTS IN THE RELIGIOUS LIFE

To probe Sisters' criticisms of the esteem their peer-group gives to aspects of the spiritual life, the two questions in Chart C were inserted in the questionnaire.

CHART C

1. Which elements of the Christian spiritual life do you think Sisters in general neglect or underestimate (e.g., spiritual direction, liturgical prayer, poverty, intellectual development, etc.)?
2. Which elements of the Christian spiritual life do you think Sisters in general exaggerate or overstress (e.g., conferences, chapel visits, community recreation, etc.)?

Conclusions from Chart C

The distribution of the 293 items in response to the first question in Chart C shows that the Sisters' rather general satisfaction with *provisions for spiritual direction* (Chart A) does not prevent their finding fault with the utilization of spiritual direction by the Sisters, for 75 responses pointed to neglect of spiritual direction. The responses confirmed the findings of Chart A that poverty is the vow most provocative of critical interest; 69 times was poverty named as an element underestimated by Sisters. Fraternal charity or other social virtues appeared 31 times among the responses to the first question, while 35 replies singled out religious exercises. Significantly, only 16 responses to the initial question were associated with exterior or apostolic endeavors.

In the 167 items answering to the second question in Chart C, religious exercises were most frequently named (48), with conferences and visits most frequently cited. Recreation and social life within the Community (42) and customs (30) scored high. But only six answers were related to the exterior apostolate or other contacts with the laity.

PROFILING THE RELIGIOUS VOCATION

One part of the questionnaire attempted to gather data for sketching profiles of an ideal Sister and of a non-viable vocation.

CHART D

1. As you think of ideal Sisters you have known, what words come to mind which are descriptive of these Sisters (e.g. prudent, detached,

independent, outspoken, docile, businesslike, approachable, etc.)?

2. As you think of religious who did not continue in that vocation, what words come to your mind (e.g. rigid, mortified, frivolous, earnest, perfectionist, sensual, efficient, determined, impatient, etc.)?

Conclusions from Chart D

Of 710 items descriptive of the ideal Sister, 306 suggested openness, approachable disposition, and other terms indicative of affability. Honesty, truthfulness, etc., recurred 32 times; terms suggesting optimistic outlook, pleasant disposition, sense of humor, etc., appeared 14 times. Feminine traits (motherly, femininity, etc.) were named only six times.

In the 379 items picturing the terminated vocation, impatience (58) scored high in frequency, as did frivolous (50) and perfectionist (45). Although the word self was not used in explaining the question, 27 responses included this word (self-centered, self-seeking, selfish, etc.).

GENERAL CONCLUSIONS

It seems in this sampling of Sisters' attitudes that liturgical formation is already achieved and is generally satisfying.

It might be that renewal does not suggest to Sisters changes directly relevant to apostolic work; perhaps renewal is construed wholly as an intramural action.

The Sisters judge their own attitudes toward poverty and obedience more critically than their view of either their institute's structure or its concept of authority. This shows a reluctance to transfer any responsibility for problems to either the design of their organization or its personnel in authority.

The survey does not reveal any magic virtue whose absence means loss of vocation. Perhaps every abandoned vocation is a unique event, with apparently no universal characteristic.

The Sisters showed a healthy interest in modifying their way of life, an eagerness to think and to express their conclusions. Perhaps the survey reminded the participants that the same Spirit renewing the Church is operative in each one of us, inspiring the enthusiastic desire for a holy and intelligent renewal.

Sisters Today, November, 1966

Sisters' Congress — A Post-Conciliar First

Sister Barbara Ann, S.N.D.

Post-conciliar implementation is the favored son in a family of many interests for Archbishop Paul J. Hallinan of Atlanta. The Sisters of northern Georgia were privileged to share in a unique way in this implementation by taking an active part in preparing for the diocesan Synod scheduled for the fall of 1966. The uniqueness? A Sisters' Congress, a first of its kind.

Previous to the official convocation of the Congress on January 6, 1966, Archbishop Hallinan called a planning committee together on December 18, 1965. This group, composed of superiors and elected delegates from each convent, met to decide on a practical course for preparations. They discussed general problems and needs, elected an Executive Board to draw up a plan for involving each Sister in the Archdiocese in the Congress.

The proposal which the Executive Board subsequently devised was basically simple. Five separate committees would investigate five different problems, to assess the present role of the Sister in the particular area under question, and to propose recommendations aiding the Sister to assume a more meaningful role in that area in the future.

The individual topics for the committees underwent heavy discussion on December 18, 1965. The topics chosen were: the individual development of the religious Sister; the liturgical life; and the apostolates of education, nursing, and social service. Since the number of Sisters in Atlanta is only 210, the proposal requested that all be members of one of the five committees. Each Sister would join the committee of her choice, and even if she could not be active in the preparatory work, because of heavy responsibilities or infirmity, she would be actively interested by way of support and prayer. The Sisters who could give of their time and energy would assemble periodically for general committee meetings at a central high school in Atlanta.

This basic operation went into effect in January, and as the members of the groups became more familiar with each other and their topics, they elected chairmen and secretaries, and in many cases divided into subcommittees for more efficient work. Properly named, the committees were: Development, Liturgy, Education, Social Services, and Health Services.

As the weeks of preparation passed, each committee — through questionnaires, tapping of resources, interviews with prominent people already involved in the area under discussion, "homework" of all kinds — gradually drew up proposals that reflected its thoughts. Consciously the committees reminded themselves of the purpose of the Congress, a discussion of the role of the Sister in the Archdiocese of Atlanta; and unconsciously there developed an awareness that any proposal involved mutually related questions: what can the Sister do to better her role in the Archdiocese, and how can the Archdiocese contribute to this betterment. The Archbishop's theme of collegiality and co-responsibility had caught fire!

At the opening of the Congress, when the Archbishop called for "unity, diversity, and creativity," these were already a reality. The separate Orders, through the close and demanding preparations of the individual committees, had quietly grown to a vivid realization of "one body" serving the Church of Georgia, and the schemata spoke boldly of diversity and creativity.

The following is a resume of each committee's proposals.

DEVELOPMENT

This committee proposed the formation of a Council of Sisters which would deal with the continuing development of the Sister as a person: spiritually, intellectually, culturally, physically, socially. It strongly recommended activities designed to promote the sharing of ideas among clergy, religious, and laity so as to insure the growth and development of all God's people within the Archdiocese. Further recommendations spelled out how the Archdiocese could exert its influence to aid the growth and development of the Sisters through provision of workshops, lectures, etc.

LITURGY

Since the Sisters feel strongly that as women of the Church, striving to serve it in the best way possible, they should assume an active role in the worship of the parish community, they recommended that a Liturgical Committee be formed within each parish, composed of clergy, Sisters, and laity, to insure meaningful parish worship. To this Liturgical Committee the Sisters would offer their services to instruct the parish community, if necessary; to experiment with music, art, and settings so as to guarantee meaningful worship; and in general to be at the service of the parish to accomplish the goal of reforming and promoting the liturgy.

EDUCATION

The committee, due to the depth and scope of its topic, divided into six subcommittees: Secondary Education, Elementary, Special, Adult, CCD, and Newman Clubs. Pertinent topics for the school system were: a proposed educational structure for the Archdiocese, spelling out the roles of all in education and showing the relation of each to the other; practical suggestions concerning the qualifications of personnel involved in the Archdiocesan educational system, and benefits such as insurance and pension plans that would be received by any teacher qualified in the United States. Other subcommittees recommended that the schools share the personnel and experience of the already active "special education" group in the Archdiocese, that adult education be given an organized programming, that schools of religious be investigated in order to find the best approach for teaching the Word of God, and that Newman Centers be enlivened through the aid of Sisters released for this work.

SOCIAL SERVICES

Recommendations for this group called for a social service organization collaborating with other agencies, local and state. This program would include the training of a good corps of social workers for the Archdiocese to meet the demands not being met by existing agencies. The possibility of each community or several communities giving a Sister to aid in this work was suggested.

HEALTH SERVICES

This committee first recommended that a commission be set up to explore the needs of the Archdiocese and then to serve in an advisory capacity to meet these needs. It suggested utilizing competent lay personnel in vital positions in Archdiocesan health institutes, and guaranteeing the same benefits to personnel involved in Archdiocesan health agencies that would be guaranteed them were they working for state agencies.

Archbishop Hallinan officially opened the Congress on May 1, addressing the assembly with words warm with hope that this Congress would "set a pace for the entire Archdiocese." The following day the congressional sessions began, with attendance just short of 100%. The chairman of each committee read every proposal aloud, and one by one each was accepted, rejected, or recommitted by the total body of Sisters. Those approved without amendment were adopted by a simple majority vote as soon as each chairman terminated the presentation of her committee's proposals. Those recommitted went back to a work session in the afternoon and at the last general assembly were brought to the floor again, this time to be finally adopted or rejected.

The liturgy encouraged the participants to stretch to meet the "depth and height and breadth of the love of God," and thus join hands with the neighbor to realize the best means of service of the Church in Georgia. Through the "breaking of the bread" in the Eucharistic banquet and the buffet dinner following it, the group knew and understood better this body which is the Christ.

Besides blazing the trail for the fullest possible implementation of Vatican II in his Archdiocese, Archbishop Hallinan provided an unforgettable experience for his Sisters. Pope John's famous "window" was opened. The breath of the Spirit "blew mightily, disposing all things sweetly," letting in fresh air and at the same time showing new vistas unattainable by one, but possible with many heads, hearts, and hands working together.

Evening

Curve my craving
to the language of light
as day funnels into silence,
tyranny of decibels
silvering to saffron,
color of calm.
And let my candle genuflect
at a cupful of rain,
a redbird bathing.

Donna Dickey Guyer
Sisters Today, October, 1975

Sisters Today, June–July, 1970

Renewal: From Cloister to National Assembly

Sister Ethne Kennedy

Possibly no group in the Church has responded so energetically to the Second Vatican Council's challenge of renewal as the Sisters of the United States. For the past five years and more, women religious of competence and experience have not feared to question the evangelical quality, style, meaningfulness and mode of inserting religious life into the culture and structures of contemporary America and to come to some radical conclusions. During the process of self-study, many have opted out of religious life. Some have chosen to experiment with non-canonical forms in small and larger groups, to verify the intuition that religious life may thrive better in a total community than cut off from the healthy interaction of clergy and laity. So far, however, the majority of Sisters — 167,167 by the 1969 count of the *Official Catholic Directory* — have reaffirmed their original commitment. They prefer to remain in the service of the Church as they once promised, hopefully for better.

To remain in religious life today offers no shelter from conflict, misunderstanding, bad press. To a growing number of Sisters it means finding new ways of spending creative energies *in* the Church *for* the Church and world. It means risking to share with the community at large the upheaval of moving from safe, functionally oriented societies (i.e., congregations of teachers, nurses, catechists, social workers, etc.) to religious communities whose common Christian vision creates an environment favorable for life and growth in love.

One of the basic structures suggested by the Council to develop unity and collaboration within the People of God is dialogue. To date the most effective way to initiate and to sustain dialogue in the Church has been the council or senate. Lagging behind the clergy but somewhat ahead of lay groups in forming councils, Sisters today have councils functioning in about seventy dioceses, with another dozen in various states of organization. Of local interest and influence generally, diocesan groups assumed national prominence recently when members joined Sisters from urban associations and Sisters from regions which possess no official channel for the public opinion of Sisters to found "the most comprehensive organization of American Sisters to date," to use the words of John C. Haughey, S.J. (*America*, 4/11/70).

The place was Cleveland. The time, April 19, 1970. The occasion, the Third National Meeting of Women Religious. In the Sheraton's Grand Ballroom about 1500 Sisters from 117 dioceses heard Sister Joann Crowley of Denver introduce a motion in favor of establishing the National Assembly of Women Religious. It was 10:35 a.m. The business meeting was already half an hour behind schedule.

The research, discussion, and debate in the fashioning of NAWR by a forty-five member Task Force from nineteen states, who had worked together for seven months, were to be weighed in the balance against the shortage of time and the unforeseen difficulties which a group so varied might surface. Would Cleveland repeat Chicago of May, 1969, when a plenary session denied confidence to the planning committee which first proposed the national organization? One wondered.

Before asking the assembly to indicate by a single vote approval or rejection of the goals, structure, financial setup, and Steering Committee (or interim government) for NAWR, Sister Joann mentioned three areas where modification had been requested: membership, representation, finance. When Resolution Chairman Sister Cel Brocken asked that someone second the motion, response came from many quarters. Silence followed, during which veteran organizer, Sister Mary Benet, nudged me. "They're not even going to discuss it." The chairman took hold of the situation: "Are you ready for the question?" "Question," replied the crowd.

Within the incredible space of a few moments, the National Assembly was approved — only three hands were raised in dissent — and applauded into existence.

GROWTH OF A NATIONAL MOVEMENT

In June, 1968, the Sisters Advisory Council of Portland, Maine, sent out invitations to councils and senates of women religious in the United States and Canada to attend an international meeting highlighting the theme, "Signs of the Times." More than 400 participants came from forty-one states and nine Canadian provinces — Sisters, major superiors, priests, vicars, bishops, and the apostolic delegate. The role of women religious, development through participation in Church leadership, the need for dynamic communications between Sisters and decision-making authority were key issues discussed. To the Portland conference goes credit for the resolution that "an international liaison for Advisory Councils/Senates of Women Religious be established.

When the Second National Meeting for Women Religious took place in Chicago in May, 1969, the Committee for a National Organization had already prepared its case. Arguments for a national group were based on consultation with priest and lay organizations like the National Federation of Priests' Councils, Serra International, National Opinion Research Center, and independent associations of Sisters, as well as on the results of a nation-wide poll of known councils and senates asked to respond to two questions: "Do you think a national federation of women religious is meaningful to the Church of the United States today? If yes, how should this organization be structured?" A summary of their replies was given to the National Meeting on May 10.

The 1500 Sisters present in Chicago confirmed what hundreds polled earlier had declared: that the vast majority of vocal Sisters in this country favored a national organization for women religious. Sisters felt a need for a corporate identity, for a voice to express their stands on issues of concern to the Church in the world. They wanted top-level communications with one another to share research, personnel, facilities, vision. They sought insertion into the ecclesial process of decision making. Without grass-roots participation, they were convinced that the creative insights of Sisters would not effectively influence Church thinking and action.

What the panel discussion revealed was the novelty of the idea of a national group and the difficulties which organizers would face regarding eligibility for membership. How was such an organization of councils to listen to and give voice to Sisters from dioceses which did not allow for councils? What relation could there be between this national organization and senates which included both men and women religious? What of alternate Sisters' groups: could they join? Not to allow problems which only study and future committee work could resolve to obstruct progress toward a national organization, the committee rewrote its proposal in favor of setting up a task force, open to volunteers from every region of the United States, representing councils as well as unaffiliated Sisters. This resolution was passed by an overwhelming majority on May 11 when sixty Sisters met to plan the next phase.

Regional meetings were projected during the summer to involve as many Sisters as possible in the long-range planning for the national association. A joint session in Toledo, June 7–8, was decided upon to discuss responsibilities of the task force and to prepare the agenda for its first meeting. Detroit and September 14–16 were chosen for the latter, which got underway at the Mercy Center at Farmington, Michigan, with forty-four Sisters who represented nineteen councils and several urban associations, as well as concerned but unaffiliated Sisters.

In view of structuring a work-planning group to initiate an extensive research program, officers were chosen and committees established. These included: chairman, Sister Ethne Kennedy (Sisters Advisory Council, Chicago); secretary, Sister Mary Benet (Urban Apostolate of Sisters, Chicago); goals committee, chairman Sister Jeanine Gruesser (Sisters Council, Milwaukee);

organizational structure and procedures committee, chairman Sister Joann Crowley (Sisters Council, Denver); communications committee, chairman Sister Maureen Cleary (BVM Religious Education Committee); finance committee, chairman Sister Thomas Mary Walsh (Sisters Council, Joliet). By a vote of the great majority, the Task Force approved the name "National Assembly of Women Religious." The name "Assembly" suggests biblical and early American notions of people worshipping and creating together.

Responsibility for involving as many Sisters as possible in the emerging Assembly was a job for each Task Force member. Many could use mailing lists of existing Councils or Senates. Where a diocese had no similar organization, Sister Cathleen Real established contact with someone willing to discuss NAWR or to distribute copies of its *Newsletter,* whose first edition appeared in November. Between November and March, orders mounted from 16,000 to 25,000 copies. Initially intended to stimulate dialogue among Sisters, the *Newsletter* went monthly to bishops, vicars, and major superiors here and abroad to keep them posted on developments. Members of the Sacred Congregation for Religious acknowledged its receipt, while the Unione Internazionale Superiore Generali of Rome requested an exchange of publications with NAWR.

Sharing its evolution with the total Church community has been important to NAWR. Thus from the beginning it has concretized several objectives: 1) to become a forum for communication among women religious and a voice through which they can speak to the Church and to the world; 2) to promote unity within the Church by working in close collaboration with the bishops and major superiors of women religious (as with similar peer groups), and by representing the interests of the Sisters-at-large in all matters pertaining to their lives; 3) to encourage women religious to bring their competence and expertise to the service of the Church and society.

Sisters Today, November, 1970

The National Coalition of American Nuns

Sister Mary Dennis Donovan, S.S.J.

Although their hopes for the future of women religious may be similar, the National Coalition of American Nuns (NCAN) and the recently formed National Assembly of Women Religious (NAWR) are sharply different.

The predominant characteristic of the Coalition is its flexibility. Minimal structure enables NCAN to give timely response on critical issues, thereby enabling a substantial and specific group of women religious to add their collective voice to that of other groups in the formation of public opinion on vital issues of our times. NCAN focuses on the social milieu rather than on the affairs of women religious as such. NAWR, by contrast, is a comprehensive organization, not particularly nor exclusively concerned with social problems.

From my position as a member of NCAN's Executive Committee as well as a charter member of NAWR, I see no conflict of interest between the two organizations. NAWR's goals are more diverse and its structure more complex. Because it will be the "voice of America's Sisters," NAWR's stance will of necessity be more conservative. Decisions to take a stand on current issues will be slowly formulated if they are to be representative of its constituency.

The Assembly (NAWR) has a complex representative structure to carry out its broad range of functions. The Coalition (NCAN) has minimal structure. Each of NCAN's 1800 members made a personal commitment to a policy statement issued in December, 1969, and agreed to support statements on controversial issues made by the Executive Committee. Periodic summary reports of NCAN are mailed to every member who has the right of person-to-person contact with any member of the Executive Committee. Members of the Coalition are polled at intervals to enable the Executive Committee to set up priorities of concern. Mailings include copies of statements that have been issued, new social issues to be considered, and background material to study.

The Coalition was actually formed in July, 1969, when eighty represent-ative Sisters from all parts of the United States spent four days together shar-ing interests, ideas and expertise under the leadership of Sister Margaret Ellen Traxler. This was their fourth annual meeting. An Executive Committee was formed from among these Sisters. All NCAN statements are formulated and issued under the signature of this Executive Committee.

"The National Coalition of American Nuns (NCAN) is a group of Sisters united to study and to speak out on issues related to human rights and social justice." So reads the Executive Committee's statement of purpose issued to the many inquiries raised by the emergence of NAWR in December, 1969. The Coalition's long-range goals for both men and women in the United States are: 1) a full participation as responsible adults in ecclesial, political and social life; and 2) equality of opportunity for such participation. These two overarching goals lead the Coalition to concentrate on relevant issues of our age and to take a stand in controversies regarding human rights and social justice.

While NCAN directs its attention to social issues affecting all persons, its special emphasis is on the contributions women can make on such issues as legislative protection of working women, the rights of welfare recipients, pro-test against the debased image of women in the communications media, and a guaranteed annual wage.

As the advanced guard of religious women who desire to speak out on controversial issues, the Coalition is dynamic, challenging, and sometimes disturbing. NCAN members are well aware that they are imminently in danger of erring. Nevertheless, these Sisters believe with Sister Margaret Ellen that, "The sun of social justice cannot come up unless you help it to rise."

One of the most encouraging aspects of NCAN is its focus upon wider issues than the plight of religious women themselves and its recognition of the universal sisterhood of all women. The formation of the Coalition suggests that a significant number of Sisters are moving outside the circle of self-sacralization; it suggests that a qualitative change in consciousness is taking place. The Coalition is for Sisters who are actively concerned about current issues, presently a minority among Sisters.

The future of NCAN rests with God. The Coalition was formed in response to conscience. The conditions which prompted us to organize as well as the precarious human rights of religious women themselves will greatly determine the course NCAN will take.

Sisters Today, April, 1974

Sisters Uniting

Sister Angelita Fenker, S.F.C.C.

The group called Sisters Uniting is one effort to bring the American Sisters together to share, support and help give direction to major happenings in each other's lives. Sisters Uniting is a council of representatives of national organizations of women religious. It seeks to promote and express sisterly solidarity in defense of gospel values when current issues call these values into question. It is an enabling group which respects the autonomy of each member organization while attempting to facilitate cooperation and coordination among its member organizations.

Sisters Uniting is a forum for the exchange of information and a channel of communication. It believes that Sisters can be agents of reconciliation among members of the human family and a force for constructive social change. Sisters Uniting hopes to further the influence of Sisters and their impact upon the Church and society in a way and at a level that can only be achieved by the concerted effort of united Sisters.

In February, 1970, a task force of the Leadership Conference for Women Religious (LCWR) was set up to explore the feasibility of establishing a center for collective relationship with/among religious conferences and associations. It was decided that what was needed was an enabling group in which and through which the national conferences and associations could collaborate in an ongoing process. This meant that religious women together would create a more effective witness to the gospel, and thus united could better serve the needs of mankind through shared information and concerted action.

Sisters Uniting was born in June, 1971. It was established to be an enabling group to help member conferences realize their separate goals in coordination and collaboration with each other through communication, information and support. Sisters Uniting is a group which meets to share agendas, programs and processes. It accepts responsibility for communicating such information to the respective constituencies and to elicit from them the response which each group is capable of giving. To end all polarizations, Sisters Uniting respects the stance of the individual member organizations on all issues. Within this very depth of mutual respect, new life is created and unleashed in the Kingdom of the Father.

WHO ARE THE MEMBERS OF SISTERS UNITING?

At the birth of Sisters Uniting, the following member organizations were present to give it encouragement, prayer and support: the Leadership Conference of Women Religious (LCWR), the National Coalition of American Nuns (NCAN), the National Sister Formation Conference (NSFC), and National Sister Vocation Conference (NSVC), and the National Assembly of Women Religious (NAWR). A representative of Las Hermanas was present as an interested party. Within the past year and a half, several other national Sister groups have joined Sisters Uniting: the Association of Contemplative Sisters (ACS), Las Hermanas (LH), and Sisters for Christian Community (SFCC).

Sisters Uniting is open to membership from other interested organizations and welcomes all efforts which will enhance communication, information and support among American Sisters. A brief description follows of each member organization, listed alphabetically.

ASSOCIATION OF CONTEMPLATIVE SISTERS: ACS

The ACS was founded in 1969 to provide a vehicle of communication and collaboration among contemplative Sisters in the United States and English-speaking Canada. The strength of the organization and its unity are rooted in the following elements:
— a strong dedication to the contemplative life, a life of prayer;
— an acknowledged need for mutual collaboration and cooperation in order to foster the healthy development of the contemplative life.

LEADERSHIP CONFERENCE OF WOMEN RELIGIOUS: LCWR

This organization is a conference of the major superiors of women religious in the United States. The purpose of LCWR is to promote creative leadership and the development of the existential role of women religious to witness to the gospel message in a continually evolving world.

The organization was initially formed in 1956 and three years later received ecclesiastical status from the Sacred Congregation for Religious and Secular Institutes. By incorporation in 1962, it was established as a civil body.

LAS HERMANAS: LH

Las Hermanas was organized in April, 1971, to be an advocate group for the Hispanic minorities, both as a response to those people's request that Hispanic religious work among them, and as an individual attempt to follow Vatican II recommendations to respond to the social message of the gospel — serving the poor and enabling them to liberate themselves from the social, economic, political and religious injustices perpetrated against them by the society and the Church.

These aims can be accomplished through such things as: Projecto Mexico, Cultural and Pastoral Institutes and the forming of mobile pastoral teams working directly with the people, or training others to do Hispanic apostolic ministry.

NATIONAL ASSEMBLY OF WOMEN RELIGIOUS: NAWR

The primary goal of this national assembly is to challenge women religious to communicate a valid concept of the role of the consecrated celibate woman in the Church today, and to study, evaluate, establish priorities and make recommendations concerning areas in which women religious are critically needed. It also intends to provide a channel for the sharing of personnel, resources and research.

NATIONAL COALITION OF AMERICAN NUNS: NCAN

This group was organized in July, 1969. It calls for full participation of Sisters in the United States in the Church and political affairs of the times, and for joint building up of the debased image of women in contemporary society. NCAN sees itself as a group of Sisters united to study and speak out on issues related to gospel values, especially those of human rights and social justice. Their purpose states: "Basing our study and response-in-action on the principles and spirit of the way of life of Jesus in the gospels, we stand for the fullest development of the human person."

NATIONAL SISTER FORMATION CONFERENCE: NSFC

This national conference was organized in 1952 to promote the professional and spiritual formation of women religious. The conference understands "formation" as an on-going process by which the Holy Spirit is constantly forming a person. The conference recognizes that the individual Sister bears responsibility for her growth; it is cognizant, too, of the fact that her congregation also has a definite responsibility. Just as the congregation seeks to aid the individual, so NSFC hopes to assist the congregation.

NATIONAL SISTER VOCATION CONFERENCE: NSVC

This group affirms itself as a national organization dedicated to deepening the understanding of the role of women, especially religious women, in the Church through the work of the vocation apostolate.

NSVC hopes to coordinate efforts at all levels of the vocation apostolate and to:

  – cooperate with other vocation-related organizations in order to help provide full service and to avoid unnecessary duplication of energies;
  – be a clearing house for all kinds of vocational/informational input;
  – communicate vocational information to many and varied publics;
  – assist prospective candidates to religious life.

SISTERS FOR CHRISTIAN COMMUNITY: SFCC

This group was begun in 1970 in response to a need for an alternate life-style for many religious women in the contemporary United States. It has branched out to include Sisters in several foreign countries as well as women who have not been in canonical structures previously. The commitment form is created by the individual, and she also decides the length of time for this according to her own vocational charisms.

The individual lives and works wherever she feels she can best respond to God's call of her to serve his people. The members are not united by rule and constitution but by mutual concern and communication.

WHAT IS ENVISIONED FOR SISTERS UNITING?

Sisters Uniting attempts to serve by stimulating religious women to look anew at their own worth as persons and to elicit their joint potential as they administer to the concrete needs of mankind in the present moment. The combined efforts of Sisters Uniting will enable the American Sister both to see new needs and to have the flexibility to meet them.

Sisters are not seeking security and protection, but loyalty and the apostolic ingenuity of a love which is by its very nature creative and life-giving. The spectrum of opinions within Sisters Uniting is of great importance. Through these varied ways of seeing God's world, members can become instruments of reconciling love and creative vision. Unity, not uniformity, is its watchword.

Sisters Uniting is living witness to a burning hope in the future of religious life, and it has the courage to continually offer something new as a response to God's wish. It realizes that creative power needs prayer, perseverance and a network of people through whom this life-giving power can be given.

The agenda of the future depends on that vision – born of prayer – which is the rock upon which Sisters Uniting is built. By the power of the Spirit,

Sisters Uniting will act upon that which it has seen in prayer, and will be truly a group of ecclesial women. Sisters today—through support and strength received in Sisters Uniting—can realize more than ever before just what great things God has done to them.

Spring: Letter from Home

It was late November,
winter in Minnesota.
The evening was blue and white and
cold. To keep warm
we walked faster than our thoughts.
I was telling you about God
and me.
He beats on my shores like
golden waves, I said,
or like waves of music
he builds and builds
inside me
until I must hold on with two hands
to stay intact and on the ground.
And it's true.
It's true.
But I watched your eyes, ice blue
and lonely
and my joy seeped away.
I believe in Jesus the man, you said,
but not in
that god
who sits laughing at this cheap joke.
And I with God crashing within me
was silent.

Do you talk of spring
in the long night of an ice-locked winter
to one already
homesick for the sun?

Sister Mara Faulkner, O.S.B.
Sisters Today, May, 1976

Sisters Today, October, 1974

Sisters' Network

Sister Camilla Shea, S.C.C.

In less than three years the Sisters' Network has grown from an idea shared by forty-seven Sisters to a reality affecting the lives of more than 2,000 members and having an influence on lobbying groups and lawmakers. The Network is a national organization aimed at channeling information to Sisters throughout the United States and encouraging active concern in political issues related to social justice.

The concept of Network was verbalized in December, 1971, and actualized a month later. Since that time the original committee of two volunteers has increased to five staff members based in Washington, D.C. The purpose of providing information has expanded to taking positions on issues and seeking to influence legislation. Even the growing tendency to drop the word "Sisters" and refer simply to "Network" is indicative of the interest of priests and laity in this concerted effort to promote justice and peace.

NATURE AND PURPOSE

The phenomenal growth of Network is closely related to the nature and purpose of the organization. In December, 1971, forty-seven Sisters of several religious congregations met at Trinity College, Washington, D.C. A weekend of lectures and discussions had been planned to study the implications of Pope Paul's "Call to Action" issued in May of the same year.

The primary focus of the Washington meeting was on the belief that Sisters can effect institutional change in government and social needs by mobilizing for better legislation – local, state, national. This political involvement is seen as a ministry, a response to Pope Paul's call:

To take politics seriously at its different levels — local, regional, national and worldwide — is to affirm the duty of men, of every man to recognize the concrete reality and the value of freedom of choice that is offered to him to seek to bring about the good of the city and of the nation and of mankind. Politics are a demanding manner — but not the only one — of living the Christian commitment to the service of others (#46).

By the time this apostolic letter was published many religious congregations and Sisters' organizations already had social concerns committees charged with the responsibility of spearheading awareness of social conditions and activity to promote social justice. It was among these that Sister Marjorie Tuite, O.P., coordinator of the Social Concerns Committee of the National Assembly of Women Religious (NAWR), began circulating the idea of a weekend meeting in Washington. She and others from NAWR who helped spread the message generated enthusiasm which they thought would bring approximately fifteen or twenty Sisters together. They were amazed at the widespread response: the forty-seven Sisters at the meeting represented twenty-one States.

Each of these Sisters represented a group prepared to take seriously Pope Paul's words in the apostolic letter already referred to:

It is to all Christians that we address a fresh and insistent call to action. In our encyclical on the Development of Peoples we urged that all should set themselves to the task: ". . .it belongs to the laity, without waiting passively for orders and directives, to take the initiative freely and to infuse a Christian spirit into the mentality, customs, laws and structures of the community in which they live" (#48).

POTENTIAL CHANGE AGENTS

The potential of the more than 140,000 Sisters in the United States to become change agents on many levels was a dominant factor in the decision to organize a network. The organization was not intended to duplicate or supplant other groups, but rather to be a service to existing groups such as the Leadership Conference of Women Religious (LCWR), NAWR and social concerns committees of various religious congregations.

The name chosen suggests the vision: an effort to influence through a network of participation, as contrasted with what the Bishops' Synod statement, "Justice in the World," called a "network of domination, oppression and abuses which stifle freedom."

Within two years the responsibilities of the core staff have assumed shape and scope related to the goals and purposes of Network. The effort to organize Sisters throughout the United States is directed toward influencing legislation, working for laws which will promote social justice. Everything in the total program has some bearing on the actualization of a network of influence.

SELECTION OF ISSUES

Two publications, the *Newsletter* and the *Network Quarterly*, keep the growing membership aware of the status of congressional bills related to issues chosen as priorities. The issues of world peace, honesty in government, environment exploitation, the poor and the aged had surfaced as the prime concerns of the original group. A steering committee of fifteen members from various states was formed to help in the selection of issues and in the direction of Network action for those chosen concerns.

The first Network *Newsletter*, September–October, 1972, gave an alphabetical annotated list of eleven issues and asked Sisters to select and rank their choice of the top three. Criteria to guide the selection were:
1. Empowerment of the poor. The poor of the world are without power to help themselves. They need the support and assistance of just legislation.
2. Timeliness – in Congress and in Sisters' interests.
3. Non-duplication of major efforts by other national citizen and Church lobbying groups.

The first Network poll determined the issues of concern for 1972–1973: peace, international justice, penal reform, welfare reform, migrants, and the Equal Rights Amendment. Subsequent issues of the *Newsletter* kept the membership informed about the progress of congressional bills related to these issues. Occasionally circumstances brought other issues to the fore.

These two organs of communication, the *Newsletter* and the *Quarterly*, are concrete evidence of the scope of the headquarters' staff responsibility. They imply up-to-date factual knowledge gained through attendance at congressional hearings and through cooperation with other national groups who share similar concern for social issues. Both publications influence and are influenced by phone alerts and contacts with state Network coordinators.

CONGRESSIONAL DISTRICTS

In several states Network used the Congressional districts as framework for organization. According to this plan the state and local coordinators, through workshops and political education days, publicized Network. They also contacted Sisters whose interest was known through social concerns committees, NAWR, LCWR, and Sisters' Councils. Membership and enthusiasm grew through the efforts of Sisters convinced of the validity and urgency of Pope Paul's call to action for legislation effecting social justice.

Volunteers set up telephone networks linking the convents in their Congressional districts. They called and visited their Congressional representatives' offices and, when possible, arranged for a meeting between the Congressperson and the Sisters in the district. In most areas this organizational work is still in process, gaining strength and looking toward effective influence during the present state and federal legislative sessions and during this election year.

Given the original goal of Network, to organize and activate Sisters throughout the United States to realize their potential as catalysts to effect institutional change through better legislation, the Congressional district organization procedure is key to the thrust of the entire Network.

It is through the Congressional district telephone network that individual Sisters can become aware of on-going legislative developments. For those who want to experience the political process first-hand, to better understand the issues and their dependence upon adequate, just legislation, an intern program has developed. Sisters in this program work at Network's national headquarters office and also in government agencies affecting social justice concerns. Currently these Sisters are non-salaried and so are generally supported by their own religious congregations. At the end of a summer session or a year in this program the Sisters have an accumulated experience to share with others in their home Congressional districts.

A briefer but also effective part of the Network program is the annual Legislative Seminar held in Washington, D.C. The several objectives of the Legislative Seminar emphasize the belief that political action for social justice is a valid and necessary ministry, and therefore aim to develop individual and corporate commitment to political action. To give this action direction, priority issues are chosen during the seminar and are set as focus for a one-year nationwide effort.

The rapid growth of Network and its effectiveness have attracted the attention of clergy and laity as well as of Sisters. This interest could lead to extending the membership to include "all Christians" as addressed by Pope Paul's call, provided Network does not thereby unnecessarily duplicate other active, organized groups.

Network is simply a creative, generous response taking the initiative in infusing a Christian spirit into the community.

Sisters Today, January, 1968

Contemplative Renewal

Sister Mary Angela, O.SS.R.

Contemplative life, like other forms of religious life, is in the process of renewal. How far will this renewal go? From many of the writings on the topic, the indication or implication is that a few minor changes will be made exteriorly and there will be a deepening of interior renewal through the study of theology and related sacred sciences. And there it will end. Much has actually been written in defense of traditional enclosure. A few brave souls who have spoken out against it have ventured to criticize only one aspect of enclosure — the grilles.

Is this really the only change the Holy Spirit is expecting us to make? Are we so smug as to think that these are the only changes necessary? Perhaps if we took an objective view of our life as contemplatives and tried to re-evaluate the whole purpose of that life, we would then see more clearly what changes should take place, in what direction they should go, and just how much they would encompass.

Of what use to the Church are contemplatives? Certainly this question can only be answered in the light of faith. Perhaps we could say that to one with faith no answer is necessary, and to one without faith no answer is possible. Yet it seems that some answer is desirable for those with enough faith to want to believe in this rather mysterious part of Christ's Mystical Body.

Perhaps some descriptive definition of the life itself is called for. The contemplative life is dedicated to an intensification of adoration, praise, and supplication in a more direct manner than is permitted by the married state, the single state, and the active religious state with all their attendant duties. While life in the other states also consists in work and prayer, the mode of expression is quite different.

There is provided for contemplatives a certain degree of separation from the world, not because the world is evil, but because the powers of human concentration and the scope of human energy are necessarily limited. Those entering this state of life find that some degree of separation is psychologically necessary in order to concentrate on the essential message of the redemption.

Although all are called to contemplation, those who are called to the *canonical state* are expected to intensify the intellectual mode of contemplation. This does not mean intellectualism as such, but rather prayer life based on community worship in the liturgy. Also, to some degree, work is chosen that allows the mind freedom to dwell on God and the things of God; or the work — writing, art, or any other form of creativity — directly focuses on contemplation and is its fruit.

There is also what the Vatican Council calls the sign value. Religious as a whole show forth and foretell by their vows the eschatological dimension. In the monastic religious, this is shown by their mode of living, their vows, and their common liturgical prayer. "Our union with Christ is put into effect in its noblest manner when with common rejoicing we celebrate together the praise of the Divine Majesty" (*Constitution on the Church*, art. 50).

Each individual in the community must have a call to the canonical state of contemplative life. To live such a life, one must be totally dedicated to a type of community living, to obedience, poverty and chastity as expressed within the structure of a contemplative community. It is a life of faith in that one does not necessarily see one's usefulness, but believes in it with one's whole being, striving for an ever greater degree of charity and understanding toward every Sister in the community and all the people in the world who will never even be known by the contemplative.

THE QUESTION OF ENCLOSURE

The history of monasticism for women has been so closely linked with externals such as grilles, keys, locks, and strict enclosure that it is imperative to look into the question of enclosure rather well. How many ridiculous things have been done because of a legalistic interpretation of the canons regarding enclosure: garbage cans being pulled into the enclosure with a rake in order that Sisters do not *step* out of the enclosure, busy housewives being called by phone to come over to the monastery to push some object through the enclosure door, lay people in prayer in the chapel being asked to leave so that the Sister can go into the chapel to change the candles without seculars being present.

Men's orders seem to have had much more freedom with respect to enclosure. In contrast, women's orders have been dominated by masculine ideas of overprotection — perhaps more or less necessary in the Middle Ages but hardly applicable to the woman of the twentieth century. Today, the purpose of the cloister and enclosure is to preserve the recollection of the nuns.

Any structures of enclosure should be re-examined in this light. Grilles, locked doors, etc., are not essential for preserving recollection. Cloister and enclosure should be reduced simply to regulations that preserve some degree of privacy and silence. Some contact with others would then not only be permitted but desired; this would, of course, be regulated.

The reason for such contact is obvious: complete separation from outsiders, both men and women, is conducive to a closed and narrow-minded outlook, and promotes unnatural attitudes. Narrow-mindedness expresses itself in the pettiness and attention to trivia which many a nun in an active Order would not think of indulging in, while unnatural attitudes are often manifested in a lack of poise and a childishness or a self-consciousness when meeting strangers, especially when there is no grille. Lacking even such a natural foundation, any spirituality that develops is bound to be, in some part at least, counterfeit. Absolute separation is not as beneficial to the balance of a well-developed nature as it is sometimes considered to be.

Just how much contact and how much separation should there be in order to preserve the balance? It would be so easy, when revising a Rule, to say, "Let each house decide." But there should be a few guiding norms.

First and foremost, grilles of any kind must be eliminated entirely in order to enable the development of a more natural, a more graceful and grace-filled approach to our fellow Christians. Viewed in the Christian light, a handshake is a kind of sacramental. How can one convey to outsiders (who are "outside" in every sense of the word), the meaning, let alone the core, of Christianity — which contemplative life is supposed to reflect — when bars, slats or chicken-wire convey as clearly as the spoken word that contamination of the cloistered inmates would result were the grilles not there. Regardless of how cleverly the theological niceties are assembled to explain the grilles, *this* is what they mean to "outsiders."

Of course, then, there are the one hundred-and-one little regulations regarding enclosure. Most contemplative Orders today recognize the necessity of simplifying and eliminating many of these rules, such as the taking of a companion to the parlor or the ringing of a little bell before the doctor, priest or plumber enters the cloister so as to *warn* the Sisters of their entrance. It would seem that all these customs should be entirely eliminated and a normal procedure observed, as is done in any well regulated institution. Here it would be well to make it clear that the elimination of grilles, etc., is not doing away with the enclosure. Enclosure is necessary to the monastic life, but the methods of ensuring it should be re-examined and updated.

There is also the question of the egress of nuns. Some think that it should never be permitted except in cases of dire necessity. But would it really disturb recollection if at least a few in each community were allowed to take courses in theology, psychology and liturgy, or in trades that would help them to pray and work more efficiently?[1]

---

[1] In August, 1967, a circular letter was sent from our monastery to all the contemplative houses in the United States and Canada. This letter asked two questions. The first asked their

If nuns are to be allowed egress, it does not seem unreasonable that lay women be permitted entrance for some relatively extended time. Pope Paul's concept of a monastery is that it should be a place which presents to others an atmosphere of recollection and prayer. Surely it would not be a disturbance of that recollection if some women retreatants were allowed to stay in the monastery for a few days of private retreat, eating, and praying with the community.

Enclosure, however, is not the only aspect of renewal. The structured horarium is another vital area that needs consideration. The monks of old came together for liturgical prayer, meals, and recreation. As for the rest of the day, it was divided according to the needs of the individual monk. The amount of time for prayer differs for each individual according to her spiritual advancement and the ways of the Holy Spirit.

It is taken for granted that the novices' horarium would remain somewhat structured, but a horarium for the professed religious which does not consider or allow for the spiritual needs of the individual inevitably constricts personal growth. There are difficulties, of course: how do we insure that the work of the monastery does not suffer from excessive freedom, and who is to tell how much prayer, work, and study an individual needs? It takes a mature individual to decide these matters — and that it precisely the point. It takes a *mature* person to live the contemplative life in community. When a person *is* mature, she makes decisions not first and foremost for herself, but for the good of the community.

INTERIOR RENEWAL

Of far greater need, of course, is interior renewal. This seems to be generally recognized, yet even here deficiencies exist. True liberty of the children of God is hard to achieve. Even when updated courses, lectures and tapes are made available to a community, the traces of Jansenistic attitudes

opinion as to the taking into their community life a few active religious who wish to spend a time in a cloistered monastery to share our life temporarily. The second question asked if they thought contemplatives themselves should be allowed a temporary stay in active communities to fill a spiritual, physical or psychological need. The results of this survey are as follows:

There were 235 communities contacted. Of these, 49 answered. Regarding the first question, 18 were against the idea, 22 were in favor of the question, the other 9 were undecided. Regarding the second question, 22 were against it, 14 were in favor, 13 were undecided. Many of those who were against it or undecided perhaps did not understand what the question involved.

In the evaluation of this survey one thing is very clear. Although there is strong opinion among the cloistered religious to keep the cloister and separation from the world as strictly as before, there is nevertheless a growing and widespread opinion that there should be a little loosening of these restrictions. As one Superior said, there would have been a horrified reaction to this suggestion two years ago, but today in their community it is felt there is a need to be met. On the other hand, it is very difficult to give any other evaluation on this survey. Many stated they did consult their community but many others, especially those opposed, did not make any such statement. Also, what are we to conclude from the vast majority who did not reply?

still survive. Fears of throwing off these chains are not entirely groundless. Again, it takes the good judgment of a mature person to decide where freedom and its corresponding responsibility enter. Thus, a basic education in theology and psychology should very definitely be stressed for *all* religious and not just for the ones being newly formed. There should be some order in the sequence of courses, and both lecturers and material should be carefully selected by those who want genuine renewal (not merely a compromise) and are not afraid of the risks involved. Possibilities might be investigated for founding a house to which finally professed members of various contemplative communities could come together to take intensive courses in theology and other areas of study.

In this spirit, intercommunication with others in the same state of life is a primary requisite in preparation for the necessary changes in both attitude and structure. For a contemplative order this might seem impossible, yet much could be done. Contemplatives should meet with other contemplatives; to some degree this has been done, but not nearly enough for many communities. It should not be just the superiors who meet.

I would like to conclude this article with the collective experience of our own community. Twenty-five in number, we had to leave our strictly enclosed monastery with papal cloister for a temporary establishment in a former novitiate for religious men. Naturally there were no grilles or fences. Having lived the contemplative life under these circumstances, we have found that grilles are neither necessary nor desirable.

The community is unanimous in this opinion, even though formerly many had favored strict and rigid signs of the enclosure. We have been made to look more deeply behind the contemplative life, and there has come a desire to eliminate the debris that obscures the true meaning of canonical contemplative life. We are still searching for deeper meaning and will perhaps continue to do so for a long time to come. But this is the age of painful renewal, and little by little we are coming to see that there is a glorious vision ahead. This vision is not without faith. Rather, by a deeper faith we see with the light of hope the height and depth of the redemption.

Sisters Today, April, 1967

Religious Habits and
the Psychology of Dress

Sister Judith Tate, O.S.B.

Often persons perceive a truth intuitively before they come to grasp it consciously and intellectually. One wonders if this is not the case with Sisters concerning the religious habit.

Discussion about habit change evokes response from a psycho-emotional level which is evidently not countered in kind by arguments based on considerations of expense, convenience, appearance, or even symbol. Since the question has not been satisfactorily resolved on these levels, perhaps the true source of the difficulty stems from deeper psychological levels of the personality. With this possibility in mind, it may be helpful — and, in the face of many recent rescripts from Rome, also timely — to consider the body of research available on the psychology of clothing. Such a consideration may enable Sisters to bring to consciousness what many of them have already perceived intuitively. Perhaps, too, a scientific approach to the discussion is the most charitable one, for it should provide enough objectivity to alleviate the personal innuendoes that often hurt others in the heat of this ever-emotional topic.

Although there is an astonishing variety of traditional religious habits, they generally have these things in common: dark color, volume, some stiffness (as in starched or celluloid pieces), and some tightness. What do these characteristics of dress generally mean?

Dark color is universally connected with seriousness. Psychologists note that somber colors become national fashion in countries that are suffering greatly, as in a war or great economic crisis. In such cases, emotions are reigned in, for there is not only a lack of joy but also an attempt to avert despair.

Bright colors, on the contrary, signify not only gaiety but also freer emotions, particularly the emotions that express themselves in spontaneity, laughter, joy, and tenderness. When a war ends in victory, for example, bright colors reappear in dress, as gaiety and a relaxation of tension reappear in the emotional life of the people. This influence of color is so important that, once psychologists and national leaders become aware of it, brightness is inserted into dress fashions in order to raise national morale during critical periods.

What is true on a national level has been seen to be true also on a personal level. Investigation indicates that those who habitually wear somber colors consider themselves to be persons of great seriousness, especially moral seriousness. By indicating emotional restraint, they also seem to be aloof, somehow superior to or at least distinct from those who express themselves more freely.[1]

Volume of clothing may be due to thickness of material or to amplitude of yardage — or both. Studies repeatedly reveal that bulk, or volume, indicates two things: distrust of the human body and unwillingness to be involved with others. Psychologists have found that when a person thinks of the body primarily as a source of evil passions, he is inclined to try to forget or to control that body by as complete a covering as possible. The Puritans, among others, exemplify this phenomenon. Bulky dress not only covers the body, it also obliterates its lines. This makes the body "safer."[2]

Besides safety, voluminous clothing often signifies aloofness. Since clothing is an "extension of the skin," thick clothing keeps one "out of touch" with others.[3] Voluminous dress — literally a wrapping up around the self — also indicates a psychological state of being wrapped up around oneself. According to psychological theses, persons who habitually wear a great amount of clothing (weather notwithstanding) are not available in any intimate or personal fashion; they may be approached as *what* but not as *who*. They create an aura about themselves as people who are distinct from the common crowd.

In all fashions, even tribal ones, this is the constant meaning of voluminous clothing. For example, in tribes where most members wear little or nothing, the chief is often totally covered, indicating his removal from the level of the ordinary tribesmen. Or, to give another example, an admiral in full uniform has more bulk to his costume than an ensign has. A dowager's dress has more yards in it than does her servant's.

Related to bulkiness is a certain pressure or tightness. Voluminous clothes are usually gathered closely about the body. This gathering of clothes about one supports the notion of aloofness. "If we find ourselves among unsympa-

---

[1] John Carl Flügel, *The Psychology of Clothes* (London: the Hogarth Press, 1950), 75ff. See also George Ashdown, *Colour in Dress* (London, 1912).

[2] Flügel, 76ff. See also W. J. Thomas, "Psychology of Modesty in Clothes," *American Journal of Psychology*, vol. 5, 246ff.

[3] Marshall McLuhan, *Understanding Media* (New York: McGraw-Hill Book Co., 1964), 119. Mr. McLuhan's comments on "hot media" may also be aptly applied to a study of clothes.

thetic people — people to whom we feel ourselves superior, with whom we have nothing in common, or of whom we are afraid — in this case also we tend to draw our clothes tightly around us, as if they somehow kept us apart or protected us from those people with whom we desire no intimacy."[4]

Psychologists also note that, whereas "loose" and "sloppy" dress often corresponds to "loose" living, so stiff and tight dress often corresponds to uprightness and/or rigidity. Extremes in either direction are seen as undesirable insofar as both indicate unhealthy attitudes toward the body. The scientific contention is that distrust of the body and personal aloofness manifest a fear of loving. Voluminous, sober, and tight clothing become, then, "a reassurance against the lack of love"; they frequently indicate that the wearers "are afraid of giving free vent to their feelings of love."[5]

If these conclusions of psychological research are valid, their implications for the religious habit are striking. Let us look at each element of the habit again.

Color. Sisters should see goodness in laughter and in the sunny experiences of life as well as in the solemn and sad ones. Their feelings of gaiety and tenderness need expression as well as those of pity and sorrow. Despite war, disease, discrimination, and human weaknesses of all kinds, Sisters should have a lively faith in the Kingdom which is here and now begun and which will come to perfection. Isn't evidence of that faith a most vital witness today? Perhaps for these reasons, many Sisters resist the idea of habitually wearing black.

Volume. As Sisters seek to be compassionately involved in society, they want to be available. They have an urgent desire to know and love — and to be known and loved — as unique persons. Sisters today do not see their way of life as superior to other ways; therefore they do not wish to be set apart from, or above, any other Christian.

Perhaps never before in history has there been such emphasis on personal authenticity and on personal relationships. It could well be that, consciously or unconsciously, Sisters feel that the religious garb sets them so much above others that they become inauthentic since, really, they are simply Christian women among other equally good Christian women. They might also feel that the garb sets them so much apart that their opportunities for meaningful and honest friendships are diminished. If voluminous clothing does indeed indicate aloofness, anonymity, and superiority, then there would be good reason for emotionally healthy and soundly holy Sisters to seek a different type of dress.

Tightness and stiffness. There may be much yet to learn about the feminine mystique, but one thing is notable: more women today are more apt to accept and to like the fact of their femininity. They are relaxed about their sexuality and so see their bodies as good and beautiful. Perhaps Sisters have understood that their celibacy is taken as a testimony against sexuality.

[4] Flügel, 78.
[5] Flügel, 77, 80.

Perhaps, too, they realize that the material symbol of their celibacy is a habit which not only covers the body but also distorts its shape, and so implies that the body is not a good gift from God. The witness of celibacy might be much more clear and effective if it is given by a woman who is joyous in her womanhood.

Without any indictment of Sisters who do wear or who have worn the traditional habit, it could be that Sisters now want to change their dress because a contemporary dress is more in harmony with their current postconciliar thinking and loving and serving.

Mrs. Kontos

Is eighty-odd years of ancient Greece
Lived in these streets of Nebraska;
On sunworthy days, she walks
Her twin Pekingese dogs, her own
Peke-faced elderliness black-mantled,
Becoming the Aegean matron. Mr. Kontos,
Who traveled, has traveled far
Beneath his stone cross in the graveyard;
The Orthodox, for the sake of his soul,
Have eaten from bowls of boiled wheat.
Speaking with rock-born hardihood,
Mrs. Kontos recalls his travels,
Her girlhood coming to this strange place,
Now her grief. In the sun, her features
Dent like a sundial, her nose
A sweep of shadow keeping time
For Ulysses' widow, in Penelope's broken face.

Nancy G. Westerfield
Sisters Today, March, 1977

Sisters Today, December, 1974

Community by Objectives

Sister Dorothy Schmidt, S.C.C.

This is a how-to article. How to take a group of Sisters, some of whom have lived together before, some of whom have barely ever communicated with each other, conservative, liberal, from the farm, from the city and in entirely different apostolates, but all of whom are going to live in the same house for the next ten or twelve months, and lay the ground work for an atmosphere of growth, support and sharing.

The how-to is the process of goal setting begun shortly after all in the group have unpacked their luggage for the year. In a business organization the process for deciding your goals is implicit in what is referred to as "management by objectives." Objectives describe goals which are related to the business' purpose in terms of concrete achievable targets.

Goal setting gives a particular local community its unique *raison d' etre* and provides a wholesome positive basis for house meetings and communication throughout the year. It sets the stage for that *espirit de corps* which, when present, makes a Sister want to sign up for another year in the same house mainly because it has been a good group with which to live and not just because it's near the place she works.

A facilitator from outside the group would, as the name indicates, facilitate the whole process. However, it is not always possible to beg, borrow or hire a facilitator, and the process itself is not that difficult. In a group of eight Sisters, for example, there are usually one or two who have sufficient personal resources and skills to guide a group through the goal setting process.

Community by objectives is a reason to leave busy phone, doorbell and other activities at home for a day or two and retreat to a house of prayer. The actual process of goal setting can take a few days at one stretch or it can be divided among a few house meetings.

There are five basic steps in the process:
1. Determine the purpose of the local community.
2. Identify the needs of the local community.
3. Set the goals.
4. Concretize the goals.
5. Evaluate the goals.

STEP ONE: DETERMINE THE PURPOSE OF THE LOCAL COMMUNITY

There is a reason why each person is physically a part of the group and why the group exists as a group. In this first step the group tries to arrive at a common statement of purpose.

The point in this step is to develop or raise to consciousness unifying elements that exist within a group. This initial step is very important because of changes in religious communities which allow and encourage greater diversity both internally and externally. This statement of purpose in a changing group can never be assumed. It has to be verbalized.

Agreeing upon a statement of purpose furnishes a frame of reference influencing future decision making within the whole group. Among all the steps this is probably the least threatening topic and consequently the best one to begin an attempt at establishing a climate of openness and acceptance. In addition to clarifying the purpose, establishing a common basis for working and sharing provides motivation for a deeper commitment to the group.

If the local community is larger than eight, smaller groups need to be formed to allow each person the time and opportunity to share. If more than one group is necessary, then in each of the succeeding instances of group work the small groups share their results and then combine them. In this case the aim is to arrive at one common statement of purpose.

STEP TWO: IDENTIFY THE NEEDS OF THE LOCAL COMMUNITY

There are hopes, concerns, needs that each person holds for the whole group. In this second step the group compiles a list of these.

Identifying the needs, hopes and concerns of the group means finding out what each person values in relationship to the group. All items listed cannot be dealt with, but the items increase understanding of each person's present and future choices within the group.

This input also gives a clearer idea of and adds greater direction to the setting of goals. The same idea surfacing repeatedly in the brainstorming session points to an area the group may want to concentrate on in goal setting. Sometimes it makes the most important goal quite obvious later on in the process.

Brainstorming makes available a greater choice of needs to respond to in setting goals. Using contrast and comparison, the more important areas of interest are singled out from a wide range of concerns.

To move into this second step the facilitator directs the whole group in a brainstorming session to write down on a large chart or blackboard the needs, hopes and concerns of the group for this coming year. Remember, brainstorming is not for the purpose of decision-making but to obtain data with which to work. Any idea is welcome, even those that at first may seem far out.

There are a number of ways to handle this particular step.
A) Positive approach: ask
   "What are the needs to which we should be responding?"
   "What do you hope will happen to us as a group this year?"
B) Negative approach: ask
   "What are your fears for this year?"
   "What don't you want to happen?"
C) Disappearing act: ask
   "What would or would not happen if we were not in existence as a group this year — if we weren't here in this situation at this point in time?"

The items listed in the brainstorming session are then prioritized in their order of importance to the group. Those items are chosen for further consideration which the group can realistically do something about.

Somewhere in the process, at the end of Step Two or the beginning of Step Three (the actual goal setting), the group has to determine how many goals it can realistically handle. If five goals are set can they be accomplished simultaneously or sequentially or not at all? Is it possible that two goals can be combined into one? Can two or three people in the group work on one goal and the others on the other or will this defeat the overall purpose of the process of goal setting?

STEP THREE: SET THE GOALS

In this step a decision is made to set goals which are achievable and realistic, specific, measurable, and acceptable to all.

The group's purpose must be supported by a statement of its major goals. The idea here is to answer the question, "Where are we going and why?" in relationship to the group's overall purpose, of each individual to the other within the group, to the group's environment and to the larger religious community.

Divergent paths of individuals and community can be reconciled in terms of the goal setting process. Here is where the needs of the community relate to the needs of the individuals, the needs of one are related to the needs of another one within the group. Community by objectives can become a key to individual and community fulfillment and effectiveness.

Each goal must somehow activate a Sister's human potential for psychological or spiritual growth. The activating of each one's potential for growth must in turn actuate the group's potential for community growth. In other words, the individual, through the goal, must find out who she is, and the community, through the goal, must find out what it is.

To proceed with this third step the group should take a look at the chart containing the rank ordered needs, hopes and concerns for the group. Here is the material from which to form goals. Satisfying some of those needs could be the goal for which the group is looking. For instance, if the group has listed praying together as a need, a corresponding goal could be to plan a para-liturgical service for the second and fourth Monday evenings of each month.

As each goal is chosen by the total group, match it against the goal criteria listed below. If it does not stand against the criteria, either reword it or drop it entirely. This is the difficult area of goal setting, particularly getting a number of people to choose goals which are acceptable to all, but it is vital to the process and achievement of the goals.

The criteria for evaluating the goals are as follows:

Achievable and realistic: "Is this goal within the power of the group to achieve within the time span that they are together? Does it realistically relate to the purpose and needs of the group?"

Specific: "What actual steps can be taken to accomplish the goal?"

Measurable: "How will the group know when the goal has been attained? What criteria will be used to measure its attainment?"

Acceptable to all: "Is the goal important and significant enough to each member of the group so her efforts and cooperation in achieving it are guaranteed from the onset?"

If it is a goal which leaves out a member of the group for whatever reason, then it is a goal of a part of the group and does not belong here. This is where the goal setting criteria differ from those of business management in which case groups go off to work on their own area or interest goals. They form separate departments to accomplish separate goals. To promote community building it is desirable that the goal be growth-oriented for each member of the group. For example, a goal stating that the teachers form a "Thank God It's Friday Club" and hold their meetings after school on Friday is not acceptable to all in the group if all are not teachers and at the same school.

STEP FOUR: CONCRETIZE THE GOALS

In this step the group should fill out a time line for each goal, listing who does what action by what date.

Making the goal as visible and concrete as possible insures a greater degree of achievement and motivation. Responsibility motivates. A person's name coupled with a specific action also lays the foundation for a means of evaluation and personal accountability covered below in Step Five.

To achieve this step the group should work with each goal individually (you are lucky if you only set one) and concretize it by developing a time line. Divide the time line into the months that you will be together. Write down the specific action being taken during each month and the name of the person(s) taking that action.

The example of the paraliturgical service is obvious because it simply entails listing the date for each service and who is responsible on that date. However, in the case where goals have not been sufficiently realistic, this is difficult. This is the point at which they are made practical or tossed out.

STEP FIVE: EVALUATE THE GOAL

In this step the group should determine who will evaluate the success of each goal, when will evaluation take place and what criteria will be used to evaluate.

Evaluation must be understood in terms of the results achieved. Personal accountability was built into the goal in Step Four where specific individuals were named for each action listed on the time line.

Personal accountability and evaluation criteria which are developed to some extent when the goals are set assure a greater degree of accomplishment. This step also offers a certain amount of control over the fulfillment of each goal during and at the end of the time the group is together.

To complete this step the group should decide who will evaluate the progress and success of the goal and when will evaluation take place?

Criteria used to evaluate goals depend upon the nature of the goals as well as the actions taken to achieve the goals. These criteria can be formulated in terms of participation, numbers, sustained interest, learning, and degree of support given and received. The time line offers the most obvious base for evaluation.

The validity of the criteria depends upon factual evidence of accomplishment, the evaluator's perception of success and effectiveness and the honesty of the group with each other.

The completing of the goal setting process is only the beginning of "community by objectives." Moment by moment tiny units of being are given to each of us by God. Sharing these units of being with others in community during the year in combined efforts to achieve one or two goals is a worthwhile means of using each unit of being before it quickly slips by and is replaced by another.

Sisters Today, May, 1971

Small-Group Communal Living

Sister Dorothy Bock, O.S.F.

I've heard the comments. You've heard them, too.

"You know, we have Sisters living on our block, right down the street in the third house from the corner."

"Why did they move out? What's going to happen to all those empty convents?"

"Mark my words, it's just the beginning. First it's living out, then it's leaving, then its marrying the first guy who comes along."

"Living's an expensive business; why don't they live off the parish?"

"I think they're great. I watch them out there raking leaves, carrying out the garbage just like the rest of us."

"After the convents go the nuns will go; the religious orders will disappear next."

"It's wonderful. They're not just at church with us; they're at the supermarket and the laundromat, too."

I've heard it; you've heard it a dozen times with a dozen or more responses to the situation of Sisters living outside the usual convent or parochial structures. Sisters today invade and remodel flats, old farmsteads, small rented homes, and apartments. The new dwellings take on a variety of shapes, sizes, and economic brackets.

All of us might speculate on real and possible assets and drawbacks of this "living out," but for me the experience is the real test. Everyone who has moved out of the traditional convent structure as a life style, whether small group or large institution, and has freely adopted a new, less structured manner of living certainly has multiple and diverse feelings, attitudes, and ideas about its benefits and its problems.

With this in mind, I will speak only from and for my own experience, not for others. For twenty years I've lived in institutional convents, some larger ones of twenty to forty women professionally connected with a high school, and smaller ones of eight to ten connected with a parish. Mine was a comfortable, orderly life of minimal personal relationships: glasses in the proper cupboards, private rooms, Mass daily in the chapel, meals organized and prepared by one or two Sisters appointed. It was a life of scheduled responsibilities and comparatively smooth professional relationships: three regular meals a day, scheduled prayer hours, programmed work and programmed recreation, designated free time which was usually consumed in getting extra jobs done that I couldn't fit into my work schedule. The borders between my life and my profession were always blurred, and my function almost always took precedence over my needs as person.

Aware of this for a number of years, I sensed the ache more keenly when the possibility of freely choosing a living group was endorsed by our Chapter in the recent years of our renewal. I knew a friend of mine who was experiencing the same. We looked for others who did not want to live where they worked.

It wasn't a case of friends clustering together; it was more like two and two and two proposing the idea, expressing desires for more quality and diverse living, projecting possibilities for growth and facing realistically our own human limitations.

Each of the six of us is fiercely independent in her own way. We met one evening at a small restaurant to talk over our community possibilities with each other. We were as different as each of our orders that night: ham salad sandwich and Coke, a pizzaburger with onion rings, a highball, milk and strawberry shortcake, a manhattan, a BLT with coffee.

On certain things we agreed. We wanted to build a life with each other. We wanted independence personally and professionally, and yet we wanted to share our communal responsibilities in regard to the house and each other. We wanted to be involved in a living process that by its very quality would enrich and strengthen our lives of mission.

A house in the central vicinity of all our commitments, we decided, was discoverable if we looked hard. Two work as musician and art teacher in a parish, one as a consultant in a diocesan religious education office, one as music teacher in a public school, one as director of formation in the province, and one as artist and writer for the community and church groups.

After presenting our plan to the executive team of our province for feedback and approval, we got the "go ahead" sign and proceeded to house/apartment hunt. In late August we rented a small house off busy North Avenue. Within our budget, the house offered us three bedrooms, a kitchen, a living room, two double baths, a basement and an old two-car garage. We moved in immediately with our private stores and common furniture for the general rooms.

PHYSICAL FACTORS UNIFY

At first the physical factors of living brought us together: cleaning, moving in and arranging things, sharing the not-too-spacious environment of two to a bedroom, laundromat trips, budget for shopping, meal preparation, repairs on refrigerator and water softener, an old garage door, and, last but not least, "Have one car; will six travel?"

Interdependence among people who care about each other is one thing, and the debilitating dependence on another for one's mobility is another. Striking the balance here is not just a family matter where parents are first on the priority list. In this living situation we have six peers, each with her own legitimate priorities; from this level we try in love and justice to work it out. Fortunately, two company cars helped. So did the province in allowing us to buy a '66 Ford.

Our lives revolved around our primary apostolic work but also around community involvements and personal commitments. We shared prayer, meal talks, recreation and cultural events. Through physical challenges and problems we moved imperceptibly to psychic levels in each other.

At this point of our group process something stirred in me: the choice between comfortable and peaceable living on one level, or real depth involvement with each other on another level that respected individuality and freedom. I chose real psychic involvement, realizing that the relationship-level with each person in the house would be constantly new and variegated. I still find it a terrible risk to be totally honest with those I live with.

I began to talk not just ideas or the run-of-the-day business matters but to communicate attitudes, feelings, and desires. Beyond the level of "good Sisters" living together patiently and with as little disturbance as possible, I longed for us to be lovingly disturbed by each other, to be impatient and challenging to each other. I had begun to grow with each one as much as I was able, as much as she was able.

Somehow at this time I began to understand that I really hadn't been too personally committed to the people I lived with before—I mean on the gut level of everyday dishes, grocery tasks, taxiing people home from school or stations, sensitivity to each one's petty or great stresses of the day. With these Sisters I'm constantly balancing the delicate weights of solitude and communality, dependence and independence, freedom and responsibility, time in for me and time out for someone else.

MY VOWS AND THE OTHERS

The vows I once took—so individually geared to a life of perfection— seem now all caught up in the communal life I'm trying to live. I'm aware now that this life together, so intensely personal, contains the possibilities for depth and extension of mission orientation for others.

Our poverty is realized in communal sharing. We do not receive any favors from parishes or central groups that we serve. We support ourselves by salaries from our respective works, turned in to the common fund. A house budget of rent, utilities, food and household expenses is met. After this each of us has a small personal budget which largely fills extra professional needs. We have to be economical, knowing our limited income and realizing our obligation to send in money for community taxes, hospital fund, Sisters' retirement fund, and debt reduction. Considering all these responsibilities, there is little left for us as a group to decide upon as far as arbitrary spending is concerned.

We come from diverse value-oriented as well as economic backgrounds. Value-one for me is often value-ten for another. But we share our talents, our insights, our values with each other as much as we can.

We know poverty of space, too. No one has a private room. In fact, there is no room in the house we can really call our own, no space we can lock off for a while unless another understands and allows. We share cars and trips, hair dryers, telephone, closets and desks.

A new meaning of celibacy is also opening up for me. We share in love our lives with each other as intensely and as wholly as we can. It is not the same for all. Perhaps out of the five others, I give and take on a much deeper level with two or three. Frequently encounters are both painful and exhilarating at the same time. There is no place for me to hide when another knows my most vulnerable points and loves me in spite of them.

In our small home we somehow all fall together, sometimes by accident and sometimes by plan. We do this not only for our own sakes but for the sake of all those with and for whom we work. It is almost impossible to become exclusive. We share renewal weekends, daily prayer experiences, shop-talk, our aches, our fears, our fun, our own human comedies.

We have other close and social friends. These are men and women from the parishes, fellow grad students, priests, Brothers, Sisters of other communities, former students, and our families. No cloister is observed here in invitations, only respect for others and consideration of the space limitations of the house.

No one pries into another's private life. We try to trust, we wait for an invitation before we enter. If I have an individual problem with another man or woman, I can talk it over honestly with one, or two, or perhaps all. Nothing is a must; everything is open to the Spirit. Intimacy is a delicate thing. If I have feelings of aloneness or self-pity or jealousy, it's up to me to resolve them within this group.

In my obedience I attempt to embrace a loving acceptance, responsible understanding and a will toward group consensus in the light of the Spirit and the needs of people. External rules no longer determine my care for others. There are no signals for: lights out, no noise, wash the dishes, now study, now pray, now talk, now be concerned, now break off concern and "be with God."

God is here in our midst more surely for me now than he ever was. He is in each of us and beyond us. Our obedience is not only responsibility to ourselves and to others in the group, but also to our community and to the Church in its mission for men. We try to listen to and be open with the Church as it attempts to alleviate human need with its many faces. Decisions are always authored by me, but hopefully in the light of others' just needs. This leaves for me less room for irresponsible and selfish choices than the loopholes I might find in rules and regulations.

This "living out" can be "living in" if I choose it to be, if I make it become. This is no safe, domesticated life, where cozy friends gather, but a risk-oriented living process wherein Sisters challenge me to more creative and profound living as well as support me by loving me in weakness as well as in strength. In this process I can become the free woman I need to be in order to really love and care for others. I live in a home where changing relationships safeguard people from being categorized or pigeon-holed into static, safe corners. The persons, the Sisters I live with, are home to me because they try to set me free to be me, but they also urge me to become even more myself. I, too, want to be this "home" for them.

Sisters Today, November, 1977

Sisters Who Live Alone

Sister Lois Spear

With the changes in religious communities over the past few years, it seems barely possible that any major problems remain untouched, readily apparent in the vital statistics of a community, yet never candidly discussed. Like the stone lying in the pathway, we often stumble over obvious problems before we are aware that they exist. I am referring to Sisters who are members of religious communities yet choose to live alone.

On meeting these Sisters on one of their visits to the Motherhouse, one is tempted, after probing to find what convent or group of Sisters they live with and discovering that they live by themselves, either to end the conversation on a self-conscious note or with embarrassed silence. More often one hears the flippant remark, "I could never do that! I *have* to live with other Sisters." This attitude — there must be something wrong because she lives alone — is shared often by community leadership, though their perceptions are advanced sufficiently to keep them from the superficial and wounding remarks often made by individual Sisters. If we value these women who live apart from the nexus of community, if we are sensitive to the pain our non-understanding can cause them, then it is time that we take a look at why they live as they do, their relationship to the total apostolate — not just the local church and their own religious community — and how we can learn from them and relate to their needs.

THE NEEDS OF THE APOSTOLATE

The chief reason, I believe, why Sisters live alone is because they put the needs of the apostolate ahead of their own urge to live in a religious community. If, for example, a Sister feels drawn to work in a black college, then she must pack up her bags and move into the areas where black colleges are located. Unless she is able to induce a member of her own community to relocate in the area, community will have to be formed around the associations she develops in her apostolate. The Sister who desires to work with the rural poor must leave the populous urban centers where religious communities are over represented and take on the life of the poor, even to the point of divesting herself of the wealth of her community relationships.

But, on a deeper level, does the choosing of work before community mean that one really cuts herself off from a religious life whose central orientation is toward living with other religious? I think not. That concept of community is far too restricting to meet the needs of our multi-apostolates today. It represents one of the few remaining strands of a philosophy requiring actual physical proximity in order to form community.

A sense of community does not always follow from living together. Older religious know all too well and can give dozens of examples showing that Sisters, supposedly joined together "in heart and mind and spirit" were often light years apart in value systems, making convent living a harrowing experience. Even when the Sisters in community shared a common perspective, one wonders if for many, living together was not just a means of propping each other up — a house of cards safe only until the strong winds of Vatican II blew it in.

ENLARGING OUR DEFINITION OF COMMUNITY

The solution, it appears to me, consists in revising and enlarging our definition of community to include all those — without regard for their living arrangements — who share with us common goals and our religious foundation's unique vision of how to reach them.

Subordinating community to the needs of the apostolate may be, for some Sisters, a way of rationalizing a more fundamental need that carries hidden guilt feelings: They may wish to live in solitude, but years of community indoctrination have convinced them that it is living with others — no matter how abrasive and frustrating the experience may be — that somehow defines them as a "good religious." Seeking an apostolate far from one's religious community, then, becomes an acceptable way of seeking solitude.

We are faced again with the need to re-define terms. Solitude too often has been interpreted as loneliness, an inevitable part of our human existence. But we cannot escape loneliness by busyness. Sooner or later, it takes us by the hand and bids us be its guest. It may come when we feel isolated among the throngs of Sisters visiting the Motherhouse on a summer afternoon or when, attending a professional meeting, we become part of the Lonely Crowd with no one to talk to and we are too timid to strike up a conversation with a total stranger. As a consequence of original sin, loneliness is something we all must bear. Fear of it leads many of us into foolish escape mechanisms: Our apostolate is so important that it consumes every minute of our time; instead of a quiet evening at home, long telephone conversations are necessary to "help others" with their problems. An excuse always can be found to postpone the confrontation with self that is integral to solitude.

AN EXPERIENCE OF DEATH

Ultimately, confrontation with self is an experience of death, unique to each person. Community may aid and support us at this crucial moment, but each of us faces death alone.

Recently I spent a quiet hour in the Motherhouse cemetery with our silent community of the dead. As I read the names on each of those simple head-stones, I mused over what they might have to say to us, the community of the living. To confront death when one is vigorous and in her prime, they seemed to say to me, will make that final meeting a welcome one and add depth and appreciation to the remaining days of life, enabling one to distinguish the fine line between loneliness and solitude.

There are other reasons, of course, why Sisters choose to live alone, many of which may not spring entirely from altruistic motives. They include a desire to extend to other geographic regions the richness of a religious foundation; a need to distance oneself from a religious community in order to re-think one's relationship to it; frustrations and resentments accumulated over the years from real or fancied wrongs in the community.

Defective though some of these motives may be, they may lead a Sister into a greater appreciation of community and a truer understanding and love of herself, making her capable of being comfortable, even supremely happy, in times of solitude.

A number of Scriptural passages describe the happy loner. Zacchaeus, apparently, was by himself up in the tree. His neighbors despised him, it is true, but not because he was a solitary. Job, as he meditated on a dung heap, was hardly consoled by his visitors, Eliphaz, Bildad, and Zophar. To realize that the confrontation with self cannot be escaped, one has only to think of Jesus in the garden, sharing our human fear of aloneness, a fear more painful by far than the physical crucifixion, and pleading, "Father, if it be possible. . ."

HOW TO RESPOND

How, then, should we respond to the community statistics showing a growing number of Sisters who live alone? Pack our bags and head for a lonely hermitage? For most of us, our needs would never be met by such a drastic move.

In a less romantic but more practical vein, we first need to listen and learn from Sisters who choose to live alone. They can show us how often our frenzied search to be busy and needed hides a deep fear of being totally alone with ourselves and the emptiness we are certain to find there. We need to listen to their observations on community and learn to sift and save those elements that nurture us in and for our apostolates while not clinging to the trivia that clutters up the basic reality of community life.

Second, we ought to listen to them for new perspectives on an apostolate daily increasing in size while its ministers wander off into other fields, unseeing and uncaring. I am referring to an apostolate to the lonely. We hear a great deal about the swinging singles these days, less about the divorced woman in her fifties whose self-image has been shattered and who lacks skills needed to earn a living wage.

Another group of lonely people, widows, has grown so rapidly that three out of every four married women can expect to face approximately eighteen years by themselves after the death of their husbands.[1] Our society's mores require them to "maintain a happy face" and gently ease into the shadows so as not to remind us of that dread visitor, death. The Sister who has experienced a state of aloneness can make a very real contribution to this apostolate.

Finally, if the individual Sister really sees herself as a member of a living, caring community, she should reach out in bonds of love and concern to the Sister struggling alone in her apostolate and facing daily the terrors of the lonely. It means the myriad of unspoken ways in which we make another person feel that, even though she may be physically absent from the community, it is one in spirit with her and needs her and the unique contribution that only she can give.

---

[1] Edward Waking, "Living As a Widow, Only the Name's the Same," *U.S. Catholic*, July, 1975, 23–28.

PART EIGHT

MINISTRIES AND APOSTOLATES:

What in the World are Sisters Doing?

To try to answer the question in the title of this section — "What in the world are Sisters doing?" — is to begin to see the many-splendored ministries that have attracted the energy and enthusiasm of women religious. The selection of essays in this part hardly does justice to the rainbow span of interests that Sisters have always shown in serving their Lord, their Church, their communities, and their neighbors.

From the beginning woman's role in the world was seen in terms of her service to others. When the Lord God saw that "it is not good that the man should be alone," he corrected the situation and gave creation its lovely crown when he said, "I will make him a helper fit for him" (Gen 2:18). If anyone still thinks that making woman a helper puts her in a subordinate and servile position, it is important to remember that when the Bible speaks of "helper" almost all the time it refers to the leader or the stronger one helping the follower or the weaker one. Thus God is "the helper of the fatherless" (Ps 10:14) and to him we pray, "O Lord, be thou my helper" (Ps 30:10).

Like the first Adam, the last Adam, Jesus Christ, knew how incomplete his own mission and ministry would have been without woman. The Lord of life had to depend on woman to give him human life, and in this first essential phase of Christian ministry the woman Mary needed no help whatsoever from man! This same woman got Jesus' messianic ministry off to an early start the day she stated so simply and so clearly the basic direction and inspiration for every apostolate: "Do whatever he tells you" (Jn 2:5). When the mission of Jesus was ready for its new phase of resurrection expansion, women were again called upon and chosen to inaugurate the action. As usual it took the men folk a while to catch up with the more perceptive part of the nascent

359

Christian community: "These words seemed to [the apostles] an idle tale, and they did not believe [the women]" (Lk 24:11).

As women of faith in the risen Lord, Sisters have never ceased carrying out that Cana command, "Do whatever he tells you." Their loving, creative service in the Church has been a consistent and welcome light and warmth amid too much darkness and cold. The schools they operated, the classes they taught, the hospitals they staffed, the social services they unstintingly provided have never been the cause of embarrassment but only the source of exhilaration on the part of the Church. Where Sisters are, there is God's work being accomplished quietly, effectively, and without frills and fanfare of titles, promotions, and plaudits.

Without intending to overlook or denigrate in any way the traditional ministries and apostolates of teaching, nursing, and the social services to which Sisters have unselfishly contributed their talents and time for centuries, the selection of articles in this part highlights some of the principles basic to a theology of ministry for Sisters. The attention given to the work of Sisters in the parochial and campus ministries serves to underline this statement of Vatican II: "Since in our times women have an ever more active share in the whole life of society, it is very important that they participate more widely also in the various fields of the Church's apostolate" (*Decree on the Apostolate of the Laity*, 9). The report of Sister Mary Anthony Wagner, O.S.B., the first woman editor of *Sisters Today*, on the first Women's Ordination Conference explores a contemporary issue of ministry that remains a part of woman's ongoing search for service, not pursuit of power.

Lest we all take ourselves too seriously and forget that it is always God's work in the world that we are doing and that in spite of our failures and successes he is still the master at creating, saving, and sustaining his people, the "Ministry of Surprise" article is offered. An uptight world and an uptight Church might profit from the episcopal author's unlikely "ordination rite of clowns." Perhaps clowns could succeed where clerics have not. Or maybe we should ask, what's the difference between them?

Clowns, clerics, and convents can be sure that there will be surprises aplenty in the future ministries and apostolates of Sisters. Provided, of course, that we have a vision of what might be, not just a memory of the way things have always been. For the Spirit breathes where she will, and there is just no telling how, when, or by whom that ministry-motto of "Do whatever he tells you" will be fulfilled.

Sisters Today, July, 1966

Women Theologians in the Church

Sister Teresa Mary Deferrari, C.S.C.

At the fourth session of Vatican Council II, Archbishop Paul J. Hallinan of Atlanta, Georgia, urged that there be a reconsideration of the position of women in the Church. He did not emphasize the ordination of women but asked that women be permitted to act as readers and acolytes at Mass and serve as deaconesses. He recommended that women be encouraged to become teachers and consultants in theology and that they be represented in various post-conciliar organizations affecting the lay apostolate and religious life. Archbishop Hallinan's remarks were given in connection with Schema Thirteen on the Church in the Modern World. They do not seem, however, to have had any great effect on the content of that document as it was finally promulgated.

If the insights of Archbishop Hallinan, which touch upon an area of the Church's life that is in great need of development, should be passed over, it would indeed be tragic. The loss here would not only be in terms of the failure to recognize the individual dignity of women but of a failure to activate an essential element of the Church's corporate life, both in its prayer and in its mission to the world. Any large organization which neglects the rights of some subgroup within itself cannot but create an unhealthy climate for the fulfillment of its own self-interest. It is in giving that we receive, and this applies to our relationships with one another in the same family as well as to the family's obligations to society.

To be specific, I suspect that there are many men in the Church, particularly ecclesiastics, who think that, if the Church is to be kept vigorous, it must be ruled solely by men. In reality, the vigor of the Church can only be stultified if the potentiality of women for leadership is ignored. In the words of Pope John, "Since women are becoming ever more conscious of their human dignity, they will not tolerate being treated as mere material instruments, but demand rights befitting a human person both in domestic and public life."

I do not intend to trace the influences, over and beyond the common cultural factors, that have caused the prejudice toward women within the Church. Much, for instance, has already been said about St. Thomas Aquinas' primitive medieval view of the origin of woman. I do not think that St. Thomas can be blamed for this attitude as it exists today. Few really take him seriously in his explanation of the origin of woman because it is so at variance with modern scientific knowledge of human development.

The prejudice against women is tied more to the kind of general authoritarianism that has been the bane of the Church's existence in the last few centuries and has made itself felt frequently toward any progressive person, lay or cleric. The fact that a lay person is also a woman affords just another opportunity for men of power who wish to dominate others to use something which really makes no difference as though it supported their own presumed supremacy.

I do not mean to suggest that this tendency to dominate is a male characteristic, however. Rather, it is a human, sinful one which belongs to women as well as to men. Women, for example, often delight in dominating one another in their own organizations.

The key to women's rights in the Church, then, is openness, or, to use a term from the Council, "collegiality." Openness and collegiality are, in turn, simply another way of saying Christian love, and it is by this term that Pope Paul VI has repeatedly described the purpose of the Council. As the Church tries to renew itself, we are all going to have to look at and treat each other with much deeper respect, without regard to rank, race, or sex. The Church as a whole must treat other Churches and all people with the same great sensitivity to human dignity under God's grace as should exist within its own fellowship.

In the judgment of men in the Church toward women there must be an appreciation of equality and need. The same must be true of women toward men and toward one another. In their effort to establish this appreciation where it is conspicuously absent in the structures of the Church, women must avoid unChristian, overly militant attitudes. On the other hand, equality will not be recognized unless women work hard for it individually and in groups.

In any struggle for equality, whether it be racial justice or the rights of women, a false principle can arise at the instigation of supremacists that the minority group must first "prove" itself if it wishes to be recognized as of equal status with those in power. In the civil rights movement, for example, the white segregationists argued that blacks are not ready for the vote because they are so uneducated. This is said despite the fact that voter registration requirements can be met by most blacks and no such class judgments are made upon groups of white people. Nor are blacks as a group considered unfit when it comes to using them in the armed services for the defense of the nation.

Moreover, it is the system of segregation itself which hinders the development of an educated black citizenry.

The same false principle operates with regard to opportunities for women in public life. A woman who desires a position of responsibility not only has to struggle with the same difficulties of competency and public relations that a man has to contend with; she also has to push against doors closed to her simply because she is a woman. Women are often prejudged by men as unequal and incapable of things which they have never been given an adequate opportunity to try. It is true that the married professional woman requires special arrangements on the part of employers sometimes in order to be able to carry out her dual role well, but since she has an important contribution to make, she has a right to expect help in working it out practically.

What is true of women in civil life is even more true in the Church. In most areas of public Church activity the doors are closed more tightly to women than they are in the secular world. One great tragedy here is that there exists within the Church through the religious life a vast potential of woman power without the problem of division of interest that married women have, but these women are not encouraged to exercise their initiative.

The argument could be given that women are not prepared to do pastoral work like priests, and this is true to some extent. On the other hand, there are some very simple but important tasks like being lectors at Mass that seem to require no other qualifications than baptism and literacy; yet these are denied to women. It is quite hard to find any other reason for the denial of functions like these to women than prejudice against their sex.

An important part of pastoral work rests, of course, upon theological training. The problem for women here is not so much one of sex as it is that, until recently, neither women nor men who were not priests could receive a training in theology adequate to meet the needs of the modern adult world. Just as the lay man is entering more into a positive apostolic and pastoral conception of his life as a Christian, so also are lay and religious women. Going along with this conception is better theological training. It remains to be seen how many handicaps active lay women will encounter in the Church when they try to use this training, that is, whether they will only have to prove their competency in order to win respect, or whether they will also have to battle an unbending refusal of acceptance by various ecclesiastical authorities, because they are lay and because they are women.

Since Archbishop Hallinan made special reference to the need for women as teachers and consultants in theology, I would like to make a few comments on this particular phase of woman's role in the Church. Most male clerical theologians, I think, would be willing to admit that the various graduate programs in theology around the country are turning out large numbers of Sisters and some lay women with Master's degrees. There is a small but steady stream of Ph.D.'s coming forth, too.

I have met priests, however, who insist that, although we have these women teachers with degrees in theology, we have no real women theologians in this country who are doing first-rate theological research. There are some women doing good popularization but none are doing real pioneering research. When women begin to publish, they say with some benevolence, then we can say that they have "arrived" as theologians.

In general, I can agree with this idea, but it needs some qualifications. First of all, if the criterion of a theologian is first-rate theological research, I am not sure that we have more than a handful of theologians in the United States even among the men. One has only to look at how dependent Catholic theological publishing houses are upon translations of European works for stimulating material to appreciate how far American Catholic theology has yet to go to become creative. Are the Catholic priests who do theology, but are not first-rate scholars, going to call themselves theologians and deny the title to women who are in a comparable situation?

Secondly, women *do* have a special cultural and perhaps psychological problem in emerging as publishing theologians. Theological research demands an ability to work alone for long periods of time. In general, I believe a woman is just as capable in temperament of doing this as a man. But there is no doubt that most Catholic women have not been conditioned to the values of this type of work by the training given in the average Catholic women's college or by the training and regime of life in religious communities for women. There are deficiencies in the scholarly aspects of the training of Catholic men, too, but the possibility of scholarship has been assumed with regard to men. Often with regard to women it has never been seriously considered. As a result, many women are unaware and unconcerned about the responsibilities they should be assuming in the intellectual world.

These women must be awakened from their apathy so that they can undertake the tasks which their personal dignity and the problems of modern society demand. Those few Catholic women in the last twenty-five years or so, especially in religious communities, who have acquired an ability and concern for scholarship in secular fields and gradually in theology, have usually had to lead lives of alienation both from their superiors and from most other women with whom they associated. There simply were not enough of them together or in leadership to make the values of professional scholarship for the apostolate of the Church commonly appreciated. They could do nothing but suffer for the truth and try to accomplish something in their own limited spheres as individuals.

The situation is beginning to change now. Archbishop Hallinan's statement is an important beginning of official acknowledgement that the Church needs trained, scholarly women, lay and religious, especially in theology. Developing these women will require not only basic intellectual preparation at a good university. It will also require a consideration of practical ways in which these women will be able to use their talents and training in relationship to demands made on them as married or single lay women or as religious women in the various stages of adaptation to the modern world in which religious communities presently stand.

As things are now, I think it is safe to say that women in general who *can* do research find it harder than men to acquire the time and the climate to do so. While there is not the same suspicion toward intellectuality that existed previously within some groups of religious women in the Church, entirely apart from the prejudice of men toward women's intellectual abilities, there is still a lack of the cultural freedom that is necessary to do a long, difficult piece of research.

One woman cannot really do this kind of work in isolation, even if she has the permission of her superiors to do so. She needs the encouragement and example of fellow scholars in her own religious family group, as well as rapport with those engaged in other types of necessary work in the community. Similarly, I would suppose that it would be difficult for a married woman to engage in scholarship without the sympathetic understanding of her husband and family.

It is not so unusual for women to give this support to men, but it is unusual for men to give it to women, and for women to give it to each other. In most situations in the Church at present, community concern for women's intellectual role does not exist. The opportunity to develop this concern is opening up, however, and now is the time that its importance should be stressed.

A question which might arise is why women theologians are needed in the Church. The answer is obvious and should not require any explanation. We need women theologians for the same reason that we need men theologians. We have an urgent need for good theologians in the modern world in order to adapt technological progress to true human values, and we want to enlist for the task as many people as possible who are capable of doing the work well.

There is absolutely no reason for excluding women from this effort. Whatever may be the differences between men's and women's thinking processes (and I am not convinced that there are any significant ones) the idea that men tend to generalize while women are preoccupied with the concrete is certainly oversimplified. Therefore, any suggestion that women are by nature not capable of scientific theology should be rejected.

It is true, as I have said before, that Catholic women's colleges have not fostered sufficiently the scientific, scholarly approach among women, and so we do not have actually in our midst enough good women thinkers; but that is quite a different matter from saying that women as such are not capable of scientific thought. Moreover, men as well as women rightly show an interest in the practical relations of general principles to human experience, especially in the area of theology.

Women theologians then are needed not because they have a distinctive intellectual contribution to make to the science but simply because they need their own leaders, not only to study the problems they share with men but also to guide the operation of functions which are carried out in exclusively feminine organizations. Male theologians, called in from time to time from the outside for consultation, certainly can give some useful advice to groups of women as they have been doing, but this advice will be even more helpful if it is followed not just blindly but with the intelligent discrimination that comes from a woman's own knowledge of good theology. Moreover, it takes an insider to know what may be the specific religious problems at *this* time for *these* women, collectively and individually.

If there is any specific contribution which women can make to theology, it perhaps may be simply to keep the male professional theologians aware in a relevant way of a large segment of the human race which, particularly as celibates, they might tend to forget. The collaboration of men and women in the same profession can be a concrete means for each of experiencing the equality as well as the differences between the two and of thus becoming more humanized and complete in their attitudes toward life. All this, of course, presupposes that the persons involved are capable of mature professional and personal relations between men and women as they cooperate in research or in other forms of apostolic projects.

Just as a professional person can become humanized in his contacts with his colleagues, so also he can become evangelized. It is for this reason that the documents of Vatican Council II on the lay apostolate, the Church in the modern world, and Christian education emphasize the need for properly prepared Christians to penetrate the world of the intellectuals, which is exercising an increasing influence on the world as a whole. For such a task both scientific competence and a continually advancing theological knowledge are indispensable.

This, too, was pointed out by Pope John, who said in *Pacem in Terris,* "Indeed, it happens in many quarters and too often that there is no proportion between a scientific training and religious instruction." If well-trained, convinced Christian men are so desperately needed in the intellectual world, the same is certainly true of women.

It is to be hoped that the Catholic Church, which has recently emerged, through the tremendous effort of the Council, as an effective leader in the general Christian effort to make the gospel message intelligible to modern man, will not neglect the role of leadership in promoting the human dignity of woman. The Church has the instruments to do this if she will only appreciate its importance. She has the biblical teaching on the relation of man and woman; she has gospel theology clarified by a strong tradition on Mary as ideal woman and type of the Church; finally, in our own times she has had the teaching of Pope John, who considered the consciousness of woman's dignity as one of the three major distinctive differences of the present-day world.

It would indeed be tragic if the Church at this point would fail to develop actions, appropriate for the needs of modern society, to manifest that she really believes the abstract principles on woman's dignity that she has always professed as part of the true Christian heritage.

Sisters Today, November, 1972

Towards a Theology of Ministry for Sisters

Thomas F. O'Meara, O.P.

St. Paul writes to the Ephesians a description of Christian community as ministry.

> And to some, his gift was that they should be apostles; to some, prophets; to some, evangelists; to some, pastors and teachers; so that the saints together make a unity in the work of service, building up the body of Christ. In this way we are all to come to unity in our faith and in our knowledge of the Son of God, until we become the perfect Man, fully mature with the fullness of Christ himself (4:11–14).

Few passages in Scripture have greater significance for us today. In those few words there is the beginning of a theology of the diocesan and parish church, a theology of ministry, a theology of the future.

Where do we begin to research a theology of mission for religious women? With what is actually done in the apostolate (those apostolates which seem so numerous but which are until recently so monoform)? With ordination for women and laymen? Do we begin with two thousand years of history in the institutions of the Roman Catholic Church? The world of Ephesians is different: liberating, creative yet normative—". . . that they should be apostles; to some, prophets; to some, evangelists; to some, pastors and teachers; so that the saints together make a unity in the work of service, building up the body of Christ."

Do we want to consider that passage in Ephesians as a norm for what the Catholic Church will be in the United States in the future? If we summon the representatives of both the Church and our society before us, they would tell us to be careful, to hesitate, to think twice. Ephesians involves action; ministry is dependent upon what you do, not upon what you claim to be or what your clothes or degrees profess. "Apostle," "evangelist," "prophet" are all action verbs rather than sacred words, status titles.

368 BLOW THE TRUMPET AT THE NEW MOON

The Christians wanted to avoid sacral titles. Action words show the universality and constancy of Christian service, excluding the facades of status in society. A prophet speaks publicly of Christ; an evangelist comes to announce good news, not bad news; a pastor and teacher actually does those things. Action-ministry implies there are going to be changes. Building up the Body of Christ, unfolding a community of service involve a variety of different things people will do. Ministry includes at its essence change and the shock of the future.

Also, the community of Ephesians demands long-time commitment. The goal is the saints, the Christians, building a community for works of service, fashioning the Body of Christ. This is an enterprise for a decade, a lifetime, for a thousand years.

Should we take the plunge into the world of Ephesians? In that pluralistic world every Christian is involved; each is called to be a catalyst, to perform a variety of services so that all human beings and Christians build up the body of Christ. Do we want to make that type of commitment? If we say yes, there are three questions which all religious and particularly religious women will have to answer:

1) May a woman, a female religious, enter a ministry at all? Can women even be part of this world described by Paul and his disciples — the same Paul who stands behind much of the controversy over ordaining women. Would Paul encourage women to enter ministry? 2) The second question is more personal. As a human being, as a Christian, as a religious, can I live in this kind of world? These ministries are demanding, open, changing in a pluralistic world. Can I live this life? 3) The third question: what should I do, what would I do in this kind of ministry?

1) MAY A WOMAN ENTER A MINISTRY?

We begin to answer the first question when we recall the difference between ministry and religious life. Ministry refers to *doing* something for the Christian community and through it for the world. Prophets, evangelizers, apostles, teachers — all Christians work together for themselves and for the world so that little by little they build a Body worthy of Christ when he comes again to earth.

Ministry, public action for the Christian community does not refer to clothes, buildings, or administration, while religious life is more concerned with *life-style*. Ministry certainly includes life-style. Our concentration on ministry neither excludes being-a-Christian nor includes activism. A Christian life-style is designated by what we do but it is also prior to ministry. People today reject being labeled by what they do. Priests and Sisters in the past were caught in an unhealthy situation: on one side they were designated by what they did (apostolate); on the other point of view they were locked into one life-style (the state of religious life). Neither was integrated with the other.

Religious life is concerned with a ministry and a life-style. For centuries life-style as state-of-life has had the upper hand, for societies reflected stability through states of life. If you went into a Bavarian village or the city of Paris, you could see its structure. There were different degrees of social life: the ruler, the nobility, the clergy, the religious, the tradesmen, the peasants. In Chicago today, that is not so evident; all kinds of people are doing all kinds of things; there are hidden levels, but even they are permeated by social fluidity.

In the past, one unchanging social stratification in the Church dictated why religious life should be connected with clothes and rules, while the idea that every Christian is called to ministry was considered Protestant. The *theological reality* of a Sister's ministry was totally neglected for the aspects of state of life, especially interior devotion. The religious woman fell under a double contradiction: she was told that although she is a full-time dedicated servant of the Church she is not a minister; secondly, the religious Sisters and "lay" Brothers are called laity. All of this is very dubious, for the people who do things in the Christian community are ministers.

In the Christian community, moreover, there is no such thing as a lay person. A lay person is someone who doesn't do anything, doesn't know anything, who isn't part of the action. The early Christian community knew nothing about Christians being inert *laikoi*. How did we reach the stage where most Christians are called "laity"? As tens of thousands of people entered Christianity, only a few were in full-time ministry. Only full-time, public ministry counted, for the universal ministry of Christians was diminished as fewer converts lived up to the gospel. By the year 200 there existed a caste of people who ran the Church, namely, the clergy. The lay person is a non-doer, a passive member outside of the special caste. Jesus and Paul knew of no such thing.

Now we are rediscovering the need for having a Christian community where ministry is pluralistic and universal. Being Christian in the global village is of such intensity that if we are going to make it we have to involve everyone. Society is so complex, even inside the local Church, that we need everybody.

Religious women will enter ministry as we rediscover that the Christian community is made up of all kinds of people, that all have some kind of action-as-ministry. There are levels of this, and eventually we reach the level where there are people professionally trained to do, free to be involved in the ministry. At this point we ordain people. Certainly we will ordain women to ministry. The theological problem is not whether women will be ordained; women were ordained deaconesses. Women can be ordained, since Christians can be ordained into a variety of ministries. The inflammatory and debatable theological question is whether they will be ordained to the leadership of a community we call the Church, to episcopacy and priesthood; yet it is secondary, specialized. But women will be totally and publicly commissioned to the ministry, since they already do exercise ministries.

The report of the Catholic Theological Society on the Permanent Diaconate states unequivocally that women should normally be admitted to ministry, and that a hastily conceived ministry of "deaconess" is the beginning rather than the end of these ministries.

Today the church is faced with the changed role of women both within the world and within the church. It behooves the church as it did St. Paul to be sensitive to its social milieu. It is the privilege of the church to have within its community not only men with spiritual and professional qualifications but also women who have proved their competence in various fields and are eager to share their talents with others in the church. Indeed, the question is being asked whether the Catholic Church can afford to deny admission to this ministry to one half its membership. Secular society employs its talented women.

The Catholic Church must be as open to the Holy Spirit in this field as it is elsewhere, for many women experience a desire to serve in capacities of spiritual leadership and sacramental service not available to them in the present structures and institutions of the church. In many countries individual women believe that they have received a call from the Holy Spirit to the diaconate and have associated together in common inspiration. The church should be attentive to this indication that the Holy Spirit may wish to enrich the body of Christ by again calling women to the diaconate. The needs of the Catholic Church are great. The world knows human suffering and spiritual need of every sort which call for those qualities not unique to but especially characteristic of women. A woman in the diaconate could do much to alleviate spiritual problems among the sick, among the divorced and others with marital problems, and among the aged. Faced, too, with the present crisis of the Catholic schools, the church experiences the need for new and imaginative diaconal roles for women in education. This need is keenly experienced in campus ministry.[1]

2) DO I WANT TO BE A MINISTER?

The second question is more personal. Do I want to be a minister within the context of the celibate religious community? New horizons open up, and yet we are disconcerted and unsettled. Is this future shock? Each individual has a task at hand: do I really want to be part of this kind of life where ministry is equal to life-style, where ministry is pluralistic, where ministry as concretely realized in what we call apostolates will encompass change?

Can we live in this world of changing ministries? We are asking about our faith and about the Holy Spirit. The Holy Spirit is at work in our society and in its institutions. He is no longer waiting for us to take the initiative. We got bogged down in multiplying buildings, neglecting the new poor. We must believe deeply in the forward move of history and in God's power in our history,

---

[1]"Restoration of the Office of Deacon as a Lifetime State; A Report to the U.S. Bishops," *Worship*, 45 (1971), 196.

since we can only minister to that action of the Holy Spirit. There is a tremendous emotional investment in some of our institutions and buildings, and we do not know what the future is.

There is uneasiness in the midst of our lives. We all depend on structures. When both lifestyle and ministry are touched by change and by an open-endedness we hesitate to call freedom, we are thrown into a dark night, the dark night of the Holy Spirit at work in our world, the dark night of the future. Our only response will be in darkness, too, in the darkness of faith.

Faith can guide us to new apostolates within honest ministry. Apostolates are the multiple, specified concretizations of larger ministries. An apostolate will more and more last for five, for seven years. A "generation" we are told, encompasses this span. The professional man or woman is becoming accustomed to a change in position two or three times in a career. We in the ministry, who are supposed to be the cutting edge of society and spirit, will see apostolates come and go. Something will flourish, needs will change, and then comes rededication to something new.

All of this takes an emotional toll. Do we find support for it within ourselves and from without? *The religious life becomes in ministry a life which needs faith for commencement and people for continuation.* Community is essential. Prayer and faith cannot totally supply for other human beings. We must have the luxury, the leisure, the effort and the understanding to develop the kind of community which is realistic for a demanding future.

3) WHAT SHOULD I DO?

The third question is: What then should I do? There are hundreds, if not thousands who in the past five years in the United States have discussed answers to this. First, we should determine that our ministry-in-apostolate be something significant. Significance is determined by real needs; it can be found either in exposure to numbers of people or in an in-depth contact with a few. The past five years have been full of calls for rapid revolution, and at times little has happened. Modesty in our goals is still a value; it does not cancel out significance. Just as detachment finds a new meaning in a response of faith to the Spirit, so perseverance even for seven years is an old value with maximum impact.

Secondly, we need to meditate upon a new approach, a new methodology for the Christian ministry. Christian ministry resembles more the catalyst rather than the organization. At first, this may make us uncomfortable. It is easier to say I organized so many people into this or that; it is more comfortable to picture the world in terms of blocks, areas processed. The catalyst has less grandiose results. But the results may be deeper, more lasting and satisfying. Mission and ministry take on a new function as Christianity rediscovers a catalytic role. We do not divide people into categories, blanketing territories. Christ is at the center of a series of concentric circles; his ministers serve the waves of grace emanating from that center. Grace is present wherever God chooses, and there is no place where he does not send grace.

God's grace tries to reach all. It is poured out far more abundantly than we can discern by simply visiting Catholic or Lutheran parishes on Sunday mornings. In his struggle to reach all, God's love becomes more intense and explicit. Man's possible response covers a spectrum of faiths, including tenuous faiths, tenuous religious commitments. Nevertheless, they are assent cloaked in persons responding to God's grace.

Do we walk out in the world and differentiate all people? Do we look only for visible signs, encouraging statistics? We may have become comfortable with buildings, uncomfortable with men and women. No matter how far we move from the deeper, explicitly Christian perspective, clothes, ideas, nonconformity do not make *the* difference. (This should not imply that external behavior is not interiorly bound or not meaningful.) Hidden, personal response to grace does.

When Jesus meets different people in the New Testament, he does not outline the catechism for them; he understands whether they have initiated a basic response to God and to their fellow man. If so, it can be built upon; if not, this is the only sin the Holy Spirit cannot forgive — the rejection of God's beginning.

The modality of the Christian ministry is, like that of Jesus, a catalytic one. Neither Scripture nor sacrament, neither Church nor ministry exists to control, to judge grace. They all exist to make explicit and firm an individual's hidden radical option for the Absolute present in history and in men. The ministry strives to draw persons involved through their freedom in the dialectic between the self-communicating God and sin towards the center of greater light and power: Jesus Christ, his Spirit, a community of belief and love.

The problem today is that there is too much to do, too many new ministries, an entire spectrum of needs and possibilities, earth-shaking problems, people who need people. Some explain the malaise of the recent past by observing that Americans reached a point where they were so bombarded by problems that they were immobilized. We must choose a few modestly significant areas and invest ourselves with competency, joy, and perseverance.

We are rediscovering what the early Christians meant by community, what they took for granted as universal, polychrome service. We are rediscovering Paul's idea of a pluralistic ministry open to all Christians, obligatory on every Christian. Often in human life the most exciting things have an element of rediscovery about them.

Perhaps a sign of this is that while in flight from inept agents with all the wonders of technology at their disposal, Daniel Berrigan chose as the framework for his diary a most unlikely book, *The Dark Night of the Soul*. What have inner darkness and little John of the Cross from arid Castille in common with American protest in this decade? Berrigan's book is a rediscovery for our times of the ancient value of "going out," "detachment," "sacrifice," "unyielding commitment." John of the Cross as activist may be harder to take than when he was safe in our cloisters in the 1950's. Both Berrigan and Juan de la Cruz urge us to go out, to choose a future goal, and to aim for it . . . in the night which is both the future and faith.

To live as a man is to face the whirlwind. More. To live consciously is to sow the whirlwind. Supposing it means something to go on somehow, how much seed reaches the furrow, how much is lost and scattered in the storm? We have the darkest forebodings — and we are right. Any student knows, to be a student, to be faithful to others, to expose the deep illness of university structure, to speak up on the war — is to be under the gun. Americans are dying for these things. Which is simply to say: we are joining the chancy fate of most men, in most of the world, as that fate is decreed by American power and method.

And what about the monks? Can they survive? Would they make it, as a community, if they were to scatter in small groups, take public jobs, take on team responsibilities, break out of the corral? There is no big prevailing evidence it would work for very long, that they could take the heat, could find ways of worship, new insights, the patience needed to turn such corners.

Still, something favors such a try. Granted certain suppositions of the Gospel, certain unfulfilled needs of men and women, ours may be a moment, not for weighing of logic and good sense against risky waters. It may be time to go ahead, the chances being large that one will die in the effort, or go down, or achieve nothing. But how else will we get out of our corner, into which we are more feverishly painting ourselves?[2]

[2]Daniel Berrigan, *Dark Night of Resistance* (New York, 1971), 48f.

Sisters Today, February, 1974

A Statement on Women in Ministry

Sister Mary Lou Putrow, O.P.

As the self-consciousness of religious women grows in response to renewal and as a deeper understanding of call and commitment evolve, various factors and expressions of religious life come to the fore. In the past several years one of the ways in which the self-understanding of religious women has expressed itself is in the concept of ministry.

Ministry is a many faceted topic which derives a variety of meanings with relative situations. The Sisters who gather in American suburbia to discuss ministry bring with them experiences which color their appreciation of ministry in much different hues than Sisters in the Philippines, in Africa, Peru and the Dominican Republic, who carry with them a day of scorching heat, heavy rains, malnutritious children and frustrated, poverty-stricken parents. Despite the variety of human experiences, the diverse activities, the divergent geographical situations, each form of ministry maintains a deep unity with all other forms through its source: the supportive, activating power of the Spirit of Jesus Christ.

To speak of ministry is to speak of human needs and the human ability to respond to these needs. Any topic that deals with human realities is profound, but when these human realities are seen in a contemplative view, i.e., when creation — both the minister and the one ministered to — is viewed in a posture before God, the topic of ministry becomes non-exhaustive. God's message always opens man to deeper and deeper realities.

Within its tradition, the Church has always entertained a continuity with the past; in her response to the signs of the times the Church has also yielded to some discontinuity with past practices. It is within this framework of continuity/discontinuity that ministry will be discussed in this paper:

What is the meaning of ministry?
What can be said of present-day ministry as continuity with the past?
What discontinuity is demanded for fidelity to a sense of ministry as discernible through study, reflection and prayer?

JESUS THE MINISTER

When the people of God look to their main past, mainly to origins and source in Jesus Christ, they cannot escape the continuity/discontinuity that Jesus' approach to life and ministry presents. Jesus arrived on the religious scene when the dichotomized view of reality had reached a peak in its influence on life and worship. The world saw itself as a divided world; a deep chasm existed between the sacred and the profane. Man realized the need for God's action in his life just as he realized that somehow he must participate in the life of God.

Within religious practice at the time of Christ, the priest was the mediator between the two spheres: the sacred and the profane. He offered prayers and sacrifices to God. Through various religious symbols, through prophetic words and ethical norms imposed upon man who lived in the profane world, the priest of the Old Testament mediated a relationship between man and God; he brought God's saving action into the life of man. The status of the priest was not a common or popular status but one that was distinguishable by power, one that was favored by the special privileges of the priestly caste. Cultic vestments and the careful observance of cultic prescriptions were a part of the priest's mediatorship.

Jesus' approach to life and to God was different. Jesus respected and built upon the past; he observed Jewish law and was conscious of Jewish tradition. His past was the foundation for the present as well as for the evolution of the future. Through his incarnation Jesus restored all of creation to another relationship with God; Jesus healed the severance between man and God in the whole process of his redemptive life. By being God in our midst, Jesus reconciled God and man; he showed us the proximity rather than the distance of God.

The priest of Jesus' time was designated within the Jewish-Hellenic tradition as *hiereus. Hiereus* means, primarily, a cultic officer. It is interesting to note that the New Testament never uses this word for persons connected to ministry within the discipleship. In fact, there is no word in New Testament language for the cultic officer; any mention of priest and *hiereus* refers to the Jews or to Jesus as great high priest. The priesthood of the Old Testament climaxed and ended in Jesus Christ. In continuity/discontinuity, not destroying but fulfilling, Jesus replaced the priesthood of the Old Law with the "one priesthood of Jesus Christ," a priesthood in which all share through word and worship. Some persons within the priesthood of the faithful continue to be called to specific service in initiation, renewal and leadership, through preaching and the sacraments.

Through Jesus' life of service for others, through his affirmation of God in our midst, through his acceptance of the call of the Father, Jesus brought about another understanding of life and ministry in relationship to the Father. Many issues of Old Testament ministry of the king, prophet and priest faded in importance as Jesus' ministry centered upon the needs and the welfare of persons.

JESUS' MESSAGE FOR MINISTERS

The image Jesus had of himself as minister contains a potent message for all who proclaim ministry in the name of Jesus Christ. According to John's gospel, Jesus saw himself as a minister whose teaching is not his own, as one teaching what the Father had first taught him, as one sent by the Father, as one who knows from whence he came and where he is going. "He who sent me is with me and he has not left me to myself." Jesus proclaimed a full awareness of himself as one who had been sent, one who had been missioned by the Father to serve others. This sense of who one is before the Father is vital to a sense of ministry.

John also records the understanding Jesus had of those to whom he ministered. According to the Jewish manner, Jesus represented a highly irregular position toward the person. For example, when the woman taken in adultery is brought to Jesus, her accusers address themselves to the observance of the law; Jesus addresses himself to the person. When the blind man is cured on the Sabbath, the source of the man's blindness is passed over by Jesus as insignificant; the suffering person is the only issue; the condition relative to the law is unimportant as is the time factor (the Sabbath), controlled by law.

Jesus' life offers a paradigm for all ministry to persons. Service is primary; a stance before the Father is vital. Religion as an organized legal structure of the Old Testament crumbled under Jesus' ministry to persons. Jesus offered little support for the legalistic demands of the old law when greater values were at stake. Through Jesus, past practices of Jewish cultivation moved from a position of centrality to be replaced by an enthusiasm for and commitment to the Kingdom of God. In Matthew, Jesus offers instruction about characteristics of the kingdom and concludes with "every scribe who becomes a disciple of the kingdom is like a householder who brings from his storeroom things both new and old."

With the old as foundation, Jesus ventured toward the new and attempted to lead all men to the kingdom of God. Jesus' attempts became recognized in the early Christian communities that ministered to the people and were committed to service and worship. Acts 2:42 offers an apt description of the ministerial community: "These remained faithful to the teaching of the apostles, to the brotherhood, to the breaking of bread and to prayers." Brotherhood implies a mutual care, concern, love, a life of service. The breaking of the bread and prayer explain the worshipping community. It is interesting to note the close connection between these two elements, service and prayer. Service lends a credibility to words, whether these words be prayer or preaching.

An overview of Jesus' ministry leads to several simple conclusions. First, in Jesus' life, the person is always the primary consideration. Any depersonalization, any failure to support human rights and dignity is a call for ministerial concern. In the Old Testament, cultic practice did not mean ministry; the word *hiereus* is not applied to one who ministers. The parable of the Good Samaritan strikes a contrast between cultic officer and minister.

Secondly, religion of any form, when it stands in the way of the kingdom, must give way with its prescriptions to the life-giving thrust of the kingdom. Any institution in its mission of bringing about the kingdom and its ministry to the people of God must always be mindful of its primary function of forming and nourishing communities of service and worship.

And lastly, Jesus, the minister, teaches that an image of man, of oneself and of the other, derives from an image of God. (This is not to deny the converse.) Herein is gleaned a strong rationale for demanding that the minister be a contemplative person. Jesus' understanding of the Father affected deeply his appreciation of man. The whole eighth chapter of John is an attempt to show who the Father is and who he is not. The Father is not judge, magician, one to be cultivated and placated by various practices of man, often touching upon the superstitious. Rather, the Father is Love and Truth, Lifegiver, Source, Protector, Teacher and the One who missions. And man is one who loves and is loved, one who seeks truth, receives life, is protected and taught by the Father and is the one who has been sent.

It was Jesus' knowledge of the Father as mission-er that gave Jesus an understanding of himself as one who is mission-ed. This recognition directed Jesus' whole sense of ministry — a recognition that is only realized in a prayerful stance before the Father.

PAULINE MINISTRY

The reflective interpretation of the words and works of Jesus as recorded especially in St. Paul gives insight into the traditional understanding of ministry in the lives of the early Christians. Ephesians 4:1-16 is a special exhortation to ministry and to the responsibility that belongs to all members of the priesthood of the faithful. "There is one Lord, one faith, one baptism and one God who is Father of all, over all, through all and within all." The one baptism has initiated all into the fullness of life in the Christian community. A view of baptism as gift only, without its concomitant responsibilities, St. Paul warns us, is an incomplete and untruthful perspective.

What does it mean to have received the "one baptism," to participate in the priesthood of the faithful? "One baptism" means that within the Christian community all maintain an equal status; each person contributes his own gift to the building up of the body which is Jesus Christ. These gifts are different in each person. Some persons have the gift of teaching; others, the gift of being able to reconcile differences; to others is given a joy of life to be shared with others. The gifts of God reside in the person and are poured forth in that person's ministry. "One baptism" means that there is no status system, no privilege/power category (except the power of Jesus Christ through man) within the kingdom and within the ministry as described by Paul.

Further in Ephesians (4:11-12) Paul reminds us that by virtue of baptism we have as a unity all accepted the gifts of Christ and the concomitant responsibility to serve. Failure to recognize this right and responsibility to serve is a loss of the sense of priesthood of the faithful. There is a need today to be re-awakened to the full practice of baptism, to a full realization of the gifts of God which have been received. The question is what continuity or discontinuity with past practices is valid and viable for service for the building up of the kingdom, for the full use of ministering by all to the needs of others.

St. Paul also understands ministry as a service rendered to the community, a service that is not necessarily a full-time service. Paul himself was engaged in tentmaking. During his daily work procedures, sewing materials together, inserting ropes and whatever else tentmakers do, Paul certainly was in a position of ministry to those in his company, but tentmaking was not his primary ministry. Paul's primary ministry was preaching the word of God.

Ministry is a service and exactly that — a service rendered according to the needs of the community. Service is not necessarily a particular, salaried position or a self-supporting role. In some situations the professional work one does may be the vehicle of ministry, but in other situations the discernible need for ministry in a given area may call one to a primary ministry outside of and in addition to one's professional work. Further, the nature of ministry and service is so evasive that it defies a job description. Could it be that many persons today are also called to a "tentmaking" life in order to be true to a sense of ministry understood through prayer, reflection and an involvement with the world?

Ministry in Pauline communities was not seen as a professional activity that one prepared for by some special academia but, again, a service and a responsibility flowing out of baptism. The esotericism effected by education brought about a situation which aided in establishing the social status of the priesthood and eradicating a sense of ministry consonant with the needs of the people. Education and ministry are not incompatible; the challenge is not to allow education to defeat ministry, to remove one from the human needs that surround, to narrow the boundaries of one's exposure, to delineate one's contacts by educational commonalities.

Paul further explained that all gifts cannot reside in one person. For the building of the kingdom all manner of gifts is needed; there is no better or no lesser. The administrator, the builder, the musician, the liturgist, the arbitrator, the counselor, the preacher are all needed.

MINISTRY OF WOMEN IN THE EARLY CHURCH

Pauline thoughts are well carried into the era of the post-apostolic Church, and the purity of the ministering activities of Jesus prevailed. The ministers who coordinated played an important part in the service of the people for the kingdom. There were the bishops who were the leaders in worship and service; the presbyters, gifted by God and chosen from among the people by the local community for specific service and leadership; the deacons in charge of specifically organized charity and possibly committed to preaching.

The Church recognized a variety of ministries and gave support to these official ministries by public recognition. Early statistics (c. 250 A.D.) indicate that the formal ministerial structure of the Church of Rome (numbering about 40,000) encompassed one bishop, forty-six presbyters, seven deacons, forty-two acolytes, fifty-two exorcists, readers and church maintenance personnel.

Significant also is the fact that women assumed an active, publicly recognized role of service, although these particular statistics do not make note of this fact. Three main groups of women are noted in the early Church: deaconesses, widows, virgins. Throughout the first six centuries the lines of distinction are sometimes clearly discernible and at other times scarcely so. Throughout the patristic writings a common thread can be seen: the exhortation of women to service, and the exhortation of women to quiet, to prayer, and to solitude.

These same sources indicate that women have held considerable and responsible positions in:

Missionary work: Frequently it was the woman who maintained the local church while the man traveled from place to place in evangelization. However, women also accompanied men on their missionary journeys.

Teaching and instruction: Those involved in preparing other women for baptism were encouraged to teach "how to keep the seal of baptism" — a form of ongoing spiritual direction. Most of the teaching was of a catechetical nature.

Healing: Women were especially encouraged in the healing which was part of conversion. Marriage of a Christian woman to a pagan was admissible because the woman ("the weaker sex") was expected to heal the pagan ways of her husband.

Comforting and consoling: The traditionally feminine characteristics of sensitivity, care, concern, sympathy, and empathy found a place in the ministerial concerns of the Church.

Caring for the sick and preparing for death: Women were called upon to "lay hands on the sick and dying," to prepare persons, especially other women, for death.

Loving and supporting.

Deaconesses are spoken of as "a type of the Holy Spirit, that active love that fills the Church." The ministry of women in the early Church was one that evolved around doing, serving, loving, and praying.

The Christian woman, in these same sections, is advised against the evil of a pagan husband who might object when she and her children eat the "sacred bread" which she has brought home from the worship service so that she and her children might daily feed on this bread before their evening meal. Other sections tell of deaconesses distributing Communion to other women. Patristic writings are filled with many other examples.

Several pertinent points may be noted: with the passage of time the woman minister found most public acceptance outside the institutional Church, and today more and more women are being ordained to ministry outside the Catholic Church. The work of women in public roles in the Church has varied with particular needs and particular times. The status of women within the Church appears and disappears with times and functions. Perhaps this fluidity and flexibility may be a normal and permanent feature of the ministry of women.

The evolution of the apostolic endeavors of religious women within the past five years is a living example of this feature. The question is whether the institutional Church needs the public ministry of women today; will it be the Church's gain or loss should women seek ministerial expression outside the Church in their participation in bringing all men to the kingdom? Does the Church recognize and allow the ministering woman's gift and ability to move out of some ministries and into others as a response to the signs and needs of the times?

MINISTRY PRIMARILY AS PRIESTHOOD

The responsibility through baptism of all persons to ministry was lost sight of, if not in theory certainly in practice, through time, circumstances, forces of history, and cultural accretions. When examined chronologically, the pastoral letters of the Fathers reveal a growing tendency toward structural forms, toward class distinction and status within the Church. The Church was growing larger, the desire to "baptize" pagan cultic practices came alive, and the Old Testament became the guidebook for the development of New Testament ideas. In subtle ways, the heresies that mistrusted human nature and saw the world as evil tainted the whole concept of Church as the people of God and, resultingly, ministry of and to those people. As early as the second century, a certain formalism had set in.

Further, as the Church began to emerge into a public role, the Church became the protector of society, and was touched with the Roman desire for order. Along with these circumstances and as a result of them, ministry as flowing out of baptism is replaced by ministry as flowing out of Orders. Because of the position of the Church, the ministers of the Church become those who are set aside, those whose status is significant for power, rather than service. Ministry becomes situated then in a power-ful rather than a service-ful person, the priest, who fills a functional, institutionalized office.

A contrast of Thomas Aquinas' treatment on ministry with St. Paul's understanding of ministry summarizes well the development of the sense of ministry. According to Paul, all persons baptized in Christ have the responsibility to minister according to the gifts that God has given them. Thomas admits to a few, chosen to minister the gifts of God. Paul sees diaconia as a service of doing for others; Thomas, situating diaconia in orders, sees the priesthood as a state characterized by particular external marks. Paul grants that there are many ministries residing in many persons; Thomas believes that all ministry resides in one person, the priest. The office of ministry in the Church was fairly well removed from the priesthood of the faithful, and certainly from women, and limited to bishop, presbyter and deacon; these offices were seen as being bestowed by God on man.

Today we struggle with this concept of ministry and priesthood. History points out to us and time has provided our own life experience of the discontinuity with the practices of the early church. Inescapable questions challenge us today:

What continuity with the past must be maintained?

What discontinuity with the past will best define our Christian life as ministers of the Word, that life which Jesus offered as a fulfillment of the Father's will?

Further,

In the study of scripture what can be learned about ministry?

What insights do the documents of Vatican II offer to ministry?

What is happening within the experience of the Church regarding ministry?

What is the level of trust in one's own ministerial experience?

Where does belief in the value and dignity of the human person direct?

TWO TYPES OF MINISTRY

There are two definite types of ministry serving in the Church today: the Pauline ministry that flows from Christian baptism and the public, official, ordained ministry that flows from the sacrament of orders. The latter is the more apparent.

The Pauline ministry is a ministry of charism, a ministry that allows a freedom to pursue service according to each one's gift, a ministry that recognizes in a non-competitive way the unique contribution of each member, a ministry without public status and without power, except the power of the life of Jesus Christ; the Pauline ministry is a ministry that is radical, i.e., one that comes from the very roots of one's being, his Christian identity; it is a ministry that is pure service and that calls forth everyone.

The ecclesial ministry, flowing from Orders, more closely resembles Thomas Aquinas' concept of ministry. This ministry affirms the cleric, the ordained male, as *the* public minister of the Church. It is a specification of baptism, a call to leadership in the worshipping and ministerial communities. It is a state with particular powers and jurisdiction and today is very much a cultic office.

Hopefully, the near future will bring about an effective appreciation of the priesthood of the faithful and a conscious awakening of every person to his ministerial gifts and responsibilities. However, even with this hope materialized, as long as the public ecclesial ministry, the leadership in worship and the leadership in service, is limited to the ordained male cleric, the ministry of the Church is incomplete.

WOMAN AS PUBLICLY ORDAINED MINISTER

"Law follows practice" is an axiom that has long been a part of the development of the Church and within the Church. Among religious communities of women especially, the exercise of the Pauline ministry is providing "practice" that could well move into "law," i.e., the practice of a woman publicly and officially ministering at a leadership level to the people of God. The present-day ministry of women is already bringing persons other than the ordained male cleric into the sacramental realm, and those who are experiencing this have begun to realize the incompleteness of official ministry within the Church.

For example, a Sister in counseling is often in a position of leading a person to a repentance or conversion, to a point where in all truthfulness one can say, "God has forgiven you." But the sacrament-consciousness of the majority of the Church will demand, "When can I go to confession?" Then a stranger, one who has not been involved directly in the whole metanoia process, is called in to pronounce the official absolution of the Church.

There are times when a woman is leading a group of other women in a deep community experience, when over a period of time the unity of the group becomes so developed that in seeking their deepest sacramental expression, a certain cleavage — almost an artificial intrusion — is required as a priest is called in to bring to a complete expression in the Eucharist that of which he may have been no part.

A similar situation may be present to the Sister who is minister to the sick and the dying, who is a hospital chaplain. One who enters so closely into the life of another in his singular experience of death or into suffering or illness ought to be able to respond to that person's need for the public and official prayer of the Church in the sacrament of the anointing. This is especially true when a hospital or a nursing home or a county home is an addenda to the already full ministry of an ordained male cleric and those who need the sacraments the most do not have frequent availability. There is an institutional halt to which all women ministers are summoned when their ministry enters into the sacramental realm.

A fact cannot be overlooked: there is one Lord, one faith, one baptism, the sacrament of initiation into the Christian life, the sacrament which opens the possibility for God's gifts of all other sacraments. But this gifting suddenly stops short when the baptized person happens to be a woman, seeking the sacrament of orders.

St. Paul once had a problem with discrimination—not the male/female kind but the Greek/Jew situation. Paul's defense was his whole understanding of the resurrection and its consequences. Paul recognized that Christ's death and resurrection—the whole redemptive process—had opened to everyone a share in the life of Christ, a reality so impactful as to render insignificant the religious distinction between Greek and Jew, the social difference between the slave and free, and the biological difference between man and woman. The resurrection, Christ's shared life, is a source of unity for all men. It is on this common ground of shared life and not on our differences that Christianity and Christian ministry are understood.

The power of Christ's resurrection, the impact of his life with us, has made it possible that we are all redeemed; that is, the life of Christ, his spirit activating all of us, is such a great thing that under the all-encompassing and all-penetrating grace of Christ all differences disappear. We are ONE in Christ.

In an age when women are filling every position in society and business for which personal competency fits them, a challenge of credibility is presented to the Church. Can the Church afford to be a medieval fortress and a sexually prejudiced institution, or even give the appearances of so being, for her own sake as well as for the sake of the personal worth and dignity of human beings?

When all other institutions, family, business, professional, educational, are recognizing the need for complementarity of both sexes in efficiently and effectively fulfilling needs and functions and relating to persons, can the Church afford to overlook the contributions of the complementarity of the male and female ministry?

Given the great variety of persons to whom the Church purposes to minister, should not the official ministry represent that variety? Minority groups seek ministerial representation and justly so. Black and Spanish-speaking groups, for example, seek ministers with whom they can identify, and the Church generally seems to realize this need. When the expanse of the Church's mission is examined, is it feasible to limit the official, public ministry to the male sex alone when fifty-one percent of the persons being ministered to are of the female sex, any more than it should be limited to white Anglo-Saxons?

As long as women are ministering at the sacramental level and the worshipping level, as long as women are being ministered to at the sacramental and worshipping level, can the contributions of women to the overall ministry of the Church be overlooked?

Can leadership be said to be complete and representative when all major decisions relative to the life of all persons in the Church are made and executed by an all-male contingent?

CONCLUSION

The call for more universal representation in ministry is not in need of historical and traditional proof of the viability of such an endeavor. Rather, ministry flows from the mission of the Church, the realization of the kingdom, the reconciliation of all men in Christ. If history teaches us anything, it teaches that the Church has it within her ministerial power to respond to the needs of those persons who, in time, are journeying toward the consummation of the kingdom.

The multiple needs of society today call for the full recognition and practice of the priesthood of the faithful, a deliberate attempt to restore the Pauline concept of ministry, the conscious service of every member of the body of Christ in a variety of ways. The multiple needs of society today also demand a creative reconsideration of the Church's official public ministry, a reconsideration in openness to the many and surprising ways in which the Spirit is leading the Church today.

Sisters Today, October, 1971

Love and Service in a Parish

Sister Mary Xavier, O.S.U.

Changes effected by Vatican II make one fact certain: Sisters who knitted and crocheted, embroidered and tatted in their spare time have gone the way of the starched wimples and boxed-in headgear that they no longer wear. Sisters today, after regular working hours, see the need for pouring their energy into more worthwhile activities.

Now one of the big questions for Sisters is: Where is the action for today's religious women? The answer is: With the people of God. Where do you find them? Everywhere. But since everyone's scope of action is limited, the locale of effort for any group of Sisters is where they are working. This paper spotlights only one of these areas for doing good: living and working, praying and worshipping with the people of God in a parish as collaborators in pastoral activities.

By no means are we suggesting that the activities we are doing in our parish must be followed as a pattern. Places differ and offer various opportunities and ventures for action. The intended message here is that Sisters will see and use the chances for placing themselves at the service of God and others by discerning what can be done in the here and now.

Belonging to God intimates that we belong to others in affection and service. The parish to which we are sent in our apostolate furnishes us with here-and-now opportunities to work for and along with the people of God. To be a religious is to be dedicated to saying "Yes" to any service asked and needed.

There is an apostolate itself in the many little things a Sister can accomplish while living among the people of God. I accentuate the word "little" because teaching is our big job, and other occupations are necessarily incidental to it. But the little things each of us does in our parish, all told, it seems to me, amount to something worthwhile.

Not all the things we do for our parish are tangible. The fact dawns on us more and more that Sisters stand for something for which people are searching: they associate us with God. By our proud joy in belonging to God, we hopefully stir an awakening and longing for Christ in the hearts of our contemporaries. God can use us in this silent way, and this, apparently, is the most important of the little things we accomplish in our parish. People need this manifestation of complete Christian living, and any facet of revealing God is precious. Sisters leading an intensely Christian life directly manifest to the world Christ and his way of life. "This," says Pope Paul, "is the main thing that men want of religious today. This seems to us to be the most urgent and up-to-date 'sign' value that religious life is called upon to offer the community of the faithful."

Our parish Church is our chapel. A few scattered incidents point out how parishioners notice us there. "What is that blue book I see you use before Mass?" It was my meditation book. Lately we moved from the front benches in church to ones further back. Said a group of ladies: "You belong up there; we like to see you in the front." When leaving for summer school, parishioners remarked, "We miss you during the summer. Things just aren't the same. The liturgy limps when you're gone. Come back as soon as you can."

GOOD WORKS IN A PARISH

Although we are eager to be in touch with the times, we do not look askance at traditional good works. In our parish, as a direct and personal service to God and his people, we take care of the sanctuary and altar, a task some Sisters might consider passé. But who belongs around God's altar more than those especially dedicated to him? In our spare time we take up the parish census. Presently one of our group, a talented seamstress, is designing and making an entirely new set of vestments to be used in our parish church. Because of the shortage of priests, the author has been commissioned at a special service to distribute Holy Communion in our parish, to bring Holy Communion to the sick or confined, and to give Viaticum to those in danger of death.

Circumstances in our parish warrant that the choir and organist be supervised by a Sister. Before Mass a Sister practices hymns for the liturgy with the congregation. One of us also trains and directs the parish grade and high school altar boys, appoints commentators and scriptural readers. High school students under the direction of a Sister help to teach catechism to children in outlying mission districts. In other words, our Sisters discover talent and direct talent. For developing parish leadership in youth, the needed inspiration, direction, and push often come from the Sisters in a parish.

The parish furnishes a pivotal point for many services to God and his people. The call to adaptation of the religious life implies that the people of God and religious be brought together rather than isolated. New apostolic ventures for us come from other faith groups: upon invitation to Protestant parishes we Sisters dialogue with various groups; recently we met with a group of Methodist ladies wanting to know more about our faith and the life Sisters lead. A Sister was asked by a neighboring Christian parish to lecture on cate-chetical procedures. To an Episcopalian parish group our art teacher presented an audio-visual program on sacred art.

For Sisters who like present changes with a dash of sociability, there are occasional dinners at the rectory with the parish priests; in turn, they dine with us at our house. Sisters are invited to meetings, dinners, and social gatherings with various parish societies. After Mass there is a chance to speak with parishioners during which time there is potential for good. In our parish we also attend baptisms, weddings, funerals; we visit sick parishioners in the hospital.

What about the time involved in doing all this? The saying is, "If you want something accomplished, ask a busy person." Most of us can find the time for what we really want to do. With time budgeting — cutting short Coke and coffee breaks, sitting before TV — the minutes snatched here and there give us time for extra-curricular activities for the Lord.

Recently a number of pastors met with a key group of Sisters to discuss renewal and updating. "Pastors like Sisters to take an interest in things per-taining to the parish," was a comment by one priest, agreed upon by all the others. When speaking of the history of his parish, a priest was asked, "Did the coming of the Sisters make a difference in your parish?" The answer was: "A tremendous difference! St. Patrick's really wasn't a parish before they came. With the coming of the Sisters in the local grade and high school, our congre-gation really began and steadily grew. If Catholic schools phase out, I fear for the parishes."

So what we are doing in our parish brings us the satisfaction of knowing that we are serving God and others, here and now, in that part of his vineyard that God in his providence appointed to us.

Sisters Today, October, 1971

Religious Women in Campus Ministry

Sister Ann Kelley, O.P.

I hear regularly from religious women who want to know about campus ministry, and how they might join it. On the one hand, I encourage them; those of us already in it regard campus ministry as one of the most important works of the Church today. On the other hand, I know there are bound to be frustrations for the new woman chaplain, and I feel compelled to point them out at the same time.

Judging from my own experiences, which I have had confirmed as typical by other women chaplains, here is what she is likely to encounter. First, getting a job will be difficult, and the scarcity of jobs prevents careful selection or placement. Right now the supply of women applicants exceeds the demand for them. As well as convincing women to join us, and their communities to permit them to, we need to convince priests to accept them and bishops to finance them.

When she gets a job she will probably attend one of the summer orientation programs for new chaplains, sponsored by the National Office of Higher Education of the U.S. Catholic Conference and the National Chaplains' Association, and she will confer with colleagues. But no one will answer her first questions, "What do I do?" and "How do I do it?" Campus ministry has not yet developed into a profession with job requirements, clear goals, accepted directions, or evaluative criteria. Some chaplains argue that situations are too varied and complex for such definition. Whether or not this is so, she will find that she is free to set her own directions. She will make her own job.

Her colleagues may be helpful to a degree. But present chaplains are unsure of their own work, and hope, rather, that a new person can find ways of bringing life to their own efforts. There are rarely internships or supervisory procedures. Priests, the dominant group in campus ministry, are not used to

388

teams, and certainly not to women as equals, and the team relationship may well become a problem instead of a help. Most of the Sisters who have left the work cite inadequate or unhappy staff relations as their chief reason for leaving.

While she will be associated with other groups, they offer little substantial guidance. The Catholic community is diffuse and inexperienced with a woman chaplain, so it has few expectations. The university itself usually does not become involved with religious chaplaincies. Religious communities are supportive of the efforts of their members, but few outside the situation really understand the work or the life style it requires.

In the long run, the lack of specificity and of expectations is probably good; the woman is free to find forms of ministry appropriate to her and to those she serves. But it means that she must be independent and resourceful when little in her religious training or her professional experience has prepared her for this.

Previously her work was well defined, and it, or her supervisor, gave structure to her life. She was subordinate and dependent. Now she structures her own time and makes her own choices. Her new work as a woman chaplain is without precedent. The only model is that of the priest, yet essential priestly functions are denied her.

NO MODELS FOR WOMEN IN MINISTRY

I think that all of the problems I have isolated relate to a basic one: there are no models for women in ministry. The work of religious women has been in professions of service, and it was the profession that gave shape to work and even to life style. Women fitted themselves into established patterns and had others' experiences to sustain them. They have not been chaplains, and people have not expected women to be chaplains.

Given this, I think the women who have pioneered in campus ministry have done well in the transition. They have made changes with grace. The idea of a woman chaplain is accepted, and the Catholic community at colleges and universities, sensitive to the position of women, finds it exciting. Most priests who have experience with a woman co-worker find new dimensions to ministry. Most important, they have gotten a new image of themselves as ministers and a new sense of equality with other ministers themselves.

Within some limits these transitional women have worked out roles meaningful to themselves and to the community they serve, and new women chaplains will profit from their experiences. In addition to the planning and administration that go with any program, women have concentrated on the pastoral mode of ministry identified in the Danforth Study of Campus Ministry. This is work related to faith commitments and life questions, primarily with individuals or small groups. It is difficult to describe pastoral work; it is usually quiet and private. Its range includes religious education, the development of awareness and response to life questions, and the resolution of personal concerns. Its expansion may include ecumenical activities, liturgical participation, and involvement in social concerns. Women chaplains work in all these areas.

All of this work is valuable; it is formative for some individuals and for the community. But little of it has a public character, and in the minds of many the woman remains in the margin of ministry. Women chaplains have not yet created new models of ministry or generally served in leadership or public roles.

EXPLORING POSSIBLE MODELS

Now that the transition is past, the time has come for us to explore possible models for the fullest meaning and diversity of ministry. The pastoral role, and even the priestly one, are only parts of ministry, and fall short of the demands of either the university community or of society. The Danforth Study lists two other roles we might develop, and there are surely others. One is the prophetic, judging the justice and humaneness of the social order and pointing to the changes required if these values are to be present. The other is the kingly or governance mode, the organization of activities for the care of men in the world through responsible corporate action. Women chaplains have been involved in these works, but without consciously attempting to create models, and without public or leadership roles.

Sisters in campus ministry have the freedom to explore new models of ministry for women, for in some ways it is still like a new endeavor, and the lack of definition permits trial and experimentation. New models may help religious women in other apostolates, for I suspect those who have made similar transitions into different works have had some of the same problems.

New models will also help men chaplains. The problems women have met in ministry are not exclusive to them; studies show men as well as women chaplains suffer from the ambiguity and vagueness of their work. Their only model has been that of the parish priest; their only job specificity has been their liturgical and official Church functions. This model is questionable for campus communities; at best it serves only a part of the Catholic community and represents only one aspect of ministry.

Along with conscious experimentation, I am convinced that we need the ordination of women. Think what this would mean – the woman would be an equal representative of the Church and clearly identified with the ministry in a public way. She could act formally in the name of the Christian community. She would have a public forum from which she could preach and exercise her leadership. The stature of her other ministerial work would be raised in the minds of people who equate ministry with only the sacramental, and her other work could be culminated in an appropriate liturgical celebration. And think what it would mean to the women's movement – definitive testimony that the Church does believe in equality of all persons.

Our ideas of ministry should widen with other models, but celebration remains a vital ingredient of a full ministry and should not be a separate mode of ministry denied to some ministers. Rather than enlarging the tight clerical circle, the ordination of women would point toward the participation of all people in ministry. Not all women would desire ordination and not all would consider it advantageous to their ministry, but I think all would agree that in liturgical celebration they should not be discriminated against.

As I say, I think women have done well in campus ministry. Now that they have self-confidence, insights from their experiences, and the opportunity to explore, there is much they can do. I hope other women will join us and that religious communities will accept this as a serious apostolate. While there are now 150 women chaplains, the number of communities they represent is so large that one concludes the work is still judged as individual and experimental. The supply may be greater than the demand, but it is not greater than the need. Well over half of the dioceses in the United States have no women as chaplains on campuses, and many more have only one or two.

Sisters Today, February, 1976

The Ordination Conference from the Inside

Sister Mary Anthony Wagner, O.S.B.

I am sure that there are many reasons why people either went to the Ordination Conference in Detroit during the 1975 Thanksgiving Day weekend or inquired about it. For myself, it was a deep attraction and desire for a fuller insight which led me there.

When I heard Nadine Foley, O.P., begin the conference by telling its 1200 registrants that we had come together not to confront the Church nor to defy its male counterpart but rather TO BE CHURCH; when I heard Elizabeth Carroll, R.S.M., begin her address by informing us that we had received a letter from a bishop in India telling us that he and a native community of religious women were praying fervently for news of the conference because of its significance for the Church; and when I heard various speakers express the prayer that we reflect and work so that the Church might be found increasingly faithful to the Gospel, then I was indeed glad to be there and ready to be challenged to listen to what Christ's Spirit is speaking so urgently to us at this time about our growing identity and understanding within the Church.

We were here in compliance with a bequest of Pope Paul that we infuse the Christian spirit within the communities in which we live. We became more aware as we continued to assemble that we had come in response to the Spirit, aware that we were not the whole Church and that we were not speaking for the whole Church, but that we had come to speak our part of the dialogue as Church.

THE ROLE OF WOMEN

As women in the Church we became increasingly aware of ways in which we have been eliminated from full activity within the Church: we had been urged to study our own role within the Church, yet we felt frustration at what we experienced; we had heard the official Church speak of openness to dialogue and decision-making in our regard, yet we found our words thinly vibrant upon the atmosphere of a patriarchal Church; we realized that there are indeed many important social issues crying for the influence of the Gospel, yet all the evils of injustice are interwoven with our own existence within that ecclesial community primarily wrought and formed by the Good News.

Our sensitivities grew as speakers helped us reflect on the role of women as it was revealed in the activity of Jesus himself who had accepted women among his followers in a manner that appeared to be a counterculture in his time, as it was exercised in the early apostolic tradition, and how an overwhelming male society several centuries after Jesus gave an inadequate response to his message by eliminating the ministries of women in the Church.

The gospel which had presented women as predominantly faithful at the cross and in the resurrection seemingly had undergone a kind of smog-effect in a society not yet totally infiltrated with its message. Though the risen Lord had brought us all the power to live on another plane with no discriminations, a culture which had cradled slavery in its homes also subordinated woman and depreciated her in the very process of exploiting her and fearing her very existence as a woman.

SET FREE BY CHRIST

The Spirit was stirring us all to see and acknowledge within ourselves that we have indeed been set free by Christ. Was this growing sensitivity and experience of women as women coming now from our secular world in which women are gradually becoming stronger in voicing their own personal growth and convictions? How ironic that the light of the Gospel had not been able to pierce the darkness in advance! Though it became uncomfortable and painful to peel accretions from the truth of the being of the Church, yet the very removal of those entrenchments and cultural appendages occasioned the true nature of the ministry of the Church to be revealed more effectively.

It became clear to us as women that we wished to participate more fully in the ministry of the risen Lord to the people of our world today, yet we did not wish to align ourselves with a caricature of that ministry: with a locus of elitism, with a power struggle, with a substitute matriarchy for an existent patriarchy. We knew deeply that a woman who would seek the priesthood as a door to power in the Church would do no good to women nor to the Church! What purification must occur in the Church if the priesthood is to become disengaged from power! Our minds must be disabused of a notion of the priesthood as possessing power separately from the Church, as a power-tool over the laity.

Women of faith, trust and love uttered convictions such as: the renewal of the Church will take place in the Spirit of Jesus; the Spirit will blow with a mighty wind to renew the priesthood in the Church to serve in love. All of us who had become aware of the voice of the Spirit speaking through Vatican II were now hearing that voice speak once again in identifying the priesthood of Jesus as one of ministry rather than of power. New models of the Church as the sacrament of Christ, as servant, as a pilgrim people seem to herald a declericalized Church, to cry for an examination of the Scripture in the light of the Church's contemporary experience of itself, and to purge the Church of those sociological accretions which led to a clerical caste distinguished from the laity.

PROVEN COMPETENCE IN MINISTRY

There was ample evidence that women were proving themselves intellectually competent, adept at parish ministry and administration; the majority of us present at the conference were women engaged in the cultural and social mission of the Church. Many are active in the teaching ministry of the Church, in the task of reconciling men, women and children, in the struggle of righting injustices, and in the delicate mission of listening to the pilgrim's search for God in our time.

Several times a day, this large conference met in small dialogue sessions; within those groups of ten we were encouraged to share and to listen to what the Spirit was saying within our hearts and within the hearts of other participants about the Church, ordination, and its mission to the world. It was particularly here that women gave witness to the ministry of Jesus which they were experiencing in their own apostolates in the Church, ministries which they experienced as truncated when they found themselves frustratingly unable to speak the words of Jesus and the Spirit within the Church in order to assure his people of their forgiveness, of their intimate association with him, and of their identification with him in the faith-community's response to the celebration of the Mystery of Faith at the heart of the Church's worship.

The Spirit was putting within the hearts of many of these women the desire to minister fully to the members of Christ. It appeared that the sacramentality of the Church would be more fully manifest with both men and women participating in the ministry of Jesus. Could the Church be faithful to its genuine mission of ministry and service of the Good News and yet relinquish outdated forms of that ministry? Would women be given the freedom to function as full ministers in the Church and not just as auxiliaries to a masculine Church? How can women truly be ministers within the Church and yet be excluded from full participation? Does the "official Church" mean to give only a token consideration to women relative to decision-making and dialogue within the Church when women are excluded from the Curia, from juridic bodies, and from diocesan councils which are almost totally male, and when subordination and humiliation of women are institutionalized in its canon law?

To most the message came clear that not to ordain women would prolong the symbol of a false interpretation of the role and nature of women, even when the Gospel message clearly witnesses to the freedom, leadership, and sanctity of women. It was manifest that both men and women have been awakened by the Spirit to challenge the past understandings and institutionalizations of the priesthood; there seems to be a growing perception of a new order, an opening up of consciousness on the nature of the Church as the sacrament of the incarnation of Christ in all humanity.

SERIOUS SEARCHING AND LISTENING

It became increasingly clear at the conference that women were serious in their scholarly search of the Scriptures and the tradition of the Church, and that they were equally intent upon listening pensively to what the Spirit was speaking within their own consciences and hearts. What women are asking for is not to claim the priesthood as a right in justice, but to seriously petition the Church to test their call to the ministry of Christ. At a Liturgy of Blessing in which we celebrated a vigil in prayer, readings and dance, members of the assembly who experienced a call to the priesthood of Christ were invited to stand and proclaim that in our midst; and members of the assembly who wished to acknowledge and support their witness were invited to sign their sisters with a cross of blessing. When over 150 women, young and old, stood, a serious silence gave clear witness to a deep response of faith and hope within the Church. Relative to this experience I heard a theologian remark that one could hardly ignore this witness as genuine "theological data" within the Church of our day.

What was it that the Spirit was saying within the Church? Many thought-provoking responses were given throughout those days of the conference. One which impressed me very much was a query of Father Carroll Stuhlmueller in his response: Is now the time for women to move from their prophetic position, or are they to acquire more ministerial experience first? Are women to continue challenging the priesthood of Christ as it now functions in the Church, as it were from the outside, rather than ministering as part of the organizational priesthood?

Father Stuhlmueller perceived a threat to the intimate connection between the ministry and the Eucharist if women are to continue in their ministries of service and teaching which more and more must perforce be paraliturgical celebrations and thus create a cleavage between their ministry and that of the Eucharistic celebration. Is the ministry of women to continue in a prophetical role outside of the structure, or ally itself with the organizational priesthood as it now exists, or should it position itself somewhere in between in order to maintain Eucharistic unity and yet continue in its prophetical-priestly role?

THE PRIESTHOOD NEWLY INTERPRETED

It became manifestly clear that women as priests were not to be men-priests but the priesthood interpreted anew; yet in order to accomplish that they are challenged with a deep-rooted structure, with a theology reflecting a male dominance dressed up in a vocabulary of divinity. As time at the conference progressed, the issue of ordination for women appeared less untimely and peripheral and more a call to fidelity to its own nature.

We as women in the Church were concerned not to get caught in forms of ministry which are liberating to neither women nor men. We realized that the freeing of women must be the work of women. We must ask the Church not just to permit our thinking but to join us in reversing history and showing forth the power of the Gospel. We had become confident that the ordered ministry as it now exists in the Church is not wrong but historic, and therefore not absolute nor unchanging. We realized that fidelity to the tradition of the Church means a readiness to relinquish outdated forms and to break with some "traditions." We felt deeply that we are a Church newly conscious of its sinfulness especially toward the poor, the oppressed and the oppressors. How, we asked, is the Church to minister in the future so that the effects of oppression and callousness to injustices will be alleviated and the causes eradicated?

There were some piercings of consciences as we heard speakers say that our priests celebrate as a caste, not hearing the cries of two-thirds of the world living below subsistence level, those priests who alone have the occasion to realize which sins of injustice go unconfessed. People everywhere want to build a "new city" in the Third World, to relieve the oppressed and to free the oppressors. The applause of the participants at the conference witnessed to the need of a new priesthood based on the need for a new society.

We were intent upon addressing ordination not from a stand of vested self-interest but from a gospel imperative of setting the oppressed free. The priest of the near future would be one ministering among the poor, struggling with them and working out actions for their Christian lives. Then the priest would celebrate a reconciliation in Eucharist with them, and not be one waiting at the altar for the return of those who have left their gifts in order to become reconciled or for those who have never left their gifts at the altar, unaware of the oppression and injustices of their brethren.

THE JOURNEY AHEAD

Our conference had revealed to us the length and nature of the journey ahead. Though women had witnessed to a call and a hope within themselves, they knew that much thought, study, continuing dialogue and probing are needed to reinterpret the priesthood in the light of today's needs. The dialectic between Christian tradition and human experience will demand discipline, reverence, creativity, courage and risk-taking. The search must look to tradi-

tion, to Scripture, to theology and to other disciplines such as biology and anthropology, and to our own experience in being the Church in today's world.

We as women in the Church must bond together in order to give witness
of what it is that the Spirit is speaking to us. We must participate in the
magisterium process of the Church; the voice of the Church may not remain
the limited vision of an all-male perspective of the world. The vision and voice
of women must be courageously given and heard. As one speaker discerned, it
does not make sense to blame the Church if the women of the past did not consider themselves oppressed; however, the meaning of the past is now in the
present: the injustices of oppression have become evident and something must
be done. Not to change at this point would be to continue the institutionaliza-
tion of the false interpretation in the past of the role and nature of women.

Thin Ice

Thin ice on the river today.
Beneath the frail skin,
the dark river moves within
its silence, no longer
proud or visible.

Behind my lids, my eyes
flow into your self; your
darkness merges with mine
in a deep stillness.
When I open my eyes,
you go on without me.

        Mary Ellen Carew
    Sisters Today, January, 1977

Sisters Today, April, 1979

The Ministry of Surprise

Bishop Robert Morneau

In the presence of a carefully wrapped package, a certain light glows in the eyes of a child, be that child four or forty. A gift to be opened: the excitement, the wonder, the anticipation, the surprise of it all. Then, as trembling fingers toss bow, string and paper aside, the glow bursts into a flame of "wow!" — and immediately the gift, and all its hidden love, wrap the child in tender embrace and emotion.

To the observant spectator, present at birthday parties, anniversary cele-brations, Christmas eve festivities, a question must be asked: who is more excited — the recipient or the giver? The glow in the child's eye may well be dim in comparison with the burning love in the one who has created this moment of joy.

To be a giver is certainly part of everyone's Christian ministry, for the Lord himself so often surprised his disciples and his people with marvelous gifts of health and joy, freedom and faith. These gifts often came in hidden, unexpected ways: being called to a full life by leaving all behind, obtaining peace through suffering, coming to faith in the darkness of the crucifixion. Jesus served by surprise, a special style of ministry much needed today in a world so highly managed and computerized that the mystery of surprise has become an endangered species.

This article has as its immediate goal to outline a theology of surprise and to state some requirements demanded of a minister of surprise. Its remote goal is to create a national refuge for all ministers of surprise who, having given their unexpected gifts, can scurry back to this haven for protection from grateful recipients and for time to package the next surprise that the Lord wants to give through them.

THREE FACETS OF GOD'S SURPRISING GENEROSITY

Any understanding of ministry must be based on our concept of God. The scriptures reveal numerous facets of God's generosity, and three of these in particular may well serve as a foundation for a ministry of surprise. These are the mysteries of creation, incarnation, and resurrection.

Is not creation a surprise and our Father a surpriser? A universe so vast we cannot count the stars! Planets that dance around a rather insignificant star! Animals created strictly for laughter: welcome the giraffe and hyena! And the caterpillar who incredibly would like to fly, and does! Water that gets angry and steams off, then becomes silent and locks itself in ice! Small yellow manufacturers of honey with sour stings! And then, that creature with body and soul, time and eternity, freedom and determinism, knowledge and ignorance, grace and sin — all mixed into one! Wow!

Is not the incarnation a surprise and Jesus the surpriser? Love enfleshed in one like us! God-become-man! The human condition deliberately and lovingly assumed in all its fullness! A hidden, humble, silent life! A few years of ministry, then a scandalous death! A life of many failures, rejections and anguished betrayals! A Lord who suffers and goes to the cross out of love. Wow!

Is not the resurrection a surprise and the Spirit of the Father and Son a surpriser? A Spirit of life flowing from death! A new presence after the "finality" of death! A power released from the powerlessness of the cross! Hope flowing through hearts of those despairing on pilgrim roads and empty gardens! Courage given to the cowardly! Peace healing fragmented souls and fearful friends! The bond of sin and death broken forever! Wow!

In an unexpected way, God as *the* minister of surprise breaks into history with a suddenness that staggers our finite imagination and intellect, with the possibility (to be realized in time) of rejection of the gift of himself, with the desire that all gifted people would treasure the love offered and come to a life of deep mutuality in him.

Though history gives volumes of evidence that many have not acknowledged the surprises of creation, incarnation, and resurrection, there have always been some who have been open to these gifts and have rejoiced in the mystery of God's love. Julian of Norwich was such a one:

And in this he (God) showed me something small, no bigger than a hazelnut, lying in the palm of my hand, as it seemed to me, and it was as round as a ball. I looked at it with the eye of my understanding and thought: What can this be? I was amazed that it could last, for I thought that because of its littleness it would suddenly have fallen into nothing. And I was answered in my understanding: It lasts and always will, because God loves it; and thus everything has being through the love of God.

In this little thing I saw three properties. The first is that God made it, the second is that God loves it, the third is that God preserves it. But what did I see in it? It is that God is the Creator and the protector and the lover.

For until I am substantially united to him, I can never have perfect rest or true happiness, until, that is, I am so attached to him that there can be no created thing between my God and me.[1]

The God of surprises continues throughout history to amaze us in sudden and unexpected ways. Hopefully we have the sense and sensitivity to respond.

MINISTERING SURPRISES TO OTHERS

Made in his image and likeness, we are challenged to minister to each other and the world as God has ministered to us: creatively, incarnationally and "resurrectionally." The specific form of how this will happen is not essential; the fact that we are willing to serve is. Often the effectiveness of service will be in proportion to its simplicity and littleness. A model of this might be the experience of Annie Dillard as a young girl:

When I was six or seven years old, growing up in Pittsburgh, I used to take a precious penny of my own and hide it for someone else to find. It was a curious compulsion; sadly, I've never been seized by it since. For some reason I always "hid" the penny along the same stretch of sidewalk up the street. I would cradle it at the roots of a sycamore, say, or in a hole left by a chipped-off piece of sidewalk. Then I would take a piece of chalk, and, starting at either end of the block, draw huge arrows leading up to the penny from both directions. After I learned to write I labeled the arrows: SURPRISE AHEAD or MONEY THIS WAY. I was greatly excited, during all this arrow-drawing, at the thought of the first lucky passerby who would receive in this way, regardless of merit, a free gift from the universe. But I never lurked about. I would go straight home and not give the matter another thought, until, some months later, I would be gripped again by the impulse to hide another penny.[2]

Silas Marner found and hoarded many pennies; the Christian finds and shares the gifts received. One form of sharing is to repackage the gift with excitement and glee, hide it in strange and delightful places, and not wait around to be acknowledged as *the* giver.

This is the ministry of surprise, a ministry done out of love and without immediate compensation. And yet the compensation is quite immediate — the more gifts that we give away, the more clearly we are able to spot the chalk marks pointing to cracks or around corners: SURPRISE AHEAD! New gifts to be discovered and shared.

---

[1] Julian of Norwich, *Showings*, translated with an introduction by Edmund Colledge, O.S.A., and James Walsh, S.J. (New York: Paulist Press, 1978), 183.

[2] Annie Dillard, *Pilgrim at Tinker Creek* (New York: Bantam Books, Inc., 1974), 15–16.

ONE ELEMENT OF SURPRISE: THE UNEXPECTED

The tripod upon which the ministry of surprise rests is the unexpected, the unpredictable, and the unnecessary. First of all, the unexpected. Surprise is the term we give to those experiences in which a person is forcibly impressed because the gift or event is unexpected, it takes us off guard. While expecting a routine response, something else is forthcoming. Many proverbs contain this element of surprise:

If I die, I forgive you; if I recover, we shall see.
He who would speak the truth must have one foot in the stirrup.
If three people say you are an ass, put on a bridle.[3]

As we turn to our faith, we see Jesus consistently speaking the unexpected: if you want to be happy, be poor in spirit; if you want to have the fullness of life, die to yourself; if you send out invitations for lunch and dinner, invite the lame and the blind, those who cannot repay you; if you want to be great, serve; love your enemies; turn the other cheek; pray for those who persecute you.

In this series of succinct adages Jesus packages the wisdom of his Father. He spoke what he heard; he spoke what was in his heart; he spoke what he lived. Jesus himself was the surprise, the unexpected one who forcibly impressed those whom he met because they were taken off guard. Sad to say, many could not accept this Surpriser and walked back to the expected, complacent, routine life of boredom, anxiety, and ennui.

Creativity, creation's source, contains the essential component of the unexpected. J. Bronowski describes the creative process in these terms:

A man becomes creative, whether he is an artist or a scientist, when he finds a new unity in the variety of nature. He does so by finding a likeness between things which were not thought alike before, and this gives him a sense at the same time of richness and of understanding. The creative mind is a mind that looks for unexpected likenesses.[4]

In another essay he states: "To my mind, it is a mistake to think of creative activity as something unusual. I hold that the creative activity is normal to all living things."[5] Thus God has implanted in all of us the creative seed that he himself enfleshed in his own creative act. Creation must be classified as an unexpected mystery. So, too, the incarnation and resurrection: events that catch us off guard and cause the mind to falter and the heart to rejoice.

---

[3] See John W. Gardner and Francesa Gardner Reese, *Know or Listen to Those Who Know* (New York: W. W. Norton & Company, Inc., 1975), 231, 233, 149.

[4] J. Bronowski, "The Creative Process" in *A Sense of the Future* (Cambridge, Mass.: The MIT Press, 1977), 12.

[5] *Ibid.*, "On Art and Science," 16.

THE UNPREDICTABLE

Unpredictability, the second element of surprise, reveals something of the interior life of the minister of surprise. Therein resides a magical process which changes the natural flow of things, even to the extent of influencing the final working out of the formula. The story begun finds its ending during the telling; the expression of concern adjusts itself as new and varied needs arise; the plan contains an open-endedness allowing the influence of diverse circumstances.

Various historical figures exemplify this unpredictable element of surprise: O'Henry, in the short story; St. Francis, in religion; Newton, in science. In praising the positive side of unpredictability, the importance and necessity of predictability is not denied; an orderly and peaceful life has need of this ingredient. However, even here, there is plenty of room for the unpredictable. Life demands a balance of each.

> Life is a series of surprises, and would not be worth taking or keeping if it were not. God delights to isolate us every day, and hide from us the past and the future.[6]

Unpredictability lies beyond the mysteries of creation, incarnation, and resurrection. Even Jimmy the Greek would have missed, if only by a few points, the conjecture that God would have seen fit to create a universe and mankind out of love; that God would assume unto himself the human condition and all its joys and pains; that death and sin would be conquered because of loving obedience and the result of that surrender. These ongoing mysteries are so incomprehensible that even the greatest fiction writers falter in trying to imagine such events. In the face of all this unpredictability of God, St. Paul can only praise, not explain what has happened:

> How rich are the depths of God — how deep his wisdom and knowledge — and how impossible to penetrate his motives or understand his methods! Who could ever know the mind of the Lord? Who could ever be his counsellor? Who could ever give him anything or lend him anything? All that exists comes from him; all is by him and for him. To him be glory for ever! Amen (Rom 11:33-36).

Those who serve the unpredictable God have an interesting challenge. Perhaps the unpredictable, creative dialogue with fellow pilgrims will foster truth where before there was only doubt and confusion. Perhaps the mandate will become clear to enflesh love in unpredictable, incarnational ways through verbalizing deep concern ("I love you more than word can wield the matter"[7]), or by being a clown in a world of heaviness and suffering, or by bringing warmth to frigid, frightened hearts. The one who serves an unpredictable God also journeys with the risen Lord, a Lord who consoles and brings hope to the

---

[6] Ralph W. Emerson, *Experience* (New York: Heritage Press, 1941), 149.

[7] Shakespeare's "King Lear," Act I, scene i, line 56.

sorrowing and discouraged. In disguise we make his joyful presence felt wherever people are in want and pain.

THE UNNECESSARY

The surprise tripod has a third leg: the unnecessary. One can eat a meal without condiments; one can live in a house without flowers; one can journey throughout life without celebrations. One can, but only at the high cost of lost joy and delight. Surprises are gratuitous, as is all grace. They need not be, they are contingent. Yet life would be dreary without them, and we all know that survival is far different from living. Life without surprises is merely minimal existence. Recently a friend of mine commented: "I don't have any ha-ha's!" Interpreted: my life is devoid of surprises, and I'm hurting.

God did not have to create, to become one of us, to bless us with the gift of resurrection. That he did in no way takes away from the gratuity of these mysteries. No necessity can be ascribed to such events of faith. What this highlights is that at the core of the unnecessity of surprise is love. Love cannot be forced or demanded; it bursts forth where "it will flame out, like shining from shook foil; it gathers to a greatness, like the ooze of oil crushed."[8]

Though it might be argued that love necessarily must give of itself, there is no forcing the manner of expression. The manner is unexpected, unpredictable and unnecessary: God is love but he need not have loved in the three life mysteries that we are dealing with here. What other forms that love might have assumed can only be guessed at by the highly imaginative.

Those who serve the gratuitous God are given a marvelous freedom to minister in ways that are not specifically "necessary." How one expresses the mysteries of creation, incarnation, and resurrection in one's ministry is surprisingly flexible. This freedom of unnecessary specificity reveals the beauty of the mutuality between creator and creature: God calls us to responsibility but allows us freedom (the heart of surprise) in distributing the gifts that we have received in diverse patterns.

As instruments of grace and channels of peace we must carefully discern the form and manner of how our Father has dealt with us and then we go forth, with the same unexpectedness, unpredictability, and unnecessity to continue the same work. The Spirit has been given to us to undertake this work: the Spirit of surprise. All this is sheer grace for us and for those with whom we work.

Undoubtedly, the official Church will never sanction an office or a ministry of surprise; there will be no ordination rite for clowns. But if there were one, I would like to suggest the following qualifications for all candidates:

---

[8] Gerard Manley Hopkins, "God's Grandeur."

QUALIFICATIONS FOR THE OFFICE OF MINISTER OF SURPRISE

1. The minister must be able to plant pennies.

   Thus, possession of pennies is a prerequisite. These would include such items as stories, jokes, insights, small gifts, smiles, tears, dreams, ideals, soft eyes, etc.

2. The minister must be able to plant and run.

   Candidates are disqualified if they stay around to watch the gift being discovered. One must be able to live without immediate compensation. Underlying this qualification is the fact that too much precious time is lost by staying around; other gifts may never be planted because of such delaying tactics.

3. The minister must be surprise-able.

   The inability to receive is an impediment to this office within the Church. The minister is one who is sent; not being able to receive implies a lack of authentic contact with the Sender.

4. The minister must be purged of avarice.

   The greatest danger for the minister of surprise is to retain the pennies given by the Lord. A second serious danger is to desire more than what is beneficial to oneself and for others. The retention of surprise pennies causes oppressiveness; the constant desire for more and more pennies fosters a discontent that makes everyone nervous, even God.

5. The minister of surprises must be involved in an ongoing education program.

   The assumption behind this requirement is that hearts tend to harden, muscles tend to atrophy, languages are lost, unless each of these is properly exercised and nurtured. These educational units would be acceptable:

   a. daily reading of cartoon (1 credit)

   b. standing on one's head for five minutes every week — helps give new perspectives (½ credit)

   c. traveling on back roads (1¼ credits)

   d. reading Don Quixote (2 credits)

   e. watching sunsets (1 credit)

   f. hugging the huggable (1½ credits)

OUR THEME CONFIRMED

In such a serious theological work as Jon Sobrino's *Christology at the Crossroads*, we find the theme of surprise verified:

It is the Father who is at work in history, and he works through human beings. He discloses his will in unexpected ways, carrying it out in ways that are a source of scandal to the world. With this realization Jesus turns to the Father and offers him thanks.[9]

We see in our God the very element that takes us off guard: the unexpected. We cannot control and manage him; his ways and thoughts are not ours. How delightful and exciting this is — to be ministers of such a reality in our own times, regardless of the scandal it might cause. The staid are many, the surprisers, few.

Ever so often those musical words are heard: "What a pleasant surprise to see you" or "Let's throw a surprise party for Sarah!" Ever so often the sidewalks are chalked with the bold letters SURPRISE AHEAD! Ever so often people are overwhelmed with laughter. Know that in these events ministers of surprise are around and active. In and through them comes life; God's mysteries of creation, incarnation, and resurrection are made visible. And one day all these ministers and their graced followers will experience what Julian of Norwich so accurately describes in her vision of heaven:

> And in this my understanding was lifted up into heaven, where I saw the Lord God as a lord in his own house, who has called all his friends to a splendid feast. Then I did not see him seated anywhere in his own house; but I saw him reign in his house as a king, and fill it all full of joy and mirth, gladdening and consoling his dear friends with himself, very familiarly and courteously, with wonderful melody in endless love in his own fair blissful countenance, which glorious countenance fills all heaven full of the joy and bliss of the divinity.[10]

---

[9] Jon Sobrino, S.J., *Christology at the Crossroads*, translated by John Drury (Maryknoll, N.Y.: Orbis Books, 1978), 155.

[10] Julian of Norwich, *Showings*, 203.

Abram in Starlight

He rode a crest of yearning out of sleep
That seemed unlike his thirst for sons
—and yet the same. Made senseless
By the sweetness, still he knew
It was his God who touched him then.
He hoped that Sarah felt this, too.
In every other way than womb,
Life was gendered in the woman.
He drew gently from the blanket,
Lest she wake to find him gone
And count herself the reason.

He stood outside the tent in April air. Spring
Was in the stars' slow winking, and the thirst
For greenness sucked the earth. His bones felt dry.
He reached them up, as if to steep them in the sky
—Then all the stars bent down! He touched their light
And felt no other pain than peace. All thought
Went white before a love whose strength
Could bring the desert stones alive.

Sarah! How he needed now to wake her,
Though he could not seem to shape
This stirring of his soul in sound.
He ducked beneath the flap: cold starlight spilled
On Sarah's face, not sleeping now, but teared.
He bent to comfort her, caressing with her name,
And she, assured, began to kiss the wonder from his face.

Sister M. Audrey Synnott, R.S.M.
Sisters Today, May, 1977

PART NINE

BULLETIN BOARD:

Musings Near a Maple Tree

Daniel Durken, O.S.B.

Every religious community knows that its bulletin board is as much a focus and forum of communication as the altar, the table, and the mailbox. A convent or monastery without a bulletin board is like a home without a kitchen or an office without a water cooler. So when editor Father Ronald Roloff, O.S.B., decided in the March, 1965, issue of *Sponsa Regis* to "experiment with a Bulletin Board, which will be open for any news or announcements that are of general interest," he picked a natural for the name of the column.

When the editor of this present volume became editor of *Sisters Today* in 1967 he began to use the Bulletin Board as the place and space for personalizing his editorial efforts. With a loving nod to the little maple tree that signalled the change of seasons outside his monastery window as well as the slowness but sureness of growth, the editor most often used liturgical and scriptural themes to provide a monthly focus.

The following sample of reflections contains musings on such topics as Christmas shoppers, the "Pow" and "Wow" of Pentecost, going for a walk, and rainbows. Hopefully a more complete collection of these Bulletin Boards will appear after this present project is completed.

Sisters Today, September, 1967

A Moratorium on Hemlines
and Horariums

When Abbot Baldwin asked me to take over the editorship of *Sisters Today*, one of my first thoughts was to change the title of the magazine. In view of recent reports that 3600 Sisters left their communities last year, I felt a title like "Sisters *Yesterday*" might be more accurate and appropriate. Seriously, some consideration was given to suspending publication of this magazine. With so many books, articles, and reports being written about nuns, by nuns, and for nuns, an editor of a monthly journal for Sisters feels that he is only adding an echo, not a new voice, to an already overcrowded rooftop. And for one to continue, as is indicated on our table-of-contents masthead, "to explore the role of the religious woman in the Church in our time" is to take the chance of looking for a treasure in a field that has been so thoroughly dug that not even vultures hover over it any longer.

And then one meets the Sisters today, in class, in conference, or in chapel, and it does not take long to realize that there is still a need for more exploration, more examination, and more exchange. If Father Andrew Greeley could write recently that only 5 or 10 percent of today's Catholics really understand and appreciate the effects of Vatican II, it seems logical to suppose that there are still some communities of Sisters and not a few individual nuns who have yet to learn that a new Pentecost has happened in the Church in the past five years.

Pentecost, old and new, has a way of shaking things up as only a mighty wind can do. For one thing it means we can no longer translate *Festina lente* as "Change—but after I die!" And yet when Sisters can say in all sincerity that hardly half the truth has been told of what goes on behind convent doors in the name of holy obedience, there seems to be good enough reason to do what must be done to convince the religious woman in the Church of our time that our time is 1967 not 1467.

408

And what must be done? Perhaps one answer was given to that question when Dr. Pollock of Fordham answered another question about a year ago. When asked, "Are nuns washed up?" he replied, "It's up to them to survive if they take the right path to survival. They have to recognize that all of life has religious import. They have to bear public witness, the sense of another dimension — give all of American life a new depth . . . . They should put the stamp of religious importance on great secular things."

As long as *Sisters Today* can be of service to the religious woman in the Church of our time there will be a need for this magazine. My preliminary plea is for ideas and articles that will further the Holy Spirit's work of renewal and adaptation among Sisters today. What do Sisters want discussed in these pages? Hopefully a moratorium will be declared on the debate concerning hemlines and horariums with the final decision apparently going in the direction of *up* for the former and *out* for the latter. But what is *in* these days for Sisters? Prayer, community, the apostolate — certainly these are but a few of the storehouses in our many mansions from which scribes abundant can bring forth the new as well as the old.

Sisters Today, February, 1968

A Joyous Revolution

The secular press has not always been kind to Sisters today. When *Ladies Home Journal* told "Why Nuns Quit" in its April, 1967, issue, there were enough reactions to print a sequel called "Why Nuns Get Angry." I have read and returned a couple of would-be answers to the *Journal* editors, answers that gave more heat than light. There didn't seem to be any point in proving to the public that there were more Sisters up in the air than the one who flies weekly on ABC TV.

But now comes *Newsweek* to prove that all good things come to those who wait. The 1967 Christmas issue of that magazine carried a cover picture of Sister Corita (before and after her habit change) and a feature article called "The Nun: A Joyous Revolution."

For those who haven't seen the issue and must now beg, borrow, or steal one, the article is a well worded tribute to those American religious women who are showing "a new sense of sisterhood — of feminine love — toward the human family." The public can now learn that the nuns who haven't quit are by no means awaiting the Parousia behind bolted cloister doors.

The article states, "In truth, there is hardly a convent among the nation's more than 500 orders of nuns that is not torn between the impulse to be religious women, wed to the church's schools and hospitals, and the desire to be creative neighbors to those in need outside the church's walls." Later the article adds, "Today's independent young nun is looking for meaningful commitment, and the religious communities are trying desperately to provide the challenge. 'In five years, nuns will be presenting such a new face to the world that their vocational crisis will be a thing of the past,' predicts Father John J. McGrath."

Towards the end of the article, the basic question is asked: "What, in fact, is fundamental to a nun's life?" A summary is given of some of the re-examining that is going on with regard to the traditional vows of poverty, chastity, and obedience. Sister Mary Evangeline, executive secretary of Sister Formation, is quoted as predicting that the three traditional vows may be replaced by one—"total availability to God and people." A concluding comment comes from clinical psychologist Dr. Mark Stern: "If the church is to be liberated at all, it will be liberated by women."

Thank you, *Newsweek*, for telling those who haven't heard and reminding all who have that 180,000 religious women in the United States are taking renewal so seriously that it has become what the Holy Spirit intended it to be in the first place: a joyous revolution.

*

More good things are said about religious in general in the United States Bishops' Collective Pastoral released early last month. "Without the public witness to the counsels of poverty, chastity and obedience which religious vow, without their generous example of community life, the Church would be sorely impoverished," the bishops state in a section of their pastoral called "Special Witness of Religious."

They continue: "Religious manifest to us the beauty and the discipline harmonized in the Christian life, a beauty that does not neglect the sinful human condition nor the reality of death, yet a discipline which is never so severe that it overlooks the redeemed status of the human condition or the inevitability of resurrection."

Offering a thought that may with profit be considered during the coming days of Lent, the bishops state, "The very presence of religious in the world is a consolation. It is also a salutary rebuke to any of us who may be tempted to make our Christian vocation an easy or a worldly endeavor."

A fitting testimony to religious is given by the bishops in these words: "The presence among us of religious is a preaching of the Gospel to the laity and the priesthood alike; in our country this preaching has been notably confirmed by the titanic work of teaching, hospital service, care of other people's children, mercy to the aged and pioneering in social work accomplished by Catholic Sisters and Brothers who, usually anonymous and too often unthanked, have borne a professional as well as religious witness of unparalleled heroism, holiness and achievement."

The bishops' statement, well balanced and positive, deserves careful and prayerful study.

Sisters Today, December, 1974

The Spirit of Christmas Shoppers

An Advent exercise that has all the potential of an Advent wreath or an "O" antiphon to help prepare a person to celebrate Christmas is a visit to a shopping center. One recent Saturday afternoon on my way to a weekend parish assignment I stopped at such a center, and despite the inflationary prices all over the place, I came away with a free lesson on the meaning of Christmas.

I chose a shopping center for this Advent adventure because of the abundant presence of the very material that gives meaning to Christmas, namely, flesh. "The Word became flesh and dwelt among us" (Jn 1:14). That sentence still remains the simplest and clearest description of the incarnation celebration. It is no accident that when St. Luke describes the Christmas event he does so in terms of a generous supply of the same flesh that is now our link with the Lord. *All the world* that went to be enrolled in Caesar's census (Lk 2:1) must have done a lot more than just sign the official roster and pay the registration fee before they returned home. Joseph and Mary probably mingled with the crowd on the Bethlehem mall, and before they looked for a room at the local inn they must have searched for bargains in swaddling clothes, carpenter tools and household essentials. And surely they bought each other Christmas presents.

Jesus so enjoyed that first incarnational interaction with shoppers, bargain hunters, and browsers that for the rest of his life he went on a kind of shopping spree, searching for what he could save. "The Son of man came to seek and save . . ." (Lk 19:10). Jesus is not out of his crib before he encounters shepherds (Lk 2:16), those who can only afford to look instead of buy, and kings (Mt 2:11), the first of the big-time spenders who don't even have to look at price tags before they decide whether or not they can like an article of merchandise. Jesus is not off his cross before he encounters two common shop-lifters, thieves who are led away to be put to death with him (Lk 23:32).

Between crib and cross Jesus goes about giving joy to local merchants and managers, for wherever he went a crowd was sure to go. And they were standing-room-only crowds. At the very start of his preaching and healing ministry, when the good news gets out that Jesus has just cured the mother of Peter's wife, "the whole city was gathered together about the door" (Mk 1:33). Sometimes there wasn't even room to stand, such as the time Jesus went to his own home in Capernaum and "many were gathered together so that there was no longer room for them, not even about the door" (Mk 2:2). No wonder that soon afterwards Jesus found a more open space and moved from shop to shore. "Jesus withdrew his disciples to the sea, and a great multitude from Galilee followed" (Mk 3:7). In case there would be a loss of crowd control, Jesus "told his disciples to have a boat ready for him because of the crowd, lest they should crush him" (Mk 3:9).

Jesus would enjoy a Christmas rush because he not only attracted bigger crowds than a jubilee sale but also because he loved crowds. He was no leg-weary and footsore clerk, aching for the last customer to leave and the doors of the store to close. "When he saw the crowds, he had compassion for them, because they were harassed and helpless, like sheep without a shepherd" (Mt 9:36), like shoppers without a salesperson. "He saw a great throng, and he had compassion on them" (Mk 6:34). He tells his disciples, "I have compassion on the crowd because they have been with me now three days and have nothing to eat; and I am unwilling to send them away hungry, lest they faint on the way" (Mt 15:32).

There was only the one time that Jesus dispersed a crowd of shoppers. "Jesus entered the temple of God and drove out all who sold and bought in the temple, and he overturned the tables of the money-changers and the seats of those who sold pigeons. He said to them, 'It is written, "My house shall be called a house of prayer"; but you make it a den of robbers'" (Mt 21:12-13). Zeal for his Father's house prompted this outburst of anger (Jn 2:17). But in a calmer moment Jesus says, "In my Father's house are many rooms" (Jn 14:2). I think he has gone to prepare a special place in that house for those who shop.

Since the kingdom of God has been revealed in such human experiences as a sower going out to sow and a woman baking bread (Mt 13:3, 33), surely the shopper has all the symbolism necessary to give us another glimpse of that same kingdom. In fact, Jesus comes close to that very comparison when he likens the kingdom of heaven to "a merchant in search of fine pearls, who, on finding one pearl of great value, went and sold all that he had and bought it" (Mt 13:45-46).

As a parable, shopping changes from vulgar commercialization to an ex-panding celebration of sound, sight and touch. It is these very same senses that give us contact with the Word of life "which we have heard, which we have seen with our eyes, which we have looked upon and touched with our hands" (1 Jn 1:1).

Heard. Seen. Touched. These are the very elements that rescue prayer from the purely cerebral activity that it can so easily become when we concentrate only on Word and forget that Christmas gives us the Word of life. Prayer, like life, is hearing, seeing, touching, not just thinking. The Word of life is the Word made flesh. Prayer is an incarnational exchange between God and us or between one person and another. Prayer that is hearing, seeing and touching can be as full of grace and truth as the Word made flesh (Jn 1:14).

We can learn a lesson about liturgy and personal prayer when we watch a shopper approach a counter. Here is total involvement when the object is touched, handled, squeezed, unwrapped, stretched, held up for size, shaken, and otherwise examined. Here is identification between buyer and object, for if the item does not reflect, extend, enhance, or fit the shopper it remains unsold. Here is where a price is paid to satisfy a need, and every shopper knows that she gets exactly what she pays for. Here patience and perseverance can be practiced, for not every counter or rack carries what is being looked for. Here is where the help of another can be asked for without embarrassment and received as graciously as that help is given. Becoming sensitive to hearing, seeing, and touching the realities around us is to start with a den of robbers and make it a house of prayer.

So there need be no tension or conflict between those who count down the number of paying days before Christmas and those who count the number of praying days left in Advent. Advent is the whole world waiting again while God shows us once more that he takes Hallmark's hint and cares enough to send the very best, "the perfect gift from above, coming down from the Father of lights" (Jas 1:17).

Advent also offers us the one thing missing from the shopping experience that I witnessed, namely, joy. With prices being what they are, I could hardly have expected to see a lot of smiling, laughing, happy looking people skipping along behind their shop carts. But I had hoped to see a few more than the two beaming faces that I did see — and those were the faces of two young lovers who obviously had found what everyone else was still looking for: the pearl of great price which is the hidden treasure of each other.

Precisely because the Advent liturgy provides us with the paradox of already possessing the One whom we still seek, we can afford to "break forth together into singing" (Is 52:9) with "abundant joy and great rejoicing" (Is 9:3). For Jesus has come, and Jesus will continue to come again and again to seal our searching with the delight of his presence. And no matter how many times the price of other items is marked up, Jesus' gift of himself to us is always free, a free gift that makes us free. "If the Son makes you free, you will be free indeed" (Jn 8:36). From now on we can start to spend ourselves for others with the generous abandon of one who has a credit card with all the charges being paid by someone else.

Advent's shopping celebration does not end with the last ring of a cash register late in the afternoon of Christmas Eve that leaves us frustrated, tired and angry after we have spent so much and gotten so little. Jesus makes certain that one good shopping celebration deserves another. And since his own birthday began with a surge of shoppers he arranges the same sort of setting for the birthday of his Mystical Body, the Church, which is fleshed out on Pentecost.

Even though it's a long, long time from Christmas and December to Pentecost and May, we can start getting our shopping list ready now. For when Jesus first sent the Holy Spirit, the shops and streets were filled again with folks "from every nation under heaven" (Acts 2:5). With all those Parthians, Medes, Elamites, Cretans, and Arabians milling around the mall, and with Peter and his troop acting so strangely, it really looks, sounds and feels as though Pentecost is just the beginning and prelude to a world-wide clearance sale and a cosmic celebration of Crazy Days.

We have just begun to see the bargains, for it is written, "The things that no eye has seen and no ear has heard, things beyond the mind of man, all that God has prepared for those who love him'—these are the very things that God has revealed to us through the Spirit" (1 Cor 2:9-10). That's the Spirit of Christmas.

Autumnal

Why do we know surprise that all things stark
Should leave us lonely? Heart-leaved poplar trees
Now naked, flights of migratory geese
Momently inhabiting the air
And leaving lonesome spaces that before
Were merely empty, gaunt stalks, stripped and gray,
Ghosts of buildings stabbing at the sky.
They are our conventional designs
For barrenness, despair, the death of hope.
Loss is one: leaves and love and life,
Primeval innocence, the fall from grace.
Eve brought end to summer. Fell together
She and autumn's first nomadic leaf.

Barbara T. Dillon
Sisters Today, October, 1976

Sisters Today, March, 1969

We Need More Passion

Passion Sunday is the one Sunday of the year that reminds us of a really important matter that we too easily forget: that our lives could use more passion.

If any age has a monopoly on apathy—that dirty word which means no passion—it may well be our own Cool Generation. Malcolm Boyd meditates on that aspect of our era when he writes,

When you get too hot (they told us), it's no good. You've got to keep cool, man, you've got to keep cool.

Don't flip. Don't get hot. Don't act mean or mad, don't shout to top the last guy's insult. The only thing you can do is keep cool.

If you're cool, you can think. If you're cool, you can laugh. If you're cool, you don't let go, you're on solid ground even when the ground's being cut out from under you. If you're cool, you can love.

But I don't know. If that means caring without getting hooked, then I'm not for cool. Maybe losing our cool would be worth it if it means caring all the way. Even wanting to get hooked, especially if a human relationship is concerned.

Let's take a chance: let's bring back passion.[1]

Unless passion is brought back we are going to remain what the lack of passion makes us—good old pseudo-Stoics who regard the presence of passion, ardor, and intense desire as unreasonable, unnatural, and the source of evil. It was the Stoics who preached and practiced the principle that apathy, the complete control of emotions, was the supreme moral task.

It is not surprising, then, that Christians aplenty have become splendid Stoics. Father John McKenzie states in his *The Power and the Wisdom*

---

[1] Malcolm Boyd, *Free to Live, Free to Die* (New York: Signet Book, 1968), 27–28.

(Milwaukee: Bruce, 1965), "Much of Stoic morality has been incorporated into the writings of Christian moral teachers . . . . The Stoic is indifferent to wealth and poverty, honor and dignity, length of life, food, drink, and sex; there is a strange echo between this summary of Stoic principles and the ideals presented by St. Ignatius Loyola in the Principle and Foundation of the Spiritual Exercises" (pp. 14–15).

But we don't have to point accusing fingers at the good Jesuits for putting out passion and prolonging apathy. (As a matter of fact, a clipping posted on the abbey bulletin board the other day told of the tribute recently paid the Jesuits by Tennesse Williams when he said he is very happy to have been converted to Roman Catholicism by the Jesuits because they "drink, laugh and love life.") Just a few days before Passion Sunday we will all pray an unworthy prelude to the whole of Passion Week when we give our Amen to the prayer that asks, "May we bring our passions under control, and thus more easily attain the rewards of heaven."

Before we say that Amen too loudly and keep passion from ever coming back, let's go back to this delightful story from the Sayings of the Desert Fathers:

Abbot Pastor said that Abbot John the Dwarf had prayed to the Lord and the Lord had taken away all his passions, so that he became impassible. And in this condition he went to one of the elders and said: You see before you a man who is completely at rest and has no more temptations. The elder said: Go and pray to the Lord to command some struggle to be stirred up in you, for the soul is matured only in battles. And when the temptations started up again he did not pray that the struggle be taken away from him, but only said: Lord, give me strength to get through the fight.[2]

To bring back passion let's go way back, back to our Hebrew heritage of the Old Testament, and then we can rejoice in the conclusion that there has to be a place for passion in human life. The Bible does not share the view that passions are disturbances or weaknesses of man's spirit. Nor does the Bible posit the premise that passion itself is evil and incompatible with right living. In fact, the Bible tells us just the opposite. It tells us, if we have eyes to see and ears to hear, that the real source of evil is by no means passion, is by no means the throbbing, hot and human heart. Rather the source of evil lies in hardness of heart, in callousness and coldness and unconcern for widows and orphans and the poor, in indifference and insensitivity to the pleading needs of our neighbor.

The God of Israel and of Christians is the jealous, passionate God of blazing fire who nowhere reproaches his people for losing their cool and being passionate. But he does rebuke them time and time again for being stubborn and stiff-necked, for being brazen-faced and hard-hearted, for being gross and

---

[2] *The Wisdom of the Desert*, translated by Thomas Merton (Norfolk, Conn.: New Directions Books, 1960), 56–57.

haughty, insensitive and arrogant, calloused, cold, and conceited. God's own passionate desire is voiced through his prophet Ezekiel when he says, "I will take the stony heart out of their flesh and give them a heart of flesh, that they may walk in my statutes and keep my ordinances and obey them; and they shall be my people, and I will be their God" (Ez 11:19-20).

That heart of flesh was the thumping source of our best prayers, the psalms. The people who sang and shouted those prayers were people with a passion. And that may be the reason we find the psalms so difficult at times. They're too passionate. There are too many O's and exclamation points in our breviaries, and we're embarrassed by such cries as, "How many are my foes, O Lord!" (Ps 3:2) and "Lord, hear the cry of my appeal!" (Ps 139:7). One of my favorite authors, Rabbi Abraham Heschel, puts the problem this way:

> Services are conducted with dignity and precision. The rendition of the liturgy is smooth. Everything is present: decorum, voice, ceremony. But one thing is missing: *Life!*
>
> Prayer has become an empty gesture, a figure of speech. Either because of lack of faith or because of *religious bashfulness.* We would not admit that we take prayer seriously. It would sound sanctimonious, if not hypocritical. We are too sophisticated. But if prayer is as important as study, if prayer is as precious a deed as an act of charity, we must stop being embarrassed at our saying, "Praised be Thou!" with inner conviction.[3]

We need the conviction of Christ, the passion of Jesus to turn our yawns at prayer into open-mouthed shouts and songs. Jesus is a passionate man, of this we may be sure. For he is prophet *par excellence.* And if there is one thing a prophet has it is passion. The prophets of the Hebrew heritage like Elijah and Hosea, the prophets of the first Christian era like John the Baptist, Jesus, and St. Paul, the prophets of our own age like Martin Luther King and Robert Kennedy — these are people who feel fiercely.

While the ideal state of the Stoic sage is apathy, the ideal state of the prophet is sympathy, empathy. While other preachers and teachers may be satisfied with improvement, a prophet insists upon complete conversion and ultimate redemption. A prophet's words burn more than they shine, Rabbi Heschel tells us, for the prophet is a man who is impatient of excuse, contemptuous of pretense, and scornful of self-pity. While people around him are content to be tolerant and timid, a prophet in his passion for God and his goodness is sleepless and suffering. In his com-passion, a prophet realizes that although few men are guilty for the world's wrongs, all men are responsible.

And that is why Christ, the perfect prophet, takes upon himself the terrible cross of all men's sins even though no man could ever convict him of sin. Christ is indeed a man of passion, and it is his passionate participation in our own life struggle that gives each one of us the promise of final salvation.

---

[3] Abraham J. Heschel, *Man's Quest for God* (New York: Charles Scribner's Sons, 1954), 49-51.

As that promise becomes actualized again in the celebration of Passion Week and Holy Week and Easter, we hear Christ accused in the Gospel of Passion Sunday of being mad. Jesus disclaims this quality, but there still comes the protest, "Now we are sure you are mad." Perhaps Christ protests too much, for surely the Lord realizes that passion and madness can look alike. Surely our Lord would have agreed then with Zorba the Greek who challenged his young English friend in these words: "You've got everything except one thing — madness. A man needs a little madness, or else he never does cut the rope and be free. . . . Life is trouble, only death is not. To be alive is to undo your belt and look for trouble."

Certainly the trouble with our times is that we don't have enough madness, enough passion. Not enough people have a passion for right, a passion for truth, a passion for peace, a passion for human dignity, a passion for prayer, and a plain old passion for other people. Not enough of us have a passion against intellectual laziness, a passion against intolerance, a passion against taking life for granted, a passion against selfishness and immaturity and irresponsibility. Not enough of us have a passion for growing up, a passion for honesty and gentleness, a passion for compassion. Not enough of us passionately agree with the anonymous author who says, "Every year I live I am more convinced that the waste of life lies in the love we have not given, the powers we have not used, the selfish prudence that will risk nothing, and which, shirking pain, misses happiness as well."

Let's not miss the point of this Passion Time — that the real Christians are those who dare to make the madness and the passion of Jesus Christ their very own.

Sisters Today, April, 1968

Alleluia Becomes Us

Alleluia becomes April; it goes with a world on a Spring Fling, a world (to quote e. e. cummings) that is "mud-lucious and puddle-wonderful." After a February of flu and fatigue and a sometime melancholy March, it is possible almost to forget that "winter's not forever, even snow melts" (cummings, again). So *Alleluia* is the label on a big bottle of Spring Tonic that gets the juices of life moving again. Shake it well, world, gulp it down, and stretch out the aches of winter's lifeless interlude. Come alive! This is the *Alleluia* generation!

Alleluia becomes the Christian; it goes with the new life that is ours, thanks to the oneness we have with the Lord of life risen and renewed. What indeed can we say to the Lord for all that he has given to us? *Alleluia* is both the least and the best response from anyone who realizes that Easter is the essence of the Good News, the "supreme solemnity" in the words of the Liturgy Constitution of Vatican II.

Again we see the eternal wisdom of the Risen One who tells us, "In your prayers do not go babbling on like the heathens who imagine that the more they say the more likely they are to be heard" (Mt. 6:7). *Alleluia* is a prayer that gives us a minimum quantity with a maximum quality. And you can hardly find that kind of prayer anymore.

Alleluia becomes the religious; it goes with the faith, hope, and love that is ours who "follow Christ more freely and imitate him more nearly by the practice of the evangelical counsels" (*Perfectae Caritatis*, no. 1).

There is a sentence in the *Rule of St. Benedict* which I have often thought should be taken much more seriously and literally than it is accustomed to be taken. In a chapter called "At What Times *Alleluia* is to be Said," the statement is made, "From holy Easter until Pentecost without interruption let *Alleluia* be said . . ." That phrase "without interruption" sets the tone and the tempo for our Easter canticle that can well become our constant prayer – a sort of sequel to the Jesus Prayer of Eastern spirituality. And we may just discover that things go better with *Alleluia*.

But we are challenged by St. Augustine to do more than pray *Alleluia*. We are to BE *Alleluia*, from head to toe. Perhaps if we had been *Alleluia* in the past as often as we had said *Alleluia* (Remember that delightful antiphon at Sunday Lauds during the Easter Season, the one that consisted of nine *Alleluias* in a row? Nine of 'em!) we would have been better witnesses to the thumping joy of Easter. If we had more positively been *Alleluia* – a living "Praise God!" – then I wonder whether Nietzsche would ever have dared to ask, "If Christians wish us to believe in their Redeemer, why don't they look a little more redeemed?" If we had more consistently been *Alleluia*, a loud and clear call to all that our God is alive and loves us, then the world could never have imagined that God is dead. If we had been *Alleluia* from head to toe, we could have renewed the world's hope that the real meaning of the resurrection is simply this: "Never say die!"

So let's go: *Alleluia, alleluia, alleluia, alleluia, alleluia, alleluia, alleluia, alleluia, alleluia.* (Nine of 'em!)

Sisters Today, June, 1968

The Explosion of Pentecost

When you come to Collegeville on your summer sojourn, be sure to take a good, long look at the stained glass window which fronts the facade of St. John's Abbey Church. The artist, Bronislaw Bak, has tried in 10,000 square feet of glass and concrete to picture the Church's year of feasts and seasons with a kaleidoscope of living color. At the focal point of the facade you cannot possibly miss the cascade of red that falls gently but firmly to symbolize the celebration with which this summer and this jumping month of June begin — PENTECOST.

Pentecost is just such a burst of brightness. A person would have to be deaf and blind to miss the tremendous impact that this event has on our Christian existence. As the primal Pentecost is once again renewed in our midst, we are reminded that when the Holy Spirit of Jesus was unleashed, his calling cards were a strong, driving wind and tongues of fire. This is the Holy Spirit, and since his coming life has never been the same.

Let's try to see Pentecost not just as a celebration but as an explosion. Fifty days ago, on Easter Sunday, Christ our Lord lit a fuse when he walked out of a tomb into his new life of risen glory. That fuse has been burning slowly and steadily these fifty days. Fifty days of waiting. Fifty days of hope. Fifty days of countdown. And now the fuse is gone and the time is up. Pentecost is POW! The pent-up power of Christ's risen life, the pulsing power of Christ's undying love is suddenly released and splashed all over the world. And we'll never finish picking up the pieces.

We hear and read a lot these days about power: black power, white power, student power, yes, even flower power. Pentecost is all about power, too — God power, Christ power, the transforming power of the Spirit's immense love which has become the radical, revolutionary power of Christian love.

A poet like e. e. cummings tries to tell us about the power of love when he writes,

> . . . and being here imprisoned, tortured here
> love everywhere exploding maims and blinds
> (but surely does not forget, perish, sleep
> cannot be photographed, measured;
> disdains the trivial labelling of punctual brains . . .[1]

Pentecost is indeed Christ's love imprisoned, tortured, but now "everywhere exploding." It maims, for love leaves law crippled and man powerless to respond until he is given the very gift of love with which to return love for love. And what a full measure that is. It blinds, for love knows no distinction of color, creed, or culture: it loves friend and enemy alike. The power of the Spirit's love cannot be photographed or measured; it disdains the trivial labelling of punctual brains. For we can never ask Christ, "How much do you love me?" Pentecost proves that Christ loves us essentially, entirely, all, completely, through and through and every which way.

Pentecost is no afterthought of Easter or Ascension, a kind of encore to make us Christians happy that we really got our money's worth. Pentecost is rather the fulfillment of Christ's promise to his disciples that not many days hence they would be baptized in the Spirit. This baptism of the Spirit does not involve our notion of baptism as a trickling, dribbling, or sprinkling of water. This baptism of the Spirit is a real plunge, as bold and emphatic a dive as the season's first swimmer makes into a sky-blue lake. Like that plunge which is a mountain removed from toe-wetting and from which (once begun) there is no return, Pentecost should take our breath away. Pentecost is WOW!

It is important, I think, to note the reactions of that first Pentecost crowd if we are to recapture the Spirit of that day. St. Luke tells us they were astounded, amazed (Acts 2:7). And this is as it should have been. The Spirit has come to teach us the fundamental response to the Good News of Christ's death and rising. And that response is one of astonishment, amazement, wonder. This is the spontaneous, unrehearsed reaction of the lover, of the poet, of the young. And it should be the reaction of the Pentecost Christian. (Is there another kind?)

Pentecost is the celebration of God's grandeur in a world of wonder. The Spirit seeks to give us a sense of the sublime, for without that sense of wonder there can be no religion, no worship, no God. Rabbi Abraham Heschel says, "The surest way to suppress our ability to understand the meaning of God and the importance of worship is to take things for granted. Indifference to the sublime wonder of living is the root of sin."

In our indifferent age when so many play it cool, Pentecost deals out fire not ice cubes! In a crowd of Cool Hand Lukes, religious have been called to be blazing emblems of the Spirit's kingdom. And one sure sign that the Spirit has found in us not burnt-out embers but highly inflammable material is precisely

[1] e. e. cummings, *100 Selected Poems* (New York: Grove Press, Inc., 1959), 45.

our response of wonder. Religious renewal may very well begin with recapturing and strengthening our will to wonder. When is the last time any of us has said, "WOW!"? We can begin by reflecting on the words of a song which I heard some time ago: "Take care to wonder at the world through which you wander. Never hurry by an open door. For you live in a universe full of miracles galore!"

Pentecost is power. Pentecost is wonder. But best of all Pentecost is people! And that's where all of us come in. The first Pentecost is full of people, jam-packed with people, people from all over the place, a regular riot of pluralism. And this is the way it is going to continue to be if Pentecost is to be perennial. The Spirit is no longer hovering over us like the blue bird of happiness. It is not altogether safe for doves to be around these days, is it? *The Spirit is within us!* The Spirit has been poured into our hearts, St. Paul tells us. He exhorts us to "Be aglow with the Spirit."

Pentecost is the explosive challenge for us to *be* the Spirit in our new Pentecost, to *be* the power of the Spirit in a world which hasn't seen anything until it sees God-in-us go to work, to *be* the wonder that the Spirit has renewed us to be. Pentecost is the answer to a columnist in a recent *New Republic* who remarked, "Perhaps the chief effect of the organized church was to innoculate the great mass of Western mankind with such a mild dose of Christianity as to make them immune to the real thing." Pentecost invites us, urges us to plunge. Come on in—the fire is fine!

Sisters Today, June–July, 1973

Let's Go for a Walk

Let's go for a walk.

This invitation may become a national mandate before we finish the summer of '73. By the time another autumn arrives we may learn that the Standard Oil Company's slogan of "You expect more from Standard — and you get it!" may still be true — as long as you don't expect to get more gasoline.

But there is a new motto of the Standard people which offers us good expectations that the coming summer will be more than long and hot. The new motto says, "SLOW DOWN." I would like to offer that slogan as a most sensitive sign of the times — a sign of the good old summertime, that is.

Even without an energy crisis to prompt such excellent advice, it is time for all of us to slow down. (Incidentally, there is nothing new about a gas shortage situation because 'way back in the Book of Isaiah it is written, "Lebanon would not suffice for fuel" [40:16].) When we start to walk instead of run or ride, we have much more than just gasoline to save. We have ourselves to save.

I suspect, however, that it is going to be as difficult to convince some religious to slow down as it is to persuade today's highway jockeys that "Fifty is thrifty." A lot of religious I know and live with drive themselves the way Jehu drove his chariot: "he drives furiously" (2 Kgs 9:20). And if that isn't fast enough, there are always the pacesetters in every community who try to outdo Jehu by taking as their model of mobility General Sisera of whom it is said, "Sisera alighted from his chariot and fled away on foot" (Jgs 4:15). If you remember that story you will recall that poor old Sisera was only fleeing from one defeat right smack-dab into another one. So what's the rush?

Most of the time most of us are in a rush. We even put a stop watch on our head and stomach aches and demand not just relief but fast, fast, fast relief. "Hurry up!" is an all too common command. And to prove to ourselves that rushing, dashing, hurrying, and scurrying are really what life is all about we squeeze, push and hustle that life between one *dead*line and the next.

But we don't need more *dead*lines. We need more *life*-lines. We need to stop equating punctuality with sanctity just as we have to stop identifying cleanliness with godliness. We need to rediscover the sixty-second minute and the twenty-four hour day. We very much need to re-read that marvelous monologue that Charles Peguy has God speak about sleep:

> I don't like the man who doesn't sleep, says God.
> Sleep is the friend of man.
> Sleep is the friend of God.
> Sleep is perhaps the most beautiful thing I have created.
> And I myself rested on the seventh day . . .
> But they tell me that there are men
> Who work well and sleep badly.
> Who don't sleep. What a lack of confidence in me.
> It is almost more serious than if they worked badly and slept well.
> Than if they did not work but slept, because laziness
> Is not a greater sin than unrest . . .
> I am talking about those who work and don't sleep . . .
> They have the courage to work. They lack the courage to be idle.
> They have enough virtue to work. They haven't enough virtue to be idle.
> To stretch out. To rest. To sleep.[1]

By this time some nervous novice has surely collected a collage of scriptural texts that prove just how heretical are Peguy and I. Doesn't St. Paul say, "It is full time now for you to wake from sleep" (Rom 13:11)? Doesn't Paul say again, "Let us not sleep, as others do, but let us keep awake and be sober" (1 Thes. 5:6)?

O.K. So you run with Paul this time, but I'll go back to Peguy who has God say,

> Poor people, they don't know what is good.
> They look after their business very well during the day.
> But they haven't enough confidence in me to let me look after it during the night.
> As if I wasn't capable of looking after it during one night.[2]

If the coming summer does not provide the night time to sleep as well as the day time to stretch out on a beach or a lawn or a lawnchair and catch a little sun and slumber, then something has got to go. I would suggest letting go of our frantic-panic compulsions long enough to realize that no matter how fast we go we can only take one step at a time, do one thing well at a time and go in one direction at a time. So if at the end of August we still have three books to

---

[1] Charles Peguy, *Basic Verities* (Chicago: Henry Regnery Company, 1965), 137–139.

[2] *Ibid.*

read, a dozen letters to write, two projects to complete, and five more people to visit — bravo! We may have wasted time, but I'll bet we haven't wasted the summertime.

When we really decide to put that "Slow Down" slogan into practice, then we will have to decide to sleep more and worry less. And during the day we will become walkers instead of riders or runners. That invitation to take a walk will then become an invitation to delight and discovery and not a call to indulge in the curse of the walking class.

If we haven't taken a walk lately, we have been missing one of life's simple, tax-free, splendid joys. I don't mean a business walk from work to home or a saunter from supermarket to parking lot. I mean a lazy-day walk through a park or a woods or a meadow or along a lake or a railroad track or a stream. I mean a walk that lets us see wild flowers and listen to the songs of birds and feel the sun on our faces and smell the wild cherry blossoms. This is the kind of walk that has no destination or purpose except to arrive at a new wonder of God's wonderful world. This kind of walk gives us time to sit on a stump and examine a leaf and think about nothing at all except "the leaping greenly spirits of trees / and a blue true dream of sky" (e. e. cummings).

And if the Spirit moves us, we can think for a while how the Lord God in his goodness began his dealings with man when he walked in the garden in the cool of the day (Gen 3:8) and a little later promised, "I will walk among you, and I will be your God, and you shall be my people" (Lv 26:12).

But what am I doing here, sitting at this typewriter while a tiny wren whistles up a symphony in my little maple tree and a million diamonds sparkle on the Sagatagan?

Come on. Let's go for a walk.

Sisters Today, August–September, 1977

Rainbows Galore

When William Wordsworth wrote, "My heart leaps up when I behold, / a rainbow in the sky," he put into words and rhythm the reaction of everyone who has ever seen that bow of beauty in the heavens. That surely must have been Noah's reaction when he was singularly privileged to be the first person to witness the Lord's flamboyant logo after the deluge. He and his weary little crew of the ark and that great big cargo of animals must have leapt and danced and sung and shouted when they looked up and saw the flourish of Yahweh's signature on his new covenant splashed across the clearing sky.

There was no need to squint for the fine print at the bottom of that contract which the Lord God was making when he said, "I set my bow in the cloud, and it shall be a sign of the covenant between me and the earth" (Gen 9:13). The flood waters had scrubbed away the world's crust of sin, and the Creator was letting the original polish of his handiwork shine forth so we all could see that God really meant it when he said he made all things good, in fact, very good.

About half-way through the Bible when the prophet Ezekiel, that unique and most creative of all the Old Testament seers and singers of God's power and presence among his people, tried his poetic best to describe the ineffable glory of the Lord, he used a rainbow for one of his brilliant props: "Like the appearance of the bow that is in the cloud on the day of rain, so was the appearance of brightness round about" (Ez 1:28).

In the Scripture's grand finale, John upstages both Noah and Ezekiel and brings on not one but two rainbows. The first one he sees when he looks through heaven's open door and beholds "a throne . . . with one seated on the throne . . . and round the throne was a rainbow that looked like an emerald" (Rv 4:2-3). That is some backdrop — a glittering, sparkling, dazzling arc of green that proves the Irish have no monopoly on that graceful color. A little later John sees "another mighty angel coming down from heaven . . . with a rainbow over his head" (Rv 10:1). That is some halo, some angel!

Now we know where we can find both ends of the rainbow — at the beginning and at the end of God's gracious dealings with his people. And lest we lose our way there is also that prophetic view of the arc right in the middle of salvation history. In other words, the Lord has wrapped our world in a rainbow ribbon. So we should not be surprised whenever we see a rainbow.

And yet rainbows have always surprised and delighted me. They are so big and so beautiful and yet so delicate and subtle — like the Lord's action in our lives. I will never forget my best-timed rainbow. I saw it one early summer evening when I was on a train going to St. Louis for a summer session. We had passed through a heavy shower, and I was reading a Second Nocturn lesson from the breviary for the Sunday within the Octave of the Sacred Heart. Pope Pius XI was speaking of the Sacred Heart of Jesus as a sign of peace and love to all nations, and he compared Jesus' revelation of his heart to the sign of God's covenant of friendship which he the Lord had made manifest in the days of Noah by an arc appearing in the sky. When I read that I looked out the train window, and sure enough. — there was a rainbow! The Lord was right on schedule.

Nor will I have any trouble remembering the most spectacular rainbow I have ever seen. Not that I don't think every rainbow is a special spectacle of splendor. But this one was really extra-special. It was a *double*-rainbow! You don't hardly get those kind anymore. And once again the timing was perfect. That double rim of color popped out of the murky sky over Steubenville, Ohio, this past June about an hour before the Charismatic Conference for Priests was to begin.

That was the Lord's way of putting his own Good Housekeeping seal of approval on our gathering together in the Spirit. That was only the first of many powerful, concrete, specific and wonderful ways that the Lord had of gently but firmly showing and telling us again and again that he is not about to revoke his covenant of mercy and forgiveness and never-ending love. Come trouble, turmoil and temptation, come hell and high water, there is just no way the Lord is going to forget that he loves us even though we are very good sinners and very poor swimmers. By the time the Conference was over, there was no one who had sat beneath the Steubenville tent and touched the Steubenville rock who could not say what the elderly gentleman had said when a priest watching and listening to him pray remarked, "You must be very close to God" — "Yes," said the man, "he is very fond of me!"

I would like to thank and praise the Lord for all the rainbows he has brought into my life. The great majority of them have not been flung upon his big-sky canvas. They have been much closer than that, close enough to touch, so close, in fact, that a lot of times I overlook my day by day rainbows and prefer to color my clouds with Apocalyptic Purple, Grievance Grey, or Too-Busy Blur.

But when I have eyes to see I discover that my world is liberally sprinkled with rainbows. For instance, living in a community means living right in the midst of a rainbow. Thank God all my confreres are not colored the same shade of pink, yellow or green. They provide a veritable riot of color. Well, at least a riot . . . Teaching in a college and for a Lifelong Learning Program gives me more glimpses of rainbows among my students. Preaching and offering the Eucharist in a friendly, small-town parish every weekend lets me behold another segment of God's wrap-around ribbon. And of course there are my family and my friends who keep coloring my life with their love.

I hope all of us have rainbows to remember and rainbows still to behold. We cannot let ourselves believe or let anyone tell us that the world is a dark, dingy, and drab old place covered over with a thick coat of Institutional Tan and decorated with cobwebs and peeling plaster. Life is a kaleidoscope of color which the Creator has swirled around the world. And all he ever uses to mix those magnificent shades are light and water.

Come to think of it, we also have that same mixture of light and water right in our own two eyes! So we should not be surprised when we behold rainbows in everything and everyone we see.

Sisters Today, November, 1978

Eternal Work

"Eternal rest grant unto them, O Lord. And let perpetual light shine upon them. May they rest in peace." How often we have prayed those words at wakes and funerals and during this month that makes us mindful of the dead. Because it is such a common prayer there is a good chance that we do not really hear what we say when those words roll off our lips. I listened closely to them recently and wondered whether we really mean what we say when we pray, "Eternal rest grant unto them, O Lord. And let perpetual light shine upon them. May they rest in peace."

First of all, if it is eternal rest we are to be granted, I hope the Lord will at least turn out the perpetual light once in a while! I find it hard to get any rest or sleep when a bulb is blazing in my eyes. I rest best at night in a dark room. When the lights are out, I am out. So if there is to be any rest in peace, please do not let the light be perpetual.

But that brings me to the other difficulty I have with this petition — the eternal rest. I appreciate the honorable monastic tradition of the mid-day siesta and even manage to take a nap once or twice a month. I enjoy and welcome a good night's sleep. I positively relish a long, leisurely weekend when the students go home and the Collegeville campus sighs and settles down and it is quiet enough to hear the leaves fall off my maple tree. And I thoroughly rejoice over the rest and relaxation that a summer or winter vacation provides.

But *eternal rest?!* No thank you. If this is all we have to look forward to — eternal rest — then I think life after death is going to be a real drag. I cannot imagine, I do not even want to imagine what an eternal rest would be like. What a dull, dreary place heaven will be if it is peopled by Rip Van Winkle types. I think we will get very tired of always resting.

That is the way it is with a lot of people. They get tired of resting. A few years ago, for instance, my mother was hospitalized for an illness, and upon her release she completed her recuperation in a rest home. Did she like it? No way! She did not appreciate or enjoy or even tolerate all the rest that others wanted her to take. So after she had rested a few weeks and had gotten to know her way around the place and what the nurses' schedule was, she called up her nephew one day, told him she was being released that evening and that he should come and get her at six o'clock that night. (That was the time when the nurses and residents were eating supper.) When her nephew arrived, my mother had her suitcase packed, she walked out the front door without bothering to check out, and went home. When the rest home called my father a little while later to tell him that his wife was missing from her room, she was in the kitchen working on a stack of accumulated dirty dishes. She had had enough of that silly rest. Now it was time for her to get back to work. And she has been working ever since.

When my father fell and broke his leg last year he, too, had to go to a rest home for seven weeks of therapy and recuperation. Was he happy resting? Not at all. It was the first time in a long time that I had seen my Dad cry because he was so depressed. But finally he was released—this time through proper procedures and channels. The next time I visited him at home, was he sitting in an armchair resting? No. He was out in the garage fixing the arm of a lawnchair that had been broken while he was away resting. And he showed me all the black walnuts he had been shucking for the squirrels that week. He was just so happy to be able to work again.

So if the Lord thinks he is going to make a lot of people eternally ecstatic by granting us eternal rest (with perpetual light shining upon us, too), he is in for a disappointing surprise. If heaven is just a glorified rest home where our added mobility and agility enable us to do better "wheelies" with our wheelchairs, God help us! Even sipping tall, frosty root beers and singing Glory songs day in and day out (remember, no nights!) will get to be mighty monotonous and terribly tedious. What do you suppose a daily root beer tastes like after you have gulped a few hundred thousand of them?

The Lord is smart enough and sensitive enough, however, to have already solved this problem of eternal rest and perpetual light. Jesus tells us that our God and his God is "not the God of the dead"—or even the God of the sleeping or the God of those who are resting—"but he is the God of the living. All are alive for him" (Lk 20:38).

And to show us that he is the Son of his Father, Jesus could hardly stay resting for three whole days after his life of strenuous and intensive work. He was too full of life to want or need eternal rest. His resurrection is a rising from sleep, not a going back to bed again.

And that is the way it will be with us. St. Paul assures us as he assured his Thessalonian friends that when the dead and the living hear "the sound of the trumpet of God" and wake up and rise up to "meet the Lord," "we shall always be with the Lord" (1 Thes 4:17). Being with the Lord is going to keep us eternally awake and busy just trying to catch up with Jesus as he continues his teaching and preaching, his loving and healing work in the world.

The prayer, then, that the Lord will hear and answer goes something like this: "Eternal work grant unto us, O Lord. And may we work in peace."

When We Dead Awaken

I

My bones lie awake
inside my body
awaiting some touch.
Delicate, small
they do not shrink
from your coming.

In the long night
I am dreaming;
someone is calling my name
in a forgotten language.
My hands answer.
There is no sound.

Somewhere there is a place I have never
entered. My body knows it.
A long dead forgotten
memory.

"When?", I hear myself pleading.
"When" wraps itself around my voice
and unending echo;
and the night comes steadily
on.

"When we dead awaken"
throbs in my hands
and is gone.
"When we dead awaken."
My body blooms into song.

II

When we dead awaken
there will be small memory
of our pastness. All that is morning
will have been seen by us
in the dark moment near dawn.
There will be vast silence
a near star
and only

a little wind.

When we dead awaken
pulses will flutter like roses
on their fine stems. The words
of an ancient language
will begin to speak themselves
inside of us. When our lovers
come to mourn our lost fecundity
they will lie marveling
as they re-awake
vivid as grass
beside us.

All this is said to remember.

The memories of silence
wearing away at the past
like a canyon. The chasms
are there
never forget it. Even when the waters
have forgotten themselves
some woman thirsting
knows how
            they were there.

Sister Galen Martini, O.S.B.
Sisters Today, August–September, 1976

The title, "When We Dead Awaken," is taken from an Ibsen play about women coming into their personhood. These two poems were read at the Women in Ministry Conference, held at the College of St. Benedict, St. Joseph, Minnesota, July 9–10, 1976.

PART TEN

SISTERS TODAY AND TOMORROW:

Onward to 2029!

A collection of essays covering fifty years of the past is an unlikely place for dreaming about the future. And yet there is the insistence that the past is also prologue. This volume, then, is prologue to a future that is certain to be as unexpected and full of surprises as Volume 50 would be for the ones who wrote and read the original issue half a century ago.

But before the future can begin we must continually deal with today. That is what a leader of Sisters and a bishop do in their interviews in this section. Only one writer could be found who was brave or foolish enough to look that far ahead at "The Church in the 1990's." When that year comes there will still be women religious around to see how accurate his prognosis has been.

These same Sisters hopefully will be continuing "to explore the role of the religious woman in the Church" of their time. What they discover then will surely prove that the Lord has hidden more than one pearl of great price in the fields of his wonder-world. Those who choose to share their discoveries with the readers of *Sisters Today* will find an audience unsurpassed in affection and attention.

May future editors, authors, and readers find the centennial year of 2029 as Spirit-filled as 1929 and 1979 have been.

Sisters Today, August-September, 1978

A Message for Sisters Today

Interview with Sister Elizabeth Carroll, R.S.M.

Sister Elizabeth Carroll, R.S.M., is here interviewed by Sister Mary Anthony Wagner, O.S.B., associate editor, and Sister Merle Nolde, O.S.B., associate professor of interdisciplinary studies at the College of St. Benedict, St. Joseph, Minnesota. Sister Elizabeth Carroll is the former provincial of the Pittsburgh Sisters of Mercy and past president of the Leadership Conference of Women Religious (LCWR). She is presently on the staff of the Center of Concern in Washington, D.C.

Sister Mary Anthony: Sister Elizabeth Carroll, I want to ask you some questions about what message you would have for Sisters today. Later, too, I would like to ask you about the role of women generally in the Church today.

Sister Elizabeth: Sisters in the Church, especially in the United States, but by no means limited to the United States, have been on a marvelous journey; there has been an awakening of consciousness among them as to the best way in which they can live the gospel. They have taken courageous steps in trying to make that gospel living a reality for themselves. Much, however, of what we have done has been in terms of the recognition of our own personhood. In this recognition of personhood there is always a trap. That trap is that instead of becoming persons we become rather individuals who might become self-centered and rather comfortable with the kind of life we have carved out for ourselves.

We are in a very interesting, challenging, and sort of scary period. I would even say, as I said to our own Sisters, that we are in the middle of a revolution. If we stop where we are now, we could become simply one more group content in seeking its own self-betterment. But if we really take seriously the kinds of skills we have learned, the talents we have uncovered and assiduously apply them to the gospel message of Jesus Christ, we would have to look outward and transfer those kinds of perceptions which we have gained for ourselves into every work that we are doing.

Sister Mary Anthony: You mention skills we have gained. Could you elaborate a little on ways which have brought us to where we are now?

THE SISTER FORMATION MOVEMENT

Sister Elizabeth: I give high priority to the Sister Formation Movement, to the fact that it was recognized by leaders of religious communities in the fifties that American Sisters could not continue to do the kinds of work they were being asked to do without education.

Sister Mary Anthony: Especially theological formation?

Sister Elizabeth: Yes, especially theological formation. When I look back at the early days of Sister Formation I see that our goals were impossible but glorious. The intent was to have Sisters become theologically well prepared, to have a grounding in philosophy and in all the arts and behavioral sciences as well as science, and to enable them to have an integration of knowledge which was theologically centered.

Sister Mary Anthony: I remember some of those thorough programs with emphasis upon all the ways of knowing in order to develop one into the full woman, the total person, and the alive religious. This began almost immediately with new members in the communities, too, did it not?

Sister Elizabeth: As I try to analyze it, I think a couple of things happened. One was that we had no perception of how contrary were the very goals we had set for religious formation to the way we were living religious life. The result was that explosion which, in our case, coincided with the explosion in the general culture. The only way I can ever say it to myself is that the world stopped revolving for a few days and then started again, because there developed such a gap between our previous understanding and the growing self-conscious understanding of the young people at that time.

I look back on that as a period of real grace as far as the human race is concerned. Young people have many things to teach us which we haven't quite learned. At the same time, relative to the goals of Sister Formation it was almost disastrous because it led many of our young people out of our communities and aroused fears in many other people. Just the same, for those who persevered in religious life and who continued with the kinds of academic preparation that had been envisaged, it was certainly a time of great grace.

This is typical of movements in the world. They never turn out quite the way the people who designed them think they will. But all is not lost. Unfortunately, Sister Formation at the time gave much attention to professional work; for some whose view of a learned person was narrow, becoming certified took priority. I have seen judgments on Sister Formation simply in those terms, which is a real disservice to the Sister Formation Movement.

Sister Mary Anthony: I am glad to hear you say it coincided with a kind of evolution in society itself. When you said revolution before, I was tempted to ask if it was not more of an evolution.

THE NEED TO DIALOGUE

Sister Elizabeth: Well, revolution comes in our way of life. It is not just in the fact that we are freer in our relations with one another, but our whole attitude toward the Church has changed decisively. Right now we are in the middle of the movement. Whereas previously we were totally controlled by the hierarchy, now there is more and more of a desire to work with the hierarchy. We are making our own decisions in conscience about where our efforts belong and we are trying to dialogue with the hierarchy about that. Hopefully we will be able, all of us, to go in the same direction. But I feel there is much potential for disappointment on the side of the hierarchy and the side of religious if we neglect to dialogue.

Sister Mary Anthony: You mentioned several times that the goals of Sister Formation were idealistic but nevertheless good goals because they set us in a right direction, even if we never achieved them. Can you recall any one in particular?

Sister Elizabeth: We can cite the theological goal which put Sisters in the path of biblical knowledge comparable, of course, to the whole Church's growth in scriptural studies. The fact that we have, and every day are developing a better biblical perspective means that the whole concept of Church and the development of the Church are strengthened. All the myths are being re-examined.

I am sure that when theological education was set as a goal for our Sisters, we thought it would make them more docile, more holy, more conformed to what our life was at that time. What we learned was that it gave us a chance to stand back somewhat and say, "This really isn't the holy way of life that we think it is. It is an institutionalized life but it may not be a deeply spiritual life." All that was coming at a time when people who had this kind of vision seemed to be rebelling against the system. Psychologically we had not provided adequately for that. We expected more of human beings than they are able to do all at once.

Sister Mary Anthony: That predated Vatican II, which is amazing because the thrust Vatican II gave to collegiality and the dignity of the human individual was one that spurred on religious renewal in our own communities. But Sister Formation was really previous to that.

Sister Elizabeth: Sister Formation put us in a position to really listen to what was happening at the Vatican Council. We hardly knew where we were until we were given the directive to re-examine our whole lives in chapters. Then all this creativity began to explode. In some congregations it was somewhat fairly easily channeled. Other communities are still struggling with how much their communities are to be affected. My position, as I said at the beginning, is thinking of those who had acted rather readily and had integrated responsibility, individuality and collegiality into their style of life, and thus becoming quite free. Now the question is whether we are going to be free for ourselves or free for other people.

Sister Mary Anthony: Do you want to elaborate on that a little?

BEAUTIFUL AND BOURGEOIS

Sister Elizabeth: What I see happening with myself and with many other people is that we have become very beautiful people. Everywhere I go I am just amazed at the beauty of religious. We have become self-determining but at the same time conscious of being members of communities. We have tried to integrate these two factors. We have become more deeply spiritual in the sense that we are trying to pray with greater integrity, greater inclusion of our whole self in our prayer. In many instances we have not yet succeeded in good community prayer but if we persevere in good personal prayer, that will come.

However, I also see that we have become pretty bourgeois people. Our old concept of order and cleanliness does not have such a high priority but it is still a part of us. It makes us like nice things, want to live in a certain style, and have nice clothes. So, we have very much the trappings of a middle class family; that scares me.

Sister Mary Anthony: I was shocked into the realization of that the other night when one of our Sisters was talking about food and diet. She said we do not live low class. We live middle class and on some feast days and celebrations we live rather high class. Our sensitivity to gospel living has much to shell off yet.

Sister Elizabeth: I think so. More and more our culture is changing tremendously. The gap between the affluent and the poor is so enormous. There is no longer that hard working, frugal ideal for the large majority of our population. Because Catholics have become upwardly mobile, we religious have tended to become upwardly mobile with them. For us to really work with the poor, which many of us were established to do, would mean cutting across the whole Catholic population except for the Chicanos, and going down and working with the blacks and the very poor whites who may or may not be Catholic. However, that is where very few of us are willing to venture.

I am struggling with myself right now because when I go back to Pittsburgh I really do not want to live at the motherhouse. But when I look around, though none of our houses is affluent, yet they are very nice. We have only one community where our Sisters are living with the blacks; I have to ask myself if I could do that, which would mean the adoption of a totally different culture. I wonder whether we really know enough about our whole social, political, economic, and cultural era in order to make choices like this. Without even thinking about it, we are swept into the life styles, attitudes, and goals of the affluent.

Sister Merle: Are you saying that we experience development in terms of understanding change in our communities without being inclined to work for that change for others? Do you see that as a kind of selfishness or as an inability to perceive that we are identified with middle class? Or is it that we do not perceive acting politically for others? Is that a skill that we have — to act politically for others?

SHARING OUR SKILLS

Sister Elizabeth: I think it is that kind of concern that needs to be pursued, more than the life style. This is an extremely important point. We have found ways through working together of developing the person and of analyzing how we have come to our own inner freedom and, to some extent, to our freedom to influence our environment. We ought to be passing this skill on to others. We sometimes think in grandiose terms like having religious people go into political office. However, we ought also think of taking positions in which we can influence the manner in which decisions are made.

Women religious particularly, because of the whole women's movement which we are witnessing today, are finding that bonding with other women is the vantage point that has opened up to us. So many married women who are raising or have raised families are not at all aware of the quality of community growth which we have taken for granted. To help them form groups to reflect on scriptures, to help them develop psychological freedom, or to enable them to become more totally human could be an enormous contribution to the basic unity of society, the family. This could be much more helpful than various action-oriented programs in our parishes.

Sister Mary Anthony: One of our religious coordinators told me recently that before she could prepare her volunteer religion teachers who would be teaching groups in the parish, she conducted a workshop with these women to build up in them some sense of self-identity and self worth. Their response was beautiful and their teaching witnessed to the joy of their liberation.

Sister Elizabeth: I met a woman in Patterson, New Jersey, whose husband had become a deacon. The diocese had allowed wives to participate in the course at the same time the deacons were being taught. What she learned was so revelatory and exciting to her; it awakened her consciousness as a woman. For her husband it awakened a consciousness for clericalism. As a result their marriage was in a very sad state and it may not have survived. But it did awaken in her a whole sense of self-identification.

Sister Mary Anthony: Ordinarily the goal of that program is to help both parties grow.

Sister Elizabeth: This is right, but in this particular case, the two had not realized the psychological problems of their marriage. The man involved had really wanted to be a priest; ordination to the permanent deaconate was more important to him than his marriage vows.

THE WOMEN'S MOVEMENT

To get back to your question, Sister Merle, this is what I meant by transferring outwards what we have gained: an understanding of ourselves, the ability to deal with scripture, the ability to recognize our own truth and to act out of it, the willingness to confront others, the assertiveness to be able to place our opinion before others, the ability to work in groups, the possibility of not dominating others and trying not to be oppressive to them. All this could be a tremendous contribution to the women's movement.

Sisters are in a really important position, not only in regard to women who are around them but to the whole women's movement. There is a great possibility of the women's movement becoming totally self-propelled, self-centered and ending up in a movement of hatred of men. A lot of men brought that on themselves. So much violence is practiced toward women. To understand that and help women live through the experience of violence and not become violent themselves is an extremely important role for Sisters.

Very large numbers of young women — about twenty percent at Michigan State University — are declaring themselves lesbian. It is not at all that they are naturally lesbian, but that they are so angry at men that that is their only protection. Unless there are counter-influences to that kind of thing, we could be coming into a very destructive age of personal relationships.

Sister Mary Anthony: I wonder how we could grow in more consciousness of the kinds of elements in society that you are talking about. Even as you speak about battered women, I wonder how can we become more knowledgeable about that information.

Sister Elizabeth: I laugh when I think of my own community. We have a tradition, from Catherine McCauley's time, of establishing houses for women who are in danger from men. We always called these "mercy houses," and the mercy houses we had in this country turned out to be pretty dark and dismal places, where women came at the age of seventy and then lived out their years there. They were supposed to be for working girls; but in many of them, the working girls lived on and on and so they lost the aspect of serving youth. It seems that at every chapter we talk about opening a mercy house, but it seems like we never get beyond the vision of starting a mercy house.

Recently I saw a television program about lay women of all races and religions, civic and community leaders, who opened a storefront house for women who needed time away from home. This happened sixteen years ago and now, after sixteen years, this has developed into a marvelous institution; they have several homes for battered women who need time away from home.

All this time we were sitting back and debating whether we should open a mercy house. All we needed to do was go out and join them. There was no need to think about money, bricks and mortar.

SISTERS AND LAY GROUPS

We need to be much more mindful of what is going on and of how our services can fit in. I think of that in terms of our own retired Sisters. One of my hopes which could revolutionize us would be if every Sister could be associated with some lay group; so much richness would be brought back to us. Our problems, our struggles in life would become more real, and our prayer life would become more real.

Sister Mary Anthony: Some of our Sisters used to volunteer for baby-sitting for poor families who could not afford a baby sitter, especially when the husband and wife needed some time to be alone together to enjoy a bit of leisure. Those Sisters came back and shared with us the really heavy burdens which are borne by poor families. We also discover this while working with students. We need to be more in touch with them. It would be great if every religious woman could be in touch with someone. It might be the lay woman who works in the kitchen with her or in some office, or whatever.

Sister Elizabeth: This was brought home to me some weeks ago. We were putting on a program for the LCWR at Estes Park. It was a dry run of the program we planned to do in August for two conventions. A Sister from Colombia was telling me about a Brazilian Benedictine community, a contemplative community. She herself was a very well educated woman; in the beginning of the religious renewal she asked this community to make the necessary changes to allow lay persons into the cloister. They then began to admit lay people into the chapel, into the parlors, and the dining room. Speaking with the laity strengthened the Sisters in their prayer life. The lay people were attracted to the elderly Sisters; and everyone grew from this experience.

Sister Mary Anthony: The Franciscan Sisters in Rochester, Minnesota, have a large motherhouse, as all of us have after the large numbers of entrants decreased. They now call it a Christian Center in which one of the floors is occupied by their retired Sisters. They sponsor institutes and workshops that meet at the Center; these people eat with the retired Sisters in the dining room. It is beautiful. The retired Sisters are in touch with the concerns of these groups, and at the same time these groups are in touch with these wonderful, calm, prayerful women.

And this is not far out of our reach. We do not have to run for Congress in order to be in touch with people; not that we belittle this for someone who can be effective in political matters.

Sister Elizabeth: When the bishops say they cannot support the ERA because of the possible effect that it might have on families, I think their analysis is not deep enough, but they are grasping at a symptom. I think the ERA movement is a symptom. It is not destroying family life at all. The bishops are not analyzing deeply enough the forces' destroying family life. They ought to take a stand against them.

Sister Mary Anthony: I had a male student in class the other day who said the ERA is not just a women's movement. He is supporting it for the liberation of men. I also had a student talk to me who is doing a paper on the aging for a medical ethics course. He worked at St. Stephen's Church in Minneapolis during January. That parish has within its boundaries homes for battered women and for the aging. The student was so excited about how he could work with these people and help them without taking them out of their social milieu.

Sister Elizabeth: You could revive a parish by getting people interested in one another in this way.

A FINAL COMMENT

Sister Mary Anthony: Sister, do you have any final comment for us? I am very happy about the areas we have discussed, and I believe there is a good message for us, a very practical one. We need to just step out the back door.

Sister Elizabeth: That is a very good way to put it. Just step out and look around. I think we need to forget some of our categories: such as always having to be the director, always having to develop the institutions, and always having to formulate the course. Rather, it is a matter of just being a good neighbor.

Sister Mary Anthony: We recently received an article from a Sister of Mercy in Rhode Island. She speaks about how their community has opened one of their local houses to lay persons by inviting them to live with them. It was a base for a charismatic community prayer group. There was some tension about whether this might destroy allegiance to their own community. The author tells how considerate their superiors were in allowing this to develop and discovered that for them religious community indeed remained a priority, but at the same time there was a significant kind of mutual learning and growth for them with the laity.

Sister Elizabeth, thank you for such a practical, challenging message.

Sisters Today, February, 1979

The Church Today

Interview with Bishop Thomas J. Gumbleton

The Most Reverend Thomas J. Gumbleton is one of the four auxiliary bishops of the Archdiocese of Detroit. Sometimes referred to as "Detroit's maverick pacifist bishop" and "the man who jabs at the collective conscience of America's Catholic bishops," Bishop Gumbleton was born on Detroit's west side in 1930, the sixth of nine Gumbleton children. After his ordination in 1956 he was sent to Rome for three years of study which earned him a doctorate in canon law. He was ordained a bishop in 1968. Sister Mary Anthony Wagner, O.S.B., interviewed the Bishop during his visit to St. John's Abbey and University.

Sister Mary Anthony: As a bishop of the Church, you have your finger upon the pulse of the Church in a different way than the laity or teachers in the Church do. At the beginning of this interview I would like to have you consider the huge question of where you think the Church is at today.

A STATE OF FERMENT AND FLUX

Bishop Gumbleton: My impression is that the Church is still very much in a state of ferment and flux, a period of real searching. It still needs to find a firm direction for itself.

I say that with a little bit of surprise on my part because I feel that at Vatican Council II a new direction was set, and it appeared that everything was going to move along very smoothly. But I am more and more convinced that is not the case yet. There is a definite direction for the Church that flows out of Vatican II, but even now with over thirteen years elapsed since the

Council we have hardly begun to put into practice the directions that the Council gave us. There is still much ferment and change, and we have to continue to search for the best ways to implement what the Vatican Council talked about. In that sense there is much growth that has yet to take place within the Church with every group — clergy, laity, religious.

All of us are finding that we still have to undergo a great deal of *personal* change and that the Church *as a whole* must undergo more change before we finally come to the point where we can say that the Church is renewed in the spirit of Vatican II. By the time that happens it will be time for Vatican III! We will have settled into some patterns again that will have become somewhat outdated, just as many things were outdated by the time Vatican II was called by Pope John.

Sister Mary Anthony: Do you think it is natural for this growth process to take a rather long time? There seems to be a beginning readiness present in the people, a readiness also in the administrative implementation.

Bishop Gumbleton: Actually, this is a short time. We ought not to be surprised. The surprise only comes because we expect too much too quickly. But when one is trying to bring about a profound change that includes a conversion within a community that is made up of 700,000,000 people, it is not going to happen very readily. For that kind of new spirit to penetrate the whole Church must necessarily take a long time. It takes quite a while for an *individual* to undergo the sort of radical change that I think the Council is calling the Church to.

I see all of this in different ways, for example, in religious life. We really have not come through the changes that were called for there, in a radical redirecting of religious life. In fact, I feel that there is still a great deal of tension. I sense that many are still trying to hang on to old forms which, I really believe, are not suitable.

Sister Mary Anthony: By old forms, do you mean structures?

Bishop Gumbleton: Yes. The forms of formation, for example. I really feel that some of the formation patterns that were current until very recently in most religious communities and seminaries were hurtful in many ways. They were sometimes even dehumanizing. Part of this flows directly out of canon law. If you have a canon law which treats, in this instance, women religious in the same category as children, then obviously they are not being allowed to come to the fullness of maturity to which they are called. To me, that is dehumanizing and very hurtful. Not only were the laws of the Church restrictive but also the patterns of formation.

Sister Mary Anthony: Made to conform to *one* pattern?

Bishop Gumbleton: Yes, no one was allowed to be a fully independent person. No one could exercise his or her full personhood in the sense of its uniqueness and its full development. We all had to be very much the same; the patterns of formation nailed it down very tightly. We re-enforced the personality patterns of those who were somewhat passive, I suppose, and somewhat dependent through our formation; that was very hurtful.

EQUAL IN FREEDOM AND DIGNITY

Because Vatican II emphasized that every person within the Church is equal in freedom and in dignity through baptism, it has been emphasized that patterns for formation in religious life enhance the possibilities for persons to come to a full maturity, so that they can really exercise their equality and dignity. No adult in the Church should be thought of or treated as a child under the benevolent or kind paternalism of a bishop. That is just ruled out by Vatican II.

Yet I do not see that it has really been ruled out by what is happening within religious life. There still has to be more change in that regard. There is still a tension. There are some who want to go back to their old patterns because to them there was something attractive about them. They did create the possibility of what could be called good order in the Church. But it stifled genuine life, initiative, and the real gifts of many people.

THE CONCERN FOR COMPENSATION

Even though religious communities have undergone a great deal of change, they still have not developed a way in which persons in the Church who want to live most radically a life of evangelical simplicity or poverty can really do it. For instance, the concern religious have for compensation is distorting their possibilities of being genuinely poor and living a life of deep simplicity. There is the whole concern about security for old age. We ought to have more of a willingness to risk being without anything when we get old, just as the poorest people among us have to risk, not by choice but by force of circumstances.

Sister Mary Anthony: Are you saying that religious men and women in their efforts to become maturely responsible for their development and their life styles, have mimicked, as it were, secular patterns, i.e., with emphasis on their own personal worth, on a salary, on security for old age?

Bishop Gumbleton: This is precisely what I am getting at. Religious life ought to be very clearly and radically different from secular life. But this is not to say that people engaged in ministry within religious life ought not be professionally trained. I suppose that is the cause of the dilemma and the difficulty; e.g., to be good teachers they have to be well trained. It is not enough just to have good will and the zeal to do a good thing. Once they think about professional preparation, some of the other things go along with it; we seem unable to lay them aside or disregard them.

I hear religious talking about the need to be compensated in the same manner as any professional in their field is compensated. I hear this also among priests. I know priests who feel that since they are professional persons and have had years of education, their salary level ought to say that publicly. I really find that a difficult thing. I also find that there are untold numbers of people who are willing to break out of that pattern, but because of the institutionalized religious life to which they belong, they cannot do it as individuals. Sometimes the communities are not quite willing to risk selling everything and giving it all to the poor to follow Jesus.

Sister Mary Anthony: I look at my own community of some 700 members. Several hundred are near onto old age and need to be cared for. Then I look at our handful of new members and believe that there must be some creative way of caring for the people who have lived under the former way.

A RESPONSIBILITY OF THE WHOLE CHURCH

Bishop Gumbleton: That is true, and I would not want to disregard that problem. I personally find it sad that we have these large numbers of older religious men and women, and also priests in our dioceses, who throughout their lives have been formed to expect always to be secure, financially and materially. At this point in their lives to expect them suddenly to be converted to an entirely different approach to poverty and simplicity of life would be expecting more than we can demand or ask of them. So something has to be done for them.

But I see this as a misdirection in the Church. I do not see that this responsibility for the older members of your community, or any religious community, should be solely your responsibility or the responsibility of those newer members who come in now. To me, that ought to be the responsibility of the whole Church.

Sister Mary Anthony: Our diocese has attempted to realize that. I recall that when I first started teaching I taught for $35 a month.

Bishop Gumbleton: The Church accepted that, and in compensation said, "Well, don't worry because you will always have someone to provide for you." Now suddenly when there are only a few to provide, then everybody else walks away from it. That is a terrible kind of injustice in the Church which the episcopal leadership of the Church is not facing.

How can people who come into religious life now be free to enter into the kind of gospel living they are more clearly called to when they have this other burden thrust upon them? I am very much aware that something has to be done to provide for those older members without expecting them somehow to be able, at this point in their lives, to redirect all their thinking on the meaning of poverty. When they entered they were formed in a notion of poverty that meant that, although they did not own anything and had to ask permission to use things, yet what they always had was security. Theirs was really a vow of security! That may sound like a terrible adjustment to make, but it is true. People did live simply, but it was not the kind of poverty that Jesus lived in the gospels. Yet that is what we are supposed to be trying to do in religious life.

THE INSECURITY AND RISK OF POVERTY

I have found large numbers of people, individuals in different parts of this country and in different religious communities and some who are not in religious communities right now, who are dedicated to and want to live that simplicity of life and that insecurity which goes with being poor. They are willing to risk everything and not know where they will be twenty-five or thirty years later when they begin to get old. They simply feel that they can leave that in God's providence. This is what it means to give up everything and follow Jesus. Religious communities still have to bring about some changes institutionally which would allow those who want to do that to be part of the community and yet have the freedom to be honestly and genuinely poor.

I see other changes as continuing to be necessary in religious communities. One is the freedom for some to involve themselves in various kinds of ministries that truly fit the needs of the Church today. Many religious communities were established at a time when the needs of the Church were different. It ought to be obvious that fifty, seventy-five, or one hundred years ago, the needs of the Church and of the community which the Church was serving were quite different from what they are today. There is a need for those who come together in a vowed form of life within the Church to do so with the anticipation and expectation that they may move out into directions that are very, very different than they were when they started as a religious community. This might require different changes in life styles, in understanding what the vow of obedience means, or again the vow of poverty.

CELIBACY — FREE TO BE TOTALLY MOBILE

This attitude enhances the vow of celibacy, because one of the things celibacy ought to do for us is free us to be totally mobile and able to respond to whatever need there is at any point. Because celibates do not have responsibilities for stability of community life required in marriage, they can do this. Yet, to a large extent our vow of celibacy has not freed us the way it ought to; this is because the forms of religious life were previously different.

The vow of celibacy merely enabled us to live in some sort of community; but most often it was a community more in form than in fact. Community members did things together at certain times, we lived under the same roof. I do not believe there was often the profound kind of personal interaction that is required for genuine community life. That is why I do not think it is possible to have communities of 500 or 1000 people.

Maybe the Benedictine style is really the style that ought to be followed: every small group is autonomous and becomes a community unto itself; but there is a larger relationship with other communities and a common spirit permeates all those who want to follow this style. One cannot have 1000 people in one pattern and expect that somehow they are going to be in community. They are *not*, because community has to be something much deeper and richer than can happen among 1000 people who hardly ever see each other at any point in their lives, especially after they are out of formation and go out into different directions.

LETTING COMMUNITY BE CREATED

Sister Mary Anthony: I think among women religious there has really been a concerted effort to let the interpersonal interactions create community, rather than expect community to be somehow organized.

Bishop Gumbleton: Here is where it seems not enough change has occurred. Even though many religious communities of women have tried to do that, at the same time they have tried to maintain the old structure for the whole community which somehow kept them as one community of anywhere from 400 to 1500 people. Instead they ought to have allowed a variety of things to happen. Small communities ought to be allowed to grow up and maintain only a very tenuous connection with each other based on a common spirit of, say, Dominican life, or Franciscan life, or Benedictine life.

As I see it, most religious communities, even if they tried to institute changes so that within the smaller communities there could be this personal interaction, yet they still attempt to do that while keeping the other form so that they are all part of one large congregation which makes expectations and demands upon them. I really think that the smaller community is necessary in order to grow into what they are called to do.

THE COMMUNITY OF THE PARISH

Sister Mary Anthony: This is perhaps true also of parishes in which we could likewise value a more intense kind of community.

Bishop Gumbleton: This is very true in parishes. More development in parishes is taking place in other parts of the world than in the United States. In some parts of the world a great deal of effort is put on what is called the "base community," the basic community. This is largely a Latin American development where within large parishes tiny cells or communities are initiated and given a sort of stimulus for growth in an intense kind of life which is possible when twenty, thirty or forty families come to know each other quite well so they can interact and share.

This is certainly much more effective than in a Church which has parishes of 1500, 2000 or 4000 families, which is common in many of our large cities. There cannot be much interaction and genuine sharing of Christian life within such a parish if one were to emphasize the reality of community. Having these very small "base" communities linked together in a parish, one could in turn have the parishes open to one another in the diocese. That is the way, it seems to me, the renewal of the Church has to go. We have hardly begun anything like that in the parishes of the United States. But it is something we must get into very soon if we want to implement and concretize the ideas that flow out of Vatican II. Those efforts put so much emphasis on the Church being a community of people rather than its being a highly structured hierarchical institution.

THE BURDEN OF CORPORATE WORKS

Sister Mary Anthony: As you talk, I can see more clearly why you are saying that it is going to take time for us to become all that Vatican II had envisioned. Relative to the apostolates, we are still burdened with the corporate works which we conduct as a community. It seems that we must gradually work through those commitments to find out if they can be dissolved or taken care of by lay people so that our membership could become freer to do new works.

Bishop Gumbleton: Yes, it is hard to let go of those. We really get attached in spite of the fact that we claim to be poor and to be living in the freedom that poverty brings. We are attached to our institutions and our corporate commitments; it is hard to make that break.

THE CHURCH AS SERVANT

A somewhat different but related area is the thrust that Vatican II gave to the Church to become more deeply involved in the world and its problems — to become a servant to the poor and the oppressed. The first sentence of the Council document on "The Church in the Modern World" clearly identifies the Church's joys, hopes and anxieties with those joys, hopes and anxieties of people everywhere, especially of the poor and the oppressed. That identification made by the Council has not really happened. It is certainly a direction to which we are called. This would mean that all the various societal problems mentioned, from war and peace, poverty and oppression, to family life and education and the humanization of people must also become the concerns of the Church.

This would really put the Church in the position of being a servant — not serving itself but serving others outside. Here we still have a long way to go. There seem to be so many ways the Church is seeking to serve itself and is afraid to reach out and serve others. There are many, many people within the

Church who are reaching out, but I do not see the whole Church, institutionally, truly moving in that direction.

There are some societal problems that are Church problems, and we get ourselves very deeply involved in them — for example, tax credits for Catholic schools. I believe that the United States Constitution would not prohibit such a thing. I really think we ought to be actively trying to promote it. However, when I see such a strenuous promotion and following through the legislative progress of all this, yet see that we do not do the same thing with legislative programs that have to do with the country's hungry and poor or the world's hungry and poor, or we do not do the same kind of thing with legislative programs that bear upon the arms race, then it seems to me that we are still serving ourselves. Tax credits, even though they would bring about justice in an unjust situation, are aimed at a justice directed toward ourselves instead of a justice that is truly concerned with the whole community.

To me that is a kind of defect in our approach to societal problems. We seem to put our greatest emphasis on societal problems that touch us directly. We give lip service, for the most part, to the others. We do put out statements; for example, the National Council of Catholic Bishops has a marvelous pastoral plan for the world's hungry, issued in 1974. Yet as a bishop I cannot remember any time that every bishop was sent a letter saying there is an important piece of legislation before the Congress now; it would be very important to call your congressperson and your senator and explain why they should vote this way rather than another relative to the implementing of our pastoral plan on hunger.

But when it comes to tax credits, we regularly get notices every time there is any progress on that legislation. This has occurred in the last session of Congress; I guess it is kind of a dead issue now. However, its progress was carefully monitored by our offices in Washington, and we were sent mailgrams and letters regularly. We do not do that about the arms race! When the defense budget comes up year after year and includes large amounts of money for the development of every new sophisticated weapon of destruction, we are never officially urged to do anything about it.

This is just one example of how we merely give lip service to this need to serve all — the whole community — and to do it in a way that would have some very practical consequences. Thank God, we do have some very powerful statements promulgated by the National Council of Catholic Bishops, but we do not have the sense that we are putting ourselves totally behind those statements in trying to see that legislation follows and that the policies of our country are changed in accord with those documents.

RELIGIOUS FOR SOCIAL JUSTICE

In regard to religious life, I have found that there are quite a few religious who have this deep sense of concern about societal problems and want to bring about the transformation of society. In the 1971 Synod of Bishops there was a very important statement, namely, that acting for justice and participating in the transformation of the world are genuinely part of the proclamation of the gospel.

There are many people who want to act for justice and participate in the transformation of the world. Their desire to do this flows out of a real sense of commitment to the values of the gospel and to the call which they experience from God himself. Yet, so often because of the institutional forms of their religious life or because there is not a community to which they can adhere and from which they can receive the support and strength they need to do this, it becomes very difficult for individuals to keep on working for justice in that way.

NURTURED BY COMMUNITY

Here is where I connect the need for changes in religious life with this thrust for working for justice. I believe that people need to be deeply involved in this prophetic and confrontational effort because of the forces of evil. They need deep personal prayer but also a faith-life that is nurtured and strengthened by coming together with a community which is ready to move with them in the same direction.

In religious communities, as in the Church as a whole, there is still much unevenness about that kind of a commitment. There are some individuals committed to efforts towards achieving social justice, but others in religious communities are very opposed to it. So the needed strength and the nurturing just are not there. In the Church as a whole that strength is not there either. People who do try to speak out on these issues find themselves opposed by other members of the Church or by their own religious communities. This is difficult to accept, but it highlights the needs for a breaking out of those old forms so that people can come together in some form of community.

One sees this most dramatically in some of the situations in Latin America right now. Through personal conversations with people involved in the struggle in Nicaragua, I know how desperately they need the support and the help of others to keep on trying to do what they are attempting. In this case it was a failure. Those with whom I spoke were trying to do it in a totally non-violent way. Instead it has deteriorated into a terrible kind of violence and oppression. Yet there are many who want to make that society more just for the poor and the oppressed in a non-violent way. However, to find the support groups needed is very difficult.

THE CHURCH SIDING WITH THE RICH OPPRESSORS

Even the institutional Church, to some extent, is siding with the wealthy who are the oppressors. To me this dramatically highlights the need for a much deeper kind of conversion in the Church. I believe we are moving in this direction in our country. However, far from being identified with the poor and oppressed, the bulk of our people are in the middle and upper classes. As the Latin American bishops have stated, those who have the system working in their favor will use every means possible to assure that the system will always work in their favor. They will use any means, even violence, to do so.

I have a dread that this could happen in our country, too. The Catholic Church, finding the system working in its favor, instead of being identified with the poor and oppressed in its midst, will identify with the powerful and the wealthy who have the system working in their favor. I have the sense that we are far from doing what the opening sentence in "The Church in the Modern World" states. We do not have identity with the poor; we even seem to be moving away from that identity. What is needed is a deep kind of conversion in the Church. I see many people ready to move in that direction; but we are now at a decision point—which way are we going to move?

A CRITICAL MOMENT OF DECISION

This is a very critical moment, for the next decade or so, for us in the United States to decide whether we are going to be the radical Church of the gospel to which Vatican II has called us, or whether we will move to the more comfortable way that will keep us very institutionally powerful, but not powerful in the way of the gospel. We are not quite ready, it appears, to identify ourselves with this choice. Are we going to choose the weakness of God and institutionally be powerless, or are we going to try to maintain our position of power in society? This decision has to be made by the whole Church and has to permeate the whole Church. I would see religious communities certainly as this kind of radical group which would choose to be powerless like the poor, and allow all their members to be that way, too.

Sister Mary Anthony: Seemingly that is what religious life should be in the Church.

Bishop Gumbleton: Exactly. It ought to be the call to become the most radical living out of the gospels possible. Yet I am afraid this is not so. Vatican II has stirred up many people to such a call. I would hope that they could form communities with a style of religious life within the Church which would allow this to happen.

A BREAKTHROUGH

Sister Mary Anthony: Do you think, formwise, such groups might break through in new and smaller groups separated from the establishment?

Bishop Gumbleton: I am not sure what will happen. I have had some experience with individuals who have not been able to find what they see as the necessary forms within religious communities. In some instances small groups have broken away and have tried to form new communities. Sometimes that is successful. Other times, because such a realization demands a legalism in order to get the approval of the Congregation of Religious and the Code of Canon Law, it becomes almost impossible to do that. So sometimes individuals have to break away and live a new kind of religious life.

How that is all going to happen, I do not know. Some persons are simply going to begin to do things; then different kinds of communities will gradually evolve. To me this would not be all that unusual or different from what has happened in the Church before. Religious life, as it came into being in the Church, was not something that someone sat down and predetermined. It began to happen, and then the structuring and legal forms came later and confirmed what was already happening.

This happened, I think, at the very beginning of many major communities. As I remember, in more recent times St. Vincent de Paul, when he established some of his active religious communities, was acting contrary to the laws which were current in the Church at the time. The need was there, and there were people who were willing to meet that need by really trying to live out a call from God within the spirit of the gospel. They began to do it, and they had the courage to face the opposition obviously arising from going contrary to the approved forms and law. Yet they had the courage to do what requires a deep kind of faith, a depth of maturity and prayer. There are people who possess these qualities and are willing and have the courage to move forward.

Sister Mary Anthony: When you talk about the poor, are you thinking primarily about the economically poor, or do you think that there are other poor, the socially poor, etc.?

Bishop Gumbleton: Sure. I have heard that we must serve in our most affluent areas because that is where, in some ways, people are far more poor than are the economically poor.

Sister Mary Anthony: Is that rationalizing?

Bishop Gumbleton: To put it very bluntly, I would say that that is rationalizing because if we went into those communities and were radically different and really lived in opposition to the values of those people, then we would be trying to say to them what needs to be said—"You are poor in ways that you do not recognize because you are so tied up with materialism and are so caught in the wasteful affluence of American society."

WE ARE CONVERTED TO THEIR WAYS!

But what seems to happen is that if we go among them to serve them, before we know it we are converted to their ways rather than our going there and living a life of genuine poverty which would conflict with their values. If we are willing to go among the affluent and be very, very different from their life style in a genuine or almost radical way, then what we would be saying to them would justify our presence among them. But when we do not do that but rather go among them and live their style of life with them, then we are not really bringing the message of the gospel to them. I have a feeling that we have to do this among them if we can. Yet in a certain sense we could not because we would be quickly condemned. The affluent would not tolerate our presence.

It is similar to when the disciples went to a certain town and the people rejected them; Jesus told them to move on. If people do not want to accept the message and put up barriers, one may as well leave that place and go where there is good soil for the word to be heard. If we had the courage to walk away, as Jesus told his disciples, and to go among the poor, then possibly, because we did have the courage to do that, some of those people would then be challenged to ask why, and maybe follow. Then the only way they are going to be freed of their riches is if they follow where we have gone. If people vowed to poverty, celibacy, and obedience within religious life were to move in among the poorest of the poor and live there, then gradually maybe others would be drawn to follow. This is how conversion could take place among those people. However, I have not seen it taking place by our being in their midst.

Sister Mary Anthony: I have heard that Mother Teresa of Calcutta has specified the drug dependent as the poor in our country rather than the type of physically poor in India. Were her Sisters to come here, that would be where she would choose to have them live and work.

A REAL SIGN OF CONTRADICTION

Bishop Gumbleton: That is true, but only if her Sisters would come in and live with the simplicity and poverty of life that they live in India. I think, however, that very quickly they would be either converted to the other way of life or they would be driven out. So if we would have the ability to live there in simplicity of life and in genuine poverty, our very presence would be a real sign of contradiction to all the values of that drug and affluent culture. Again, if we could not be that sign of contradiction, maybe the only way we could free them from their drug dependency and from what flows from that affluence would be to show how the poor can live a life of significance and a life of joy and happiness in "Blessed are the poor."

We could show that our living among the poor with the gospel commitment to be poor gives a profound meaning to our lives and a sense of joy and optimism that comes not from material things but from something far deeper. That could happen rather by our being a sign among the poor than by our being a countersign among the rich.

Sister Mary Anthony: We perhaps need to live among the poor in order to become that sign ourselves.

Bishop Gumbleton: Yes. That may be part of how we become more radically converted ourselves. Then maybe we would be able to go among the rich as genuinely poor people without any restrictions on how we live because we are celibate, we are obedient, and we are poor. Then we could also go among the affluent and be a sign of contradiction to them.

WOMEN IN THE CHURCH

One of the points that we should touch upon before we conclude is the role of women in the Church. We have talked about religious in general. Reform of women in religious communities is obstructed in part by the tight control that is maintained over those communities by the male dominated, legal structure of the Church. Not only religious women, but women as a group in the Church have been kept out of important decision-making and out of the possibility of truly being heard and being able to participate in the full life of the community.

It is very clear, in the institutional Church and otherwise, that decision-making is something extremely important to persons; if they do not have some responsibility and at least some control over their own lives, they are not really functioning as fully adult, mature persons. Neither are they exercising the equality of freedom and dignity that the Vatican Council said was the right of everyone in the Church. So if decisions are always made for them, they just are not enabled to live out that dignity and freedom which is their birthright, if you will, by baptism.

Sister Mary Anthony: What I find, too, is that one's own search for values upon which those decisions are made is frustrated and obstructed if one is never faced with personal decisions.

Bishop Gumbleton: You mean that if someone else is making them for you, you are absolved from having to struggle with the search and the decision?

Sister Mary Anthony: Yes, and you do not grow in the process of being engaged with the painful struggle involved.

Bishop Gumbleton: Yes, that is true, and that is inhibiting to one's own growth. One really does not grow as a person unless one has to struggle with that oneself. If someone is imposing a decision on another then not much can happen internally. Not to develop is a very genuine loss.

I believe that this is another change which Vatican II pointed towards; but we are a long way from having it happen. A year ago that National Council of Catholic Bishops took a survey of all the dioceses of the country to see how many dioceses had women in various positions of decision-making. It was put forth as a sort of positive declaration of how far we have come. My own feeling of it is that we really do not have very much to brag about. In fact, it is almost pathetic if we were to look at the real situation in the Church and got behind some of the figures that were given as a result of the survey.

Sister Mary Anthony: Thank you, Bishop Gumbleton, for your insights.

Reflections on Luke 21:25-38[1]

At the Harvest Dance
the silver-studded people
laugh in shreds and spill
their drinks too soon.
Women with numb desire
lean against dull men
with fat, vulture eyes.
They move into null dance steps
drifting like floating debris
toward plunging rapids.
Music festers in coffined corners
and oozes a maligned melody,
dripping, dripping into
cankered ears.

In the shadows
beneath hesitating balloons,
a white, ignored, moon-faced man
sits in wrinkled pants.
Grain bits bunch and sag,
half swallowed in the cuffs.
"The wind whistles in my bones,"
he says to a woman passing
under a limp light.
"Outside it twists the oaks
and strips the forests.
The moon turns blood red. . ."
Pulling needlessly on a strap
beneath her silk, she says
with her cracked eyes,
"This is not the time.
No, this is not the time
at all."

Sister Colleen Scully, R.D.C.
Sisters Today, November, 1977

[1] "There will be signs in the sun, the moon, and the stars. On the earth, nations will be in anguish . . . Be on guard lest your spirits become bloated with indulgence and drunkenness and worldly cares. The great day will suddenly close in on you like a trap" (Lk. 21:25,34. *Editor's note*).

Sisters Today, September, 1968

The Church in the 1990's

Arthur C. McGill

This past summer I attended a conference on the problems of American life in the last quarter of this century and the implications of those problems for the Church, particularly for the Church's educational task.

In this regard we found it useful to ask about the conditions for fruitful human life, the minimal conditions necessary for a human being to be human at all. For what do men fight? For what sorts of things do they rise up and take decisive action?

A list has been compiled by Harold Lasswell, a political scientist from Yale, on the basis of a study of political life of a good many societies. He lists eight ingredients as the essential constituents of a human life: wealth, power, deference (or respect), health, enlightenment (which is provided by education), skill, rectitude (this term emphasizes the uprightness, the fulfillment entailed in living morally), and finally affection. These are not a final list, but they provide a convenient summary.

We might use the list in this way, saying that in order for any person to be an adequate human being he must have access to these eight conditions. The term I use here is "have access," not "possess." Possess is the capitalistic way of having access. But there are other ways of having access. The point is not simply to possess these goods but to have them available in whatever way the society decides.

All this has bearing for the Church because the Church is called to see that the hungry are fed and that the naked are clothed and the wretched are comforted. The Church—and by the Church I mean the people of God, the community of believers—are commanded to see that all have access to the basic conditions for human existence.

Jesus' address in Matthew 25 on the last judgment puts the whole weight of his redemption on this single point. The community and the individual will be judged, not on the vigor of their churchmanship, not on the orthodoxy of their faith and not on the sincerity of their religion, but exclusively on how they helped and nourished Jesus himself when he appeared to them, not in the form of their priest or bishop, but in the form of *their needy neighbor.* Jesus' brothers, those he makes his own, are the poor, the sick, the sinful, and the deprived. These are the ones for whom he came and died. Because he has indeed made them his own, so far as we do to the least of these, his own, we do to him.

Lasswell's eight conditions, therefore, are simply a useful catalogue of what people need to be minimally human. These are the things which the Church should be passionately concerned to see that all have.

One set of questions to ask about the next thirty years is to consider how well people will then have access to these eight goods. And what can be done to address the kinds of deprivation that will afflict our brothers and sisters in the coming decades. The following diagram will indicate how people today have access to the goods.

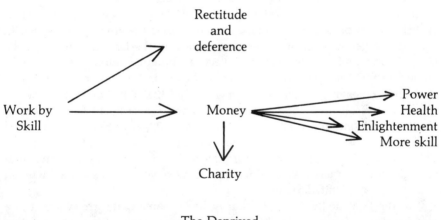

The Deprived

The foundation of everything is work by skill. In return for that work money is given. The most decisive mark of money is not so much the money itself, but rather the recognition of work which money entails. By virtue of that recognition a man enjoys a feeling of rectitude. I suppose the good worker is the dominant form of rectitude in our culture. Out of rectitude comes deference shown to that good worker. Money itself is able to provide power and health facilities, enlightenment through education and the means to secure more skill. Our culture is essentially therefore a culture where access to these essential conditions of life is predicated on work and on the acquisition of money by work.

Underneath this group on my diagram, excluded from the goods of life, are the deprived. The question to be asked is who, during the coming years, will be the deprived and how may they be given access to these goods.

THE END OF PRIVATE CHARITY

The first problem that the Church will face in the last quarter of the century is a problem that is already upon us: what will be the best form of charitable work? At present, the normal idea of charity is to contribute such money as one has available for the sake of the deprived. This is the pattern of Christian charity that tends to be most prevalent. One may give not only money, but also one's property, or one's blood. Generally, however, Christians try to help the deprived have access to the goods of life by a practice of monetary charity. This pattern of personal charity goes back to ancient times when it was known as almsgiving. Each Christian gives what he can, and Christians as a group gather their contributions together.

Already today this is an outmoded, an unnecessary and therefore an irresponsible form of charity. Why? Because of the existence of governmental agencies. I can dramatize this in the simplest way by relating some figures. In 1967 the largest almsgiving type of operation in the United States was the United Fund and it was able to collect six hundred million dollars. This amounts to $3 for every man, woman and child in the country. By contrast state governments spent on welfare in 1967 $7,832,000,000 or 15% of the entire budget of all fifty states. The United States Government Department of Health, Education and Welfare spent $11,739,000,000 or 8% of the national budget, and this outlay was second only to the expenses for national defense. Thus through public programs, through assistance given by governmental agencies in 1967, there was spent for the deprived $497 for every man, woman and child in the United States.

In the light of this, private charity has become quite irrelevant. It is a waste of time, it is a negligible remnant of a past age that is kept up out of habit. In the next thirty years indications show that the government will be playing an even larger role in welfare, that the volume of public assistance will continue to increase. If private charity is now a negligible enterprise, this will become even more fully the case as time goes on.

The task facing the Church is therefore a simple one: to find a new mode for participating in the work of charity. The answer is clear — in the coming decades the Church must learn to use its energies to affect the decisions of governmental welfare agencies. The Christian passion for nourishing the deprived can lead only in this direction. The Christian community must enter the arena of political pressure groups, influencing Congress when it forms its

welfare budget, influencing national welfare agencies and their policies, keeping an eye on the committee that handles the welfare funds for each local
county.

In our day and increasingly so in the decades ahead, the Christian community and the Christian individual will follow the command to nourish the
poor that belong to the Lord by *political action* and not by monetary gifts.
One letter to a congressman is worth twenty people's private charity. The
churches and their members must learn to apply whatever political pressures
they have. They must become informed about welfare laws in their cities.
They must learn where their influence must be applied. For the individual and
the Christian community, then, the days of charity by the gift are over; the
days of charity by the vote and by the pressure group have now begun.

TWO OBSTACLES

There are, however, two obstacles to the Church's moving in this direction, two pervasive ideals that stand in the way.

First, there is the normal desire that charity be the exercise of my private
virtue. Whether or not my giving helps others is perhaps secondary to the
principle that it should be personally and distinctively mine with my name.
Not a governmental decision with tax funds . . . but my personal check,
sending a CARE package with my name.

In this particular habit there is too much self-indulgence. Charity is essentially to help the other, not to indulge in our own virtue. Charity is primarily
concerned for the other. If, as is now the case, governmental agencies are
flooding billions and billions of dollars into welfare, the Christian task is to see
that this money is channeled well, to see that the poor are fed and the naked
clothed as well as possible, even if this means that we cannot put our own
name on the service.

There is, however, a second obstacle here, and one that is even more subtle. It is the capitalistic belief in the fecundity of money. In the diagram above,
the significance of money, the meaning and not simply the utility of money
becomes quite clear. Money is that which generates power, which gives access
to health, which is the key to education. Furthermore, by virtue of interest,
money is able to beget money, to generate money, to make money. Karl Marx
developed a devastating criticism of this whole preoccupation with money.

In a middle-class country like the United States, the Church has, on the
whole, adopted unwittingly this capitalistic viewpoint. It has tended to
measure the help a Christian gives to another person in terms of money, as if
money itself were the measure of good. This is a very deep notion in the imagination and not simply in the intellect of American Christians today. They do
not feel that they are helping others unless their gift can carry weight in
monetary terms.

To tell Christians in our country that the most important thing which they
have for the support of the poor is their political power, their power to affect

political decisions — this is to speak a language which they do not yet understand. It seems to me that a great and urgent educational task now faces the Church: to enable each person, each diocese, and each hierarchical structure to realize that what it has for its Lord, insofar as its Lord stands before it as the poor, is political effort. And woe to those Christians who through sloth or pride or indifference fail this call.

LACK OF CONCERN FOR GOODS AND SERVICES

There is a second problem which faces the Church in its service to the deprived. Considering the eight conditions that Lasswell names, there is now going on a shift of emphasis as to which ones are considered most important. The standard view now held by propertied people in the United States is that the poor should be given *goods* and *services*, that which money can buy. But it is already clear, even now, in 1968, that the deprived of this world, in the underdeveloped nations of the world and more the American poor, are no longer primarily interested in goods and services that money can buy. It is dignity, it is deference that has become first and foremost in their minds.

There was repeated this summer a television series on black America. On one of these programs there is shown a class of three and four year olds in Philadelphia, where the teacher seeks to teach the young blacks to stand up to the white people, to help them realize that their main vocation in life is to be black and beautiful, to be themselves. At one point the teacher offers a little boy a dollar if he will say that he is an American Negro, instead of saying he is an Afro-American black. "Negro" is a name which designates black people as unworthy of deference. The teacher turns to the boy and says, "You're an American Negro." The boy replies, "No, I'm not."

Then the teacher pulls out a dollar (goods and services) and says, "I'll give you a dollar if you'll say you're an American Negro." The boy says "No." "You know what this dollar can buy? Why don't you say you're an American Negro?" The boy's eyes begin to roll with the tension of uncertainty, but he sticks to his guns and again the teacher praises him.

This is a very piquant parable of the way in which goods and services are no longer the primary concern of the deprived of this world. What they demand before and in all else is deference. The teacher in Philadelphia is teaching the young blacks to scream at the whites, to frighten the whites and perhaps to kill the whites in order to compel deference, whatever it may cost them in the realm of goods and services. From this point of view the blacks' first task is to stand up to the whites and to compel deference in whatever way possible.

Then the next question arises: How do the deprived secure deference today? Again the standard middle-class way is to secure deference by your work, by work that brings an income and that thus bestows rectitude and respect. But work does not bring goods and services for the poor these days. The government does this.

In this new situation the deprived may secure dignity by participating, by having a role in the government decisions which affect them. But how do the poor effect this, except by political pressure — Black Power! For the poor man today, the first blessing is dignity, and the way to dignity is not to receive it as a gift — dignity is never, never "given" — but to seize it by the exercise of political power. Governments and peoples must take account of them, must compromise, must come to terms with them, must consult them regarding the decisions that affect their lives. The day of goods and services is over.

This is very hard on the American middle class. There is no more dreadful example of the American inability to understand this than the bombing of North Vietnam. One assumption behind this policy was that by the bombing of North Vietnam, by depriving the North Vietnamese of their goods and services, the North Vietnamese would submit to the indignity of coming to the conference table. It has now become clear that for the North Vietnamese, like the blacks in our country, no amount of loss of goods and services will compel the loss of dignity. The North Vietnamese are quite capable of being subjected to incredible lacerations in terms of the goods and services for life rather than compromise their dignity.

This means that what the Church must seek for the deprived in the next decades is a place in democratic decision-making. Political activity is therefore not only how the charity of Christians should operate (that was the first point), but political activity is what Christian charity should seek *for the poor*. The days of welfare will soon, in this sense, be over. The dole is not going to be tolerated either by the blacks or the poor whites here at home, or by the underdeveloped countries abroad. While the dole may give goods and services, it takes away dignity, and people today will not pay that price. Therefore it is not self-determination at stake here. Self-determination is rather a childish dream. It is to have a shaping role in the decisions that affect people; it is really participative democracy.

The Church therefore should stop worrying about getting food and medical supplies to people, and instead work to unionize them, to organize them politically, to see that they get political leverage. That also means political leverage within the life and decisions of the Church itself. College students today do not want education if the price is that they have nothing to say about how it is done, if they are simply to receive it like a dole. The Christian no longer wants truth and guidance if he simply passively receives it. The poor do not want goods and services; they would rather suffer if the price is the indignity of a handout. Participatory democracy then is what is at stake everywhere today, and this will continue to be the case for the rest of this century.

It seems to me that this problem of participation becomes most difficult in the matter of revolution, in the matter of breaking the law. Today it is pervasively believed by the deprived that a law or a rule to which I am subject is not just, no matter how well it treats me, unless I myself have had a part in shaping it. The logic of justice is not thought to rest on what the law requires but on how it is fashioned. There is a lessening tendency, therefore, for the poor to seek redress for their injuries within the framework of present law. Do not expect the deprived to obey the laws which they did not shape, even the laws intended by lawmakers for their benefit. They will violate those laws as the first act of political dignity.

It seems to me, in this situation, that the Church's role is not to repress the poor in their revolutions against the law, not to insist that the poor must submit to laws which they had no role in making, but rather to turn in the other direction, and to prepare the civil order to remake its law-making practices quickly and drastically, so as to include the poor, before the poor carry their revolution to a point of anarchy.

LIFE WITHOUT WORK

A further problem regarding access to the eight goods of life is posed by automation. Automation vastly increases the range of the kinds of tasks which can be done by machines. The need for workers thus becomes seriously curtailed. The new jobs required to produce these machines will not compensate for the number of workers displaced by them. If we look at the diagram above we can see the implications of this development. In a world where work is the tap root for access to the goods of life, automation cuts this root and thereby promises to increase the number of the deprived.

The only possible direction is clear: access to the conditions for life simply can no longer be a reward or a payment for work. What is the alternative? One suggestion is that access to these goods of life be considered a natural right. No one has to *do* anything to have access to health, to some wealth, to enlightenment and to deference. In other words, automation may make work such a minor factor in the lives of so many people that work will lose its value and currency. Does every human being have a right to some money, to medical services, to an education, quite apart from whether he works or not? Those advocating a guaranteed annual income would answer this question affirmatively.

The problem for the Church and for our religion and culture in general will be this: What will people do with their time if they do not have to work for a living? What will become of motivation and incentive, of their sense of purpose in their existence? This may lead to such boredom that people will be driven to violence and depravity. As far as I know very little work has been done on this problem.

THE WORSENING PLIGHT OF UNDERDEVELOPED COUNTRIES

A very different kind of question will be posed concerning the deprived in underdeveloped countries. Perhaps I can express this difficulty in a rather simple way. The kind of economy now present in the world is a technological economy. It is not pastoral nor agricultural; it consists in the use and transformation of natural resources by machines. The question regarding underdeveloped countries therefore is this: How can they develop a successful technological economy?

It is quite clear that three things are necessary for a technological economy. First, there must be a technically competent personnel. This is not a serious problem. The underdeveloped countries can produce an educated class. Secondly, there must be capital to pay the personnel and to develop the resources. This, too, is not an impossible difficulty. It means that the nations with capital, the developed nations, must find ways to channel their capital into the less developed areas.

Third and finally, for a technological economy there must be enough raw materials to allow enormous *waste*. Technology depends on waste. There is the waste involved in the trial and error method of the developing of products and devices. The new items that are developed but not produced and the inventories that are not consumed all mean great waste. In addition a strong technological economy must have a variety of resources available so that if the use of one of these resources ceases to be profitable the country can shift to another. But unused resources represent resources being wasted. From the viewpoint of resources, no economy has ever existed so inefficient as modern technology.

The fact is the underdeveloped countries do not have resources to waste. Most of them are one-resource countries. Almost none of them has such a vast amount of resources as to maintain over a long period of time and through several kinds of economic phases its own technological economy. And finally few have a small enough population to be supported by their resources.

Here then is an authentic crisis in international life. The poor nations, in order to become self-sufficient, must develop their own technological economy. But they do not have the resources to do this since a technological economy depends on waste. Thus they are doomed to perpetual poverty, and stand as constant sources of instability among nations, at least until some new kind of economy is developed.

The problem sits heavily upon the Church because of the millions and millions of people subjected to deprivation by this situation. No suggestions have been clearly proposed. One possibility is for underdeveloped nations to become integrated economically and therefore also politically with the developed nations. The disadvantaged people would live off the resources and technology of the developed nations. The United States and Latin America would suggest such a marriage.

But this is not a very practical proposal. It requires that national identity be eroded in the economic sphere. It is not just a matter of reducing duties and other trade barriers. It is a matter of pervasively integrating the impoverished nations into the economic life of successful nations. This will be a monumental task, to which the Christian Church, perhaps because of its international character, might provide some assistance.

OVERPOPULATION

The most serious international problem will continue to be overpopulation. The rate of birth increase in the last two years has diminished slightly in Asia and Africa, but the lessening of the rate of increase has not been decisive. One can perhaps dramatize the problem in a rather simple way. If the rate of increase of births which marked the period from 1950 to 1960 were to continue until 1998, in that year there could be a total nuclear interchange between Russia and the United States and all the people killed would be replaced in eight years.

We should not be distracted by the future, however. The problem of overpopulation is now very real in certain limited areas of the world, and there it represents a kind of nightmare. One situation described to me concerns a woman in Calcutta who had her eighth child. The food necessary now for this child and for the preceding one had to be taken from the mouths of the other children. But because of the low subsistence level at which this family lived, if the available food were distributed to include these two youngest children, none in the family would receive enough to sustain life and before long all children would starve to death. Therefore there faces this woman a terrible question. Should she continue the even distribution of food, leaving it to chance which ones die, but in the process weakening all the children and perhaps subjecting many of them to death? Or should she deliberately decide which of her children to let die immediately so that the others may live? Nothing the Church can say about the morality or immorality of artificial birth control mitigates the nightmare in which these people are living.

The issue facing the Church here is a very peculiar one and a very practical one. Overpopulation means that life for the first time in history becomes an agent of death. There seems to be no preparation for this in Western history. Life has always been precious at the practical level. That is to say, each individual by his existence has contributed more to the common good in productivity than he drained away because of what he consumed in order to subsist. We now have the situation where human life, which all instinct and all morality and all religion teach us to cherish, becomes the most terrible threat for existence. There are simply no resources in the Christian imagination to come to grips with this kind of a problem.

THE PROGRESSIVE DETERIORATION OF FAMILY STRUCTURES

Turning to a rather different area, there appears to be a peculiar crisis developing in the area of affection. In the kind of society with which we are familiar, affection has found its natural expression in the family. In fact the family has existed less as an economic unit than as a unit for the nourishment of affection.

In the next thirty years the present erosion of the family as a context of affectional life will increase. It is not that the family will disappear, for children will continue to be nourished by their parents. It is rather that the family will not be the exclusive area for affection.

We already know the effects of taking the children out of the family at an early age for education by the state. This causes the child to look to his peer group, to his companions, rather than to his parents as the guides and primary shapers of his expectations and values. At the same time – and this, too, is already happening – television means that family life itself becomes filled, not with the life of the individuals in it, but rather with an endless stream of stimulations and situations from the outside world. For children this seems to empty the family on its own interior dynamism, and to foster the impression that even family existence depends for its real substance on life that is going on elsewhere.

Finally, and most important, there is a growing tendency for sexuality no longer to be rigorously limited to the husband-wife relationship. Not noticing some of the radical proposals made to normalize extra-marital relationships, it is certainly the case that the family matrix is no longer felt to be naturally, essentially and properly the exclusive setting for sexuality. In the next thirty years it appears that the momentum of this deterioration of family life will increase.

The crisis that this poses to the Church can be expressed at two different levels. At one level, the erosion of the family deprives people of having access to affection. We might therefore ask: What kind of structures will people create in their efforts to alleviate this suffering? Will the Church try to hang onto the family and authorize no alternative structures, leaving those who have an eroded life to pay the penalty of being cut off from having access to affection? Or will the Church be open to new kinds of inter-personal structures that compete with the family? At present the community of the hippies is the only alternative structure that has appeared so far. But we can expect many more.

There is a second level of the crisis facing the Church. For the Church itself has tended to let itself become grounded on the family. This has happened in two different ways. In sociological terms, it has identified itself primarily with its *parish form*. It chiefly serves and nourishes itself, not from work institutions, but from family institutions. The Church so far has been completely unable to relate itself creatively to the work life of modern man. It is almost exclusively grounded on the home of the parish community. As family life becomes eroded, what becomes of the reality of the Church, as it finds itself growing weaker with the progressive erosion of family life?

Secondly, the family not only affects the Church by giving it at present its chief social basis. It also affects the teaching of the Church. For the Church still takes as its model for love family intimacy. It still tends to think of charity in terms of this kind of close, direct, I-thou, interpersonal kind of relationship, which only the family setting can provide.

This may be one reason that the Church is completely unable to interpret the work life of our modern age as a work of Christian charity. It has been unable to move very affirmatively into the great urban arena where nobody knows anyone personally, and where therefore the kind of intimate love of family life is largely irrelevant. The Church thus finds itself caught up in this problem of the erosion of the family, not simply in terms of those who suffer from it, but also in terms of its own identity, its own tendency up to now of identifying itself both socially and also in its concept of love with the family context.

THE INDIVIDUALIZING OF RELIGION

A rather different kind of problem, religious in character but also crucial for the general life of our culture, concerns the vacuum of ultimate meaning which already seems to plague a good deal of modern life. This sense of having no ultimate meaning will probably increase in the United States, especially if it continues to maintain its high material standard of living. There is a widespread feeling that, while the day-to-day life goes along well, it really does not mean anything in the long run. It is all pointless. This anguish is fed by the experience of boredom, but it issues out of an inability to know anything or have any sense of anything or to believe in anything beyond the arena of immediate experience. American pragmatism and American empiricism all feed this anguish of a lack of any sense of ultimate meaning.

The very existence of this feeling now shows one thing: it means that the official religion of our society is unable to make much of an impact. It is now quite clear that whatever religion people have, whatever sense of ultimate meaning they possess, they do not receive this because society says so or because some Church says so. The official religion is no longer functioning as a religion. It has ceased to give many people a sense of ultimate purpose in life. And this seems to be true both among those who are still going to church and among those who have no connection with any religious institution at all. The interesting question for the future is this: What will be the *style* of religion in the next thirty years? What form will religion take, and how will it give our on-going life a sense of ultimate things?

What is already emerging is the fact that people seem to try to deal with this problem in *consumer terms*. They shop around and each individual fabricates a temporary and provisional sort of religion of his own from what he finds available. This is now true, whether one is a Protestant who shops on Sunday at the various Protestant churches in town; or a Catholic who consults different priests for a morality that seems right; or whether one is an agnostic, who reads the different novels recommended by the *Times Sunday Book Review* in order to find some ultimate significance to last for the week ahead.

This pattern of not expecting society or any group to speak with authority on ultimate matters is now, it seems to me, generally taken for granted. However much the Church may want to pose as the spokesman for the society or to pose as the exclusive source of light for a group, as bearer of ultimate truth, people in fact think of ultimate questions as matters which they themselves decide on eclectically out of their own individual experience.

The style of religion in our culture will increasingly become individualistic. For this, quite truthfully, the churches are not at all prepared. This again is a religious crisis that promises to become more intense. It is a religious crisis for which the Church itself must bear a heavy responsibility. For in continuing to try to identify itself as the official religion of culture that is pluralistic and unchristian, the Christian churches have falsified and discredited themselves. There is no "official religion" on whose coattails the churches can ride. What we trust in our public life is not the "God" mentioned on our money, but the Congress or the President or the Defense Department.

RESOURCES FOR COPING WITH THE DAY

As a last problem, I would like to draw attention to the problem of what is most required for people to cope with the day. Formal education doesn't attend to this. It is the parents who try to give the young such resources as are necessary for this task. But the Church, since it is not limited simply to the public arena but may also give direction in the personal arena of life, has rather neglected this problem.

For what is the foundation of modern existence? What emotional experience is the most real and the most pervasive, giving shape to everything? I will take my cue here from some remarks by Norman Mailer in *Cannibals and Christians* (Dell Publishing Co., N.Y., 246–247). He says that in our day the foundation of existence is not love. It is not passion or fear. It is not the mind, not mood, not interest, not dedication, not responsibility. It is annoyance. "Annoyance is the foundation of modern existence, and the progressively most common condition for everyone alive is interruption and annoyance, interruption and annoyance.

"One plans one's life—there is a war to interrupt it. . . One plans to eat—one has to wait for the food to unfreeze. One calls a friend on quick impulse—the line is busy;. . . look to pour your friend a drink—the telephone will ring; begin to watch a show—a commercial comes in. Contemplate a city vista—an ugly building will smash the view."

The list can be continued endlessly into every corner of modern life. Mailer continues, "Is a man reading a newspaper? The story is broken by the turn to another page. Is there coffee for breakfast? No cream. The wife has forgotten again. Rush to catch the subway? Wait for the change teller. In a hurry to take the elevator? The doors won't close—they are automatic, and their timing is not yours. . . .

"In fact, we are talking of the modern man's ability to swallow nausea. From infancy the very style of his nervous system is built not so much on the sensuousness of his mother's breast, but on the click of the electric light switch. Born in a sterile room, the baby does not die of fever, nor does his mother.

Rather at eighteen months he shows his first sign of genius—he turns on the television set by himself. Soon his consciousness is formed on collisions and interruptions, trips on highways with billboards, radio blasts, car horns, construction blasts, brakes. . . What does each interruption signify but shock— shock to expectancy, shock to nerve, shock to rhythm, and at last—apathy. Then there is need for stimulus, a shock that stimulates rather than stops.

"In the nineteenth century children were raised on frustration. The children who came after the Second World War grew up not on frustration but interruption. Their physiology now runs on two systems—the old one, sympathetic and parasympathetic, act and rest; now, with it, an electric overlay of a new system: depressant and stimulant, apathy and shock, depression and mania, flipped-out, back-on.

"Animals subjected to constant interruption go mad, but not humans, not yet."

Here, then, is a serious anguish for the Church to understand and to interpret. It is not a matter of eternity. It is a matter of coping with the daily interruptions and annoyances. This brings about a deprivation that eats away at the sanity and the psychic resources of every human being alive today.

We have to ask in the time ahead: what will the Church do for this misery?

INDEX